# THE MARINER'S CATALOG

### Edited by George Putz and Peter H. Spectre

**Volume 7**

**International Marine Publishing Company**

Copyright © 1979
by International Marine Publishing Company
Library of Congress Catalog Card Number 73-88647
International Standard Book Number 0-87742-115-3
Typeset by A & B Typesetters, Inc., Concord, New Hampshire
Printed and bound by the George Banta Company, Menasha, Wisconsin

All rights reserved. Except for use in a review, no part of this book may be reproduced or utilized in any form or by any means, electronic or mechanical, including photocopying, recording, or by any information storage and retrieval system, without written permission from the publisher.

Published by International Marine Publishing Company
21 Elm Street, Camden, Maine 04843

## CONTENTS

**Shoptalk** 4
**Ship's Gear** 46
**Power** 57
**Tophamper Happenings** 73
**Steering, Navigation, Electronic Sundries** 86
**Interesting Boats** 101
**Models and Modeling** 126
**Shoreside Structures** 132
**Books and Things** 139
**At Sea** 159
**Index** 183

## THE COVER

The photograph on the cover was taken by Joe Upton of sometimes Camden, sometimes Vinalhaven, Maine. Joe is a commercial fisherman/photographer and is the author of one of our absolute favorite nautical books: *Alaska Blues* (Alaska Northwest Publishing Company, 1977; see review in MC-6, p. 120). The cover design is by Ingrid Beckman.

## OUR THANKS

Our thanks go out to the legion of people who have helped us in ways big and small. Our special thanks go to Julia Littleton for her index, Kathleen Brandes for her soothing words as she wielded her editorial axe, Nan Kosntantolopoulissteinenbaum for her artful dodging through the minefields of productionland, and Norma Whitman for her uncommonly fine layout of the book.

## PETE CULLER

Here and there throughout this volume of the *Mariner's Catalog* we have included notes and items from Pete Culler that did not find a place in previous volumes and so have pined away in our files. Pete died last year, so these few remaining notes are the last of his unpublished wisdom. He is sorely missed.

## THE PRICES

We used to make jokes about loading up the wheelbarrow with one dollar bills to buy a loaf of bread until the local beer store put a big box filled with pennies on the counter with the sign, "Need a few pennies? Help yourself." The box is still there, filled with the same pennies, because nobody has any use for them. The moral of the story is that inflation rages onward, so don't take any of the prices listed herein as ironclad. Last year we didn't know who to blame; this year we haven't even had time to think about it, what with chasing around town trying to find a gas dealer who will condescend to take $20 for a fillup.

 24¢

 12¢

 14¢

 11¢

 16¢

 16¢

 10¢

 10¢

 77¢

 10¢

# SHOPTALK

*There is no reward in another life for not building a boat in this one.*

**Brooks Fredrington in**
*Goferit Boatbuilding*

Any subject can be "covered" forever. An earful at any lunch counter will show, for example, that in ten thousand years we still have not yet finished covering the weather as a topic of conversation. Still, after a bit, one feels that perhaps the weather will happen anyway, with or without further coverage, and one moves on either to more profound things or to details.

And so it is with our *coverage* of tools, boatbuilding, and related materials; it would be inappropriate to move on to, say, man's fate or his capacity for good and evil, but it is time—some would say high time—to move on to details. Here are some shoptalk shavings, notations, and noticings over the past year of wondering where boats come from.

We have listed the Wooden Boat Foundation in the past; but not a list of the subjects covered in their Boat Study Workshops, which may be of interest to readers in the Northwest. Wherever such programs have been created, a terrific interest has been generated in a very short period of time, and boatbuilders with a pedagogical bent might do well to take entrepreneurial note. There is no place in the land where such a program would not be welcomed.

**The Wooden Boat Foundation**
**Point Hudson Marina**
**Port Townsend, Washington 98368**

Hey, we found another source of fastenings, especially good in stainless, but all things and materials offered; "anything in metal," their note says.

**Ayres Screw and Nut Shop**
**6676 Arlington Boulevard**
**Falls Church, Virginia 22042**

## We've Come to Cease Your Berry, Not to Praise It Dept.

Dear Editors:
For some time I have been trying to obtain old-fashioned laid cotton caulking.

The enclosed letter from Massasoit Company gives the reason why this type of caulking is no longer available domestically.

I disagree with Massasoit's opinion of their Bristol Caulking. To me, this single strand material is no better than sleazy absorbent cotton.

Do you know of any source for a substitute material similar to the old Security Caulking? What do they use in Canada, Scandinavia, and Great Britain?

May I have your ideas on this subject?

**Lane Lovell**
**Edgartown, Massachusetts**

Mr. Lane Lovell
P. O. Box 414
Edgartown, Massachusetts 02539

Dear Mr. Lovell:
In reply to your letter of November 2, we appreciate your kind comments about our Security Caulking Cotton, which had a strong following in the New England area.

Unfortunately, the combination of rising costs and limited demand forced us to discontinue the manufacture of the Security grade several years ago, and the machinery used to manufacture this caulking cotton, after many years of meritorious service, has been scrapped.

Our Bristol Caulking Cotton is carried by all of the major New England marine distributors. While we do not claim it to be the same quality as the Security Caulking Cotton, we have no hesitation in offering it as a quality grade under the raw material conditions that exist today.

Yours very truly,
Massasoit Company

Dear Editors:
I work with Maynard Bray, and he insisted I should send you a sketch of the water heater for my steambox, as you might want to include a picture of it in your catalog. Enclosed find my crude drawing.

The can is a one-gallon varnish tin to which I attached a piece of radiator hose with a hose clamp. I punched a hole in the top center of the can and attached a 1000-watt water-heater element. I poked a hole in the corner of the can for addition of water.

To operate, I plug it in, add water through the hole. Oh, the steambox sits above the can on the planking bench. That's about it. It boils pretty well—don't let it go dry.

**Andy Davis**
**Thomaston, Maine**

*Left: From Ayres Screw and Nut Shop catalog.*
*Below: Andy Davis' water heater.*

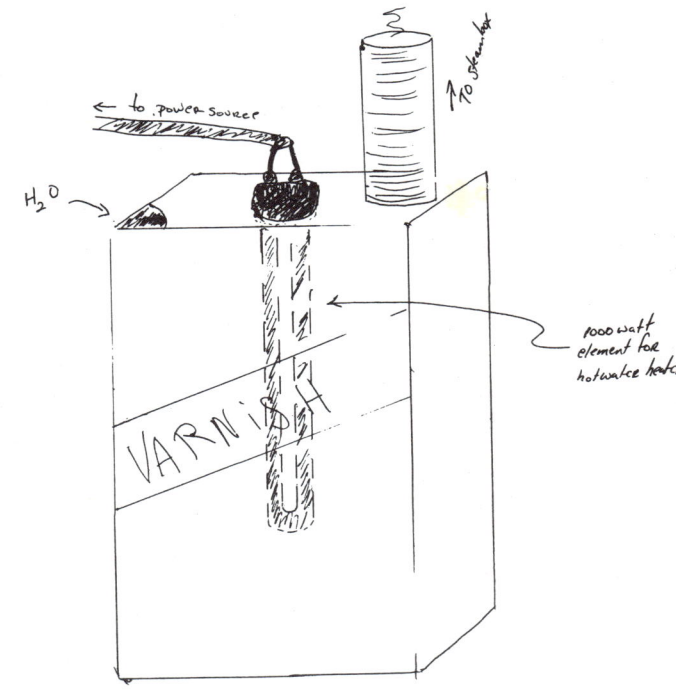

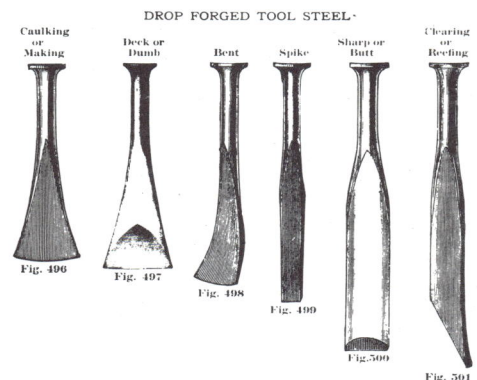

## Trunneling a Small Craft

### by Pete Culler

I've been asked more than once how small a boat I thought might be trunnel-fastened. I feel this is a very hypothetical question, and one that can be answered both simply and at length, neither making much sense in these times. It's the sort of thing it's fun to hash over on a long night watch, or around the stove in a blizzard. The answers that come up in such sessions often do make sense, though no one ever does anything concrete about it, simply because there is no real need to do it in this day and age.

I feel that in a situation where wood was plentiful, and metal nonexistent, there would be a very good reason to trunnel a very small craft. It has been done for the above reasons in many places, as the only possible way of building a boat. To do it now, in civilized areas, is quite possible, but to me not sensible. The argument for doing it now is the cost of fastenings. I think the cost of labor involved, plus the type of small boat suited to it (the question originally was how small a boat) make it simpler for the would-be builder to do some outside work, say, mow lawns or cut wood for others, to make some money for fastenings, which, if I were running things this close financially, would certainly be of galvanized iron. Even in these outrageous times, when a head of cabbage is becoming a luxury, iron fastenings are still not out of sight. This, of course, brings up the point that the boat must last. Well, like the Marine said, do you want to go on forever? A stout iron-fastened boat is capable of being refastened at least once, if the wood is sound, which usually places her in the 25- to 50-year lifespan, if she's had good care. If the wood is not sound, the kind of fastening doesn't matter.

Not wanting to end the discussion here, so as to spoil the fun of it, this is the way I would go about it if I felt ambitious enough to try and prove a point. I assure my readers that I don't.

I would choose a boat model suited to heavy scantlings, say, a small yawl such as shown in Chapelle, or a Bahama-type dinghy, jolly boat, or similar craft. She would, of course, be natural-grown frame, or double-sawn frame like a ship, or sawn single futtock, like some of these were done in the past. Now, most builders would use a bandsaw for framing, and if you can afford that, you probably can afford nails and bolts. (Seems I keep being a killjoy.) Planking, of course, must be stout, and the backbone, simply a small ship in miniature, or tiny shallop.

This may not be exactly the craft you really would like, but it's one suited to trunnels. Naturally, if you have never done trunneling before, you will have to learn as you go. The usual first troubles are that they are too loose to hold well or too tight to drive without breaking. And you will be making wedges for one end, both ends, "feathers," or blind wedges—all of which takes a small amount of learning. You will probably need to make a splitting chisel, or more than one for different sizes, for the chisel you have on hand is apt to be not just right. Wedges you will need in great number, and these can be made by power, in very small sizes. You will need a fine blade, but again, is a power saw available? Or does it fit in with such a project?

Locust has been the time-honored trunnel material, where it's available, because of its low shrinkage and durability. Other woods have been used; it's simply a matter of where you are and what you can get. The material must be dry. Some old builders in out-of-the-way places dried their trunnel stock by a fire, slowly, for long periods, a form of kiln drying. These same ones felt stock split out was superior, because it was sure to give a straight grain. They have a point. In recent times I've seen power-made trunnels for a large craft that I thought had a lot of poor grain in them. Probably some gave trouble in driving. I think a lot of it is up to the man who saws the stock; if he's intent on saving wood at all costs, he will turn out cross-grain stuff and be more wasteful in the end.

The trunnel was not much in use where I learned the trade at the period I did. We did sometimes assemble sawn frame with it. Having done it both ways—the other being with short iron drifts—I see little difference in the finished vessel, in spite of the arguments pro and con. Occasionally trunnels were used in assembling a "collar," or the massive wooden rim required in building a round stern. The idea was that there was much shaping and dubbing to do on such a structure, so wood pins of any kind could be trimmed off with the rest. Trying to plan bolts in the early stages of such a structure can lead to "striking iron," and delays cutting it back. Such structures were then metal-bolted when they were about finished size.

I'm no expert on big trunnel work, but have done quite a lot connected with smaller stuff—not from lack of metal, but because it was handy. Sometimes it's best at least to start a job using them. Most of the same principles apply, be they large or small.

First you should choose the bits you are going to use, see that they are sharp, and stick with them. If it's a big job and two bits the same size are used, be sure THEY BORE EXACTLY THE SAME SIZE. If they do not, and many don't, they will be too tight or too slack for the trunnel.

I don't think it matters how you shape your trunnels—by hand, in a lathe, in a trunnel machine, or with what I have, a hand-operated dowel machine. Some of these machines have adjustable cutters. Try to adjust closely but slightly oversize. I find some of these machines not wholly accurate. Make a sizing block, or more than one for different sizes. This is simply a hole in a metal plate. This can take time to make, as the metal bit can bore differently from the wood bit. If it's too small, ream out a little at a time, until things are right; if too big, peen the edges carefully with a ball hammer. To make sure things are right, test a trunnel in a thick piece of stock. You probably won't have many hangups if you follow this procedure.

You can turn out trunnels ahead of time, in as many different sizes as you want, provided the stock is dry and they are slightly oversize—not much, but some. I find some woods are much affected by humidity, or lack of it; some puff up in foggy spells. On some very dry days, they just *feel* different. Hence the need to make them oversize, something few builders seem to take into account. Some hardware stores catering to home workshop furniture makers get complaints that their dowels are under-size, especially in winter.

This is what the sizing block is about. Bore your hole, drive a dowel or trunnel thru the sizing block, and drive it in the hole at once. You seldom have trouble if you follow this system. Even so, I notice there is a difference in driving on dry days, wet days, and with different dowel or trunnel stock, as well as with the kind of stock you are driving into. If things begin getting sticky, I always use some tallow in the hole.

I was asked to write about trunneling a very small boat. Never having done it entirely, I simply give some opinions based on a lot of past wooden pin work. I leave it up to the reader if he wants to attempt a totally trunneled small boat. I look at it this way: I think I could if I just had to, but I see no point in it if there is no need. At the present minimum wage, a very short spell of outside labor will bring in enough to buy galvanized boat nails with reckless abandon—and maybe even a beer.

◆◆◆◆◆◆◆◆◆◆◆◆◆◆◆◆◆◆◆◆◆◆◆◆◆

Detco offers a pneumatic caulking gun. As we said two volumes ago, air is a coming power delivery mode in small shops, a simple matter of having a few electric motors instead of dozens. Detco also carries a full range of caulking and surface preparations.

Detco Marine
3452 E. Foothill Blvd.
Pasadena, California 91107

*Below: From the Detco Marine catalog.*

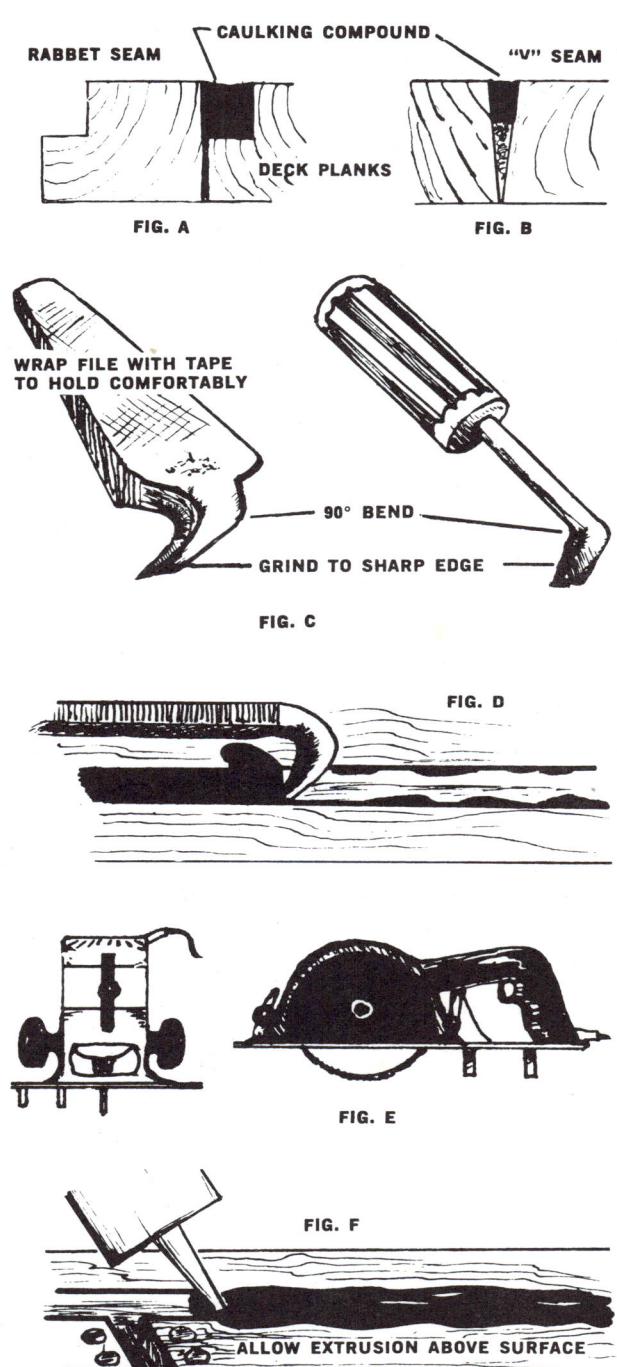

## Metallic Sundries

A couple of marine metal workers wrote in to say that the liquid galvanizing compounds on the market are *the* way to go on metal surfaces once the welding, grinding, and smoothing are finished up—better than the pigmented primers of common use. One such compound is called Liquid Galvanize and is offered by:

> **Ross Chemical Products Company**
> **Hingham Industrial Center**
> **P.O. Box 99**
> **Hingham, Massachusetts 02043**

Another source of zinc coating is ZRC.

> **ZRC Chemical Products Co.**
> **21 Newport Ave.**
> **Quincy, Massachusetts 02171**

*Below: From ZRC Chemical Products catalog.*

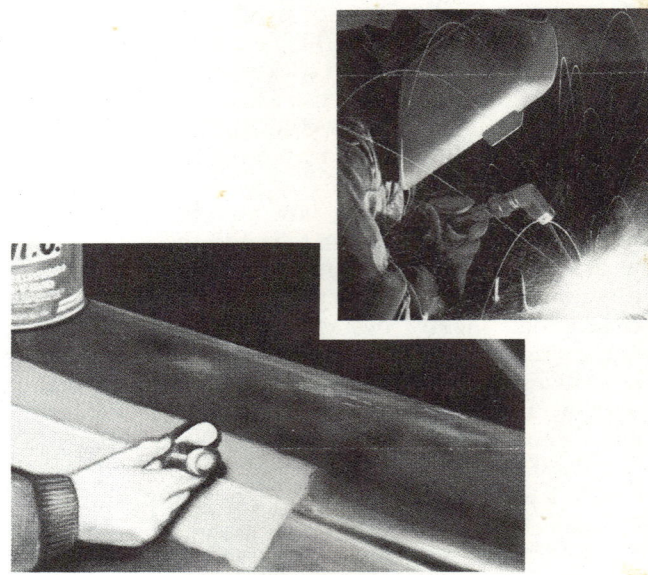

We've always been fascinated by the quick-and-dirty applications for aluminum. As you might know, modern offset printing uses vast quantities of thin aluminum printing plates, which are usually thrown away or sold for scrap after use. We have seen fishhouses and ice-fishing shacks sided with these discarded plates and have heard they make excellent, though noisy, roofing shingles. We can't get an aluminum-plated kayak out of our minds, but we're stuck on the edge-fastening problem. Welding is too heavy-handed. Epoxy, perhaps? Has anybody tried this stuff?

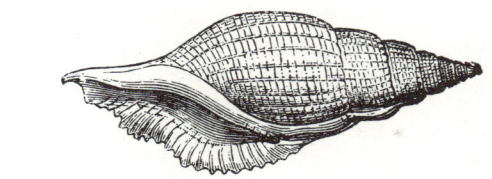

*Boatbuilding in Aluminium Alloy*
**by Ernest H. Sims
Nautical Publishing Company
Lymington, Hampshire, England
110 pages, illus., index, 1978, £ 5.50**

A book on aluminum boatbuilding has been a long time coming, which is surprising considering the number of aluminum boats that have been and continue to be built. But then again, it's not surprising, because there are few amateur boatbuilders involved in aluminum, and most boatbuilding books are written for the amateur because that's where quantity sales lie. Be that as it may, this book presupposes that the reader is a professional boatbuilder and has plenty of experience in his craft. It is more of a general guide to principles than a step-by-step, how-to tract.

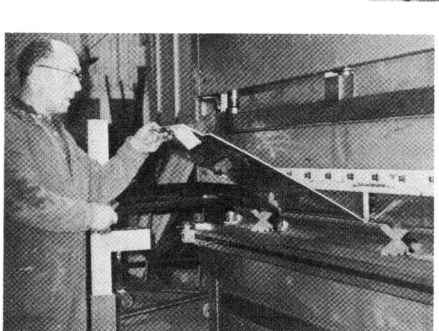

*Above, right, and below: From* Boatbuilding in Aluminium Alloy.

**Forming**
Straight line bending of thin material up to about 18 gauge can be dealt with by the hand folder, (see figure B-3) which is adequate and also simple to operate; for thicker materials of not too long a bend, a hand operated flypress of adequate size (about No. 6) is used. All other bending requires a press brake (see figure B-4), this should have at least an 8 ft. bed, and be capable of about 80 tons pressure. In the hands of a competent and resourceful operator, a wide variety of shapes can be produced with a minimum of tooling. A multi-vee block, and about three segmented bending knives, with say radii of $\frac{1}{8}$ in., $\frac{1}{4}$ in. and $\frac{3}{8}$ in. would be adequate for most bending jobs.

Wrappers—i.e., lengths of thin aluminium, bent around the knife edge, can be used for intermediate gauges. The knife selected for bending, would be dependent on the thickness of metal to be bent, and its hardness condition. Bend radii could vary from $\frac{1}{2}$T to 3T, (T=sheet thickness), whilst in practice, the material used in boat construction is fairly soft, usually O, or M, condition (see chapter 1), and $1\frac{1}{2}$T or 2T is normal. A certain amount of 'spring back' is to be expected, the actual amount can only be ascertained by experiment, so the punch or knife should have an included angle of about 86° where a 90° bend is required, to allow a slight overbend initially.

## Laminating Rollers

The plastic laminator always appears to be a rather voluble chap compared to the wood boatbuilder, perhaps because he has to shout to be heard above the noise of his jangle box giving nonstop-pop as he splashes jallop from his bucket onto the molding. However, like the traditional boatbuilder, plastic laminators will argue for hours over a tool; the only type of tool one can argue over in that trade is the impregnating roller used to compress the layers of glass reinforcement, which are daubed with resin and then smoothed out to build up the structure.

Venus Products Inc. offers 34 choices of rollers in aluminum or Teflon to suit almost any laminating job. These range from 2 inches in diameter x 8 inches long in aluminum or Teflon down to 2 inches x 6 inches and 2 inches x 3 inches; one-inch diameter of the same lengths; barrel rollers 2 inches x 3 inches, 1 inch x 2 inches, 1 inch x 3 inches; ¾-inch diameter x 3 inches and 6 inches long; and wheel-like corner rollers of ⅛, ¼, ⅜, and ½-inch radii.

Teflon rollers have excellent release characteristics in the grooves, even when the abrasiveness of the glass reinforcement has worn away the coating at the tip of the roller. Venus rollers have nickel-plated steel roller supports and a recessed headnut that will not catch in the work and is readily removable. Venus claims their rollers have improved vertical wall space between the fins to allow air to escape, compared to thicker-finned rollers with angular fins, which require more pressure and longer rolling to achieve compaction. This latter type is a contributing cause of too thin a laminate, which is undesirable in a hull or deck molding where adequate finished thickness as well as weight per unit area of laminate is important. The rollers are made from a single piece, in contrast to many others which are built up in segments.

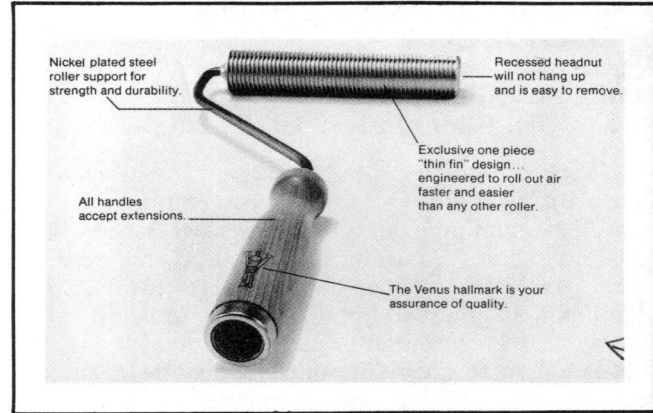

*The Venus laminating roller.*

They also make Delrin rollers of ¾ inch and 1 inch diameter x 3 inches and 6 inches length. Cured resin can be removed from these by taking the roller off the handle and flexing it. However, the wider fin necessary with this material results in less efficient operation.

Venus offers replacement handles of any size, grip rings for corner rollers, and nylon end caps.

**U.S. distributors:**
Venus Products Inc.
1862 Ives Avenue
Kent, Washington 98031

**British distributors:**
C.T. (London) Ltd.
3 Hobart Place,
London SW1W OHW, England

—John Leather

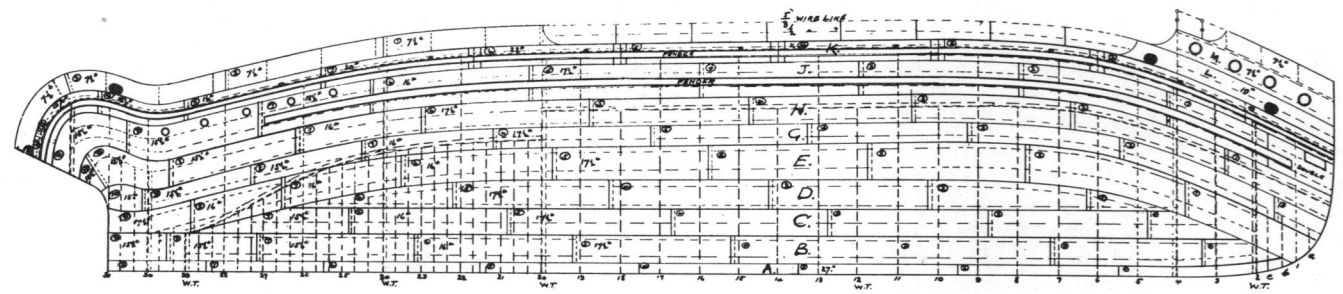

*C-Flex Construction Manual*
by Barry Kennedy
92 pages, illus., 1977, paperbound, $5.95
(plus 30¢ postage)
Seemann Plastics, Box 13704
New Orleans, Louisiana 70185

We've had our downs and ups with C-Flex, the miracle material that allows you to "plank" a one-off fiberglass boat (see MC-3, page 50, and MC-4, page 54). It *is* an option for custom glass boatbuilders and is seeing increasing use for a large variety of craft, from small boats to large yachts and from working craft to competitive racing machines. This book is a how-to manual published by the manufacturers of C-Flex and simply must be on hand if you are planning to use the material.

Previously unlisted sources of broad lines of wonder goos have been discovered. But listen. The evidence is piling up on the possible carcinogenic properties of many of the resin and hardener ingredients they contain. Goggles, gloves, and respirators *designed for use with vapors* should be part and parcel of their use. Be careful. Be neat. Be ventilated. Be protected.

**Allied Resin Corporation**
**Weymouth Industrial Park**
**East Weymouth, Massachusetts 02189**

**Allied Resin**
MARINE ADHESIVES • FAIRING COMPOUNDS
• COATINGS • RESTORATIVES & LUBRICANTS •

**Astro Chemical Company, Inc.**
**1205 Godfrey Lane**
**Schenectady, New York 12309**

**Fibre Glass/Evercoat Company Inc.**
**6600 Cornell Road**
**Cincinnati, Ohio 45242**

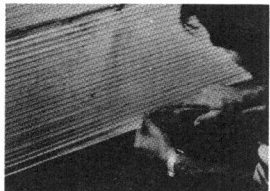
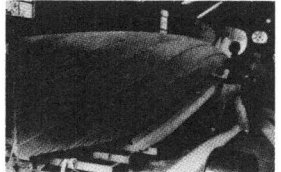
1. C-Flex is attached to the frames with narrow crown staples (3/8" long). The butted edge is stapled first, and the free edge is pulled taut to insure fairness and then stapled.

2. Generally, stapling starts in the midsection and proceeds to each end of the hull. It is easiest to have one worker hold the C-Flex in place and help pull it fair around the framework while another staples the plank to the frames. Notice the icepick holding the C-Flex temporarily in place.

3. To insure smooth, fair contours without ripples or distorting especially in round sections, the plank might require some tension from an end while it is stapled in place.

4. Individual rods stripped from C-Flex planks can be used to hold planking in place in a concave section, such as this deck structure or the flare of a boat hull. The rods are positioned on top of the C-Flex and over the frame edges and are stapled in place. After the C-Flex has been wet out with resin and it has cured, the rods are stripped from the surface.

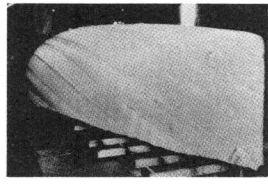
5. The C-Flex planking was started at the centerline on this round bottom sailboat and was trimmed where it ran off of the stem and sheerline. Notice that full length planks are butted side by side around the girth of the hull, and there are no overlaps, no stealers, and no joints.

*Above: from C-Flex Construction Manual.*
*Lower left: Gel-Paste from Fibre Glass/Evercoat.*

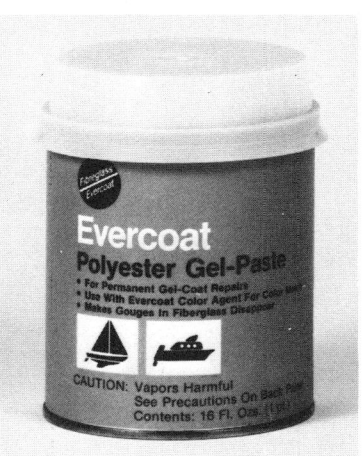

## The Hazards of Urethane

We received a frantic telephone call from Mark Roeyer of Lawrence, Kansas, one night. He had just finished exploring the advantages and disadvantages of urethane foam as an insulator and discovered that the material does indeed burn—contrary to some previous reports—and it burns faster than many thought possible. More disturbing, however, is test data showing that CYANIDE (!) is produced by urethane that burns at temperatures greater than 800 degrees C.:

> According to Wooley, cyanide is produced at temperatures over 800° C. This is not an uncommon temperature in compartment tests (UCB Fire Tests No. 3 and 9). In an extremely hot fire, such as a house burning, a lot of cyanide could escape into the surrounding area and be hazardous to the neighbors. One example of the danger from cyanide is an airplane crash that occurred near Chicago in 1972. The downed plane caught fire and all the passengers died. Autopsies later revealed that many had not died from the crash but possibly from cyanide poisoning. The cyanide may have come from the flexible urethane foam in the airplane's seats which burned in the fire.

The above quote is from *Dome Notes* by Peter Hjersman (Erewon Press, Box 4253, Berkeley, California 94704, 1975, $7.50). This book is filled with test data on urethane foam and is must reading for anyone using urethane anywhere for anything. Now that you're properly scared, think about all that foam you have in your boat.

*Tools of the Maritime Trades*
by John E. Horsley
International Marine Publishing Company
Camden, Maine
304 pages, illus., 1978, $15

A history and description of the tools used in wooden boat- and shipbuilding, including specialized tools used by the sailmaker, rigger, ropemaker, sparmaker, shipsmith, cooper, and tinsmith; there is much information on why and how these tools were used.

Boatbuilding in sizes over 20 feet involves a tremendous amount of crawling, climbing, stooping, twisting, and contorting. In cabin work particularly, the measuring, wood selecting, cutting, and fitting operations can have a builder over the rails more times in a week than the owner will experience in years! And so when we saw the Workmate ads on television, out came the ole three-by-five card saying:

> Workmate (for finish work below, etc.)
> at hardware stores, made by
>
> Black & Decker Inc.
> Towson, Maryland 21204

*Black & Decker router.*

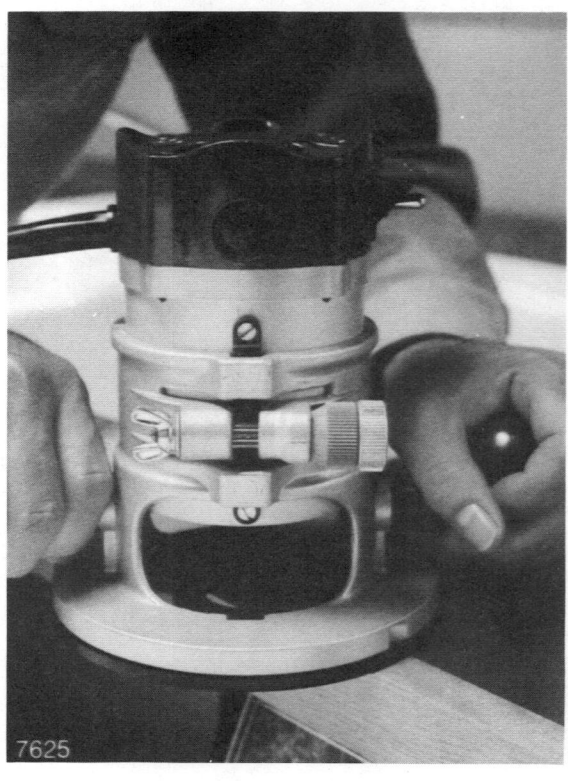

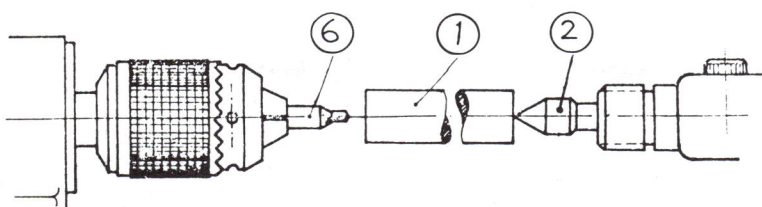

Fig. 6.5 Work being centred with centring drill in drill chuck prior to running between centres. 1. Workpiece. 2. Centre. 3. Centre drill.

The nominal horse power of the current Unimat is $\frac{1}{10}$th h.p., and its speed 4,000 r.p.m. Under load and with the friction of one, two, or three rubber belts this will drop to 3,450 r.p.m., or even lower and speeds given take this into account. The higher speeds offered for the watchmaker's spindle is because it has a smaller step pulley and tends to be used for lighter work of a high precision nature.

Another factor to reckon upon is a slight variation in the current available from the local power station. At certain times of day, or days of the week, there may be a heavy demand from both industrial and domestic users and hence slightly less power. If it is possible to borrow a tachometer (such as used to test speeds of model aircraft engines) this can be used to check your own motor and see for yourself the effect of different pulley combinations. All motors are not *exactly* the same; they are tested to be within a certain range so hope that yours is among the best of the bunch!

*Above: From* The Book of the Unimat.

## The Unimat

Back in MC-2 (page 148), we discussed the amazing Unimat, the miniature shop tool for machining, sawing, and jointing. Modelmakers just getting used to their Unimats will find a lot to ponder in:

**The Book of the Unimat**
**by D.J. Laidlaw-Dickson**
**Model & Allied Publications**
**Watford, Herts., England**
**128 pages, illus., biblio., 1977, £ 2.75**

Neat folding extension table for this-and-that shop situations, from:

    L.D. Kreitz Ind. Inc.
    P.O. Box 60
    Pequot Lakes, Minnesota 56472

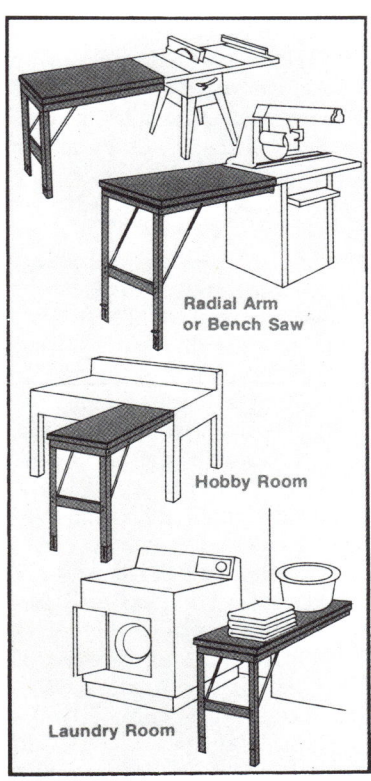

*Left: Versatile extension table from L.D. Kreitz.*

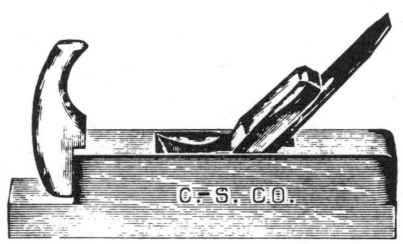

## Sharpening Saws and Planer Knives for the Small Boatshop

#### by Pete Culler

Every small boatshop has a bandsaw, that boatbuilder's friend, and usually some sort of planer—or is living in the hope of acquiring one. There may be a jointer, and several other power tools. I pass on some ways and ideas for maintaining sharp tools of this nature, that starting young builders may find useful as well as economical. There are good books on sharpening tools, and they should be referred to; however, I'll pass on some things I've picked up over the years. Metals have changed somewhat over these years, as well as ways of treating them.

Shops that build small craft, and the ones just starting out, don't need a very big bandsaw; you can get by quite well with 12", 14", and 16". A stout 16-incher will build quite some craft. Some fortunates may own an old 36-incher, which is great. When I started, all bandsaws could be filed; now, with the advent of the very hard skip-tooth blades, this is no longer true. Here is a fine blade, and not cheap, so what do you do when it gets dull? Forcing it is hard on the machine and hastens breakage. By the way, you can still get blades in the larger sizes that can be filed.

The hardened disposable blades CAN be sharpened—not by filing, but by grinding. They are good for two or three grindings, and one or two breaks; then you find there are apt to be so many gullet cracks that the blade is no longer useful. Junk it. These saws are too hard to set, so you lose a little at each grinding, though it hardly affects the use. You have gotten two or three times the normal life out of a blade, which, for what they cost, is a big saving. Here's how I go about it.

I use a ⅛-inch by 6-inch bonded metal cut-off grinding wheel on a mandrel set up in my wood lathe. You can do it on some standard grinders, but often they are so protected there is limited room. You can do better with a polishing head run by a small belt-drive motor. I only turn my wheels 1500 to 1800 rpm, so an open polishing head is safe enough. I like coarse wheels run at modest speed; they heat up less. Have an adjustable rest, metal or wood, for the saw blade to rest on; this should be set at an angle that agrees with the hook of the teeth. Don't get too much hook, or the saw will grab in some woods. Overhead you need a rod or stick to support the saw more or less in its natural shape. Set the blade rest very close to the wheel. Take your time and grind lightly on each gullet, backing into the tooth and forming a point. I usually start at the splice, or you can mark your start with chalk, which is good to have handy in case of an interruption, so you can mark where you have to leave off. It's square-across grinding, so you work from one side of the blade only. You can skip a tooth all around, then reverse the blade, but I've not found any advantage to that. Until you do a couple and get the hang of it, it seems slow work, but I find now that I can do 14 inches (16-inch saw) in about 12 minutes. At that rate, without rushing it, I can do quite a lot of blades in a couple of hours.

These blades break, of course, like any other blade, but they are quite spliceable with silver solder and a small torch. My system is this: I use a wood jig, simply a rabbeted piece that is true, with a cutout in the middle for the splice and torch flame. It's important that this jig be true in the rabbet. Broken saw ends are carefully ground back to matching bevels. (One tooth is enough lap, and make sure in a trial fit that there are no bumps.) These ends are then clamped in the jig with small C-clamps. Carefully line things up so the back of the blade is true and straight, otherwise the saw will pound during use. Place sheet silver solder with its flux in the lap, or use rod already fluxed; it does not matter. Have a big pair of pliers whose jaws fit well. Heat the splice dull red until the solder flows, and immediately clamp the pliers on the splice. The reason for this is that the light saw blade tends to warp open when heat is applied. This all cools quickly, so then examine the splice, and if it looks good after removing it from the jig, and if it sights straight along the back (most important), clean up the job by careful grinding and filing. If the splice is bad, melt it open and try again. You now have a reconstituted saw that will give many more hours of sawing. As mentioned above, you can do this two or three times, then gullet cracks appear and the blade is done. What you have accomplished is to convert a $6.00 throwaway blade into a $2.00 blade—or less.

Although most really big shipsaw blades now go out to a professional shop for service, it might be interesting to know how these were handled when I was learning the trade. There was a jig as I've described, only quite a massive one, of course. Splicing was done in the "engine house," where the big railway hauling machinery was, massive in the extreme. There was a forge in the engine house for general maintenance. The big blade (and some were near 2 inches wide and many feet long) was prepared about like I've described for the smaller blades, then it was set in the jig with all the above-mentioned precautions, and solder and flux were put in the splice. Then a big pair of tongs, with large, flat "coppers" similar to a soldering iron, was heated in the forge. The tongs had a locking ring on the grips and there was also a rest attached to the jig for the grips to set on. When the tongs were heated to a red heat, they were clamped on the splice and locked, and the whole thing was allowed to cool. Then it was all finished off as

I've described for smaller saws. When torches were not readily available, things were a bit different!

These big saws could be both set and filed. There was a big pair of wood wheels (somewhat adjustable to hold the saw horizontal) and a clamp that was similar to a hand saw filing clamp, only bigger. These saws were filed and set by hand, and a good filer was much sought after in any busy yard. Now, jointing, setting, and filing on these big saws is all done by machinery. So much for the old ways; we do have to borrow from them somewhat to fit the economics of the young and strugling small boatshop.

Planer knives, jointer knives, and those for power planes have things in common as far as sharpening goes. For these, use a ½-inch or ¾-inch flat-face grinding wheel. If it's too wide there is too much heat. And run it at moderate speed as mentioned. On your tool rest, which should be about twice as long as the longest knives, have a wood piece with a rabbet in it. This is for the heel of the knives. Mine is a clamp-on affair. It must be adjustable for the correct bevel. My system is this: When all seems adjusted correctly, check the knives to see if their widths are equal. Check the ends with calipers. Knives totally alike are in balance. Start the grind by making only one pass to a knife, laying each on a heavy, flat, steel surface, such as a saw table, which prevents overheating. If knives need matching, do it a little at a time as you proceed. When you have a sharp, straight, clean edge on all, and their widths match, that's it. Though it is not really necessary, I hone these edges lightly on a stone—it's surprising how well the machine runs and cuts. It's assumed your machine has a jig for setting the knives. If it does not, make one before removing the knives—it's just a couple of pieces of wood or metal connected by a bar, about the same length apart as the knives. There are other ways to set a planer, depending on make and model, but I like a gauge.

Jointer knives are done just the same way. My jointer sets from a straight edge working from the front table; some work differently, but the principle is the same. My power plane has its own jig for setting, which is most simple and rapid. After a grind, it's good to run a trial piece and check it against the machine's scale, which may need slight adjustment.

A word of warning: be sure you replace the knives correctly and have them all equally *tight*. You don't want to go through the experience of a thrown knife; at the least it probably wrecks the machine and the worst is too much to think about. I was close to one knife-throwing during the World War II years, though I was not actually employed on the machine, a huge 12-inch spindle shaper of most massive proportions. We got out keel stock for 110-foot craft on it. Shapers are horrible things, and this giant was as wicked as a lake full of crocodiles. Anyhow, one day she threw a knife, a 12-inch x 4-inch x ¾-inch piece of steel said to be turning 12,000 rpm, whether that was true or not. How they shut down that machine without wrecking it, no one knows. The knife went through the tin side of the mill shed on the flat. It went so fast it cut a nearly clean hole like a punch. We later found out that it missed the bow of a new craft on the railway by inches, crossed a truck unloading area, missed an eight-bay building shed by inches, and, still gaining altitude, crossed a fitting-out basin and went into a field, where someone mowing found it months later. The person mowing was a yard employee, so he knew about it and set up a stake. Sighting from the hole to the stake, it was obviously a miss by inches all the way. The mill crew was badly shaken for weeks. I bring up this yarn as a bit of past history and a warning.

Circular saw blades are other items that are often incorrectly sharpened; yet with the aid of a grinding rig, various thicknesses of round-nose wheels, and files, plus a little know-how, they can run sweet and true and be easy on both the machine and the operator. Some time back a friend brought in maybe a dozen blades he had had sharpened by a so-called pro shop. He said they would not cut, or they cut very poorly. Yes, they had been sharpened, but for the most part they were badly out of round, the gullets needed deepening, and there was no set. Besides not cutting, the saws ran with a lot of commotion. This shop charged about 75 cents per blade for this work; with the way I do it, I can't compete.

I went at restoring the mess in my usual way. Each blade is put on my table saw and run down just below the table. I place a castoff industrial grinding wheel about 12 inches x 3 inches thick over the slot on the flat

(continued on following page)

(continued from previous page)

(any stout flat stone will do) and gradually raise the blade until it just touches the stone, at the same time rotating the stone so it wears evenly. Stop often and check the top of the teeth, because flats develop. When all teeth show contact with the stone, the low ones barely touching and the high ones sometimes showing as much as 1/8 inch flat, you have the saw round. Now raise the blade, and turning it by hand, chalk both sides for about an inch all around near the teeth. Figure the amount of deepening you think the gullets need, put a pencil flat on the table, turn the blade by hand, and mark a ring of gullet depth, both sides. Take off the blade, put it aside, and round others the same way if you have many, not forgetting the gullet bit. Then set up your round-nose gullet grinding wheels for the proper thickness. Adjust the tool rest so the blade is square with the work—you want no bevels here. Grind the gullets a little at a time, going round and round; you can easily burn the blade by trying to do too much. When this is done you can file the teeth to near-points; don't quite complete it. Some big hook-tooth ripping blades can be brought pretty close by grinding; try to maintain the bevels and hook as nearly as possible. You now have a round blade, near sharp, but not set. If you set it before rounding, it will naturally not give you a true set.

My set is simply a big block of iron with the corners ground off to various amounts; the "gauge" for this set is simply to place the blade on the iron so the tooth fits a bevel to my fancy (coarse saws need more bevel) and chalk the hole, since all used blades vary slightly in diameter. Using the chalked hole as a gauge, and noting how the original set was, I simply belt every other tooth with a hammer, then turn the blade over and do the others.

Since the saw was badly out of round, setting before rounding would not be accurate. I now put it back on the saw table and wipe the points once again to make them really true. Take off the blade and file to points if it's a combination blade, not forgetting to have the raker teeth 1/64 inch to 1/32 inch low and filed or ground square across. Some coarse hook-tooth combinations can be largely ground to points, the rip blade square across, and the combination with a bevel. A lot of set is better than too little.

You will now find the blade runs quietly and cuts like crazy. If the cut seems a bit rough, rotate the blade by hand, passing a stone against the side of the teeth, a little at a time on each side. Try and hone, try, and hone lightly; what you are doing is evening the set, and the less of this the better if you have a planer blade to use

---

Ridgid Tools are very highly regarded in the industrial world. Their hand and power tools alike are very rugged and forged not only of the best materials, but uncountable hours of work on the job everywhere. One of the most fascinating items in their line is the No. 700 Portable Power Drive. In addition to doing all manner of wrenchy-twisty things, it has something like a machine shop with a handle capability. I want one, from:

**The Ridge Tool Company
400 Clark St.
Elyria, Ohio 44035**

My brother has pointed out that even a poor man can save up to own and wear the world's finest socks. Tool freaks don't think this way. Would you believe a whetstone for $250 (at time of writing)? From:

**The Buckingham Tool Co.
P.O. Box 25
Crondall
Farnham, Surrey, England**

*From the Buckingham Tool Company catalog.*

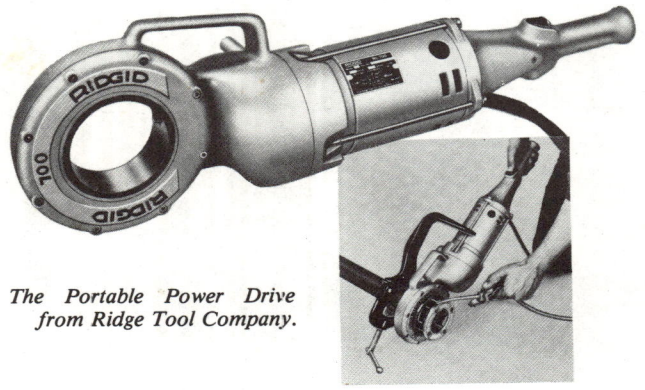

*The Portable Power Drive from Ridge Tool Company.*

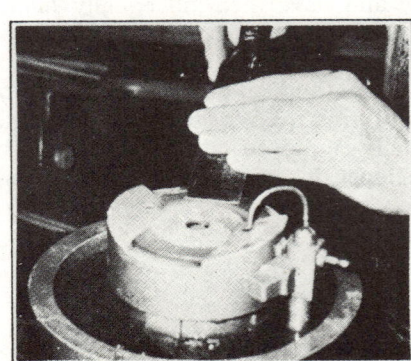

for the fine work. These blades are treated just the same way but need no set, as they are hollow-ground. If blades are taken care of, there is nowhere near as much trouble involved. But I repeat: I can't compete with the 75-cent pro shops.

Dado heads are restored about the same way, although usually they are not in bad shape: people who use dados do careful work. One dado problem is that it is hard to get a true, smooth bottom in a dado cut, in spite of careful jointing. There is a bit of unavoidable slack around an arbor that prevents getting all cutters set true each time. Usually it does not matter much.

For really clean bottom dados and plow cuts, I find a converted milling cutter is tops; industrial areas are apt to have these around on scrap piles for the taking. They often need a lot of regrinding for woodwork and are usually somewhat damaged—they are quite hard. The amount of reworking often seems too much, but once you have a good one in the shop, it's a prized tool. With the grain, across, or at an angle, one of these can produce very fine work. I spent several weekends bringing one of these back to my liking, and I have not regretted it. The principles for fixing it up are about the same as for reconditioning any circular saw, except that there is no set due to the great thickness, and no need for set, because there is enough clearance for grinding the teeth.

I've said nothing about filing hand saws; this is an art in itself, but it's not difficult to learn. I suggest using one of the filing guides now on the market until you get the hang of it, which does not take long. I think many beginning craftsmen tend to shy away from much sharpening simply because, as with lapstrake planking, they think it's too difficult—which you will find it's not, once you get into it and do it a step at a time as outlined above.

The usual contractor's circular electric hand saw is most often a dull blade out of round, and maybe it also lacks set due to sandy lumber and the rush of construction. A quality saw of this kind with a perfectly balanced and sharpened blade is a different matter, and much safer.

One more word. Before beginning to sharpen any saw blade—band, circular, and planer knives, too—check for warp or cracks. Junk the piece if there's any sign of them. This is not only unsafe, but it is then impossible to do a proper job. Break up the blade and grind the pieces into scrapers.

---

O.K., now, if Papa Bear is more to your liking, and you've slept on the Eiger, won at Monte Carlo, and are tiring of your sixth spouse, how about a circular saw 16 inches in diameter?! This one by Makita is 12 amps and the largest available anywhere. There are outlets nationwide. We heard of it from John Harra via the *CoEvolution Quarterly*. Go ahead. I'll hold your coat.

**John Harra Wood & Supply Co.
39 West 19th Street
New York, New York 10011**

*Below: The Makita 16" circular saw.*

We have never met any shopman (no, Virginia, there is no such thing as a shop-person) with any kind of working planer that did not simply squirm with smugness. They turn coal into fire, ore into ingot, sweetness into light, love into marriage, sickness into health, dead ducks into l'orange, aching feet into backrubs, and so on and so forth. Here's one (we've listed others before) from:

**Williams & Hussey Machine Corp.
Milford, New Hampshire 03055**

*W & H's molder-planer.*

*From the* VNR Illustrated Guide to Power Tools.

**VNR Illustrated Guide to Power Tools**
**by Rudolf F. Graf and George J. Whalen**
**Van Nostrand Reinhold, New York**
**240 pages, illus., index, 1978, $18.95**

Like the argument over auxiliaries versus pure sail, the argument over hand tools versus power tools is a thing of the past. To be sure, one or two unadulterated purists are still to be found, but most of us are thinly disguised schizophrenics. We love that old Disston, but given actual work to perform, we'll take the Skil every time.

With the power you get from power tools comes complexity and danger. More maintenance, more operating knowledge, and more safety consciousness are required. To get the most from your power tools takes study and experience. The latter is your responsibility; the former can be aided with the *VNR Illustrated Guide to Power Tools,* a guide to the set-up, use, maintenance, and repair of just about every modern shop tool available today.

Once in a while, not often, but sometimes now and then, you come onto a batch of wood that can only be described as in the bloody way; hard knots on crooked stock, burls, and so on. Sculpture knows all about it and has the tools. Here are three smallish sculptor's adzes from Sculpture Associates for such situations. I own the middle-size one and use it three or four times a year. Be prepared to pare down the handle. The ones supplied just aren't right. Then, for humungus and truly obnoxious stuff, there is the Super Hog-Power Adze! It doesn't have much to do with boatbuilding, but it's kinda interesting, all from:

**Sculpture Associates Ltd., Inc.
114 East 25th St.
New York, New York 10010**

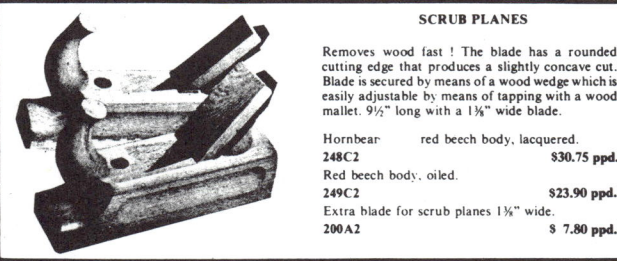

*From the Frog Tool Co. catalog.*

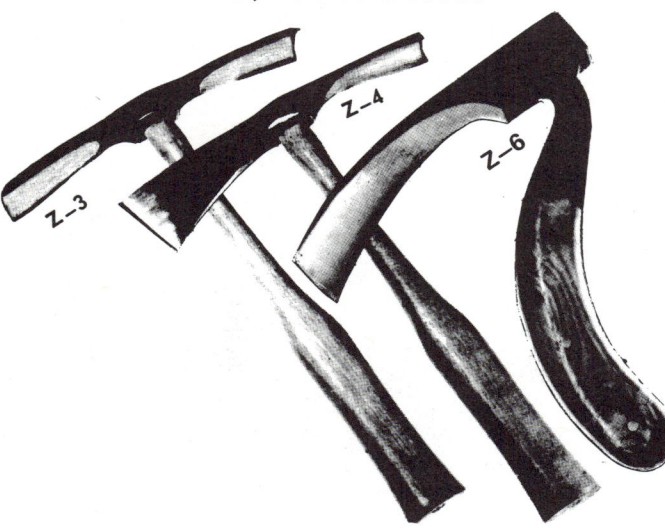

| SCULPTORS' ADZE |
|---|
| Made of the finest alloy steel, these well-balanced tools are hand-forged. 8" long head. |
| Z-3 — 2" gouge and 1½" gouge    2 lbs. |
| Z-4 — 2" straight and 2" gouge    2 lbs. |
| Z-6 — 3¼" gouge    4 lbs. |

*Above and below: Hand and power adzes from Sculpture Associates.*

Anyone who likes woodworking, and boatbuilding especially, enjoys hanging out around the older workmen, not just for the technical learning, but also with the subconscious sense that perhaps some of the *ease* will rub off. They have that uncanny knack of getting more done by going slowly! Drives ya nuts, if you think about it.

Anyway, these guys aren't romantics about their work—not as much at least as a lot of their younger onlookers—and almost all of them have given up the old scrub planes for the powered hand plane. The onlookers perhaps don't think to ask how they did the work in the old days, and probably assume that all our forebears were pleased to plane their hearts out for half a day to get out one piece of wood. No, they were not pleased, and they didn't. They used scrub planes, and do they ever get rid of wood fast! It will amaze you! And they cost a fifth to a tenth of what a power plane would. These shown are from:

**Frog Tool Co.
541 N. Franklin St.
Chicago, Illinois 60610**

Otner-Botner makes the nicest little pocket and finger planes of brass. Though they belong perhaps more appropriately in the modeling section, we'll stick them here, saying something like keep one in your shirt pocket while fitting plank.

**Otner-Botner
P.O. Box 6023
Providence, Rhode Island 02940**

*A whale of a plane from Otner-Botner*

There are a few exceptions, but generally it has been our policy right along not to re-list sources from other volumes. One of the exceptions, three or four times, has been Woodcraft Supply. They have this nasty habit of always coming up with new tools of obvious interest to boatbuilders!

Three items that appeared in recent Woodcraft catalogs (a buck each) are: (1) the Ulmia Auxiliary Vise—canoe and kayak builders are constantly faced with the problem of fairing ittybitty flimsy strips of wood over several feet, and only a vise of this configuration allows you to do it without screwing around a lot; (2) the Hollowing Plane No. 100½—rounding the inside of planking at turns, particularly bilges and tucks, can be exasperating without such a tool, particularly since all the old-time wooden ones now hang on the walls of bars; and (3) Abrasive Belt Cleaner—I don't know about you guys, but I'm paying over a buck each for belts these days, and anything that'll give another quarter hour is a good buddy, from:

**Woodcraft Supply**
**313 Montvale Ave.**
**Woburn, Massachusetts 01801**

*Some goodies from Woodcraft Supply's catalog.*

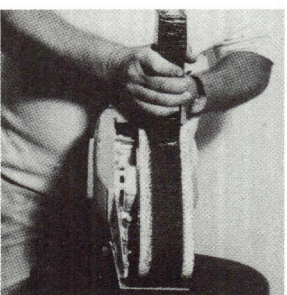

**ABRASIVE BELT CLEANER**
This cleaner will increase belt and disc life from 2 to 4 times. Simply hold the stick firmly against a moving abrasive belt or disc until all loaded particles have been removed—usually a matter of a few seconds. It can also be used to clean wood, plastic, copper, brass, aluminum, lead and other soft metals on both stationary and portable disc and belt sanders. Stick measures 1½" × 1½" × 8".
04W11-HH                                    $7.55 ppd.

**HOLLOWING PLANE NO. 100½**
A truly unique carving and modelling plane incorporating the popular palm plane design and a sole radiused in both length and width. The 1" blade is made of high carbon tool steel with an edge ground to match the shape of the sole. This grind enables it to rough out a hollow or contour easily with or across the grain. The cast iron body has sufficient weight to make planing a pleasure and the raised handle provides for considerable control. Overall length of the plane is 3½". The sole has a radius of 12" in length and ⅞" in width.
02A31-D                                     $14.45 ppd.

Replacement blade for 02A31-D
02F42-D                                      $2.50 ppd.

---

Dear Editors:

A source of sandpaper is a cabinet shop where they've got a surfacing sanding machine. These things use continuous belts, paper or cloth backed, in grits from 80 to 180. The belts are huge—36 inches wide and 5 feet in circumference.

Well . . . the belts break. Brand new ones. Offer to take out the trash.

Quick 'n' Dirty Thoughts—A cardboard (corrugated) mold for a cruddy one-off fiberglass job. You could wash out the mold once the glass set up. Yuk.

Think about it: "shop grade" plywood is sometimes a good bargain. It's all exterior-glue stuff where I shop, except the edges are a tad scroungy and sometimes you see impressions in face plies that are from plugs or plies that got pressed in the stack. It's cheap(er) though.

Chris-Craft used a plywood in their wood lapstrake boats that has various names depending on where you are. "Harborite," "Crezon" (long "e"), "Duraply." The guy at Champion Paper Products in Kansas City, Missouri, told me they invented "Duraply." It's a phenolic impregnated kraft paper covering that's applied to exterior plywood, mainly to sheathe houses. I can get ⅜" by 4' x 8' sheets at my local lumberyard. I got a stack of ¾" by 4' x 10' sheets through Champion for the art museum where I work. We made all our painted walls and pedestals with it. It takes paint perfectly, it's incredibly smooth, with no possibility of surface checking like straight-up fir ply invariably does.

It isn't cheap. But for certain things, it's great stuff. Champion says they'll make it up in 12-foot lengths if you want to order it from the mill. Champion claims that there are fewer internal voids in this stuff than in AC or better grades of plywood. (I think I read a confirmation of that in *Fine Woodworking*.) Same is supposed to hold true of the junkier B face (and worse) grades of other plywoods. I think it's true.

—Mark Roeyer
Lawrence, Kansas

*Okkake-daisen-tsugi,* the Rabbeted Oblique Scarf Joint  Because the *okkake-daisen-tsugi,* or rabbeted oblique scarf joint, resists tension and bending stress, it has many uses, such as in splicing beams or lintels or in underpinning. Since the male and female halves of this joint are cut identically, even down to the tapered keyholes, the half driven home is considered the male half. Usually the face in the center where the joints lap is cut at an angle, as shown in the drawing at right. When cut this way, of course, the male half can be driven home from only one side, but it is a bit easier to get a tight joint. Sometimes, however, the center lap is cut at a right angle to the edge of the work, as shown in Figure 23, and then the joint is also known as a *wari-tsugi,* or divided joint.

The *okkake-daisen-tsugi, okkake-tsugi* (a variation that does not use keys), and *kanawa-tsugi* all belong to the same general class of joints and are really not very different from each other. They were devised and greatly refined as carpenters' skills increased with the development of new tools and techniques in the last few hundred years; however, these joints are not particularly strong. For example, tests conducted on a 9 cm. square beam (about 3 1/2" × 3 1/2") spliced with an *okkake-daisen-tsugi* revealed that its tensile strength was only one-tenth that of a sound 9 cm. square beam of the same wood. In general, then, it would seem that this joint should be used in framework only where it will not be subjected to great tension stress. However, it is sometimes used for the underpinning of pillars being restored in ancient Japanese architecture.

In a horizontal member, whether the joint is made so that the keys enter from the side or from the top depends on the type of stress the joint will have to withstand. For example, if the joint will be subjected to bending stress, then the key side should be uppermost so that the rabbeted ends of the joint can be brought into full play to resist both bending and compression force. However, when this joint is reinforced with bolts, straps, or plates, it seems to work equally well in either position.

*From* The Art of Japanese Joinery.

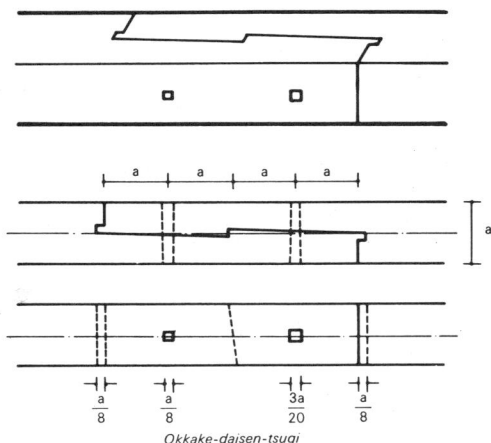

*Okkake-daisen-tsugi*

## The Art of Japanese Joinery
## by Kiyosi Seike
## John Weatherhill, Inc., New York
## 126 pages, illus., 1977, $8.95

The revival of high craftsmanship in wooden boatbuilding has taken on all the elements of a contest to see who can execute the best, most elaborate joinerwork. The joint that holds is the joint to use, but who can deny that the toughest joints are usually the most beautiful? So if strong, durable, and *gorgeous* joints are your goal, you have nowhere else to turn but to Japan. The Japanese have elevated wood joinery to an art form. Through excellent photographs, fine diagrams, and clear text, this book shows you what it's all about. The only thing lacking is step-by-step instructions on how to cut the joints, but you can't expect the masters to reveal *all* their secrets, can you?

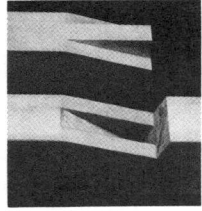

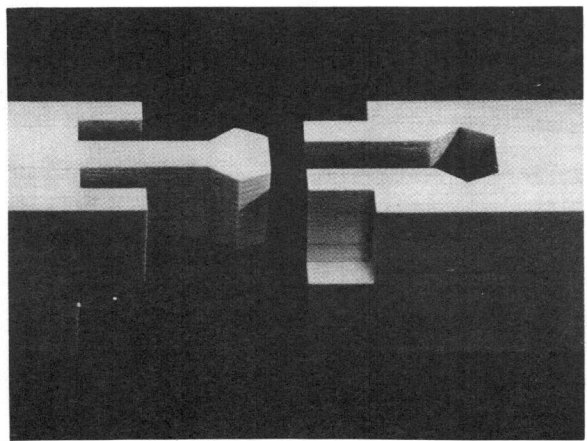

*From* The Art of Japanese Joinery.

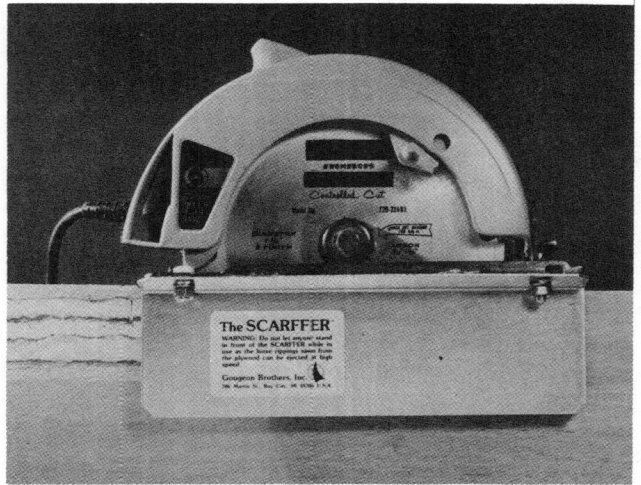

*The Scarffer from Gougeon Brothers.*

*Fred Clark's blank handle.*

Scarfing up long sections of plywood is not the Big Problem one's mind tends to make it; but that doesn't mean that making it easier is a bad idea. It's a good idea, for heaven sakes! Try the Scarffer, from:

**Gougeon Brothers, Inc.
706 Martin St.
Bay City, Michigan 48706**

Here's a neat wrinkle in a small business: a brass-jawed colleted blank handle that you can carve to your own specs and that accepts a host of knife blades and carving tools. From:

**Fred Clark
Warren Tools
P.O. Box 289
Rhinebeck, New York 12572**

Another nice feature offered by Warren Tools is their leather tool roll carrying the carving gouges as well as blades. Good for traveling and to have aboard.

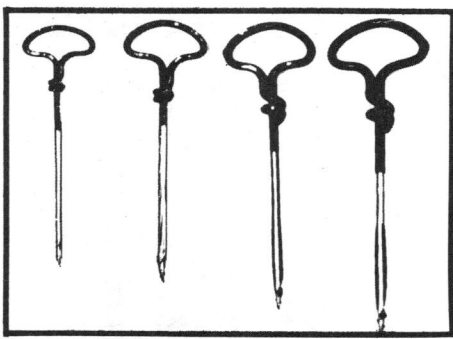

*Nonalcoholic gimlets from Fair Price.*

*Greenlee's Nail Eater.*

The Greenlee Tool Company is reintroducing many of its long-discontinued quality hand tools. Great. The drought of the fifties, sixties, and early seventies is drawing to a close.

**Greenlee Tool Co.
2136 12th Street
Rockford, Illinois 61101**

In canoe, kayak, and ceiling work an electric drill can often be used excessively, what they called counter-productive back in Great Society days. Here's a set of gimlets for five bucks, minus the vodka, from:

**Fair Price Tool Company
P.O. Box 627
La Canada, California 91011**

Hole alignment is an every-other-day concern in almost all boatbuilding, and here's an item to help ease the suffering of it all; the Precision Drill Guide from:

**Portalign Tool Corp.
P.O. Box A-80547
San Diego, California 92138**

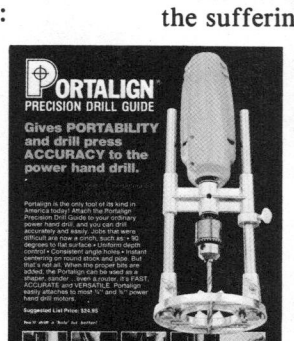

*Portalign says with this, "You'll drill a 'hole' lot better."*

Like so many activities ancillary to nautical skills, carving can become a habitual fun thing to do. In addition to the *National Carvers Review* (Drawer 693, Chicago, Illinois 60642, $6.00/yr.), aspiring buffs will want to know about *The Mallet,* a National Carvers Museum publication that is free to museum members. There are several levels of membership, the basic one costing $10. Write to:

> National Carvers Museum Foundation
> 14960 Woodcarver Road
> Monument, Colorado 80132

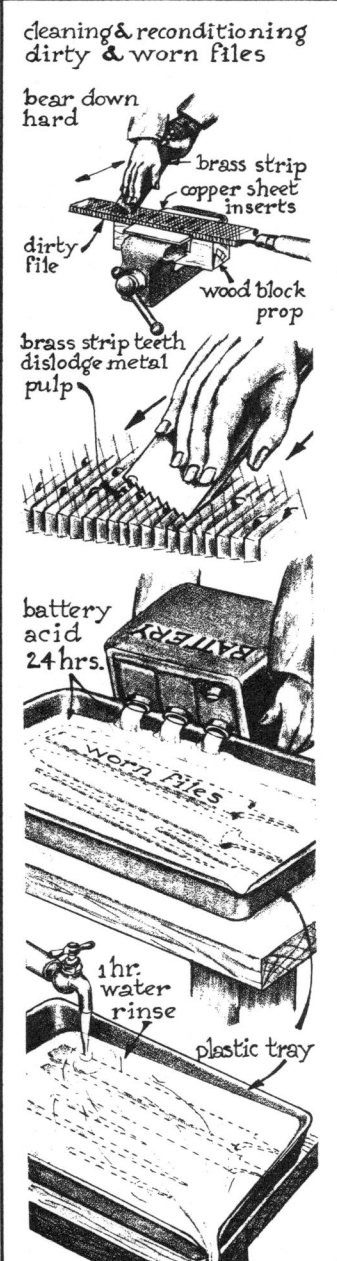

*Left: From* The Recycling, Use, & Repair of Tools.

***The Recycling, Use, & Repair of Tools***
**by Alexander G. Weygers**
**Van Nostrand Reinhold, New York**
**112 pages, illus., glossary, paperbound, 1978, $6.95**

We have been fans of Alexander Weygers for a long time now. His *The Making of Tools* (MC-2, page 54) and *The Modern Blacksmith* (MC-4, page 34) are two of the most intelligent, clearly thought out, and informative books we have ever seen. They are inspirations.

This latest is everything we have grown to expect. The premise is that the scrapyards of the world are not the ends of things—rather, they are the beginnings. With rebuilt these and recycled those, he shows us how to make such things as tool handle ferrules, a wood-turning lathe and tools, chisels and punches, makeshift bearings, and files. In the process he tells us how to drill square holes, punch small washers, use a trip hammer, and sharpen tools. As in Weygers's other books, to do what he describes, you'll need a fair amount of metal-working tools before you start.

THE SEA-BAT.

## Getting a Handle on Things
### by Pete Culler

Time to consider the hafting of tools, or putting in suitable handles, in old tools, or altering new ones that seem unsatisfactory.

First question is what wood, and where do you get it? Simply use your head, and think ahead: the woodpile, and local woods nearby, supply all you will ever need. If you are a real city feller, better buy what's available, and it often won't be quite right.

Any handle should be seasoned, dry stock. This is where you have to plan ahead—some woodpiles automatically supply dry-enough stock. Some storage time in a heated room before using helps things along.

Chopping and striking tools have things in common: they have some sort of eye that the handle must fit into. These eyes vary in shape depending on the particular tool, which is an obvious statement, but not really thought about by some greenhorns until confronted with it. I've seen deerfoot chopping axe handles put in an axe head designed for hewing, and an adze handle put in backward more than once—incredible, but these things do happen. My shop has been a crossroads for hanging adzes; most come in hung backward, or, if not, they have no hang at all, so they are impossible to use. (I go into the details of how to hang an adze in my book *Skiffs and Schooners*, so I won't repeat it here.)

As to kinds of wood, many are available. Hickory can be found in some places, ash, white oak or any other dense oak, maple, birch, most of the hardwoods—locust, apple, and pear are fine, the two latter especially if the handle is curved—plus many other hardwoods not so common. A wood that continues to warp, even though dry, is no good.

It's obvious which side of an axe head, whether for chopping or hewing, is supposed to be up. Not so some striking tools. Examine the eye; good ones show a taper in the eye in favor of the wedge—that is, the wider part will be the top, although this is not always the case with some cheap tools.

Once you have fitted the right handle to the right tool (and previous *Mariner's Catalogs* have shown some very fine tool handle shapes and what tools they suit), note that it must be wedged. A saw cut is made fore and aft, not quite to the depth of the head; say, three-fourths of it. It should fit so the handle must be driven into the eye by modest taps on the end of the handle. Take care tapping a deerfoot handle or you can spoil it. I like to make wedges of oak or locust. Be sure the wedge is of such length that it does not "bottom out" before fully spreading the handle. If this is a re-handle job, and there were one or two corrugated steel wedges in the original, put 'em in again, usually at a 45-degree angle. These steel wedges, by the way, are available in some hardware stores. It's sort of obvious that you trim off the excess wood and smooth things up before driving any steel wedges. Most of my driving or chopping tools don't have these wedges; I simply salvage from those that do in making a new handle.

Sometimes, due to long storage in a very dry place, a handle will become loose in spite of proper fitting. Simply soak the head of the tool in water for a short time. This usually fixes it right up. If a handle persists in becoming loose, it's time to refit it; nothing is more apt to get you in trouble than a loose-headed tool.

On the other hand, consider this: heavy bolt sets, handled spike and nail sets, and blacksmith sets of all kinds, including hot and cold cutters, should be handled loose, wobbly loose. The heads are retained by a pin (a cutoff nail will do) through the top of the handle, which in this case should stick beyond the eye an inch or more. Any tool struck by another is never quite square with the work, and the slack lets the head line up with the maul, or hammer, and the work; otherwise you end up with a badly stung hand at best, possibly a broken wrist. I save discarded handles from repairs, cut them down, and use them in these various sets, because such handles are not critical in shape and are somewhat expendable—being loose, they wear in the eye. So much for striking and chopping handles. You learn what you like the feel of, and make it accordingly.

Handles for cutting tools such as chisels and gouges are easily made on a lathe or simply cut out by hand. The same above-mentioned hardwoods do very well. For light paring tools that are never struck, lighter, softer woods seem to do okay—mahogany scrap is good for these. Some pointers here: some hands are big, others small, occasionally somewhat crippled or arthritic; try shapes you think you will like. If it's a replacement, did you like the original or not?

Handles should not bottom out or fit to a shoulder in socket tools, artistic as the latter may be. They won't stay tight and usually start splitting off the shoulder. For stout socket chisels and gouges I make ferrules from readily available electrical conduit, which is easily cut square with a tubing or pipe cutter. If you use a cutter, file or scrape out the burr on one side. Here again, don't set to a shoulder, because it will cause splitting as the handle wears under blows.

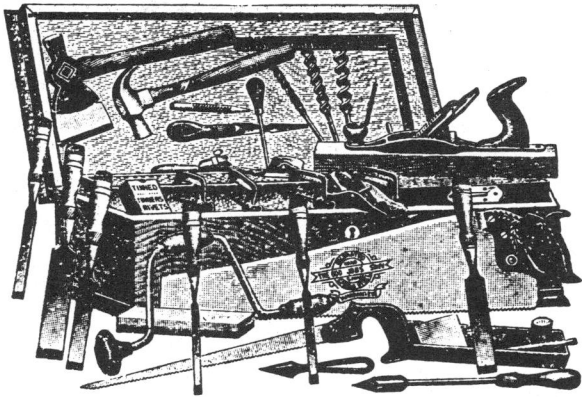

Tools with a tang and shoulder, intended only for hand pushing or very light tapping, need a ferrule on the lower end of the handle, so I use conduit again. Often a ferrule is fitted on top too; if so, it should be set well down. Setting to a shoulder is okay here, but leave enough wood to round the end nicely for comfort. If you pound very hard on this tool, you are going to wreck it anyhow—reach for a socket tool instead.

Some like a hexagonal shape on part of a paring tool handle, others like a round with four shallow flats, and there are all sorts of shapes in between. Here again, develop a shape you like. Some new paring and carving tools come with very nice handles; others sometimes lack a proper feel.

Pretty much the same principles apply to many other tools, knives, turning tools, and whatnot. Saw handles get broken, or you might need to restore an old one. You can buy plastic and plywood saw handles in many hardware stores if you like them, but I much prefer, if the saw blade is a nice one, to copy some nice-feeling old-timer, say, in beechwood, including the fancy carved work. Replacement screws for saws are available.

Planes often need restoring, both metal and wood. It's not much of a trick to carve a new wood handle or turn a knob for a Stanley. Same with wood planes; some have sort of a sawgrip and knobs, or a horn. Many wood planes are simply their own handles, and they are often uncomfortable. Analyze what's wrong and do some whittling—this often turns a brute into a nice tool. The standard boxy wood plane, especially if it is of some length, is often helped by cutting it down aft of the bit and resetting the grip. If it has no knob, it often helps to add one.

I've never learned to use the readily available wooden European planes, which are nicely built and expensive. They simply feel awkward and top-heavy. I'm sure one can get used to them, but I simply never learned to use the type.

With the above suggestions, a person who is the least bit handy should have no trouble restoring and repairing handles that just suit his fancy and in many cases are better than can be bought.

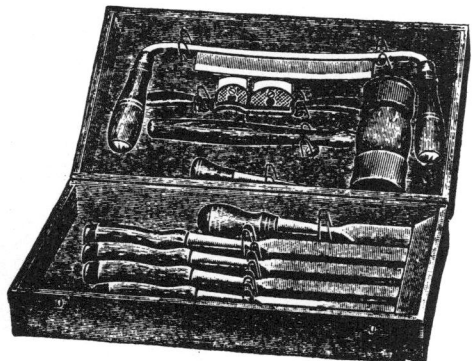

## Coopering

We haven't seen a copy, but we understand there is a book in print covering the history and art of coopering, including the methods, tools, and timber used:

**The Cooper and His Trade
by Kenneth Kilby
Humanities Press
Atlantic Highlands, New Jersey
1971, $18**

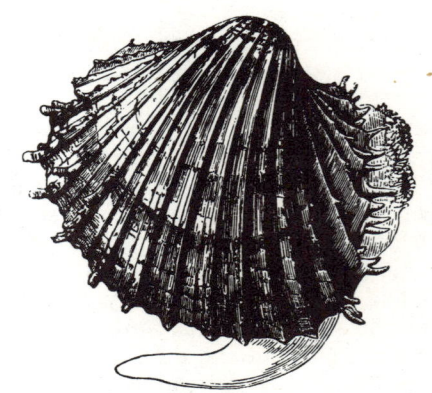

### NOW! Polishing Blocks for Spot Work

These durable polishing blocks will remove rust, light scratches, gunk and other blemishes on your knife blade. They will clean up tarnished brass and scrub any other material that you have on your knife—wood, micarta, stag, etc. **Just like the polishing wheels above these blocks are polyurethane based, impregnated with super cutting silicon carbide.** They measure 3″ long by 1″ by ½″ and so are comfortable to grip while you clean up the hard-to-get-at places. We have them in the same three grits as the polishing wheels above so you can match up your blocks and wheels.

Some people like to use these blocks when they want to touch up only part of a blade. Generally, the coarse grit blocks are great for cleaning up tangs in preparation for soldering and the finer grit blocks are better for final appearance touch-up work. They're also great around the house for speeding up innumerable other clean-up tasks.

Order No. 8-CH-175 .......................................... (60 Grit Block)
Order No. 8-CH-176 .......................................... (120 Grit Block)
Order No. 8-CH-177 .......................................... (220 Grit Block)
$1.50 each. Set of three/$3.95.

Boatshops tend to be near water. Now that you've picked yourself up off the floor after that terrible secret was let fly, you'll note or imagine that iron and tool steels respond to these hydro-exigencies by trying to rejoin their Earthmother, beginning with pits. That one little oxygen molecule (two atoms loosely bonded) will find that one little micro-crystal just dying to be oxidized, and it's the pits. Knifemakers deal with this problem all the time, so, when you emerge from your winter I-ain't-goin'-anywhere-near-that-shop syndrome

*From Atlanta Cutlery's catalog.*

and come to find your tools a mass of chickenpox, get the polishing blocks they use for spot work, from:

Atlanta Cutlery Corp.
Box 839
Conyers, Georgia 30207

A heretofore-unlisted general tool source, Conover also was active in creating *The Tool Catalog,* a 288-page book surveying tools and tool sources from around the country. Selling for $14.95, the book offers a unique roundup on the subject, is conservative and commonsensical in its choices of what to review, and is only a little reticent to make comparisons. Not a bad place to begin for someone shopping for a shop. From:

Conover Woodcraft Specialties
18125 Madison Road
Parkman, Ohio 44080

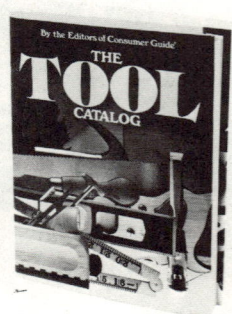

## Knife-Making

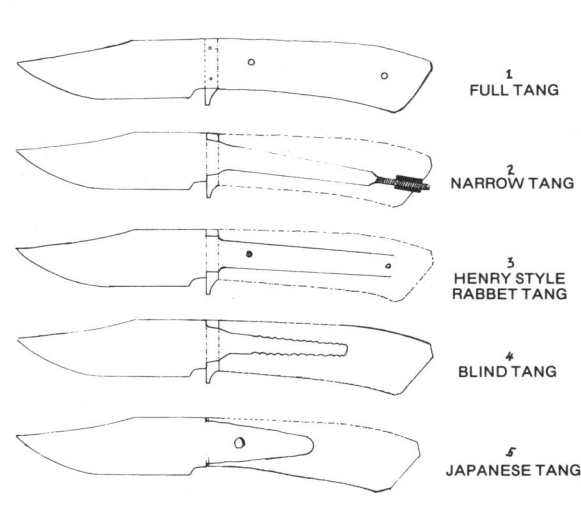

A few pointers may be of help. Foremost in the authors' opinion is always the question, "Will the knife function as designed for the purpose intended?" Obviously we are not talking about minimums here. It's possible to gut a deer with a penknife, and some enemy sentry can be dispatched quite well with a fifty-cent ice pick. In the context of this book, function means not just well but superbly.

A remark by R. W. Loveless has real meaning to the maker who would earn his daily bread by making knives. "A knife must not only be made from the best steel available, the best handle material, and the best construction possible, but it must also have visual and tactical appeal so that the customer will just have to pick it up, fall in love with the feel of it, and maybe buy it."

It is extremely important in knife design to have or develop the ability to put your ideas about knife design on paper.

There is no other practical way for the knifemaker to see his ideas develop, to make changes, and to visually appraise his efforts. By making overlays, subtle line changes can be made, shifted slightly, widened, shortened, narrowed, etc. If you think you can't draw, practice until you can.

*Left, above, and below: From* How to Make Knives.

 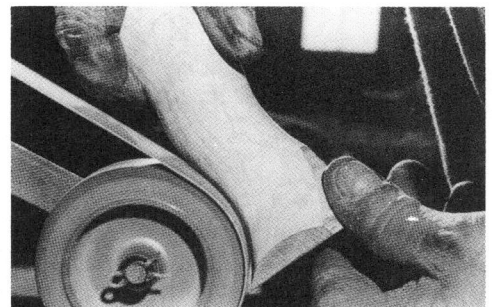 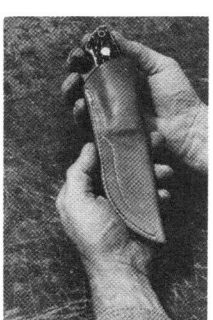

Further to our descriptions of books on knife-making in past *Catalogs*, we have found another book:

**How to Make Knives
by Richard W. Barney and Robert W. Loveless
Beinfeld Publishing, North Hollywood, California
182 pages, illus., 1977, $15.95**

One of the authors, Robert Loveless, is generally considered to be one of the best custom knife-makers alive today, so this book is worth studying if only to determine how a master performs. Especially valuable is an annotated listing of sources of knife-making services and materials. Even so, however, we prefer *Step-by-Step Knifemaking* by David Boye (see MC-6, p, 39).

Another interesting publication, primarily for hard-core knife buffs and collectors, is:

**The Gun Digest Book of Knives
by B.R. Hughes and Jack Lewis
Digest Books, Northfield, Illinois
288 pages, illus., 1973, $6.95**

It's filled with articles on knife-making, both custom and production, collecting, design, sharpening, history, etc.

*Below and left: From* The Gun Digest Book of Knives.

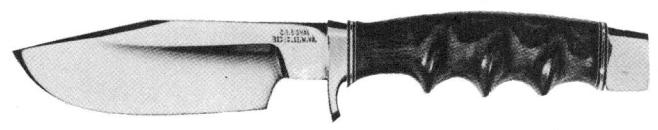 

First, don't order this $3.50 catalog we're about to review here unless you are a large industrial lab or factory that will be doing some major ordering in weird categories of stuff. That said, know that the Abbeon Cal Industrial, Laboratory, and Plant Buying Catalog is one of the most unusual, interesting, idea-stimulating,

*Left: The Flexbar from Abbeon Cal.*

and simply splendid pieces of industrial literature we have ever had the pleasure of reading. It is 895 packed pages of incredibly diverse and otherwise hard-to-find products. The people who run it obviously care about their business—love it, in fact—and to read their philosophical rap about the nature of life, love, and the pursuit of honest profit is enough to wipe the most sheepish grin from the most doctrinaire Marxist. The book has a trillion things in it. We're showing this really odd holding device that could be a third arm for some boatbuilder.

**Abbeon Cal, Inc.
123 Gray Avenue
Santa Barbara, California 93101**

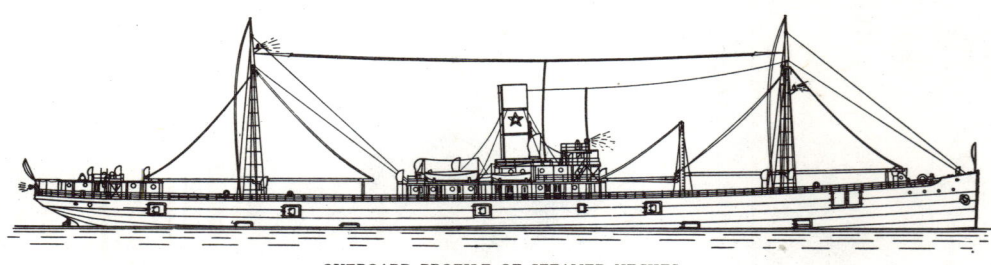

OUTBOARD PROFILE OF STEAMER NECHES

### WOOD - OUR ONLY RENEWABLE NATURAL RESOURCE CONSTRUCTION MATERIAL

We read very little these days about the traditional methods of boat construction using wood except in the pages of those admirable periodicals: "National Fisherman," and "Woodenboat," and the newsletter of the Traditional Small Craft Association. Wood is a favorite boatbuilding material of mine and many others, partly because we feel at home working with it, and partly because a few of us believe that the use of petroleum-based plastics for such frivolous applications as skimobiles, automobiles and yachts is a scandalous squandering of a soon-to-be scarce commodity. Except possibly for steel, sheet plywood may still be the least expensive material for the amateur boatbuilder.

I am indebted for the following information to a paper published by H.O. Fleischer of the Forest Products Laboratory of the U.S. Department of Agriculture. Wood is our one renewable material resource which, with wise husbandry, need not be in short supply. It takes over 67,000 kw.-hr. of energy to produce one ton of aluminum, over 12,000 kw.-hr. to produce one ton of rolled steel but a mere 1500 kw.-hr. for a ton of lumber. There are many other good things to say about wood. Environmental damage incurred in its harvest is much less than that for other materials. C.W. Dane estimates in a published paper that the social costs of aluminum, concrete and steel are: 28, 24, and 9% of the respective finished product selling prices. The same costs for lumber are rated at only 2%.

One of my favorite authors: George Snyder, published an article entitled: "Endangered Boatbuilding Materials," in the March/April issue of "Multihulls" magazine. To my surprise, in the next issue of this periodical, poor George was attacked strongly in two articles and one letter. Statements were made leading the reader to believe that there never will be a petroleum shortage. Bunk! Writing from a background of 20 years in the energy field (nuclear), my own strongly-held belief is that this generation will be cursed by our descendants for our lack of concern with conserving petroleum and its derivatives and other irreplaceable minerals. Three arguments are usually advanced by laymen I talk to in this area to support their contention that there is not and never will be a scarcity of oil: 1. It is all a plot of the oil companies. 2. Technology will save us. 3. Economics - the more we are willing to pay for oil, the deeper we can drill, etc. etc. This is not the place to argue out these well-refuted and rather naive points, but the lack of concern of the majority of people with this problem appalls me.

Build a wooden boat! Use Epoxy resin and glue, as it is coal tar based and not a petroleum derivative as is polyester.

*Reprinted with permission from the* Experimental Yacht Society Journal.

## For Aesthetes Only

Not too long ago, before synthetics and other imitations gained the upper hand, wood was an accepted building material and was used, period. No philosophical preference had to be proclaimed, no positions had to be staked out and defended. You wanted to build a boat, or a table, or a mast—you didn't think twice; you went down to the mill and asked Joe for so many board feet of pine, cedar, oak, cherry, or what-have-you.

Modern technology changed all that. Now if you want to build a boat, you have big choices to make before you start. Should you build it out of fiberglass, ferrocement, wood, steel, aluminum, or rolled-up newspaper? Each material has its advocates, and each has its place. But it's funny how the preferences for a particular material have come to be stated. The defenders of fiberglass almost always bring up glass's easy maintenance, but have you ever heard it called beautiful? Aluminum is always touted as having strength with light weight, but have you ever heard it termed warm and soul-satisfying?

Wood, on the other hand, has almost always been defended in terms of aesthetics. It warms the heart, it satisfies deep, inner yearnings, it represents Nature rather than Man, it signifies reservoirs of good taste in the user. When sentiments reach such lofty planes, you can be sure that the time has come for academics to get into the act. It has and they did:

---

None of us who have visited Japan have failed to be bowled over by the Japanese approach to living—exemplified by their handling and feeling for wood. This is true in modern work as well as the traditional work which still exists and is still practiced in Japan. This is a natural outgrowth of Japan's very beginnings in the eighth century under the Shinto religion. The attitude of man toward trees, as to all nature, was a very sympathetic one. The woodcutter never cut down the tree without appealing first to the kami or spirit which he believed resided in it. Today as then the Japanese woodworking is done with the same respect for the spirit of the wood. For instance, Langdon Warner tells us in his book *The Enduring Art of Japan* that thirty years ago a fresh log for the repair of the huge Daibutsuden temple in Nara was laid out on blocks to keep it from the damp earth and a mat shed was built above. He was told it had been felled three years before, three more moons must pass before it was hewn, more moons still before it could be sawn and then the planks wedged apart for air in the pile, still an unspecified number of moons before the planks could be pegged in place on the great building. By that time the spirit, Kino Kami, who writhes in agony and splits the log, would have made her escape. Mr. Warner goes on to say it is neither sentimental nostalgia nor worship of the good old days which makes us recognize the large measure of human good in this society. Their material culture was fostered by a natural system of craftsmen priests compared with the complex structuring of today's industrialized society. It is certain that fewer conveniences were produced, but one necessary thing we lack today was then available. This necessity we lack is the prime requirement that a man's trade should permit and train him to grow into a complete man. Our growing specialization quite blocks the complete development of potential skills of hand and mind and soul. Without it no one can be called whole or wholesome.

The confidence in one's ability to create wood objects which are beautiful and useful, or, to reformulate that slightly, to create ourselves the objects we desire in a real material, grows in importance as we realize that it is a key on the one hand to the world of art, and on the other, to a personal involvement with the objects of everyday life. It is here that our present educational system shows its flaws most vividly. Woodworking is just another drill where children make someone else's thing without any real desire or understanding. The child is induced to make poorly designed towel racks, napkin holders, and other trivia instead of beginning at the beginning to relate his effort to real needs through the creation of useful, beautiful objects. Here is certainly a chance, which is going to waste, to create both a market and an indigenous art. Public knowledge of wood is limited, and need not be. Skills with tools, confidence, and respect for the material could be taught in schools, but is not. The child is confronted with another tedious adult exercise which does nothing positive, but is seemingly contrived just to waste his time.

I believe that the lumber industry, the tool makers, and producers of quality wood products of all kinds have a great challenge and opportunity before them which I hope they are visionary enough to pick up —to encourage, educate, and reward the craftsman-artist who uses wood well.

---

**Design and Aesthetics in Wood**
**Edited by Eric A. Anderson and**
**George F. Earle**
**State University of New York Press**
**Albany, New York**
**223 pages, illus., 1972, $20.00**

This book is a compilation of papers presented at a symposium on "Design and Aesthetics in Wood." It is divided into four parts—wood as an art and artifact, wood as architectural material, design in a dynamic technology, and wood as a material—and it represents some of America's best thinking on wood. If your choice is a wooden boat, and you can't find the words to explain why, this book will help you out.

*Above: From* Design and Aesthetics in Wood.

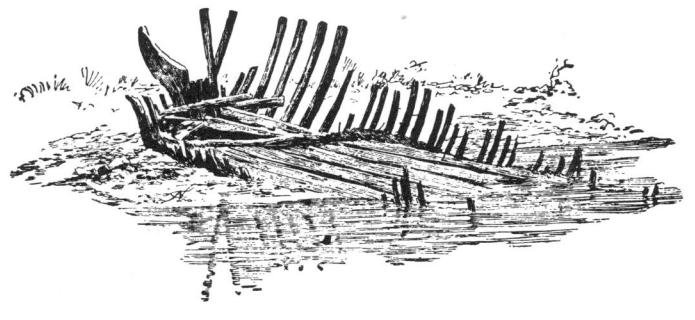

While we're on the subject of aesthetics and design, some time back we reviewed David Pye's *The Nature and Art of Workmanship* (MC-3, page 48) and recommended it as an excellent treatise on what constitutes good, bad, and mediocre workmanship. Since then, Pye has written a new book, *The Nature and Aesthetics of Design,* in which he discusses utilitarianism versus art, and techniques in relationship with intent. We're always talking about boat "designs"; it's about time we started thinking about what we mean. We found this to be a first-rate essay:

***The Nature and Aesthetics of Design***
**by David Pye**
**Van Nostrand Reinhold, New York**
**159 pages, illus., 1978, $12.95**

---

Where then did the idea of the doubling round the pivot come from? There is a certain element of invention or creation in the idea. Joining timbers by lapping or doubling is commonplace. Pivoting timbers on a bar through the middle is commonplace. But the idea of making a joint in a lever precisely at the point where it needs most strength is by no means commonplace. Moreover the act of neatly killing several birds with one stone, as we have done here, is not commonplace. It is in its degree ingenious.

But I do not believe that this or any such ingenuity is unprompted. Invention involves an antecedent of some kind.

In the present instance, when I set out to trace in my unconscious mind the antecedent for the doubled lever I found that there was persistently in my mind's eye a picture of something not only doubled but also crooked (Fig. 14). I realised that this was probably a recollection of an oar, called a Yuloh, used in China for sculling Junks and Sampans by the stern. The analogy then became apparent. The Yuloh, being an oar, works like a lever. It has a doubling in it which serves to make it crooked, *and it is pivoted at or near the doubling*. It is pivoted in a different way from our lever and produces a different though analogous result. The 'creative' act was the unconscious selection of the Yuloh out of all the innumerable devices stored in a designer's memory, as an analogous device to this very different

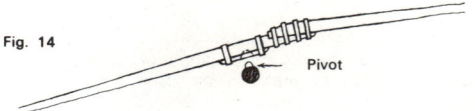
Fig. 14

lever. Fig. 14 shows a Yuloh.

It is of course possible that I have unconsciously produced the Yuloh as a cover for unconsciously lifting someone else's invention of a doubled lever (which would be pretty ingenious in itself!). It is also possible that this way of working is a personal eccentricity of mine. But I do not believe in either possibility. I believe that this is the normal process of inventive 'creation'.

*From* The Nature and Aesthetics of Design.

---

Three more wood sources to add to the files; F. Scott Jay deals specifically in boat stock, the other two in general and exotic furniture and related woods.

F. Scott Jay & Co.
P.O. Box 146
8174 Ritchie Highway
Pasadena, Maryland 21122

Unicorn Universal Woods Ltd.
137 John Street
Toronto, Ontario, Canada M5V 2E4

Amherst Wood Working
Box 464
Sunderland Rd.
North Amherst, Massachusetts 01056

F. SCOTT JAY and COMPANY, INC.

AMHERST WOOD WORKING

### Advantages of pigment oil stain

Of all the stains discussed, this is the most simple to apply. You merely put it on the already-prepared surface and wipe off the excess. More will be said of this later in this chapter. It is not a fast-drying stain and, consequently, need not be applied with the haste and care required for other stains. A reasonable length of time may elapse before wiping off the excess. Then, too, the ingredients for making this stain are common household supplies; and, where they are not available at home, they can be purchased from your local paint dealer. The oil color pastes are not wasted if they remain unused. They can be stored for future use without losing any of their strength.

This stain is important also as a blending and antiquing medium. When a dark stain is applied to a light-finished surface and then wiped off lightly, a contrasting soft color will result. See Chapter 13 for further details.

### Disadvantages of pigment oil stain

The main weakness of pigment oil stain lies in the fact that it is not a deep penetrating stain; it is a superficial stain just covering the top layer of the wood surface. It fades when subjected to light for a long period of time and, consequently, is not recommended for very fine work. Also, it does not possess the clarity and transparency of the other stains mentioned and must be wiped off after it is applied to assure some showing of the wood grain. On soft woods like pine and gum, the stain has a tendency to darken the wood more than if used on hard woods like maple or birch; therefore, a good practice is to coat these soft woods with a wash coat of shellac or linseed oil before applying the stain. More uniformity of color will also result. As with the penetrating oil stains, fillers cannot be applied directly over the surface stained with pigment oil stain. The filler will combine with the stain, forming a muddy film over the surface. The stained surface should be coated with a wash coat of shellac in order to protect it before the filler is applied. Finally, the length of time required for drying should also be considered. At least twenty-four hours should elapse before any other material is applied.

### Applying pigment oil stain

The piece to be stained should be thoroughly prepared with the usual sanding and checking. Then you must prepare the desired shade of stain according to instructions.
1. Use a stiff, flat bristle brush. Fill it to capacity, but not dripping wet.
2. Apply the stain to one section of the job. Direction of brushing and amount of stain applied is not important at this stage.

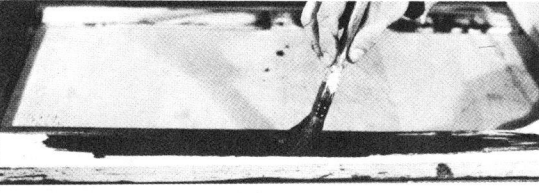

Pigment oil stain is brushed on, then the excess is wiped off with a rag. Use a dry brush to get the excess stain out of crevices.

*From* Wood Finishing and Refinishing.

***Wood Finishing and Refinishing***
**by S.W. Gibbia**
**Van Nostrand Reinhold, New York**
**271 pages, illus., index, 1971 (rev. ed.),**
**paperbound, $6.95**

Though aimed at cabinetmakers, this book has immense value for those boatmen who are hung up on brightwork (there is a chapter on paint, but the main thrust is varnish, shellac, lacquer, and oil). It is so good, in fact, that we suspect it has been for years the primary reference book for the writers of those obligatory spring fitting-out articles in the slick boating magazines. Besides the clear, unvarnished (heh, heh) text, what we like best about this book is the discussions on the advantages and disadvantages of various types of finishes. And the chapter on stains is enlightening, to say the least.

---

And a fascinating place offering flitches and free-form slabs of unusual woods (dimension stuff, too) is:

**Willard Brothers Woodcutters**
**300 Basin Road**
**Trenton, New Jersey 08619**

## Wood Bibliography

The American Crafts Council publishes a number of books and monographs of interest to craftsmen, among them a bibliography of wood that lists publications in such fields as woodturning, veneering and marquetry, finishing, woodcarving and sculpture, restoration and repair, and tools:

**Bibliography: Wood**
**American Crafts Council**
**44 West 53rd St.**
**New York, N.Y. 10019**
**23 pages, 1978, paperbound**
**$3.40, members; $4.40, nonmembers**

Dear Editors:
I have been working with osage orange for some time and find it a great wood. Very heavy, hard, weather-resistant, finishes well, etc. I enclose a small piece, in case you are not too familiar with it. I have made a few cleats, deadeyes, belaying pins, etc.

As you may know, it was a native of Arkansas, but about 80 years ago it was introduced here (western New York state) for fence posts, etc. Still some left here and there.

**Robert Gilmore**
**Wyoming, N.Y.**

Not a breakthrough, but certainly a development, the new line of portable chainsaw mills offered by Sperber is state-of-the-art stuff. If this is how you've *got* to go, then this is how you *ought* to. Hard work, but what slabbage!

**Sperber Tool Works Inc.**
**Box 1224**
**West Caldwell, New Jersey 07006**

*The double engine portable chainsaw mill from Sperber.*

---

Not long ago there was a bunch of us (eccentrics don't come in groups) standing about watching a fellow use BlockBond. This is cheap (inexpensive) bagged goop that you mix up and spread over cinder-block foundation bricks to fix them in place and seal them from moisture. Well, this stuff has a hardener of some sort in it, and by and by it hardened up and we began to play with it. It's tough stuff, rather like fiberglass in some ways, and we began to wonder whether it could be used in boatbuilding somehow; paper boats or in mold-making er sumthin'.... Anybody tried using the stuff? You surely can't beat the price, which, if it does turn out to have some nautical applications, will no doubt skyrocket the minute "marine" gets stuck onto its label.

—Eds.

---

Convinced of the general conspiracy against boatbuilders, a bunch of cutthroat THEMS keeping us from our Right to Wood, we continue our occasional listings of timber tools. Snow & Nealley offers a full line, and we just had to list and show this breakthrough in woodsplitting technology from Chopper. It's the first advance since the Iron Age and a note to note for the faint-hearted nothing-new-under-the-sunners.

**Snow & Nealley Co.**
**155 Perry Road**
**Bangor, Maine 04401**

*Left: Timber carrier from Snow & Nealley. Below: The Chopper 1 log-splitting axe.*

**Chopper Industries**
**P.O. Box 87**
**Easton, Pennsylvania 18042**

# The Mariner's Catalog / 33

*From* Fine Woodworking Techniques.

**Fine Woodworking Techniques**
**The Taunton Press**
**Newtown, Connecticut 06470**
**190 pages, illus., index, 1978, $13.95**

*Fine Woodworking* is one of the best and classiest magazines you'll ever see, on any subject. This book, which contains a selection of 50 articles from the magazine, is the creme de la creme. The emphasis is on furniture and cabinet work—no specifics on boatbuilding per se—but it's the techniques that are important here, not the applications. Wood, tools, joinery, finishing, turning, marquetry, shaping, carving: it's all here in a book as elegantly produced as its subject warrants.

## METHODS OF WORK

### Ball plane

I was recently asked to make a double-curved "ball plane" with which to smooth a laminated cherry sphere five feet in diameter.

The wooden sole of the plane is curved throughout its length and width, combining the traditional sole design of the wheelwright's compass plane and the joiner's hollow molding plane. I followed the plane-making methods set out in *Fine Woodworking*, Winter '75 to make the basic plane, which is 10 in. long by 2⅞ in. wide and high. The blade angle is 47 degrees and the iron is 51-mm (2-in.) "Record" tungsten-vanadium iron and cap set.

After making the block, a template was used to trace a section of a five-foot diameter circle on the sole. The sole was then chiseled to within 1/16 in. of true, and a flat scraper was used to finally reach the true line. This operation formed the curve throughout the sole's length. The plane bottom was scraped slightly hollow so it would function like a Japanese smoothing plane, hitting the work at three points only: front, back and cutting iron. This helped level the ball in every direction. A spokeshave and another scraper, ground and shaped to the same 5-ft. arc, were used to curve the sole across its width.

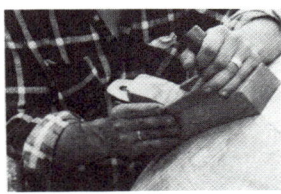

The iron was then roughly ground to the same curved line and finally brought to the exact curve with a sequence of increasingly fine sharpening slips.

I used white beech for the sole and the main part of the block, oak for the top plate and wedge, walnut for the front horn and cherry for the rear palm handle. The handles were shaped to fit the hand whether pulling or pushing. The entire plane weighs only two pounds, an important consideration since many days were spent bringing the sphere to within ¼ in. of a five-foot diameter.
—Eduardo A. Rumayor, Bronx, N.Y.

### Vee-Block for resawing

I have had only mixed results using a rip fence on a band saw for resawing wood. Unless the blade teeth are perfectly set and sharpened, the blade tends to drift even though the board is firmly held against the fence. This

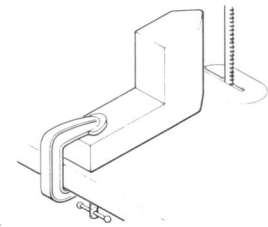

drifting can cause the wood to bind and will leave a wavy surface.

The blade's tendency to drift can be sidestepped by using a vee-edged block attached to the band-saw table, as in the drawing. The block is located so that its rounded point is even with the toothed edge of the blade, and at the desired thickness of the board from the blade. The block must be carefully made so that the radius at the vee is square to the face of the blade.

To use this approach the board to be resawed is scribed along its edge at the desired thickness. The vee-block provides a guide to hold the side of the board parallel to the blade. The board is fed into the blade with the operator free to swing the unsawed end to counter the drift. The surface will still need to be planed before it is of furniture quality, but this setup is much easier, faster and more accurate than using a rip fence.
—M.G. Rekoff, Jr., Minneapolis, Minn.

### Darkening glue lines

Glue lines of polyvinyl and aliphatic resin glues (white and yellow) can be darkened with tincture of iodine. This turns the glue a dark purple, perfect for walnut and dark mahogany. It should be applied after wet-sanding as it does not penetrate deeply, but it does go through oil nicely. I have also had good results using it under lacquer.
—Richard S. Newman, Rochester, N.Y.

The only thing better than *Fine Woodworking Techniques* is a subscription to *Fine Woodworking* magazine. Get it from:

**Fine Woodworking**
**The Taunton Press**
**52 Church Hill Road**
**Newtown, Connecticut 06470**
**$12/year (6 issues)**

It was three short years ago that we first listed *Fine Woodworking,* a magazine devoted to excellence in the woodshop. It has become *most* successful, now with over 100,000 subscribers, and hooray says us!

Now there is a rival publication in England with much the same format, paper, style, and feel. In fact, they have clearly copied *Fine Woodworking,* except for the fact that the sources and articles are British. Their first issue reflects a quality job on a par with its American counterpart. So, gang, now there are two! It's:

**Working Wood** (quarterly)
**Quailcraft**
**Pankridge Street**
**Crondall, Farnham**
**Surrey, England**
**Subscription: $15, surface; $20, air**

---

Very soon after presstime last year we received a note from Robert Nicolait in Belize informing us about his plans to offer Swampscott dory kits, the pieces being fabricated of Honduras mahogany, famous among boatbuilders as *the* finest planking wood in the world. So, this year we wrote off to him and said heck yes. His response here tells The Story.

—Eds.

Dear Editors:

The Swampscott dory kit project has been dormant since I last wrote, primarily because of the lack of evidence which would indicate a suitably large market. I have not deluded myself that the sale of these kits would number in the thousands per year, but I am having difficulty convincing myself that I could peddle 50 to 100 per year!

I am certain that if the kits were to sell for under $500-$600, they would move. But hell, you can hardly buy hamburger for that these days. So with one thing and another, the price would be about $2,000-$2,500 in your back yard. That is the stopper.

While everyone who has seen the prototype, rowed and sailed her, is quite ecstatic, the people who like it also happen to be the people who have no money. They'd like it for nothing.

On the other hand, I would refuse to put on the market a bunch of junk wood, second-rate hardware, and cotton sails. Getting first-rate Honduras mahogany requires a great deal of effort, and its selection and aging simply costs money. I am told the current price in the States is $2.40 per foot wholesale, if you can buy it. And on and on. . . .

Enclosed is a picture of the prototype showing her in the completed state without sail, although sail is included in the kit. Not very evident in the picture are the four oars, the rudder, the tiller, and the centerboard. The beach rollers on which the dory rests are not part of the kit.

—Robert Nicolait
Stann Creek District
Belize

---

Dear Editors:

Some suggestions which you might wish to pursue for the next *Mariner's Catalog:*

Perhaps the ultimate in Quick and Dirty boatbuilding is the Norwegian style of small craft, refined over more than 1,000 years into an esthetically superior boat with excellent performance and a long useful life. Perhaps you could prevail upon Paul Schweiss, of Clinker Boatworks, 8906½–35th West, Tacoma, Washington 98466, to write an article for you—with pictures of his lovely creations. Briefly, the method involves building a beautiful boat by a set of rules that contravene most North American practice.

• There are *no* rabbets.

• Plain slash scarfs, without stopwaters, are used in posts to allow use of straight-grained stock to make curves.

• Only 5 frames in a 20-foot boat—3 main frames with crossbeams, 2 cant frames in ends. None are fastened to the keel. No floors either.

• No molds are used—the shell is built to "formula" with the shape established by shores—and by eye.

• *Every* plank is scarfed, with most scarfs falling within about 2 feet of the midships section.

While Paul uses clear spruce for planking, the boats I have seen from Norway are extremely knotty, and the oak used looks awfully red to me.

All in all, there is a high level of skill involved, but there seems considerable food for thought—and a jolt or two for the dogmatic "true believers" who act as though *a* way were *the only* way.

Another source of plans for models:

Anker-Modeller
Jernbane alle 28
DK. 2720 Vanlose
Danmark
(Catalog costs 2 Danish crowns)

An interesting book, *Danske badtyper,* by Christian Nielsen, is available from:

Danish Maritime Museum
3000 Helsingor
Danmark

At the moment the price in Danish crowns is 85.00, plus air post 30.00, or by sea 10.00. A personal cheque requires an added bank fee of 8.00 crowns. This is a collection of Danish coastal vessels, mostly small sailing beach boats. Full-size plans of each boat are also available—same source—for about 50.00 crowns each set, plus postage. Most of the book is in Danish.

—Dante D'Alessandro
Tofino, B.C., Canada

## Letters

Every boat deserves a name, and every boat with a name deserves a nameboard. Plastic letters, decals, and transfers are used with abandon, but the result is discouragingly ugly for the most part. So, too, are hand-painted or carved nameboards when the maker fails to pay attention to the aesthetics of lettering design and placement. To charge ahead with no plan, or worse, with stencil in hand, is to make a good intention bad. A good, quick, easily grasped introduction to "form & skill in the design & use of letters" is:

*From* Lettering Design.

***Lettering Design***
**by Michael Harvey**
**Barre Publishers**
**Dist. by Crown Publishers, New York**
**160 pages, illus., 1975, $10.95**

## There Are More Than You Think

When it comes to discussing boatbuilders, especially builders of traditional craft, the names of a few "grand old men" (we don't mean to be sexist; there just don't seem to be any "grand old women") keep coming up. We aren't trying to deprecate the achievements of these builders, since they are obviously men of experience and integrity, but it bothers us no end. For every one of these well-known few, there are probably a hundred more with the same amount of capability. These men are just not recognized. Perhaps it is because they are reticent, or unpublished, or buried in backwaters where journalists never tread. Chances are they live right in your town.

Yet when a question must be answered, the immediate tendency is to pose it to grand old so-and-so, or to check it out in grand old so-and-so's book, or, if you are an editor, ask grand old so-and-so to write an article to explain it all. And if he can't answer the question, then there obviously is no answer.

What we ought to be doing is seeking out the craftsmen who have the skills but who have gone unnoticed—not to create a new class of grand old men, but simply to find out what they have to say. Traditional boatbuilding is rigid enough as it is; it will soon suffer from rigor mortis if we don't hear from new voices belonging to builders from the past who are still plying their trade.

—Eds.

***Fitting Out Ferrocement Hulls***
**by Robert Tucker**
**Granada Publishing**
**29 Frogmore**
**St. Albans, Herts., England**
**187 pages, illus., index, 1977, £ 11.50**

Once you've built your ferrocement hull, or any other for that matter, you're only partway there. With the exception of only one other book we are familiar with (*Ferro-Cement Design, Techniques and Application* by Bruce Bingham, Cornell Maritime Press, Centreville, Maryland), most ferrocement boatbuilding books tell you all about building the hull and give short shrift to finishing it off. There are special problems to be faced when finishing ferro hulls, and this book tells you what they are and how to deal with them.

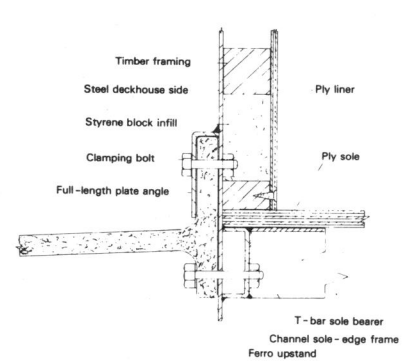

Ferro has a built-in problem: it has a low materials cost. This has manifested itself in a great many ways which will show up time and time again through this book. At this point let it only be stated that the cost factor has tended to obscure the excellence which ferrocement can achieve as a material when it is correctly put together by experts. It has great longevity, can survive with minimal maintenance, is little affected by changes of temperature and humidity once it is fully cured, is virtually fireproof and is impervious to rot and similar bacteriological degradation.

This panegyric sounds as if low cost is the material's only drawback; this is patent nonsense, otherwise it would be a perfect material in the fullest sense! Technically its prime drawback is that it is heavy; moreover, it is very easy, by quite minor inattention to detail, drastically to increase its weight; again, the wrong mortar–one which is too wet, too dry or too lean, or made with the wrong grade of sand or impure water–can be disastrous.

*Right: From* Fitting Out Ferrocement Hulls.

# 36 / The Mariner's Catalog

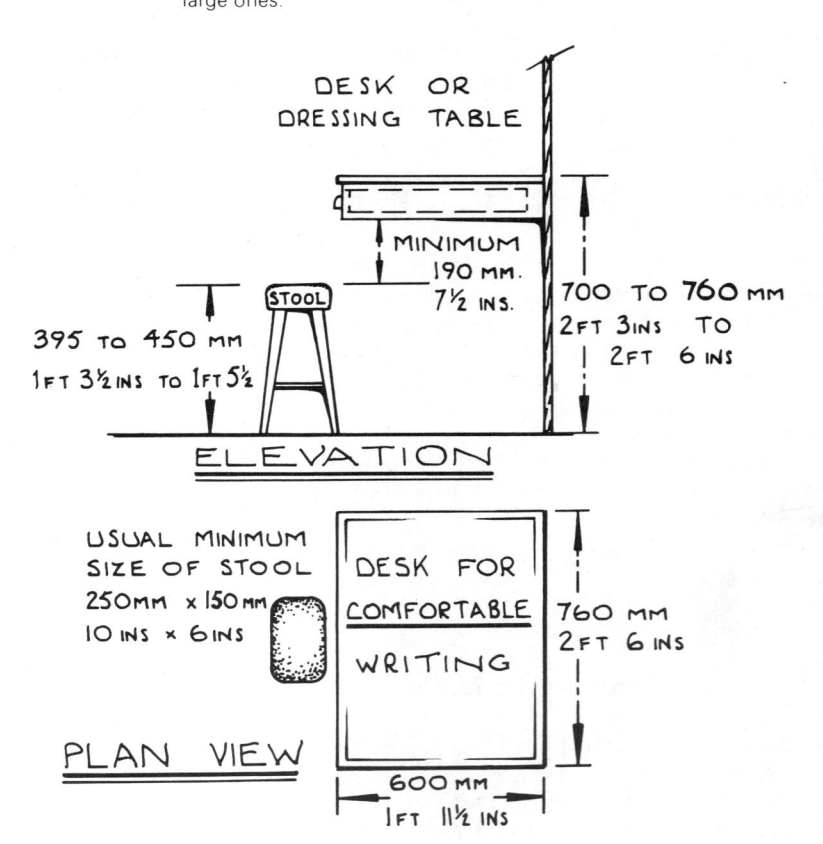

### Desk, dressing table, stool—sizes

If necessary desks can be much smaller than the one shown in the plan view. In large yachts' engine rooms, for example, an under-size desk is better than none. However the dimensions given here should not be under-cut without good reason.

Likewise the seat size of 250 mm (10 in) wide by 150 mm (6 in) deep at the top can be reduced, especially if there is good padding. But small seats become uncomfortable sooner than large ones.

*Right and below right: From the* Boat Data Book.

**Boat Data Book**
**by Ian Nicolson**
**Ziff-Davis Publishing Company, New York**
**191 pages, illus., 1978, $9.95**

Just the thing for designers, boatbuilders, outfitters, etc. All sorts of useful tables and lists, from breaking strengths of bolts to sheave specifications, from tool kits to rudder stop spacing, from rigging load requirements to paint coverage considerations. The author is a well-known yacht designer and knows of what he speaks, but, because he is English and this book was originally published in England, you can expect a certain amount of confusion with the terminology.

Mechanical properties of woods

| WOOD | WEIGHT | | | TEARING FORCE | | CRUSHING FORCE | | BREAKING FORCE | | MODULUS OF ELASTICITY | |
|---|---|---|---|---|---|---|---|---|---|---|---|
| | SPECIFIC GRAVITY | KGS PER CUB METRE | POUNDS PER CUB FOOT | KGS PER SQ CENTIM | POUNDS PER SQ INCH | KGS PER SQ CENTIM | POUNDS PER SQ INCH | KGS PER SQ CENTIM | POUNDS PER SQ INCH | KGS PER SQUARE CENTIMETRE | POUNDS PER SQUARE INCH |
| ASH | 0.75 | 750 | 47.0 | 1190 | 17,000 | 632 | 9,000 | 855 | 12,200 | 115,500 | 1,645,000 |
| BEECH | 0.70 | 700 | 43.8 | 800 | 11,500 | 658 | 9,360 | 657 | 9,340 | 950,000 | 1,354,000 |
| BIRCH | 0.75 | 750 | 46.9 | 1050 | 15,000 | 450 | 6,400 | 820 | 11,670 | 115,500 | 1,645,000 |
| CEDAR | 0.49 | 492 | 30.8 | 800 | 11,400 | 412 | 5,860 | 522 | 7,420 | 34,200 | 486,000 |
| ELM | 0.54 | 540 | 33.8 | 945 | 13,490 | 725 | 10,330 | 427 | 6,080 | 49,200 | 700,000 |
| GREENHEART | 1.00 | 999 | 62.5 | | | | | 1160 | 16,550 | 186,000 | 2,656,000 |
| LARCH | 0.50 | 496 | 31.0 | 720 | 10,200 | 392 | 5,570 | 417 | 5,940 | 957,000 | 1,363,000 |
| LIGNUM VITAE | 1.33 | 1330 | 83.2 | 835 | 11,800 | 647 | 9,920 | 800 | 11,400 | 39,000 | 558,000 |
| MAHOGANY, HONDURAS | 0.56 | 559 | 35.0 | | | | | 810 | 11,480 | 110,000 | 1,593,000 |
| MAHOGANY, SPANISH | 0.85 | 848 | 53.2 | 1530 | 21,800 | 576 | 8,200 | 531 | 7,560 | 882,000 | 1,255,000 |
| OAK, BRITISH | 0.93 | 929 | 58.3 | 700 | 10,000 | 700 | 10,000 | 700 | 10,000 | 102,000 | 1,451,000 |
| OAK, RIGA | 0.68 | 687 | 43.0 | | | | | 905 | 12,890 | 113,000 | 1,610,000 |
| OAK, RED | 1.02 | 1021 | 64.4 | 720 | 10,250 | 421 | 5,990 | 745 | 10,600 | 142,500 | 2,149,000 |
| PINE, RED | 0.58 | 576 | 36.1 | 1010 | 14,300 | 378 | 5,380 | 621 | 8,840 | 102,500 | 1,458,000 |
| PINE, PITCH | 0.66 | 658 | 41.2 | 550 | 7,820 | | | 688 | 9,790 | 861,000 | 1,226,000 |
| PINE, YELLOW | 0.46 | 460 | 28.8 | | | 383 | 5,450 | | | 112,300 | 1,600,000 |
| SPRUCE | 0.51 | 511 | 32.0 | 700 | 10,000 | 457 | 6,500 | 865 | 12,350 | 126,500 | 1,804,000 |
| TEAK INDIAN | 0.88 | 879 | 55.0 | 1050 | 15,000 | | | 1030 | 14,600 | 197,000 | 2,800,000 |
| TEAK AFRICAN | 0.93 | 934 | 61.3 | 1470 | 21,000 | 656 | 9,320 | 1050 | 14,980 | 161,500 | 2,305,000 |
| WALNUT | 0.67 | 667 | 41.8 | 570 | 8,130 | 467 | 6,650 | 562 | 8000 | | |

**DUCK.** A strong, heavy cotton fabric employed for sails, awnings, tents, heavy bags, shoe uppers, machine coverings, and where a heavy and durable fabric is needed. It is woven plain, but with two threads together in the warp. It is made in various weights, and is designated by the weight in ounces per running yard 22 in. wide. It is marketed unbleached, bleached, or dyed in colors, and there are about 30 specific types with name designations usually for particular uses such as **sailcloth.** When woven with a colored stripe, it is called **awning duck. Russian duck** is a fine variety of **linen duck.** Large quantities of cotton duck are used for making laminated plastics and for plastic-coated fabrics, and it is then simply designated by the weight. **Belt duck,** for impregnated conveyor and transmission belts, is made in loosely woven soft ducks and in hard-woven, fine-yarn hard fabric. The weights run from 28 to 36 oz. **Conveyor belting** for foodstuff plants is usually of plastic fabric for cleanliness. The **Transilon** of Extremultus, Inc., is a belting of good strength and flexibility to operate over small-diameter rollers. It is made of nylon fabric faced on both sides with polyvinyl chloride sheet. It may have a variety of surface finishes such as tetrafluoroethylene.

**Hose duck,** for rubber hose, is a soft-woven fabric of plied yarns not finer than No. 8, made in weights from 10 to 24 oz. The grade of duck known as **elevator duck** for conveyor belts is a hard-woven 36-oz fabric. **Plied-yarn duck** is used for Army tents instead of flat duck as it does not tear easily and does not require sizing before weaving. **Canvas** is duck of more open weave. The term is used loosely in the United States to designate heavy duck used for tarpaulins, bags, sails, and tents. But more properly it is a heavy duck of square mesh weave more permeable than ordinary duck, such as the canvas used for paintings and for embroidery work. The word duck is from the Flemish doeck meaning cloth, originally a heavy linen fabric. The word canvas is from the Latin cannabis, originally a coarse, heavy hempen cloth for tents. **Osnaburg cloth** is a heavy, coarse, plain-woven fabric used for wrapping and bailing, and for inside sacks for burlap flour bags. It is made from lower grades of short-staple cotton and from waste. In colored checks and stripes it is used for awnings.

## *Materials Handbook*
### by George S. Brady and Henry R. Clauser
### McGraw-Hill Book Company, New York
### 1011 pages, index, 1977 (11th ed.), $26.50

We don't know how you can be without this book if you are a boatbuilder, no matter the size of your operation, amateur or professional. A *readable* technical manual for nontechnical people, this book tells you what all those ingredients are and what they are used for. For instance, who hasn't read the boat specifications that call for Tobin bronze? The specs demand it so you get it, but do you know what it is? For that matter, do you know what makes brass different from bronze, or Monel differ from brass? The answers are all in the *Materials Handbook*, along with "the composition, methods of production, major properties and characteristics, uses, and commercial designations or trade names of some 13,000 substances." We wish we had had this book a long time ago.

*Left: From the* Materials Handbook.

## *Lapstrake Boatbuilding*
### by Walter J. Simmons
### International Marine Publishing Company
### Camden, Maine
### 184 pages, illus., index, 1978, $10.95

A fine book for the boatbuilder who has progressed past the beginner's stage and wishes to learn the advanced wrinkles that mean the difference between good and excellent work; written by a professional boatbuilder with years of experience.

## *Building the St. Pierre Dory*
### by Mark White
### International Marine Publishing Company
### Camden, Maine
### 240 pages, illus., index, 1978, $20

A step-by-step guide, exceedingly well illustrated, to building one of the most seaworthy and salty-looking small boats ever designed.

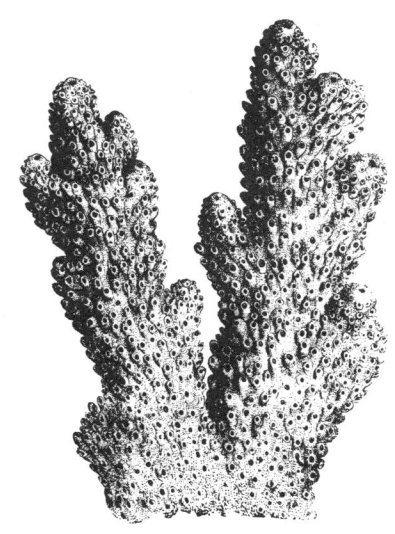

## *Instant Boats*
### by Harold H. Payson
### International Marine Publishing Company
### Camden, Maine
### 152 pages, illus., index, 1979, $12.50

Dynamite Payson, the king of instant boatbuilding, describes how to build good-quality plywood boats without lofting lines or building elaborate jigs; the plans for six small craft were conceived by Phil Bolger.

***Build and Sail Your Own Boat***
**by Norman Dahl**
**Stanley Paul, London**
**Dist. by Merrimac Book Service**
**5 So. Union St.**
**Lawrence, Mass. 01843**
**112 pages, illus., index, 1978, $4.50**

They must have some very interesting television shows in Great Britain. This book is based on a television series broadcast in Ulster on how to build a dinghy from a kit. It's intended for people who hardly know how to sail a boat, never mind build one, and features the 12-foot Ideal dinghy designed by Jack Holt and sold in kit form by IDTV Enterprises, 15-17 Craven Hill, London, England. The Ideal is built from plywood and the seams are sewed together with wire and then fiberglassed, as in the Mirror dinghy building method. Because building from a kit is about the same no matter the brand of dinghy, this book could be used as a guide for building the Mirror and a number of other types.

*Below: From* Build and Sail Your Own Boat.

---

*Aerolite 306 urea-formaldehyde glue*

Aerolite 306 is a two-part adhesive; a resin, which is supplied in powder form, and a liquid hardener. It is described as a gap-filling, water-resistant adhesive, unaffected by moulds and fungi. It was used to glue the wooden Mosquito bomber together during the Second World War, which is probably as good a recommendation as you can get. Equally important from the amateur's point of view is the fact that it is relatively cheap and very easy to use.

The powdered resin is mixed with water to form a syrupy liquid. The approximate proportions are two parts of powder to one part of water (by weight), or four parts of powder to one part of water (by volume). Use a dry, non-metallic container and add the water to the powder gradually, stirring well to prevent lumps. Continue stirring after all the water has been added until the resin is completely dissolved. Warm water (20–25 C) assists in the process. If you are able, let the solution stand after mixing, to allow any bubbles to disperse. The mixed resin has a life of about two weeks, so do not mix up more than you can use in this time. The dry powder has a shelf life of two years at least.

To use Aerolite, first make sure that the surfaces to be joined are clean, dry and free of dust, and that the joint fits as well as you can make it. Apply the resin to the smaller of the two pieces by means of a spreader or brush. Then apply the hardener to the other surface with a pad or sponge, using enough to make the wood uniformly damp. Now put the two pieces together, make sure they are in the correct position, and then hold them firmly together with clamps, weights or panel pins.

The two pieces must be held together firmly, so that there is no possibility of them moving, but the joint should not be over-clamped, which would squeeze the glue out of the joint and lead to starvation and weakness. It takes a little practice to judge how much resin to apply. You have got it right when a small bead of resin oozes out all round the joint as you clamp it up. Too much is better than too little, provided that you clean off the surplus before it sets. In making a long joint, as when fixing a rubbing strake along the gunwhale for example, it is possible for the hardener to dry out before you get round to clamping the far end. If there are signs that this might happen, re-apply hardener to the dry areas before clamping.

---

***Building and Repairing Canoes and Kayaks***
**by Jack Brosius and Dave LeRoy**
**Contemporary Books, Chicago, Ill.**
**134 pages, illus., index, 1978, paperbound, $4.95**

Short and to the point, this book tells the person who has never worked with fiberglass before how to build his craft. Though the title mentions canoes, the example shown is a kayak, but this need not be a problem, since small-craft fiberglass work is all the same. The section on repair is short and inadequate. On the plus side, however, the authors give a list of canoe clubs around the country that are likely to have on hand, or assist you in finding, molds for fiberglass canoes and kayaks.

---

Ventilation is most important. The person who builds in his basement may find the smell of resin and acetone lingering throughout the home for a month to six weeks. Even when building in a carport, the smell may linger for you and your neighbors for about 24 hours.

More than smell is involved, however. The person who builds in his basement must ventilate thoroughly against the danger of a fire set off by a buildup of fumes around a furnace and/or a water heater, or from their pilot lights. The best way to ventilate is to open a window at one end and to set a big fan exhausting at a window at the other end. This draft, of course, could blow out your pilot lights—which is another good reason not to build in a basement.

To build with polyester resin, you need air temperatures ranging from 50 to 80 degrees Fahrenheit, with relative humidity below 70 percent. There are catalysts available that can be added to the resin to let it set up as low as 35 degrees Fahrenheit, but you should ask the supplier what this addition does to set-up time.

*Above and right: From* Building and Repairing Canoes and Kayaks.

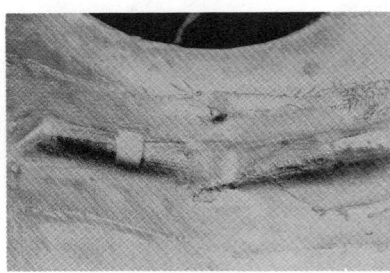

This is a reinforcing deck rib—a piece of rolled-up newspaper just glassed into position.

The final layer of cloth is placed on a deck.

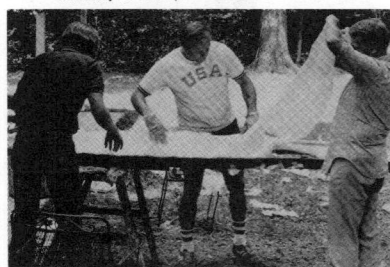

# Maintenance

It begins when you notice that little spot that won't hold paint. You might push on it with your thumb a couple of times. Doesn't seem too bad—just a little damp spot you didn't notice while painting. So you scruff it up a little, brush some primer over it, and paint it again. And again it peels off.

So this time you try your fingernail. Then a knife. And that sinking feeling begins to grow within your breast. If it is in the middle of a piece of wood, your mind marshals its forces of rationalization and puts it all off 'til next fall's haulout. If it appears where many pieces of wood come together, your mind marshals its forces of rationalization, paints over the spot, and places the boat on the Caveat Emptor list. Or . . . you do something about it.

Now what one *ought* to do about it is tear it all out and spend the season (groan) scarfing and worrying and puttering and rebuilding the damn spot. What one *can* do is use one or another of several rot-penetration preparations, several of which we've listed in the past. Epoxybond Cure-Rot is another one, by:

**Atlas Marine Products
Farmington Rd.
Mertztown, Pennsylvania 19539**

*Below: Epoxybond, available from Atlas.*

### EPOXYBOND® CURE-ROT

Restores dry rot, ends leakage, reseals spring joints. Easily applied by brush or by applicator bottle.

| Cat. No. | Packaging | Unit Size | List Price |
|---|---|---|---|
| 112111 | 6 doz./carton | 4½ oz. | $ 4.25 |
| 112113 | 1 doz./carton | Pint | 12.25 |
| 112115 | 6 qts./carton | Quart | 21.95 |

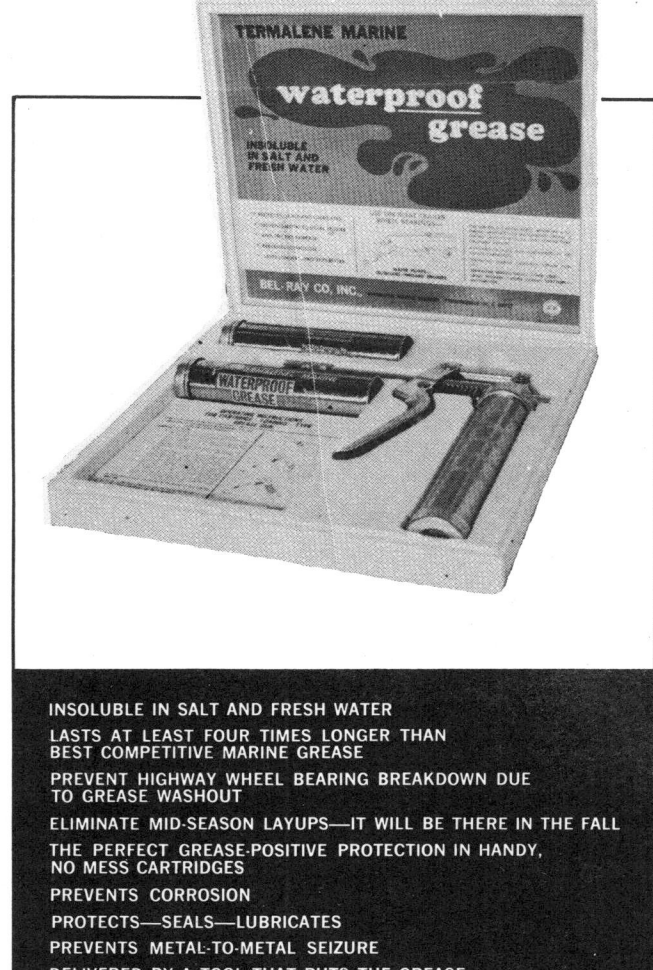

*Above: From Termalene.*

Waterproof grease has numerous obvious uses around boats, and some not so obvious. A common trick in yards we frequent is to use waterproof grease on the seams of wooden boats on launching day. The grease keeps out the water and gives the planking time to swell, so it rejuvenates the integrity of the boat. A very high-quality grease for this purpose (available only through dealers) is offered by:

**Termalene Marine Division
Bel-Ray Company, Inc.
P.O. Box 526
Farmingdale, N.J. 07727**

## Refreshing Pause

Many of the smaller working boats of the United States achieve engine cooling by running piping in a long "U" along the tuck of the bottom. In time these pipes rime up with deposits that not only obstruct water passage within the pipe, but also reduce the system's ability to exchange engine heat with the cold ocean water.

Here in the Northeast, a fairly common trick performed by the fishermen who would like to get an extra season out of their systems is to open up the joints on the inside of the boat and fill the pipe with cola, leaving it in there to work for an hour or so, usually with satisfactory results. We're not sure, but it would seem as if this treatment could have other applications in and through marine gear. (We already know what it does to our teeth.)

Dear Editors:

You asked for user reports on Deks Olje as a teak system. I have been using it for a little over a year on my Mariner 32 ketch, in Hawaiian waters subject to our strong tropical sun. My experience has been that, if properly applied in the first place, it holds up remarkably well and much better than the alternatives—varnish, teak oil, etc. With relatively minor touching up, my first application lasted a year. I then redid the job by wet sanding, application of a coat of #1 followed by several coats of #2. This was a lot easier than the original job, and restored the brightwork to "like new" appearance. I have had countless compliments and inquiries about my "system" of maintenance during the past year.

—W. B. Althoff
Honolulu, Hawaii

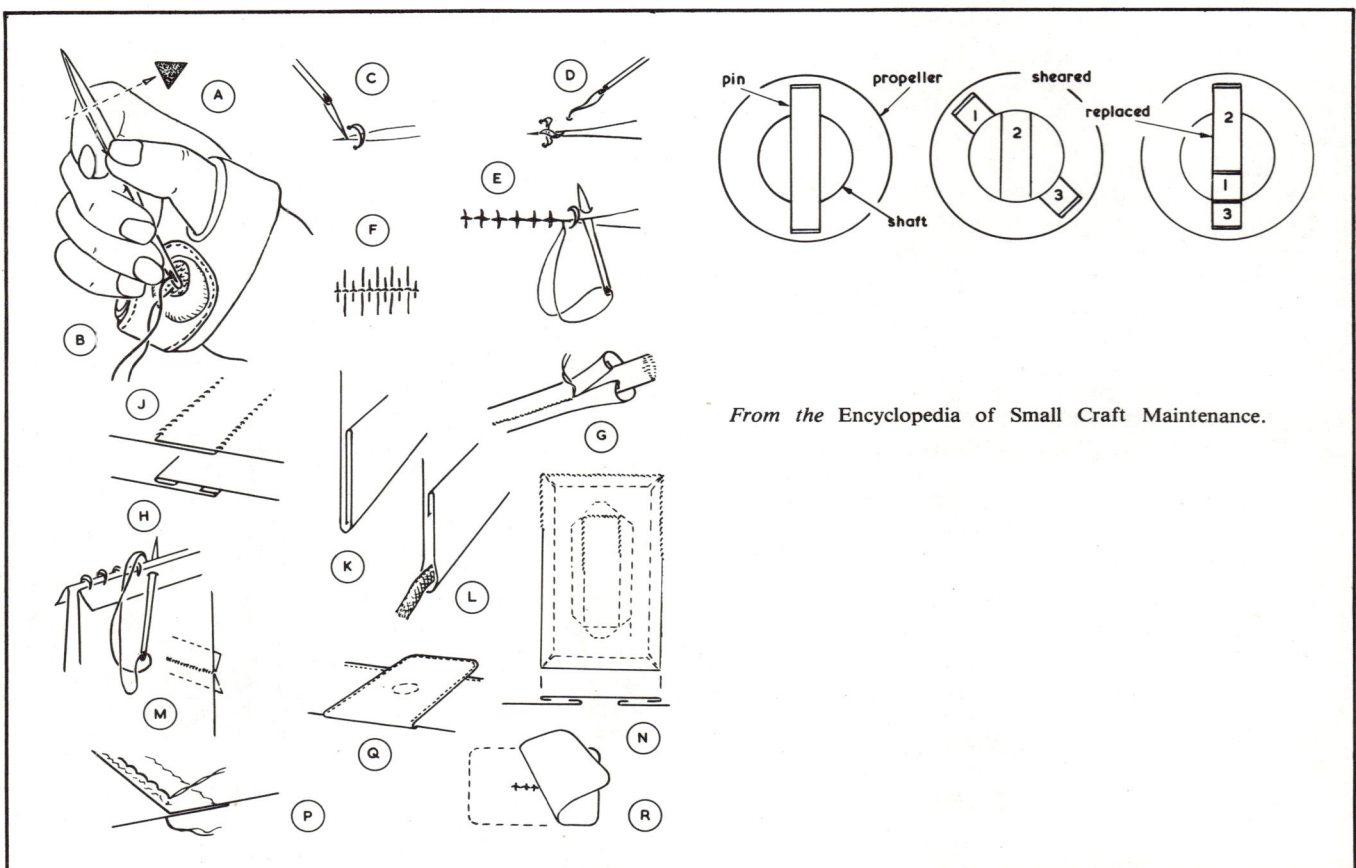

*From the* Encyclopedia of Small Craft Maintenance.

**Encyclopedia of Small Craft Maintenance
by Percy Blandford
Pelham Books, 52 Bedford Square
London, England
192 pages, illus., 1977, £5.50**

If Percy Blandford isn't the most prolific writer of nautical books in the Western World—his biography claims over 50 books and thousands of articles—we don't know who is. Blandford's material is journeyman stuff and for the most part can be expected to be reliable. This latest book on maintenance is good, but like all others on the subject, doesn't cover all the problems you're likely to encounter. On the other hand, it has some tips we've never seen before, like how to reposition a broken propeller shear pin so you can get home when you don't have a spare.

Another book by Blandford, recently published, is *Modern Sailmaking*. It's one of the better books on the subject, especially in its sections on enlarging and reducing sail area. The index, though, is hopelessly inadequate.

**Modern Sailmaking**
**by Percy Blandford**
**Tab Books**
**Blue Ridge Summit, Pa.**
**320 pages, illus., 1979, paperbound, $7.95**

And while we're on the subject of sails, Jeremy Howard-Williams, the well-known British author and editor, has a new book out on small-boat sails, which is actually a revision of his 1971 book, *Racing Dinghy Sails:*

**Dinghy Sails**
**by Jeremy Howard-Williams**
**Granada Publishing**
**St. Albans, Herts., England**
**152 pages, illus., 1978, £4.95**

This is not a book on sailmaking, though there are sections on the subject; rather, it emphasizes theory, design, and usage. Small-boat sailors, both cruisers and racers, will find this a good manual on how to get more from their sails and rigging.

*From* Dinghy Sails.

*Jumpers.* Jumper stays will also control bend at the top of the mast. *Figure 55* shows how jumpers which are tight will keep a straight mast head, while slackening them off allows it to bend back. Any

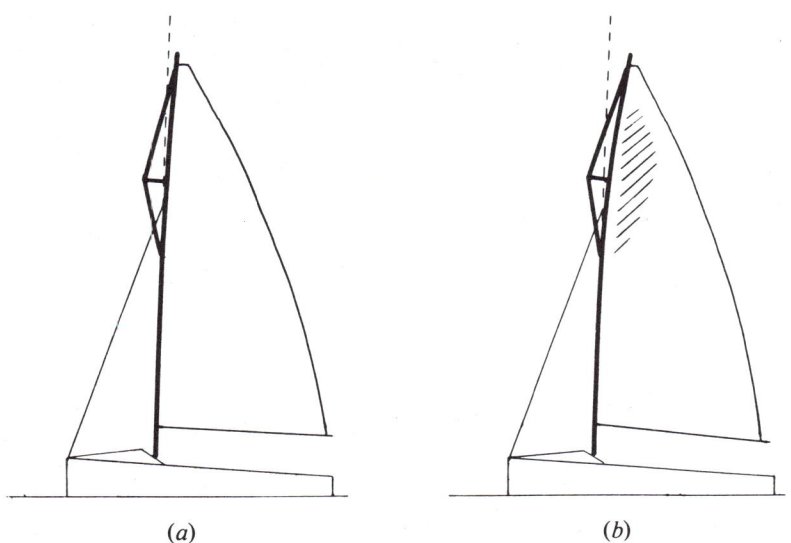

(a)    (b)

*Fig. 55. Jumper Stays.* Tight jumper stays as in (*a*) mean that the mast head is stopped from bending back. When the jumpers are eased off as in (*b*), the mast head is free to bend more, thereby flattening the sail in the head. More or less the same effect can be produced by chocking the mast at deck level as in *figure 54* (*a*), without the damaging wind resistance produced by jumpers.

unnecessary weight and windage aloft is a handicap you can well do without, however, and you want to think twice before you start making your mast look like a radar aerial; about the only time when jumpers may pay is if there is a lot of unsupported mast above the hounds, such as on the 14-ft International.

## Termites

Dear Editors:

She looked so nice—*how was I to know she had the sickness no mariner likes to talk about?* Definitely homey, and with a nice build. One day in poking around her plywood stringers I noted a little heap of peppery particles. Now—who would spill the pepper right there? I consulted the marina yacht salesman who immediately viewed me like a leper in the maternity ward. Yes—we were "infested" (as they say in the service). This result of our relationship was stunning *news* to me; I consulted the Resident Marina Expert-Emeritus who drawled, " 'Bout every wood boat around here has termites—mostly they come from the untreated boards on the docks. . . ." But he had no recommendation for treatment. The Resident Marina Expert-Senior advised that his rental properties also had the *sickness*, but not to worry—just find the tiny hole where the "pooty" comes out and pump in Cuprinol. I caught the little bugger pooping out digested particles and deluged him, satisfied that we were "cured." Two days later—no dice. Marinas Terminitus undoubtedly had SCUBA capabilities.

A Pest Contol Contractor bid about $100 to bag the boat—but what with the Marina Busybodies and economic-fear outfall, I declined. Someone said burn formaldehyde candles; the Pharmacist implied this was a strange request from a like-kind individual. Someone said burn Flower of Sulphur; this turned out to be a nice 80-cent can of Sulphur the same Pharmacist was glad to sell me. A "flame test" revealed a nice little glow, non-propagating. So I made up a little "safety oven" of two tin cans, lit the lethal fire, closed up the boat, and let it burn overnight.

The next day a ghastly smell exhausted from the opened hatch, but it disappeared within a few hours. With tempus fugiting, I noted no recurrence, and the subsequent picky-choosy new owner stayed happy. I felt shaken but sanitary with this experience—but it should be noted that in actuality many, many social diseases are never really cured—just "arrested," as the medics say. . . .

—Norman Benedict
Lomita, California

Dear Editors:

If any fish factory does not know what to do with the fish oil, I would like to recommend an experiment of long ago, when I could no longer obtain whale oil. Fish oil worked as well.

Mix two cans of oil to one can of any choice paint. It lasts nearly seven years near the waterfront, longer inland.

I hope this will find an outlet for the fish industry.

—John G. Ammells
Plaistow, N.H.

Readers who are unhappy with the toxic strength of bottom paints available on the market may want to try adding Biotox by Dana Marine Labs.

**Dana Marine Laboratories
5445 Mariner Street
Tampa, Florida 33609**

Dear Editors:

You will find Biotox to be compatible with your favorite bottom paint—just add and stir in very thoroughly.

The efficacy of Biotox is achieved by an approach based on the naval research laboratory's theory of controlled leaching of toxins in antifouling paints (see article by Winston Groom in *Boating,* June 1976) combined with a nontoxic, antifouling repellant developed by the chemists at Dana Marine Laboratories.

Remember that your boat, which represents a substantial investment in money and time, is protected from the elements by only a few thousandths of an inch (the thickness of a fingernail) of paint, so use a recognized good-quality bottom paint and follow the paint manufacturer's instructions with care.

—David Navarre
Dana Marine Laboratories

*The tools of the trade at Paul Schweiss' shop.*

Three years ago we got a letter from this guy named Paul Lipke. It said something like, Dear Sir, I am very interested in boats and boatbuilding and boatbuilders and I would like to go around the country and visit with every one of them. Do you have any suggestions? Sure, sure. Pat pat. Well, Paul Lipke likes boats, boatbuilding, and boatbuilders, so he got into his car and went all around the country and talked to maybe not every one of them, but one heck of a lot of them. He's writing a book about it. It's going to be *some* book.

## A Tale of Two Builders
### by Paul Lipke

In the course of 45,000 miles and 180 interviews researching my book, builders and their views often grouped themselves together in unusual ways. For instance, Ray Speck of Sausalito, California, Paul Schweiss of Tacoma, Washington, and Chip Stulen of Suttons Bay, Michigan, are all reasonably young, professional wooden boatbuilders who trained outside the U.S. Furthermore, they have similar building techniques that are interesting variations on plank-on-frame practices around the U.S. today. Remarkably, their attitudes about "quality of workmanship" are much the same, while their opinions on other topics can be so different as to represent the full spectrum of boating opinion.

As a biographical footnote, Paul and Chip (by purest coincidence) apprenticed under the same man in northern Norway, Einar Eisenlohr. The similarities in their workmanship, attitudes, and of course designs (the faerings) are striking. Since they are alike in so many ways, I will let one represent both and spotlight Chip and Ray Speck, who apprenticed in Yorkshire, England.

Here is Chip Stulen on the subject of a Bjorkedal faering.

The stems are sawn to shape and then tapered in both cross and longitudinal sections, the latter being accomplished by roughing out with an ax and then smoothed and faired with a plane. I even use the ax for roughing out plank scarfs. [I have seen Paul Schweiss do this, and all the joint needed was a couple of touches with a plane to make it "perfect."-P.L.] .... The fineness of the scantlings of a faering ... has come about from the boat's long period of evolution, at least a thousand years. There seems to be nothing oversized in the boat, nor anything in the construction that is not a necessary part of the whole.

The faerings are built without benefit of molds by a method Paul Schweiss calls "lofting in air." To cite Chip again . . .

After the stems are scarfed and riveted to the keel, the assembly is plumbed and secured to a beam directly over the keel (right side up). As each strake is added, it is first clamped at its hood end and then to the preceding strake (or keel). At the same time, shores are wedged between the top edge of the strake and the overhead beam, bending the plank out to the proper angle—giving the hull its proper shape. At three predetermined stations you check this angle with a Batlodd (?). This is basically a protractor having a long arm with a plumb bob attached. The other factor that must be known for this type of moldless construction is

(continued on following page)

*A Bjorkedal faering in progress in Chip Stulen's shop. (Photo by Chip Stulen)*

(continued from previous page)
the width of each strake at these points. It is . . . lofting as you build, in 3-D: bending and shaping these planks to follow these points in space. . . . As planking proceeds, many of the shores on the lower strakes can be removed.

Only five sawn frames are fitted after the faering is planked. Due to the faering's resultant flexibility, Norwegians ask not how the faering rides in the seas, but rather how it "swims."

This system lends itself very well to modifications in the hull lines to adapt specifically for rowing, sailing, row/sail, or even to accommodate a small diesel. It helps me be much more in tune with the lines of the hull, and gives me insight into the particular shape and lay of each strake for the development of those lines.

Chip's shop is on his farm, out of town. "My basic attitude is one of striving for self-sufficiency, looking toward my own woodlot, for instance. Things I don't supply myself are basically a source of uneasiness."

In contrast to Chip's rural farm/shop, Ray is located smack in the middle of Sausalito's Waldo Point and its polyglot lifestyles. In this one small area there are exotic, Bohemian houseboats with bubble windows and hanging plants; the Bank of America with its manicured parking lot—the establishment and all; and a third section with dozens of classic and not-so-classic cars, trucks, and boats in various stages of reconstruction and neglect. Amidst the chic hipness of this ultimately Californian collage, Ray is a bedrock pragmatist with only a touch of romanticism about his vocation.

The method he uses in building lapstrake traditional small craft, and his "Sid skiff" in particular, is midway between the largely "by eye" Scandinavian technique and the "by rule" traditional molded standard. He uses three *removable* molds with the same spiling system and shores to an overhead beam to control the planking's pitch. His frames are steam-bent. He has built a number of Whitehalls this way.

In contrast to Chip's self-sufficiency, here is Ray on the subject of lumber and other things.

I've grown dissatisfied with lumber—cedar, for instance. Rather than pay $2,000 a thousand board feet for better cedar, I'm thinking of going over to Honduras mahogany. I'm also looking for a new future in crook material. If we can interest the "redwood burl" people in milling locust, oak, or cedar crooks, the boat lumber market will be greatly enhanced.

By the nature of the beast, boatbuilding doesn't hold dilettantes. The work is too demanding. It takes a couple of years of long, steady work to achieve a modicum of skill and efficiency. Yet the people this business attracts are not into a nine-to-five routine. And seeing that my routine is eight to six, I find myself alone for the most part. It takes a special fiend to roll this boulder uphill; my hope is that I will soon find another fiend, since it takes two to make a truly efficient boatshop.

One truly gratifying reward to all this is the public's appreciation for good craftsmanship. I've done a number of shows . . . and come out with hand-rubbed boats. People from machos to grandmothers are humbled by the sight of a "real" boat. Not that plastic, aluminum, or epoxy boats aren't real, but these lapstrake boats have a heritage—and I'm proud to be able to contribute to keeping this heritage of honest joinery and workmanship alive.

There are two morals to this tale of two builders. Whether a person's thing is self-sufficiency or the development of support industries is immaterial on a personal level; they still have to push the rock up the hill. Second, both professionals and amateurs should examine other methods for their unique advantages. [From a half-model, planking width and pitch could be deduced and a great many designs (both new and old) might be built using these European methods or some variation.]

I'm pleased to report that Chip, Ray, and Paul are doing well, and I feel this is in no small way the result of their faster, businesslike approach to an old challenge.

*A 14-foot Sid Skiff nearing completion in Ray Speck's shop.*

# SHIP'S GEAR

*Anybody want to trade a bucket of tuckgammons for a dozen triple-ought wiskets?*

—Fred Brooks

## The Cedar Bucket

**by Pete Culler**

I'm often asked where I got the small-size cedar bucket that is part of the gear for my open sailing boats. Here's how. Large wooden buckets seem occasionally available from recent makers of wooden ware, which seems to be having a comeback. Small buckets suited to a small open boat I've yet to see. Needing one not too big to stow on a small craft, the only answer was to make it. Never having done Tight Cooperage before, I gave it some thought and came to the conclusion that there is no great mystery to it, or skill beyond anybody who likes to work with wood.

The first reaction usually is to panic about getting the shape, taper, bevels, and hollows of the staves. Don't. Simply draw a full-size profile of the amount of bucket you want—width of bottom and top, and height, not making it with too much "draw," or the hoops won't pull properly. Use about what seems common in buckets; just eyeball it. The sides of my bucket are about ½ inch thick, finished. Draw a bottom diameter, inside and outside of staves, and do the same for the top diameter. Divide up these double rings in a convenient number of staves, based on your available stock; cedar, pine, or other soft woods will do. I can see a nice bucket in redwood, western red cedar, cypress, or several other woods.

Using the height drawing, plus the two others, you now have the length, tapers, and bevels of the staves, plus the round, inside and out. Make up these staves a little long, and one a little wide, for final fitting. When all is shaped and more or less set up for fitting, I simply try it and trim, having the thing set bottom up and held with a string and twisting stick. Large rubber bands might do, although I've not tried them. When you are more or less happy with it, lay off the bottom true with another string, trim this, set up again and mark inside, about ⅜ inch from the edge, the place to cut the vee for the bottom. Knock it all down again and cut each piece with a small chisel. Set her up again and get the diameter of the bottom, by simply sharpening to chisel point two very small sticks, each a little shorter than the opening, and using them as a gauge or trammel, making a pencil mark when they fill the greatest diameter. I cut out the bottom (of, say, ⅜-inch stuff) about 1/16 inch larger than the actual diameter, and work a double bevel of somewhat sharper angle than the grooved bottom, which is about 90 degrees. The idea is that you will get a crush fit on the bottom so it will be tight.

Assemble again and take the length of the hoops with a piece of marline or a strip of paper, allowing for a scarf. My hoops are simply 9-gauge galvanized fence wire (very stiff) ground to lapping ends and silver brazed. Copper transmission wire is good if you can get it. Drive the hoops on so they are snug, trim the top, maybe trim some more on the bottom, and sand inside and out. It's surprising how nicely it will shape up. I made little one-legged staples, somewhat like J-bolts, out of something smaller and similar to galvanized pot nails, and drove about four of these, equally spaced, over each hoop to prevent them from drying out and falling off, but they never have.

Varnished outside, and much oiled inside, this bucket does just fine and is always tight. Each spring it gets "fitted out" just like the boat: sanding, varnish, oil. The bail is traditional for these buckets, at least aboard ship. There are pinked leather washers, stopper knots on the ends, and the rope bail is snaked and then lightly tarred.

The reactions to this bucket are interesting and diverse. Many are quite attracted by it, a few I don't think notice it, or know what it is if they do. It's sort of like a hog looking at a fine tapestry—it's not for them, so no matter. Others covet, but as yet none have taken the bull by the horns and made one. The construction description shows it's no great feat. Making regular strap hoops out of sheet metal is no big thing either; you simply wrap some paper around it in one of the trial setups, and a string over that, pencil mark it, and you have the curve of the hoop. There are "scientific" ways of arriving at all these shapes, but why make it scary when you can do it simply?

Same for wooden bailers. Either made of pieces or carved from a chunk of pine, they add something to a nice boat. I, for one, can't go the plastic bucket and Clorox jug bailer route.

*The proper cedar bucket from A.G.A. Correa.*

## The Holding Device

Living on a Maine island built out of sturdy granite, we're often amused at state officials when they come by to remind us about the state codes for the proper disposition of what the daily seven forty-five does with the food and drink we had yesterday. Seems like we're supposed to dig a hole in the granite and so not pollute the ocean. My hundred-pound dog laughs about this too. Also, we've got this little 26-foot daysailer with the bad manners to have a cuddy and head. It seems as if the state has some codes about this, too. Managing only 20 or so decent sails a year, the looming costs for pollution control devices on the head bode to make 'vacuation positively unworthwhile. I figure that by holding it I could afford a new genoa jib.

It's another one of those deals where people in the countryside have to pay for the sins of the tightly packed. Anyway, I'm going to pull the damn thing out of the boat and install a bucket. If I get boarded and they protest that it isn't a proper head, I'll tell them that that's right, it isn't a head; that it's a holding device. I'll say it sort of threatening-like. Here's a cedar bucket for $40 (cheap), from:

**A.G.A. Correa**
**Wiscasset, Maine 04578**

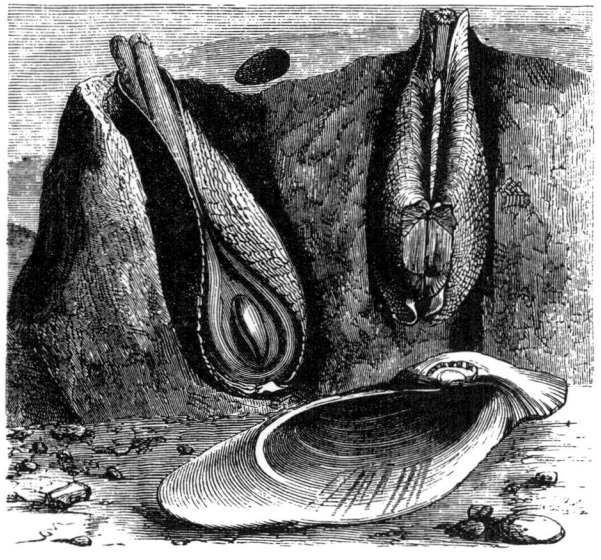

Speaking of buckets, what could be nicer than a small company that makes oak cleats and *canvas* buckets. It's:

**The Oak Cleat and
Canvas Bucket Company
R.R. 6
Napanee, Ontario K7R 3L1
Canada**

*Navigator's dividers from H.M.S. Association.*

## Cast Your Own

Daring souls who are dissatisfied with the range and quality of marine fittings on the market today and who are ready to do something about it will welcome:

***The Backyard Foundry*
by Terry Aspin
Model & Allied Publications
Watford, Herts., England
102 pages, illus., 1978, £ 2.25**

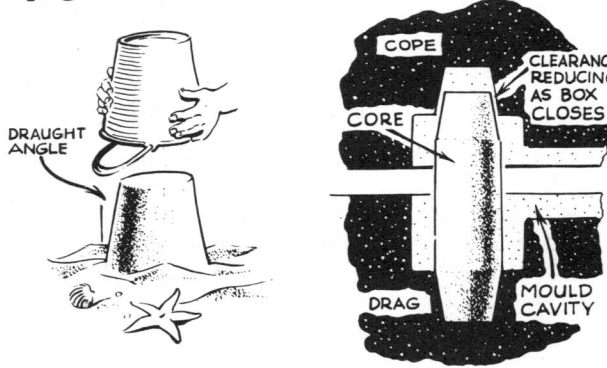

*From* The Backyard Foundry.

Those who have a real penchant for traditional nautical instruments will be interested in another replica, these chart dividers offered by Jay Stuart Haft. They're copies of an instrument excavated from the wreck of the H.M.S. *Association*, which sank off the Scillies in 1707.

**Jay Stuart Haft
8925 North Tennyson Drive
Milwaukee, Wisconsin 53217**

The Opahl Absorber automatic bilge pump looks to us as if three things have happened: (1) genius continues to emerge from our stew-pot gene pool; (2) obvious simplicity remains the best form for good ideas; and (3) we gotta have one. From:

**Elvström-USA, Inc.
151 River Rd.
Cos Cob, Connecticut 06807**

*The Opahl automatic bilge pump.*

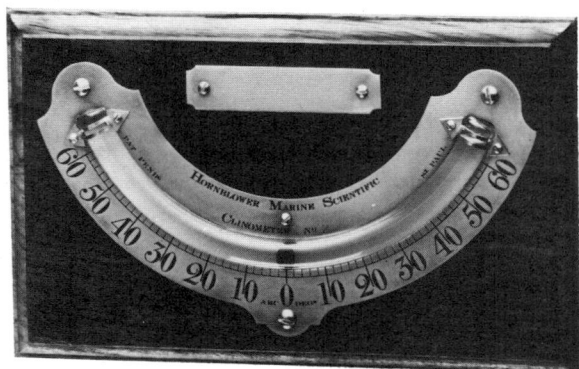

*The clinometer from Hornblower Marine Scientific.*

Dear Editors:

We intend to develop a full selection of nautical and navigational devices in the style and materials of the last century. Our philosophy is to create the things *we* would like to work with or look at during a long cruise. We hope other sailors, especially those with the traditional boats that have become popular, or those who just have a strong sense of history, will agree with us.

Our parallel rule is patterned after a 19th-century English ebony rule. We use teak because ebony is prohibitively expensive. Our rule is slightly heftier than the traditional ebony one and the knobs are larger (more comfortable) but of authentic design. However, ours is more accurate than the old ones were, and less likely to "chip out" at the corners as the old ones did. It's 15 inches long, 1⅜ inches wide (1 leg), ¼ inch high.

The clinometer is an original design of ours based on the typical design characteristics of nautical instruments in the mid-19th century. It has a solid brass engraved (not printed) register plate and a precision vial with fluid-dampened ball, all attached to a teak plaque with traditional fastenings. It works, as I'm sure you know, by gravity—the ball always stays at the bottom no matter what the boat does. One reads the number of degrees of heel wherever the ball alights.

Our thermometer recalls the days when Fahrenheit and Celsius values were meaningless to most people and the familiar "blood heat," "summer heat," and "freezing" were more understandable. Once again it is of teak and brass construction with, like all our instruments, deeply engraved artwork and polished brass. The design is typical of thermometers of the time, especially what was called a deck thermometer, except that we have dubbed ours a "cabin" thermometer. While not considered a true nautical instrument anymore, these were, as I'm sure you'll recall, valuable instruments in their day, as they were used to predict fog.

All 3 of these devices are individually numbered and we will register them for those of our customers who enjoy the thought that some day some nautical sleuth will be able to trace an instrument back to them.

The parallel rule and the clinometer are able to be personalized and we provide a blank nameplate for this purpose.

—John V. Geisheker

**Hornblower Marine Scientific**
**2101 Princeton Ave.**
**St. Paul, Minnesota 55105**

Dear Editors:

Your mention of the Tung Woo copper navigation lamps "in all the traditional patterns" (*Mariner's Catalog*, Vol. 6) left me wondering.... If Tung Woo actually manufactures good lamps, the copper anchor lamp of their make marketed in this country by James Bliss at a hefty price is certainly not one of them. It is not only unnecessarily difficult to fill and light, but also refuses to stay lit in anything approaching a breeze. They do tarnish nicely, and mine now serves as a handsome and salty decoration on a bookshelf in a farmhouse in Vermont, where it has given no further cause for complaint.

An interesting chapter in the modern-day lore of the oil lamp was written by David Blagden in his *Very Willing Griffen,* a useful account of his effort in the 1972 OSTAR. He sailed with no electrics at all, relying on a bevy of oil lamps including the Simpson-Lawrence Force 9, the Tilley Storm Lamp, and a hurricane lamp. Blagden said that, of all the lamps on board, a bicolor lamp "made by Davey and Co. from a pattern that dated from the turn of the century, was the only one that was totally reliable."

I bought one of these and agree that, unlike the various lamps presently available in marine hardware outlets in this country, it is truly reliable and useful at sea. Unfortunately they also are becoming unavailable. I have a deposit down on another Davey lamp. We correspond about it from time to time. It has been three years, so far.

Enclosed is a cut from the 1924 edition of Francis B. Cooke's *Single-Handed Cruising*. It shows yet another type of Davey lamp which apparently has been out of production for years. Mr. Cooke describes it as follows: "The lamps should be of the *windproof* type, which have a glass cone inside.... The windproof type of lamp can be obtained at almost any yacht chandler's, and is by far the most efficient I have ever seen. It will burn steadily in a gale of wind, and I have never known one to be jolted out by the motion of the yacht."

Why isn't anybody selling a lamp like *that*?

—William Cheney
Rupert, Vermont

*An early Davey lamp.*

Your hands are cold and wet. Your snaps are corroded. AAhrrgh! Snap-Ease to the rescue, from:

**Andrew Adams Development Corp.
765 Eagle Ave.
Bronx, N.Y. 10456**

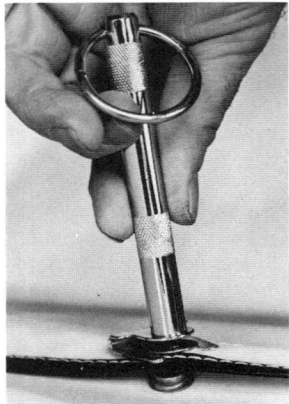

*The perfect gift for that friend who persists in sailing in polar climes.*

***The Outdoorsman's Guide to Government Surplus*
by David Leroy
Contemporary Books, Chicago, Ill.
225 pages, illus., index, 1978, paperbound, $5.95**

Everyone dreams of the Army Jeep for $50, or the Navy launch for $150, or the sextant for $3.50. The author tells you the how, when, and whatfor of Government surplus sales, with a lot of extraneous information thrown in—for example, almost half the book is a listing of publicly owned facilities open to outdoor people (i.e., where to use your government-surplus pyramid tent once you get it). We wouldn't recommend this book at all, except that buying from the government is such a hassle that anything that halfway explains the system is worth something if you want to play the game.

> The Department of Defense is responsible for the sale of its own personal property and is the source of large quantities of varied types of property, including commercial, industrial, and consumer items. Property generated as surplus by the military services is sold through Defense Property Disposal Sales Offices. The mailing addresses of these offices are shown following.
>
> A centralized mailing list is maintained for sales conducted by these Defense Property Disposal Sales Offices. You can obtain a Department of Defense Surplus Property Bidders Application to have your name placed on the mailing list by writing to:
>
> DoD Surplus Sales
> P.O. Box 1370
> Battle Creek, MI 49016
>
> You should complete the application and mail it to the above address. Only when the classes of property you specify on the application are placed on sale in the geographical areas designated, will you be sent an Invitation to Bid (IFB). IFBs contain descriptions of the property, specific locations, dates and time for inspection, and other detailed information concerning the sale.

*From* The Outdoorsman's Guide to Government Surplus.

## German Gear

Our German correspondent, Karl Freudenstein, kindly sent us the catalog of a supplier of traditional-style chandlery items. German not being our second language, we can't make out whether the goods are genuine or reproductions, but they show lanterns, binnacles, compasses, engine-room telegraphs, wheels, mechanical signaling devices (among them, a rare hand-cranked foghorn), and bells.

**General and Maritime Trading
Winsener Landstr. 3
2105 Seevetal 4
Hamburg, West Germany**

There is a simplicity and elegance (in use if not design) about the cast bronze and hardwood outboard motor mount by Spartan. It's good for motors up to six horsepower, from:

**Spartan Marine Products, Inc.
160 Middleboro Ave.
East Taunton, Massachusetts 02718**

*Spartan's outboard motor mount.*

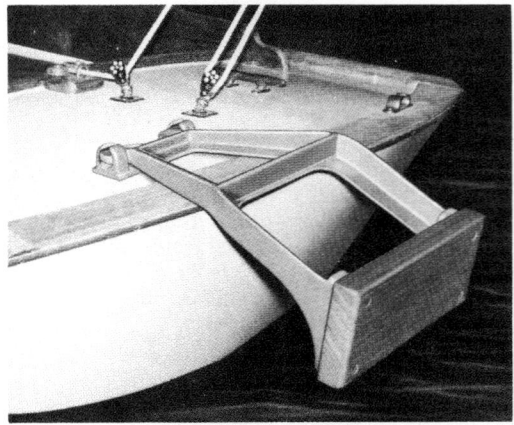

Some time ago we listed Briggs Marine, a distributor of nautical hardware in Australia. We did not realize that they carry really handsome ship's bells, including handled bells, and that they have an American distributor. It's:

**Sterling Hardware-Marine Division
1605 East Kalamazoo Street
Lansing, Michigan 48912**

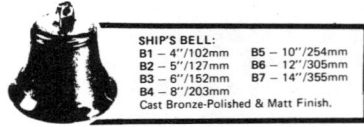

*Briggs Marine's ship's bell.*

## Matches Dept.

Dear Editors:

In Volume 5 (p. 130), you mention Green-lites matches, which I use all the time. You can buy them in the supermarket chains here in Australia. The matches are produced by Bryant and May, 51 Raymond St., Bankstown, Sydney, Australia, but they don't at the moment have an American distributor. They are available in Canada under the label, "Koghlane's Waterproof Matches," and a company called W.S.T. Sales will be attempting in late 1978 to develop an American distribution at least in sports shops.

The matches themselves are very good—I have let them sit in water and still had them light by the third stroke on the side of a wet box (just to prove the matter to friends). I hope this information is of use to you.

—Murray Isles
Kensington, N.S.W., Australia

---

## 519 HIGH–CAPACITY PUMP / PERMANENT MOUNTING

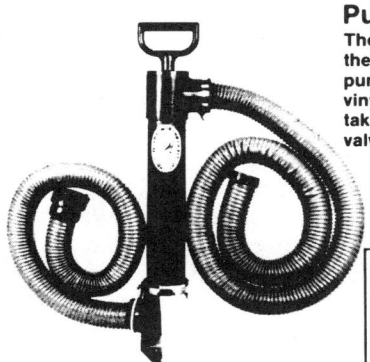

**Pumps 22 gal./min.**
The 519C pump has the same capacity as the U.S. Coast Guard approved pump. This pump is provided with 2-inch reinforced vinyl hose on both intake and discharge. Intake hose incorporates strainer and check valve.

Pumping Capacity per min. 22 gal.
Length Intake Hose 4 ft.
Length Discharge Hose 6 ft.
Weight 9 lbs.

*Available for Life Boats or Commercial Vessels.*
**U.S. Coast Guard Approved Pump**
Approval No. 160.044/14/0
*Write or Call for Quote.*

**Flush Deck Permanent Mounting Pump**
The 519 FD is a permanently installed high capacity pump designed for offshore yachts. To operate, remove deck plate cover and pump. Deck plate cover has a stainless steel chain attached to avoid loss. Note discharge hose is reduced to 1½" for thru hull fitting.

Pumping Capacity per min. 22 gal.
Length Intake Hose 8 ft.
Length Discharge Hose 4 ft.
Packed 1/ctn.
Weight 11 lbs.

*Pumps from the Beckson Manufacturing catalog.*

---

Always on the lookout for good bilge pumps, that is to say, SOMETHING THAT'LL GET THE BLOODY WATER OUT-OUT-OUT, we spotted these high-capacity jobs from:

**Beckson Manufacturing, Inc.**
**Box 3336**
**Bridgeport, Connecticut 06605**

---

Fred Brooks was mentioning the other day that he had a warm feeling just thinking about how frigid the ol' girl was. Several people got up slowly and began backing out of the room, until Nordy Pilts had the presence of mind to ask who was frigid. Fred said Gerty, his ice chest. Two people who weren't taking chances had already left by then, but the rest laughed and began to relax. That icebox of his has been spreading rot and disease throughout an eight-foot radius in his boat for years—a good trick in a boat with 7 feet 9 inches of beam. Asked how come she's so frigid, Fred allowed that he'd used one of the new low-current units. Smart fellow, Fred.

We found a low-current conversion unit from:

**West Marine Products**
**850 San Antonio Road**
**Palo Alto, California 94303**

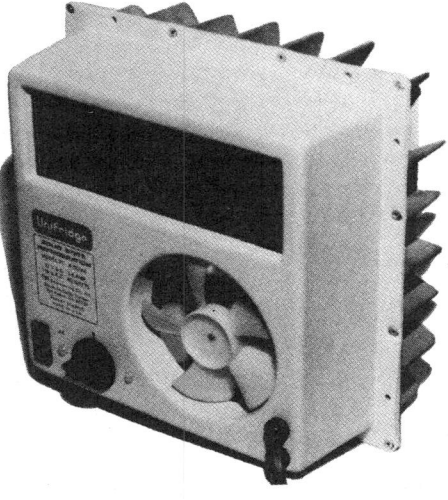

*West Marine's refrigerator conversion unit.*

And if you feel like going berserk on yacht refrigeration, here is a place that specializes in custom systems:

**Adler/Barbour Yacht Services
43 Lawton Street
New Rochelle, New York 10801**

*The ColdPump from Adler/Barbour.*

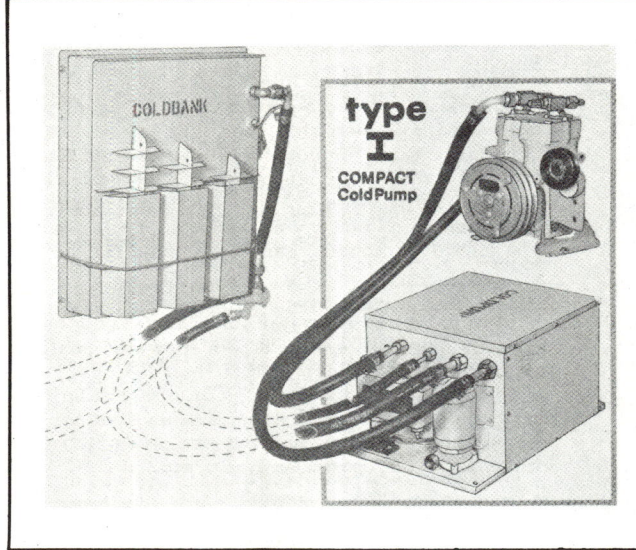

IMMC specializes in tie-downs and accessories for boat trailers, lots of them in many variations. They are wholesalers, so tell your distributor.

**Indiana Mills and Manufacturing Co.
120 W. Main Street
Carmel, Indiana 46032**

*Tie anything down with help from IMMC.*

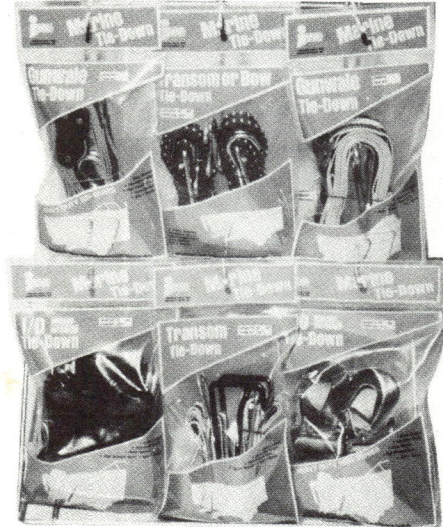

## Towing Lines

Dear Editors:
Regarding the nylon tow line comments on page 144 of MC-5, the precautionary note is indeed properly put forth; boat builders are solely responsible for the lack of hull stress distribution from fittings normally used for tow line attachments. Even then, the cross-section and length of tow lines are of substantial importance in the "shock absorber" characteristic, and must also include some consideration of the weights of the craft involved.

—H.H. Durr

Midland manufactures Twin-Tow lines, which are prerigged towing lines of prestretched nylon and polypropylene for small-craft use. For more information, send for their "Twin-Tow Fact Sheet."

**Midland Safety Systems
Box 37503
Omaha, Nebraska 68137**

Years ago Captain Nat of Bristol developed a line of hollow cast bronze cleats. There were several things about them besides the saving of weight that he had in mind. They held more rope, more turns, and you could get a hold on them—better for boarding situations. Lines were more easily fair-led through them, and they had a way of snagging a bight thrown at them, much better than other configurations. Anyway, there are now copies of these being made in Taiwan. It's:

**Holywell Development Corp.
Hao Ran Mansion No. 2-12 Lane 180
Kuang Fu South Rd.
Taipei, Taiwan**

*Hollow cast bronze cleats from Holywell Development.*

Look at this neat dinghy oar holder, from:

**R.C. Plath Co.
337 N.E. 10th Ave.
Portland, Oregon 97232**

**1. For 14' – 19' Boats.**
Components:
(1) 303-30 Cheek Block
(2) 78-31 Eye Straps
(2) 70-14 Cleat

Kit 99-15  8 oz.  $19.15

Once in a while the racing boys come up with gadgets most interesting to the singlehanded cruiser; these vertical halyard/sheet stoppers, for example, and this jiffy-reefing system, both offered and described in the Schaefer Marine catalog.

**Schaefer Marine, Inc.
Industrial Park
New Bedford, Massachusetts 02745**
or
**17945 Sky Park Blvd.
Irvine, California 92714**

*Above and right: Work-savers from Schaefer Marine.*

Too, the Clamcleats developed by Sneve-Nysether and the magic boxes by Harken also would seem to have their places aboard the shorthanded craft where things can become much too busy much too fast. (Question: Is it the winners who think up these things or the losers who have more time to think?)

**Sneve-Nysether Inc.
Box 1201
Everett, Washington 98201**

**Harken Yacht Fittings
1251 East Wisconsin Ave.
Pewaukee, Wisconsin 53072**

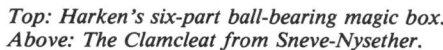

*Top: Harken's six-part ball-bearing magic box.
Above: The Clamcleat from Sneve-Nysether.*

Dear Editors:

I recently obtained my copy of Volume 6 of the *Mariner's Catalog* and was interested to note that there is still some confusion over gronicles.

Mr. McClure, in his letter on page 85, is obviously referring to "gronicals," not gronicles—an understandable confusion over spelling. Certainly gronicals are banned by Catholics, as they are by Baptists, Methodists, Presbyterians, Seventh-Day Adventists, Latter Day Saints, and all other true Americans dedicated to preserving the sanctity of home and family.

As to gronicles, attached is a photocopy of a clipping from the catalog of the firm of Finlaysen Forge and Foundry. As you can see, gronicles are readily available in eight sizes with other sizes to be had on special order. My copy of the catalog is a few years old and I've misplaced the price list so can't give you the costs.

The catalog listing does not indicate the amount of beryllium or antimony in the alloy, nor is banding with phosphor bronze mentioned. In view of Finlaysen's fine reputation, however, I'm sure that the assurance of "highest quality materials" is sufficient.

Finlaysen's is an old family firm now enjoying its third generation of family management. Some may wonder how and why gronicles happen to be manufactured in Nebraska. The Finlaysen firm began with the production of quality equipment for the Nebraska citrus industry. They soon expanded into a number of unrelated fields where forgings and castings of great precision were needed.

I hope that this information will help clarify the whole subject of gronicles.

—R.G. Maxfield
Hightstown, N.J.

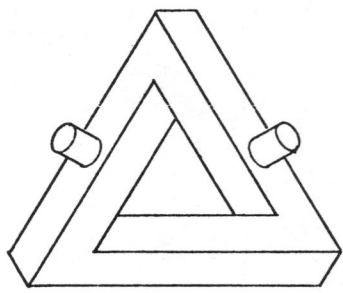

Dear Editors:

Your exchange of letters about gronicles in the *Mariner's Catalog*, Volume 5, was amusing but wide of the mark.

Gronicle is actually a generic, though now little used, term for any kind of scoop bailer. It is a corruption of the earlier and directly derivative term gronicker, or sometimes gronnacher.

This in turn stems from the original word *Greenacre,* the name of the dairy imprinted on the plastic milk bottle cut off slantwise on the bottom by the genius who gave us the original bailer.

Realizing your interest in traditional gear, I knew you would want to be informed.

—Neil Wilson
Annapolis, Md.

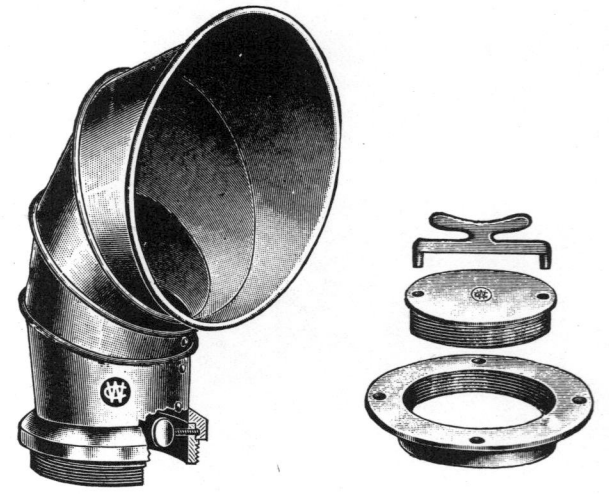

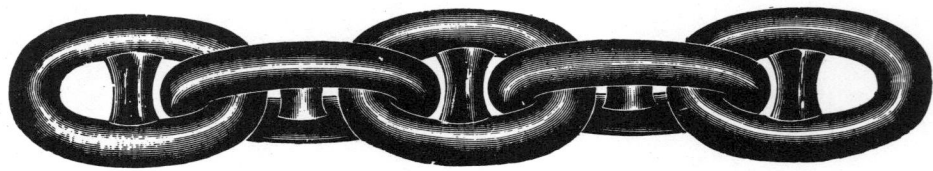

# Notes from the Companionway

*There comes a time to be in your ship, not on it.*

**—Fred Brooks, in a late-night radiotelephone call to the Editors.**

The energy crunch, a peculiar term at best, has caused considerable review of solid fuel combustion devices, stoves (heh heh), and it was inevitable that someone would develop an "airtight" model for use below decks. Called the Pansy Mark V, it is designed for charcoal and boasts an eight-hour burning time, remarkable for its 18-inch by 7-inch size and 5000-BTU average output. From:

**Faire Harbour Ltd.
44 Captain Peirce Rd.
Scituate, Massachusetts 02066**

*Left: The Pansy Mark V from Faire Harbour.*

Our Northern Climes chauvinism naturally prejudices us toward iron and solid fuels, and most of the stoves we've listed in the past reflect this. But the past decade has seen the emergence of safe, reliable, and accepted gas units, not only on yachts, but on working craft as well. Corp Brothers manufactures a line of stoves in many sizes built expressly for compressed *natural* gas.

**Corp Brothers, Inc.
1 Brook Street
Providence, Rhode Island 02903**

*Left: Corp's CNG cooking system.*

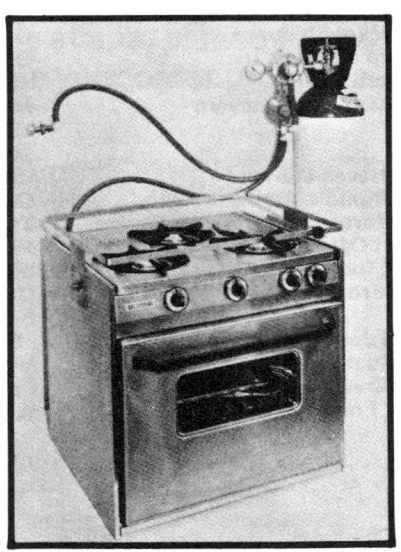

## 56 / The Mariner's Catalog

*Right: The Purette portable water filter.*

Stoves are made of earth, and burn more earth by combining it with air to produce fire (tomorrow, Kids, we're going to look at gravity. . .). Anyway, where's the water?

It's here, coming out of Purette, from:

**Andene Sales Associates
Suite 306
927 15th Street N.W.
Washington, D.C. 20005**

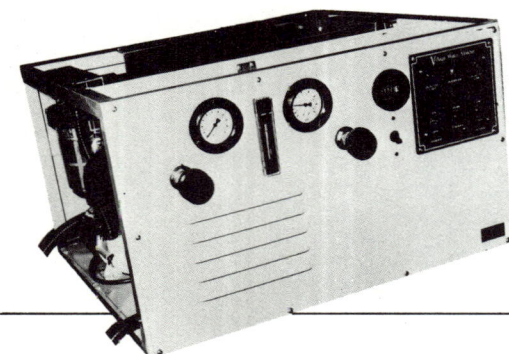

Or, for much more serious water usage, Village Marine carries a line of water purification systems producing from 100 to 2,600 gallons of fresh water daily.

**Village Marine
8888 West Washington Boulevard
Culver City, California 90230**

*Left: The Village Water Monitor.*

Another source for freeze-dried foods has come to our attention; it's:

**Mountain House
Oregon Freeze Dry Foods, Inc.
P.O. Box 1048
Albany, Oregon 97321**

*Left: From the Celestaire catalog.*

At $16.95 (or whatever bit more it will be by the time we get into print), this ingenious solar still by Celestaire really belongs in every life-raft kit that could possibly find itself offshore.

**Celestaire
416 S. Pershing
Wichita, Kansas 67218**

By the way, a book on marine refrigeration is now available, that is, it has been available for some time and is now out in a revised version. Good, clear, and based on solid experience, it's:

***Marine Refrigeration
for the Do It Yourself Sailor*
by Art Smith
P.O. Box 6538
Fort Lauderdale, Florida
42 pages, paperbound, 1978, $9.95**

**Order from:
Sailor Boy Products, Inc.
408 Lakeshore Drive
Palestine, Texas 75801**

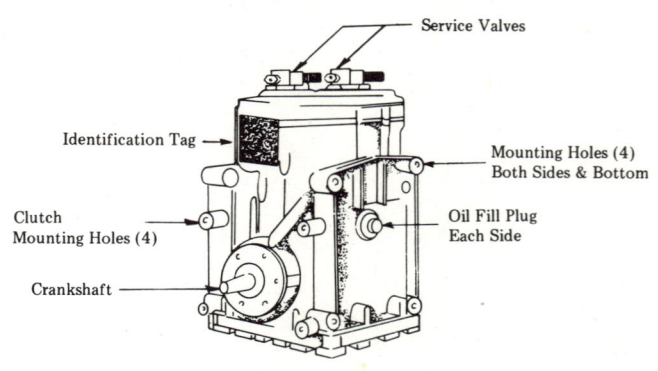

*From* Marine Refrigeration for the Do It Yourself Sailor.

# Power

## Engine Installations in Present-Day Boats

**by Pete Culler**

Having referred to sensible engine installations and my ideas on them in my book *Skiffs and Schooners* (International Marine Publishing), I've been asked to elaborate on the subject, especially with regard to today's modern wooden sailboat. Personally, I can't see what difference the material used in the boat makes—wood, glass, steel, cement, and any combination thereof—the installation can either be sensible or not.

I think this is a loaded subject anyhow. Forty or fifty years ago there were large fleets of oystermen and crabbers working the Chesapeake; these craft were, for all practical purposes, open boats. A fire or explosion was almost unheard of among such craft. Engines were of the simplest sort, installations fundamental, sometimes crude. Government-required safety equipment, if it was there at all, was usually in deplorable condition. Among motor yachts of the times—and granted there were not many compared to now—fires and explosions were more common, no doubt because many were decked and were more complicated in layout in the interests of yachting.

This is all food for thought. Looking back on it, even a pleasure motorboat of the old days was far simpler than what we think is necessary for even a small launch today. If you will closely examine the current Coast Guard rules and regulations for the installation of engines, piping, batteries, wiring, tanks, and all that goes with it, you will quickly see what complicated equipment, poor installations, and the penchant for jamming machinery out of sight have brought on us. I don't hold in toto with all these rules prescribed. Sometimes I find the ideas on venting hind-side-to, but generally it's all pretty sound, considering what Man has brought on himself in his love for complicating what could be simple things.

Going by The Book now makes engine installation very expensive. How to cut back on this? Simply eliminate what is not essential. In planning a new auxiliary sailboat, figure the engine as part of the crew and give it room and air. If this happens to eliminate a fancy chart table, full-length hanging locker (much beloved by the present generation), a bar, or even a bunk, consider the sacrifice well worth it. Any fuel tank, gas or diesel,

(continued on following page)

(continued from previous page)

is better off on deck in the cockpit under open seats, with a cutoff at the tank. You have eliminated a lot of ventilation problems right there, plus you've simplified future repairs or servicing.

Now, it seems, everyone wants an instrument panel, and gadgets of every kind in the cockpit, where they eventually suffer from water and salt. If you possibly can bring yourself to do it, eliminate this junk as much as possible. How? Like this: Place an oil gauge anywhere high up in the cabin, in view through the companionway. Same with an ampmeter if you have a starter and some electricity. Put the regulator box up high and dry too. These things can arc, you know; gas vapor is heavy. You don't need a temperature gauge. Put the excess water discharge through the hull up high, where you can see and feel it. Some people can't run an engine without a tachometer; you certainly can. What sounds good is good. Cultivate the knack of judging a boat's speed by looking over the side, plus gauging the sound of the engine. Once learned, this knack is far more accurate, simpler, and faster than trying to do it scientifically, because a small craft's gait has too many variables to attempt to treat her like a big craft.

Where practical, use the lifeboat tee exhaust, it being fairly simple. Often it's not practical, so you do the best you can. Through-hull fittings must be stout (therefore expensive) and very accessible. I think that for some waters at least, a Clear View strainer is worth having, even on a small engine. If it can possibly be arranged—and this is not easy in a small boat—the fuel strainer should be next to the tank on deck. Keep any vapors outside when you clean the thing. Have a cutoff valve right next to the carburetor (assuming you have a gas engine).

Assuming you have a small diesel, you simplify things a bit more if you want to. Many of these engines can be totally hand-starting, so you can eliminate wiring and batteries altogether. Remember, a battery is a source of explosive gas, so install it accordingly. Whether you have self-starting or not, there always should be a way of hand-starting a small auxiliary engine.

And although ALL engines should have a pan under them, I think it especially important with a diesel. A gasoline spill is no good, but with care and a little luck, the stuff will evaporate. Not so diesel; once wood is soaked, that's it: a cause of most fires aboard fishing boats these days. True, diesel fuel won't explode until it reaches very high heat, but hear this! oil-soaked wood can burn.

The little diesels take care of a lot of the requirements that would complicate things if you were using a gas engine, but at the expense of the most fussy sort of engine room housekeeping. Look at it this way: what you don't really need does not cost money and can't give trouble.

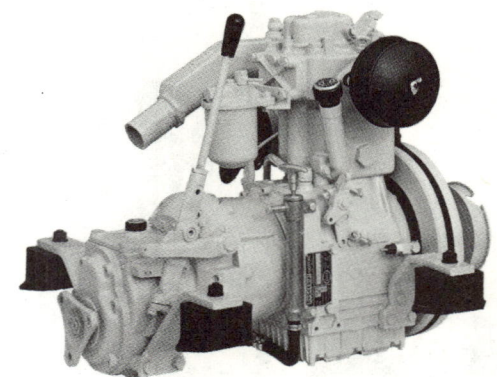

*The Ruggerini RDM 901 model.*

## Diesel

A fine, rugged-looking line of small diesels made in Italy has appeared in the U.S. The Ruggerinis, 5 through 45 horsepower, are distributed in this country through:

**General Propulsion
5522 Research Drive
Huntington Beach, California 92649**

The Atomic 4 auxiliary engine has resided in as many bilges in as many harbors for about as long as any other make one could name. But did you know that Medalist-Universal, manufacturer of the Atomic 4, also makes auxiliary diesels? They do; in 11, 16, 24, and 32 horsepower. Not only that, did you know that there are Atomic 1s and Atomic 2s? Yes, there are, and the Atomic 1, rated at 5 horsepower, they call "... the smallest four-cycle 100% marine engine on the market," at 20⅞ inches long, and 130 pounds. From:

**Medalist-Universal Motors
P.O. Box 2508
Oshkosh, Wisconsin 54901**

*The Atomic 1 from Medalist-Universal.*

## Engine Parts

Two years ago Fortune shined and the Fates allowed me the privilege of owning a cheery little ketch of Nielsen design, Luke construction, and 30 years of excellent care. She carries a four-cylinder Redwing in her slippery nethers (ouch) and, wanting gaskets, I began calling around for parts.

This engine had not been manufactured for some years, so I began calling some of the better yacht yards to find out where parts might be secured. In retrospect, my brain must have been at half-mast not to think of Red Wing, Minnesota. My dad came from close-by there, and so on. But these things did not come to mind; nor, oddly, did they occur to anyone I called. Instead, everyone said, "Call Stokes." After about the eighth "call Stokes," the residual half-brain remnant began ever so slightly to stir itself. Why not call Stokes, say I originally to meself. In fact, why not list Stokes in the *Mariner's Catalog*?

So, first things being first, ladies and gentlemen, Stokes is one of the foremost marine engine and engine conversion outfits in the country. They work with and carry parts for a dozen engine brands in both fuels in all sizes. They are especially adept at and useful for auto engine block conversions to marine applications. All kinds of boatyards use them as a matter of course and we should have listed them long ago.

**Stokes Marine Supply, Inc.**
**Main Office**
**740 York Ave.**
**Pawtucket, Rhode Island 02861**

**Sales Office**
**Coldwater, Michigan**

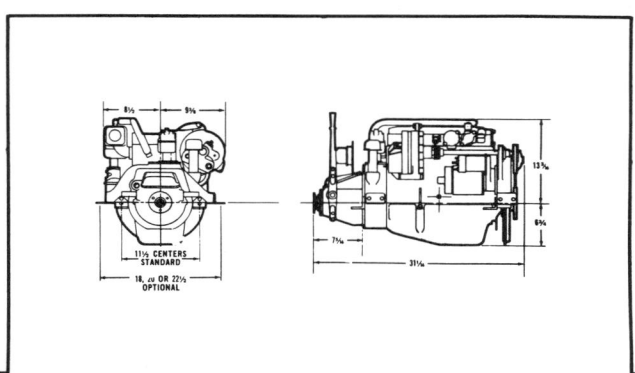

*From the Stokes Marine Supply catalog.*

While Stokes is well known for its supply of defunct engine parts, they didn't have anything for the Red Wing. So finally an ole guy says, "Well, 'course there's Red Wing, Minnesota," and before he could finish his sentence, I dialed information and asked for any Red Wing Engine Company that might exist. Nope. Well, how about the Chamber of Commerce, then? Fine. Dialed it. Hello, yadayada, what do you suggest? Well, she said, you could call the Red Wing Marina. Perfect, give me the number. Dialed the number. Hello, the telephone said. Hello I said in reply, is this the Red Wing Marina? Well, it said, that's up on the wharf, this is a telephone booth on the dock. Oh, I said, well, see, I'm calling from Maine and. . . . Oh, how's the weather there? Gee, I hear it's really nice there. Yeah, it's nice in Minnesota too. Look, are you the guy that works at Red Wing Marina? No, I was just standing here; any messages I could tack up for you? No, thanks, I was just trying to find out what happened to all the parts left over from the Red Wing Marine Engine Company. Oh, he said, they're all in Virgil's garage. Who's that? Just a minute, and I'll look it up here in the phone book. Here it is, it's:

**Red Wing Engine Parts**
**211 Main Street**
**Red Wing, Minnesota 55066**

---

Dear Editors:

The Red Wing Motor Co. made engines from about 1910 until 1962. Most parts for these engines are still available. We keep a good stock of parts here in Red Wing.

I purchased this business about 10 years ago and have been operating it on a part-time basis since then. It has been quite a challenge to try to supply parts for engines you have not seen. Red Wing had blueprints on most parts, which helped very much. We do not sell complete engines, only parts for Red Wings.

I have met, talked to, and written to many wonderful people who thought their engines were great. Because of their age, a lot of our engines have been junked out. What are left will soon become collector's items.

A lot of Red Wing parts will be available only as long as our stock lasts. For others, parts should be available for many years.

—Virgil Mischke
**Red Wing Engine Parts**

## Antique Engines

The day a friend of mine dumped a stripped-down jump-spark one-lunger, caked with grease and dirt, flaked with rust, into the trunk of my car was the day I began to understand marine engines. Old-timers for a long time now have been decrying modern marine engines as mere shadows of their former selves, yet to someone who grew up with complicated, high-speed machinery, what they were saying was completely beyond my experience and was shrugged off as nostalgic raving. My logic told me that modern technology is progressive, that machinery (and everything else) *has* to get better as time passes—if for no other reason than our generation is, indeed, the best and the brightest, that the good and the bad are always replaced with the better. My recent experience tells me otherwise.

After lugging the parts of my 50-year-old Detroit down to my workshop, I spent a day or two circling them warily. My knowledge of engine mechanics is elementary to say the least, and the parts looked to me to be just pieces of this and that, some barely recognizable, others lumps of brass, bronze, and iron. By the process of elimination, and using the small amount of 2-cycle engine theory I knew, I gradually figured out how things went together. And I discovered a most indisputable fact about antique marine engines—they are so simple that they can be put together and taken apart with a monkey wrench, a crescent wrench, a screwdriver, and a pair of pliers.

Now who can say that about a modern marine engine— a perfect jungle of wires, belts, piping, cams, gronicles, starters, generators, and assorted gizmos? The only thing the average person (that is to say, just about all of us) can do when his engine breaks down at sea is wait for a tow. Except for the most elementary chores, fixing it takes the services of a factory-trained mechanic wielding thousands of dollars of specialized tools, and you and I know what that means.

An antique marine engine is the only way to go. Naturally, low rpms, high torque, low horsepower, and heavy weight mean that it will serve only in a displacement boat, but we aren't in a hurry anyway. And, of course, we'll have to live with a certain amount of thumping vibration, but most would agree that a slow thump is far easier to handle than the high-pitched whine of today's engines.

Antique engines aren't that hard to find at all. News that I was restoring a marine engine spread around town pretty fast, and people who dropped by to gawk soon plugged me into a subculture I hardly knew existed. Buying, selling, and trading is going on all the time, and the prices of engines (except the rarest ones) in the best shape are still well below the price of a brand-new modern one. Parts, too, are fairly easy to find. Joe here knows a fellow who has a bunch of grease cups; Fred can put you on to a timing lever; Sam has a spare lubricator. I even discovered through the grapevine that there is an old-timer a couple of towns away who has the twin to my engine installed in a boat. I'll be going over there to compare notes when I'm ready to install mine.

My Detroit looks great now. It's all cleaned up, painted dark green, and the brass and bronze parts have been buffed to a bright luster. I put her back together by myself, with a little advice from an expert—and because I did it all myself, I know exactly why and how it works. I am confident that if it should break down in the bay, I can fix it. I know and understand my engine.

The best way to plug into the antique engine underground is to ask around. Next best is to subscribe to a great little magazine:

***The Gas Engine Magazine***
**Stemgas Publishing Co.**
**Box 328**
**Lancaster, Pa. 17604**
**$9/yr. U.S., $10 Canada, $12 foreign**
**Published 6 times a year**

Filled with short articles, restoration tips, and pages of classified ads, *Gas Engine Magazine* is the convert's delight. It's almost exclusively devoted to stationary and tractor engines, but they do carry marine material occasionally. Best yet, the publisher, Stemgas, has reprinted a number of ancient engine catalogs and instruction manuals. Among them we found:

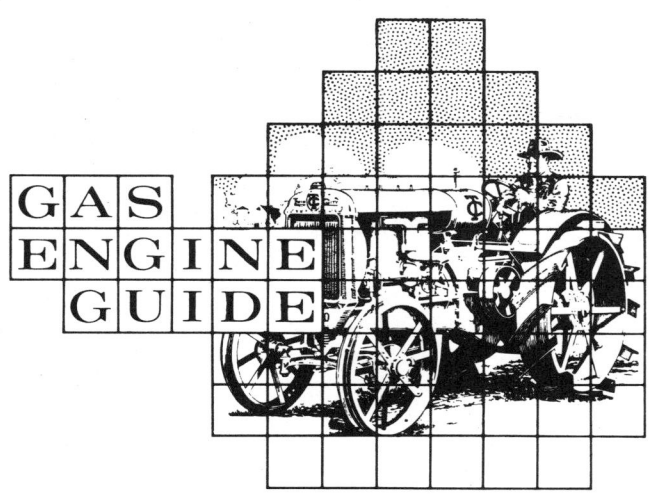

*Gas Engine Guide*
**Stemgas Publishing Co.
(address on opposite page)
$2.75**

Covering both 2-cycle and 4-cycle engines, this little book tells all about ignition, operation, carburetors, batteries, wiring, etc.

Another book, originally published in 1911, that will be helpful is:

*Gas Engine Troubles and Installation*
**by J.B. Rathbun
Ron Lachniet
867 Crampton Ave. N.E.
Ada, Mich. 49301
$10.95**

With this book, repairing and maintaining your antique engine is made easy.

Once you get really involved in antique engines, you will undoubtedly want to learn more about the history of their development. A most interesting, well-written and researched chronicle is:

*Internal Fire*
**by Lyle Cummins
Carnot Press
Lake Oswego, Oregon
351 pages, illus., biblio., index, 1976, $18.95**

The author, son of the founder of Cummins Diesel, has written a book on developmental technology that is not only readable but also enlightening. He discusses the progress of the internal-combustion engine from 1673 to 1900, both in terms of engineering and of the people who were responsible for the great breakthroughs. By the time you turn the last page, you will no longer see gas and diesel engines as inanimate lumps of cast iron.

*Right and left: From* Internal Fire.

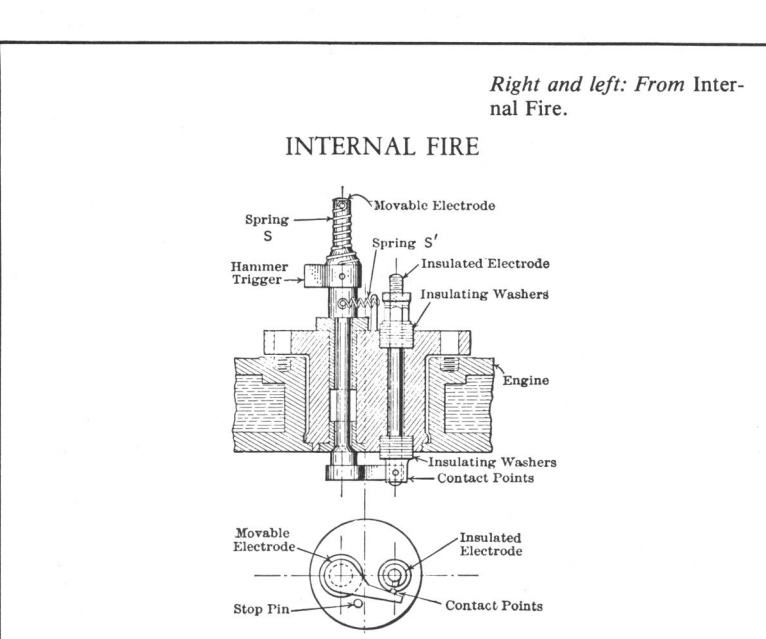

Fig. 12-26 Typical construction of a "make and break" igniter block as installed in an engine. (Hirshfeld, *Gas Engines for the Farm*, 1914)

## Quick-and-Dirty Power

With inboards and outboards getting so expensive that you almost have to sell your boat to get the wherewithal to power her, more and more people are becoming interested in the 2- and 4-cycle air-cooled engines manufactured by Briggs & Stratton, Tecumseh, Clinton, et al. (See past discussions in previous *Mariner's Catalogs*, specifically Pete Culler's piece in MC-5, page 54.) They're cheap, light, fuel-efficient, and, most important, easy to maintain.

There are a number of books available today on the operation and maintenance of small engines, but one of the best we have yet to see is:

*Small Gasoline Engines*
**by George E. Stephenson**
**Van Nostrand Reinhold, New York, N.Y.**
**256 pages, illus., index, 1978, $7.95**

Set up like a course book for a trade school, it has test-yourself questions at the end of each chapter and laboratory-experience checklists to aid in self-study. It covers everything from theory to practice and will put you on intimate terms with your engine.

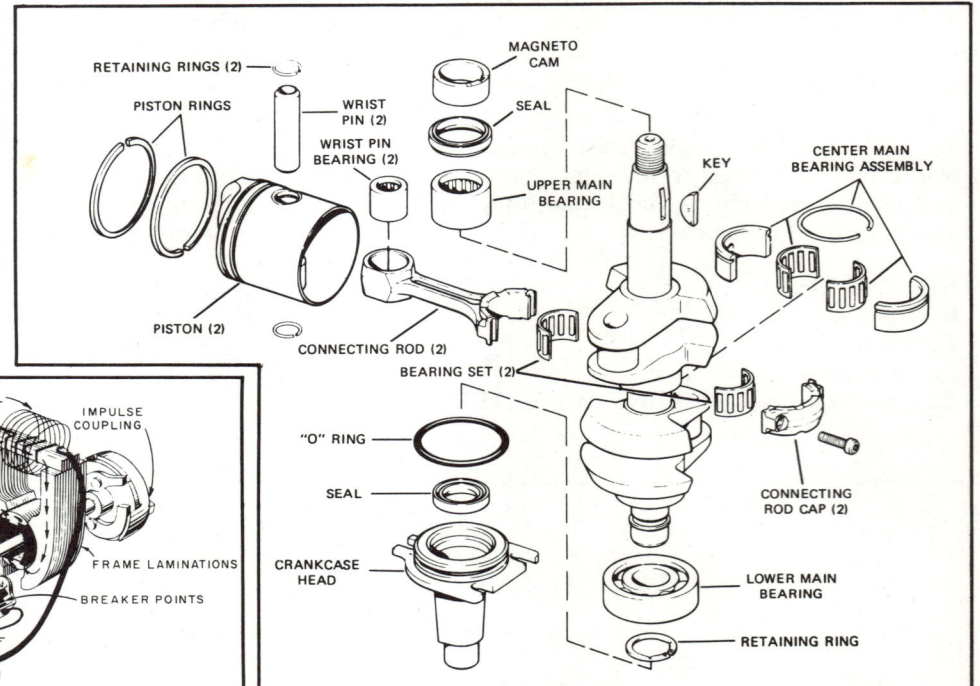

*Right and below: From* Small Gasoline Engines.

Dear Editors:

Your MC-5 quick-and-dirty boats section, with emphasis on Pete Culler's superb "Motorboats for the Masses" (Briggs & Stratton powered) dissertation, was most heartwarming. I suggest we belatedly (like a few or several decades) formalize our background experiences to ensure a real putzy future. I don't necessarily agree with everyone, including the concerned factory folk, that the little Briggs should shake around so much. First, whenever possible, scout around for the cast-iron block oldies—they came down to about 1½ HP, I believe. Check the crankshafts mostly for roundness; the newer aluminum connecting rods seem quite adaptable. This happily should put you into your lawn mower fixit shop trash pile.

Mainly, there are flywheels AND flywheels—considerable weight differences, all of which affects easy starting, good idling, and reduction of vibration. The reason for the differences is that some installations, like rotary mowers, include the weight of the rotating blade for reciprocation—remove it and you've a rougher operating motor. Watch to see if the carburetor is there in the older models—they seem to be cannibalized otherwise. The upright or horizontal crankshaft motors seem to lubricate better than the vertical crank types, which require a slinger ring to distribute the oil.

While I like Pete's fore-and-aft "clutch" (the helmsman), I did see one neat installation here that had a simple centrifugal clutch and 3:1 chain/sprocket drive. As an engine hobbyist, and not necessarily a mechanic, I believe *Mariner's Catalog* readers could contribute immensely to Briggs & Stratton selection and understanding—the old-style cast iron flywheel makes 'em run like a true boat motor.

—Norman Benedict
Lomita, California

# SHHH!
### by David L. Register

The outboard motor industry in 1921 was a noisy, struggling infant with several serious birth defects... and noise was one of the worst. If you could get one of the contraptions started at all, you were rewarded for your exertions by a cacophony that battered the eardrums, and sometimes even by gentle burghers along the shore hurling rocks and abuse.

Ole Evinrude at the Evinrude Motor Company, sensing that his advertising budget was going down the drain, determined to do something about it. What he did do was invent the first through-hub underwater exhaust to help still the hubbub. That this was a giant step forward is an understatement. He would certainly be encouraged, were he alive today, to learn that the exhaust is now only the third major noise source in an outboard. And he would be overjoyed to note that the underwater exhaust is now practically universal throughout the world. Quiet scavenging of the outboard has been an expensive and demanding discipline, and several systems in use today approach the ultimate in sophistication. Yet, after 57 years, we're still not there—some indication of how difficult noise suppression is.

Nevertheless, exhausting underwater was so successful that the concept of quieting its motors became a cornerstone of Evinrude's research and development and still receives much attention even today at Outboard Marine. There is here a solid record of achievement that's hard to fault. As early as 1928, opposed cylinder blocks began to give way to quieter alternate firing arrangements. Rudimentary motor hoods began to appear in 1929, intake silencers and reed valves in 1935, and then, in 1942, OMC converted to war production. Both the Army and Navy, however, wanted super-quiet "invasion" motors. With research and development funding on virtually an unlimited basis, OMC collaborated with acoustical people at Harvard and developed these powerplants... which were seldom used.

The quieting techniques were too bulky and expensive for civilian production; but if OMC learned what it couldn't do after the war, it began to get some inkling of what it could. For example, it had been evident for some time that the boat itself acted as a sounding board for the motor, and that some means of isolating the two would have to be found. By 1950, OMC had developed a spring-mounted outboard whose entire power component was allowed to float freely of the transom clamp. This was another giant step forward, comparable to the underwater exhaust. Rubber mounts were found to be more effective than springs and soon replaced them. By 1955, several other important noise sources had been treated by rubber isolation, and quieter spiral bevel gearing made its appearance. Since 1955, OMC's efforts at noise suppression have resulted in numerous refinements but only one major innovation—that of water-jacketing almost the whole exhaust system of its 50 H.P. and larger motors. Actually, this

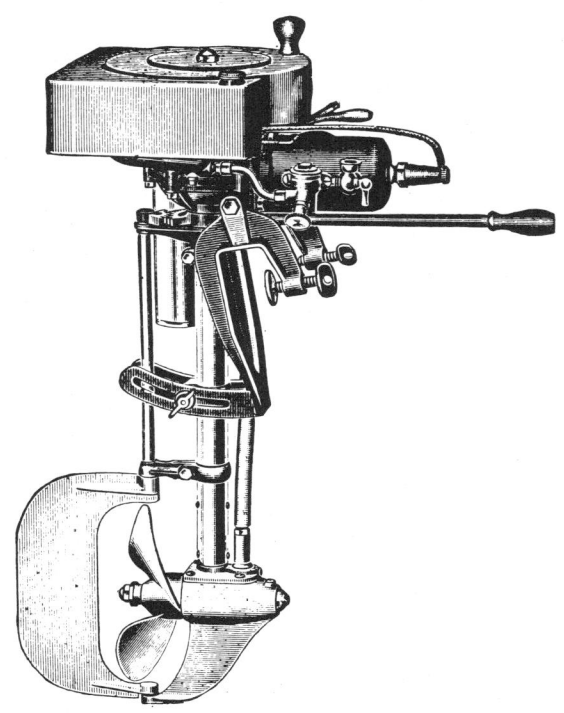

was done primarily for cooling reasons, but it also served to muffle the exhaust note substantially.

As the outboard motor advanced technologically, so did the science of sound measurement and analysis, itself a struggling infant at the turn of the century. Despite the complexities encountered, our knowledge grew apace, and with it the development of sensitive and costly equipment. People interested in noise abatement had to go back to Square One more than once, as the new equipment seemed to be raising more questions than it answered. But accurate noise analysis also proved to be a two-way street, dispelling a number of cherished misconceptions and promising always a better handle on the subject.

In any case, the whole rather murky scene crystallized suddenly in what's known as the Clean Air Act of 1970, which included noise as a pollutant and classified outboard-powered craft as "pleasure vehicles," along with snowmobiles and motorcycles, among others. Happily, the outboard motor promptly went to the head of the class as "the most effectively silenced application of the widely used two-stroke internal combustion engine" (EPA's *Report to the President and Congress on Noise,* dated December 31, 1971). This was certainly getting off on the right foot, but the specter of Federal regulation now loomed menacingly, and the outboard community reacted with some vigor.

The situation was a bit delicate to say the least, for here was an industry that had forgotten more about noise than the EPA currently knew and was therefore in a position to tell the regulator how to regulate. Pre-
(continued on following page)

WHAT TO DO WITH YOUR MOTORBOAT IF YOU MOVE INLAND

(continued from previous page) dictably, the EPA shirt-tailed in on nearly 50 years of abatement effort and began mumbling that the outboard people would have to do better. So what else is new? Theoretically, there's almost no limit to what can be achieved in noise abatement, but at what cost? And who would pay for it? Indeed, who even agrees on what's noisy and what isn't? The aeronautical engineer rejoices in the sound of his jet taking off, but the people living around the airport don't. Clearly, the EPA would have to be shepherded through this maze with tender loving care.

A variety of conferences took place, but the field tests proved the most interesting, although their industry sponsorship raised some questions about objectivity. One, under the aegis of OMC at its test site near Stuart, Florida, was unusually elaborate in an obvious attempt to pinpoint many of the problems underlying regulation. It was discovered, for example, that towing outboard hulls, with motors locked down and propellers free-wheeling in neutral, produced noise levels not all that much below those recorded when the boats were operated at full throttle. This was a test of boat, or "transit," noise, and one might wonder why the lower units were in the water, since they're part of the motor, not the boat. Be that as it may, this test was significant in that it proved the hull itself produced a great deal more noise than had been supposed . . . and suggested that further quieting efforts might justifiably be the joint responsibility of the boat and motor manufacturers.

Thrown in for good measure were several well-established characteristics of sound propagation as they applied to outboards. It was pointed out, for example, that each doubling of distance from the source attenuates (weakens) the sound level six decibels. OMC was anxious to make this point because the SAE, which had established the test standards, insisted that the sound pickups be made at only 50 feet. It's illegal in many waters to operate a boat within 100 feet of other boats, swimmers, the shore, etc., so the results of this test were really 6 dB(A) too high. In point of fact, they weren't all that bad even at 50 feet, averaging about 76 dB(A), which is equivalent to a busy office. In-boat levels were, of course, substantially higher, and here perhaps lies the crux of the problem: For whom do you abate the noise? Reducing the in-boat levels to, say, 75 dB(A) may well prove to be a most difficult and expensive effort. Boat design is going to have a great deal to do with it in terms of the semi-enclosures that may be required, as these will fall in the bailiwick of the boat manufacturers.

Another interesting characteristic of sound is that multiple sources are additive in a most peculiar way—not just the sum of all levels. There's a rather complicated formula to compute this total sound level, and we will therefore avoid it like the plague. Suffice it to say, in a very simple example, that twin outboards each generating 80 dB(A) produce a total of only 83 dB(A)— not 160 dB(A). I hasten to concede that this is a purely academic observation, since the sound level meter automatically shows the total level. Only in the anachoic chamber, or "quiet room," can several separate noise sources within a single piece of equipment be identified and measured.

In the midst of all these prestigious data, OMC stumbled across another little gem: Just back off the throttle 1,000 rpm, and you reduce the decibel level by 5. That doesn't seem like much, but the idea behind it isn't to be dismissed lightly. Why not run a larger motor at half throttle? A reduction of 2,500 rpm means a reduction of almost 13 on the dB(A) scale, and that will just about put you to sleep, not to mention the gas savings.

Apropos of rpm reduction, another important phase of the Stuart tests was a study of boat usage based on the percentage of time spent at a given rpm. The preconception was that outboards are operated at WOT (wide open throttle). The results were astonishing. They indicated in general that motors are seldom operated at more than 80 percent throttle, and that the average boater runs his motor at half throttle or less nearly half the time he's afloat. As you might expect, smaller motors are operated faster for longer periods than larger ones. Owners of the larger units turn out to be reluctant dragons. Unfortunately, the objectivity of this usage test is especially in question because the data were recorded by OMC employees using their personal motors. On the other hand, the extensive nature of the test suggests that disinterested data are likely to substantiate the results.

But what really muddied the waters was another OMC-sponsored field test that took place at the University of Windsor in Ontario, Canada. Someone had noticed that wind noise seemed pretty loud sometimes. Would the U of W care to look into the matter? The U of W would, and did. Test subjects were equipped with sensitive ear "bugs" and subjected to various wind velocities at various angles. What was this? Incredible! A 25-knot breeze created a sound level, right in the ear, of 96 dB(A), while bicycling produced a level of 92 dB(A)! These values approach that of a jackhammer and represent nothing but ambient noise, over which we have no control except the use of ear plugs. What effect will these findings have on regulation? Probably none. Technically, marine life pollutes the waters, but we can't dump our sewage overboard.

Whither away? At the present time, we're in a gray area, a sort of uncertain limbo. Objective data are still in the process of development. Obviously, the EPA will feel compelled to justify in some manner its regulatory status in terms of noise abatement. But the outboard industry needs very little, if any, regulation, as its record in this area indicates. Would it not be better to allow the industry to proceed on its own initiative? Current thinking about regulation involves product compliance at the manufacturing level, with continued compliance the responsibility of the consumer. Enforcement, however, will be another matter. The manufacturer's motor will be in compliance if it's just barely in compliance at the time of sale. But outboard motors loosen a bit with age and generate a little more noise each year. A motor could well become illegal with 10 or more good years of life still in it. And how will we know if our motors are legal or not? Will dealers become inspection stations for annual noise checks? We can hope the Clean Air people don't next require catalytic converters!

There's no doubt the industry will continue its efforts at noise abatement—indeed, would have done so without the Clean Air Act of 1970. Future research will concentrate on in-boat levels, which are a bit high at cruising speeds and often bothersome at WOT (even though we spend very little time there). Hoods will become slightly larger to accommodate sophisticated noise-absorption material molded to the inside. It might even be more effective to mold the entire hood of closed-cell foam about an inch thick with a protective layer on the outside. The underpan on which the hood is clamped will have to receive comparable foam treatment, as this is usually aluminum.

The carburetor air intake has always been a major source of noise; but, as if that weren't enough, there's the additional problem of supplying air through the hood, which should really be a perfect enclosure. Automotive-type "pancake" silencers could easily be developed for the carburetors, but admitting quietly through the hood the vast quantities of air needed for combustion is a most baffling problem. *Nota bene,* you motor macs and home tinkerers!

The bottom line? Oh, hell, just crank up and enjoy yourselves!

For our friends with irritable neighbors, here's the Super Trapp from:

**Gil Marine
4935 Santa Anita Ave.
Temple City, California 91780**

Dear Editors:

On my wife's list of most cherished things, boats are two lines below root canal surgery. But last May, while I was doing some things in Stamford, Connecticut, she waited in a bookstore. She found four volumes of the *Mariner's Catalog* and bought them for me because "They really looked neat." Later that day, the new infection became even more severe and, in a yard in Old Saybrook, she bought a basket-case Rhodes 19 with a busted plank, which I now have to go after.

Now, some other things.

I am a small craft designer (Westlawn) and operate a used boat business at a large inland lake in Indiana. I support my habit by working as a graphic designer. I am, and have been since I was a kid on Great South Bay in the 30s, intensely interested in any kind of a boat no one else is. This falls right in line with your Quick and Dirty Department.

But I think there is a serious case to be made for something that I've started calling Pragmatic Boats.

Item: My friend Steve Tiebout, who has been in the marine publishing business most of his working life, and who is now a rep out of its New York office for *Motor Boating & Sailing*, and who has been sailing seriously since he and I were small boys, built a boat while he was living in California. It was a double-ended sharpie, flat-bottomed, with a gaff rig and a jib on a club. It had rope rigging and a taffrail with actual belaying pins. But the interesting part is the way it was built (on a severe budget). The hull was quarter-inch *interior* plywood. But as he built, Tiebout painted every inch, inside and out, with good old porch enamel thinned with turpentine and applied in multiple coats.

This was several years ago—10 or so—and the boat is still in use, but now on Long Island. Steve had it out somewhere off L.A. one day and got hit by a Santa Ana, and survived as greater vessels foundered. He thinks the only thing that saved him as he rode it out, unable to get his mainsail down in time, was the porosity of his homemade former-bedsheet sail.

Now this is a real boat, built and sailed by someone who knows boats and takes the whole subject seriously. But it's a Pragmatic Boat. Given the factors of little money, ultimate use other than extended cruising, trailering and dry land storage between uses, and the fact that the whole purpose of small boats—at least in most American 1970s situations—is strictly to have fun, Tiebout's boat made abundant sense.

So the boat may not last for eternity. So the plywood will probably craze and eventually delaminate. And the only really good piece of wood on the boat, a Sitka spruce mast, will rot and split. And so what? If the alternative is no boat at all . . . if you can't go first class, stay home . . . then this kind of a Pragmatic Boat answers all kinds of needs.

Item: Right after the war (WW2, the Big One), a friend and I went partners on a 20-foot sloop that had lain a-rotting for at least four years in a yard in Mamaroneck. We patched and painted it, and got it into sufficient shape to be launched and sailed. We got an engine with the boat, for our $400, but it was rusted solid, so we bought a 2-hp Briggs & Stratton. We mounted it off-center on the old engine bed (down inside the cabin, in a totally airless cavity) with a V-belt from a 1-inch shaft pulley to a 4-inch prop shaft pulley. This gave us a 4:1 reduction, at whatever speed the engine was capable of running. We ran it wide open, and moved our heavy, cement-ballasted old boat very well through all sorts of water for three seasons. As far as I know, the guy who bought it from us kept our engine installation intact and carried on with it in the Hudson River, where he moved the boat after we sold it.

Certainly the installation wasn't right, nor was it scientific. The propeller was one we picked up in the yard and used because it fit the shaft diameter, not because its pitch was right. But it worked!

Item: The Toro lawnmower people came out with a high-torque engine last year. I have a push mower with one of the engines on it, and it's a gem. The dealer says it's made by Clinton. But whoever makes it, it's a fine, small air-cooled engine. It runs at dramatically noticeable low speed, makes far less noise (with one of those cardboard mufflers lawnmower makers specialize in), but cuts its way through weeds and wet grass like its far-larger, far-faster predecessor, which was a two-cycle.

It occurs to me that this would be a superb small boat engine. I suppose a horizontal shaft model is made, but know only of the vertical shaft, which leads to still another lump of pragmatism.

Making a cheap, workable clutch has always been a problem when an engine is adapted to marine use. Forgetting, for this paragraph at least, a reverse gear, consider this idea: mounting a vertical shaft engine on a simple, flat base which is, in turn, mounted on a hinge. A lever extends upward from the base, with some sort of positive lock to hold it in two positions. The shaft of the motor, as it sticks out below the base, is equipped with a small abrasive wheel 2 inches or less in diameter.

The propeller shaft is fixed in place in its log and equipped with a flat wheel, about 4 inches or so—whatever it takes for a 2:1 or 3:1 reduction, according to the size of the abrasive wheel on the engine shaft—positioned so that the shaft abrasive wheel can make contact with the flat surface. It would probably be best if the surface of the propeller shaft wheel were abraded or covered with a tough, glued-on sandpaper or whatever.

The engine runs, the shaft turns, the small abrasive wheel runs in contact with the flat wheel on the prop shaft. To disengage, the lever is moved and the engine rocks forward on its hinged base. To engage, move back and let the two wheels make contact.

It shouldn't tax anyone's ingenuity too much to take this arrangement one step further and devise a way to raise and lower the engine a few inches. Thus, with the engine in the down position, the shaft wheel contacts the bottom of the prop shaft wheel, causing it to turn in one direction. But when the engine is raised, the small wheel engages the large wheel on the upper half of its diameter and turns the shaft the opposite way. If you have a hollow in the center of the large wheel, where the small wheel engages air, you have a transmission with forward, neutral, and reverse.

We always think in terms of rigid engine mounts, but when we're dealing with engines that actually weigh less than a case of beer, it seems practical to consider the engine as the movable element, rather than a complicated set of belts or gears.

This small wheel—big wheel, incidentally, was the basis of the old Locomobile car transmission. Old-timers who drove them swore that these were the greatest, smoothest transmissions ever. And they probably were, predating any sort of fluid or automatic drives. Seems as though the simple concept could be easily applied to all sorts of marine configurations (see crude sketch below).

Item: A couple of weeks ago I was talking to Charles Stokes, who founded and ran the engine conversion plant of the same name, in Coldwater, Michigan. Charles told me my memory was working; that his highly popular Model A and flat-head Ford V-8 conversions did indeed have automobile transmissions but no clutches. The guts of the transmissions were removed, all except reverse and second gears, and were shifted simply by shoving the original gearshift lever through a straight line pattern. The trick was not to equivocate; throttle down, seize the lever, and ram 'er home! He who hesitated got

(continued on following page)

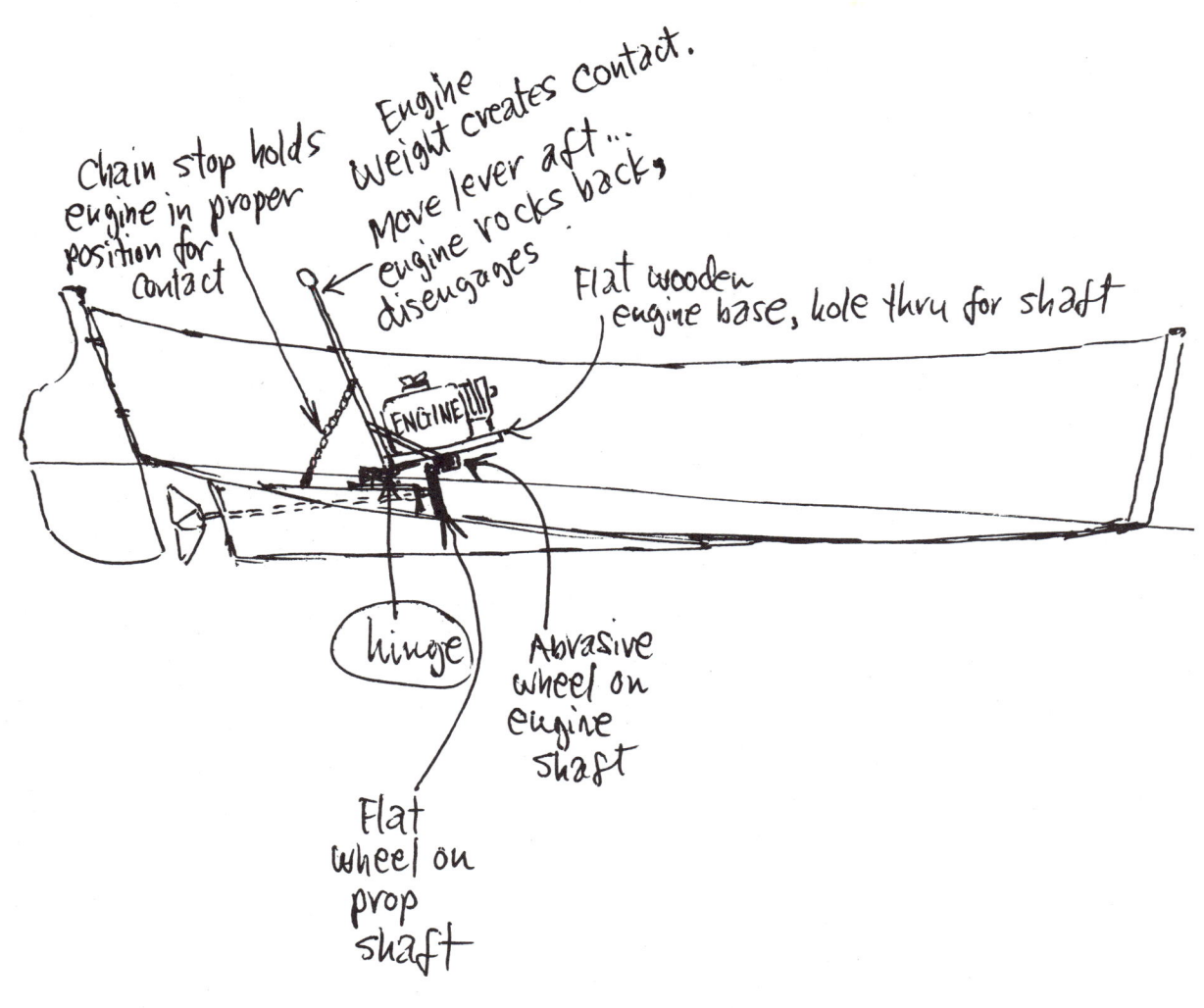

*(continued from previous page)*
a grinding noise and little pieces of gear teeth inside the gearbox for his timidity. But the process worked, obviously, for hundreds—Charles thinks more likely thousands—of boatmen who bought and used the old Ford conversions.

OK, why not reworked car transmissions hooked up to air-cooled engines, Acadias, et al., where ready-made gear sets are not available (or cost too much). No clutch, just gears. Make the engine-to-transmission connection with flat flanges welded on, or rigid metal sleeves or whatever. Transmission-to-shaft connections, where lower speeds are involved, can be made with short sections of high-pressure hydraulic hose, clamped in place. Don't laugh. The kind of hose I'm talking about is used on 100,000 psi industrial hydraulic equipment (big bulldozers; draglines, etc.). There isn't a small engine made capable of twisting a four-inch section of this stuff into the breaking point, yet it will give enough to make a very practical universal joint. You can even fudge a small difference in diameters simply by clamping tighter.

Item: Still haranguing about Pragmatic Boats, I'm in the process of eating my own cooking. This winter, I expect to finish a 19-foot flat-bottomed, double-ended yawl with a ballasted fixed keel and lateen sails. Now if this sounds insane, at the most charitable, consider the pragmatic factors. Flat is simple, thus cheap without resorting to bad materials. Amateurs can build flat-bottomed boats; they have a helluva time with round and often as much making the stem connection on a vee bottom. The keel is long and shallow; no loss of space inside the already minuscule cockpit. And it gives stability to a very long (over 4:1 length-width ratio) hull which would otherwise have the characteristics of a surfboard. It's designed to fit any of hundreds of commonplace, standard boat trailers without modification. It has a pounds-per-inch-immersion factor of almost 200 pounds, so it will carry a lot of weight and people.

Why lateen? I can rig the whole boat for what a single extruded aluminum spar would cost, and probably have enough left over for at least one of the sails. There are three sail combinations, which takes care of the inherent lateen fault of being unable to be reefed. No standing rigging means changing from one configuration to another in a matter of seconds.

This isn't a boat to cruise the Maine coast, nor to cross the Pacific. It's a simple, cheap daysailer or possibly an overnighter for the folks who like backpacking. A 90-pound girl can launch it, rig it, and be underway with both sails in less than five minutes, which is more than you can say for any conventionally rigged trailerable boat.

Certainly this is not the ultimate, nor is it even in the race for sailing perfection. But if the whole point of messing around with boats is fun, then for God's sake have fun and forget about the IORC and MORC and who knows what other chicken rules mankind has imposed on himself in the pursuit of enjoyment.

That's the basis of Pragmatic Boats. It's too bad the Nixon administration had to give a good word a bad connotation. Maybe you or somebody can come up with a good synonym. Meantime, I have to go back to work on some milk cartons I'm designing. Somebody has to pay for the new plank in my wife's old boat.

—Joe Reisner
Fort Wayne, Indiana

## Know Your Motor

If you watch television, no doubt you have seen the ad: A pleasant, smiling, good-looking woman, probably a mother, looks forthrightly into the camera and announces matter-of-factly, "Hi! I'm Peg Bracken and I hate to cook." Substitute "I hate my auxiliary engine," and you'll have reached the heart of the sailor's psyche. Is there a sailor alive who doesn't hate his engine? Of course not, and therein lies the problem. Dislike breeds neglect—neglect breeds dysfunction—dysfunction breeds contempt—contempt breeds ignorance—ignorance bodes ill when the engine won't start as you enter a yacht harbor on a Saturday evening in the summer on a fast tide when the wind dies and every other sailboat, skippered by a person of like mind, is trying to do the same thing. Good luck.

You don't have to love your engine. Just like it. And if you like it, do something for it: keep it maintained, accessible, and orderly. *Learn something about it.* If you don't, there isn't a mechanic in the world who can save your ass when you need it.

***Engines for Sailboats***
**by Conrad Miller**
**Ziff-Davis Publishing Company, New York**
**183 pages, illus., index, 1978, $9.95**

*Below: From* Engines for Sailboats.

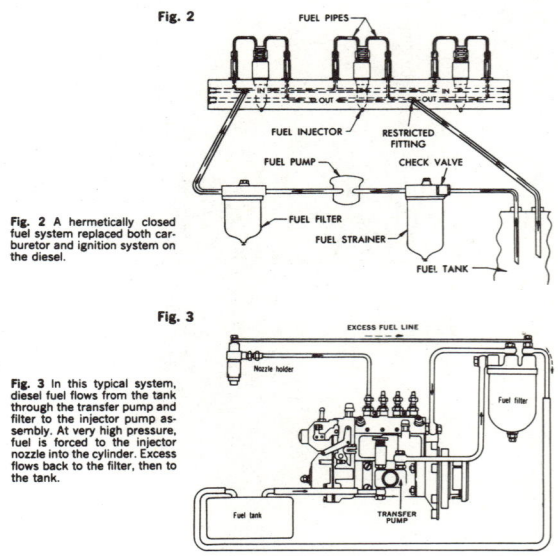

Fig. 2 A hermetically closed fuel system replaced both carburetor and ignition system on the diesel.

Fig. 3 In this typical system, diesel fuel flows from the tank through the transfer pump and filter to the injector pump assembly. At very high pressure, fuel is forced to the injector nozzle into the cylinder. Excess flows back to the filter, then to the tank.

"The yachtsman's guide to selection, installation, first aid and maintenance of sailing craft powerplants." Up to date and understandable to the most unredeemable engine-hater.

Owners of outboards needn't feel slighted either:

**The Outboard Book
by Nigel Warren
Hearst Books (Motor Boating & Sailing),
New York
186 pages, illus., (no index!), 1978, $8.95**

*Below and below left: From* The Outboard Book.

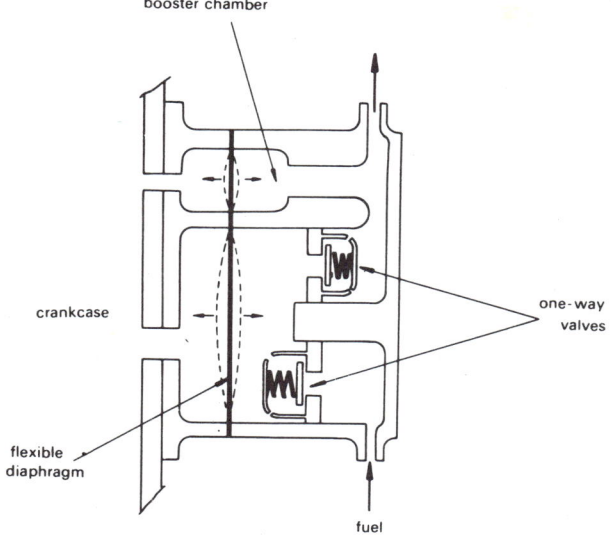

> **Generators**
>
> The smaller outboards on the market often do not have the option of electric starting and charging. Exceptions include the Johnson and Evinrude 10 and 15 hp, Chrysler 10, 15 and 20 hp, Mercury 20 hp, Ocean, Selva 20 and Archimedes 9 and 14-hp. Some of these can be converted by fitting an electric start kit. Other small non-electric start motors have a flywheel generator incorporated as a standard fitting; some can be adapted with a battery charging kit. There are two important things to determine before one buys an electric start or battery charging version of an outboard: will the charger cut in at *normal* cruising revs, and will the current delivered at these revs be sufficient? On some motors the generator does not cut in and commence charging until the revs are quite high, and this may be inherent in the design of the generator.
>
> The current output of most generators on outboards is usually quite small. For instance, Johnson 10- and 15-hp electric start motors give 2 amps (24 watts) at 2000 rpm rising to 5 amps (60 watts) at 4000 rpm. The Chrysler 10- and 15-hp auto-electrics give 10 amps (120 watts) at 3800 rpm. The Mercury 10- and 7½-hp motors can have a coil generator giving 10 watts (watts = amps × volts, and many systems are 12 volt). The Yamaha 8, 12, 15 and 20 have 40 watt coils, and the Archimedes motors range between 17 and 60 watts output. Normally the wattage quoted is the maximum developed only at high revs.

## Sticking It in the Water

Whatever the fuel or power system, water has to be made to move or otherwise be pushed against. The conventional wisdom reduces this problem to propellers or jets, and we have always tried to identify the new or unusual variations and sources of either. We continue in that vein and here show the Outjet from England in four models for engines from 5 (unusually low for a jet) to 200-horsepower output. From:

**West Beach Components Ltd.
Stephenson Way Industrial Estate
Formby, Liverpool L37 8EG, England**

*Right: Two Outjet models.*

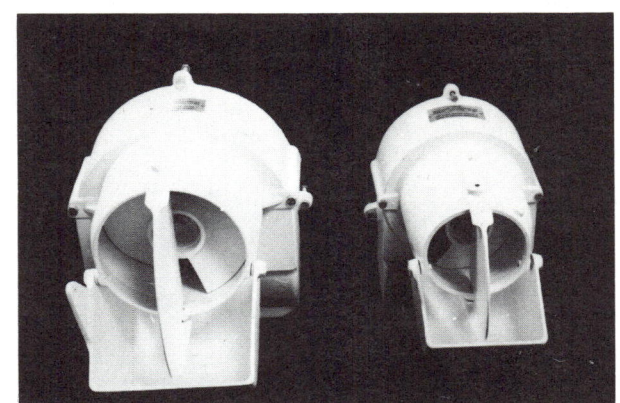

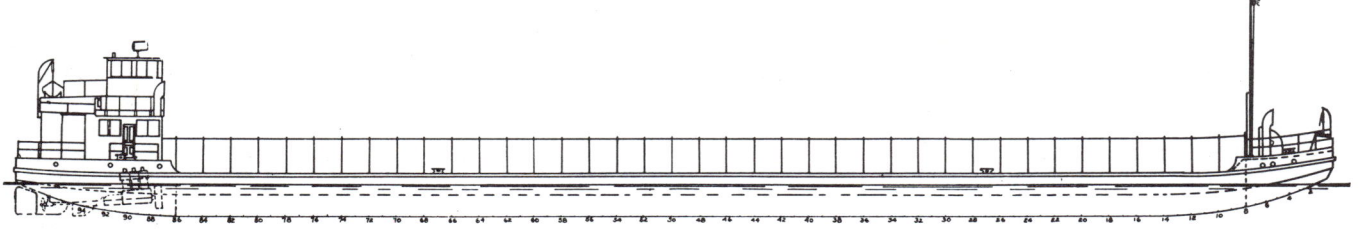

In the past, lateral motion in ships (and, of course, tugs) has been supplied by side thrusters. Since we had never listed side thrusters before, we looked around for a small one that might find a practical place in some reader's special needs department. Here is the hydraulically run Marco T50 from:

Marco
2300 West Commodore Way
Seattle, Washington 98199

Marine Construction and Design Co.
P.O. Box H3045
New Bedford, Massachusetts 02741

*Below: The Marco Side Thruster.   Right: Maytag's 2-cylinder motor.*

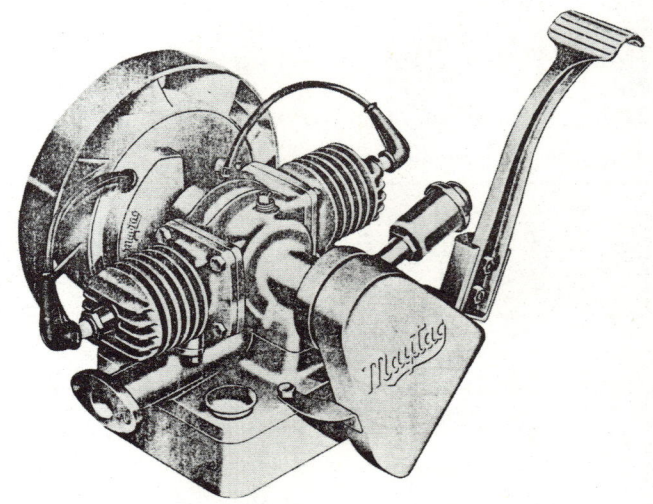

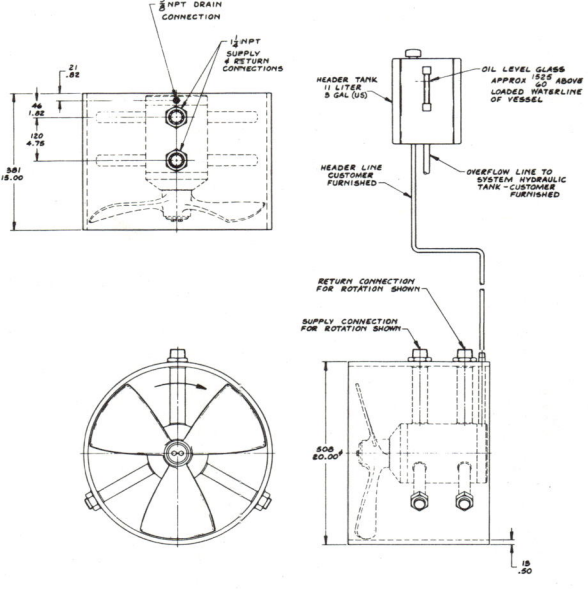

## Maytag Power

A great many Americans are surprised to learn that much washing by machines beginning in 1914 was done by gasoline-engine units in the home—namely, by the Maytag Company—and these fascinating engines are still around in limited quantity. The Maytag Company advises that the original motor was a vertical one-lunger that was discontinued in 1923 with no available parts or data. The predominant motor was the horizontal single-cylinder Model 82 rated at ¾ HP at 1050 RPM and manufactured from 1923 to 1937. From 1937 to 1952, the two-cylinder horizontally opposed Models 72D and 72DA rated at ⅝ HP at 1650 RPM were manufactured. All these motors were 2-cycle and used a 1:16 mixture of outboard motor oil and regular gasoline. The Maytag Company Service Department, Newton, Iowa 50208, has a supply of small parts, such as washers, etc., on hand, but no major components anymore. The old-time motors fire in the typical "Bang-Bang-Bang, Chuff-Chuff-Chuff" manner as a governor arm in the magneto holds firing down to the maximum rated speed. These stout and reliable motors were beloved by young homebuilders in the "ol' days"—who knows, maybe we should have an elite powerboat class today?
—**Norm Benedict**

Dear Editors:

The T-50 and T-80 Side Thrusters are manufactured both in aluminum and steel while the T-200 and T-350 are manufactured in steel only. The aluminum units use a stainless steel propeller while the steel units use a bronze propeller. The T-50 and T-80 are powered directly by a hydraulic motor incorporated within the Thruster hub. The hydraulic oil may be supplied from any convenient prime power source such as an electric motor, auxiliary diesel engine, or front power take-off from main engine. Both units may be controlled from single or multiple stations, depending upon the needs of the boat operator. Should multi-station full throttling control be required, the system becomes rather complicated and expensive.

The T-200 and T-350 Side Thrusters may be powered electrically, hydraulically, or directly with a marine diesel engine by coupling to the input shaft of the Thruster. Power is directed to the bronze propeller by means of spiral bevel reduction gears within the Thruster hub.

—**R.D. Keegan**
**Marco**

## Outboard Note

Recently the Fiat giant in Italy sat down to rethink the outboard motor in the lower power ranges. They had to, really. Anyone who has been to Rome or any other large Italian city soon discovers more fellow tourists than natives. The reason is that a significant portion of the middle-class population simply takes the summer off and goes to the beach. And, once at the beach, they find a need to get off the beach because it is so crowded. As a consequence, Italy offers an extraordinary number and variety of small boats on the retail market. The powering for these craft is by necessity very efficient. Inflation generally, and fuel prices specifically, are very high there, and so Fiat's efforts are inevitable. The Fiat Nautica line is now offered in this country and we received this note from the importer.

**Fiat Nautica
Voyageur Motors, Inc.
Suite 21, Yacht Haven, First Street
Annapolis, Maryland 21403**

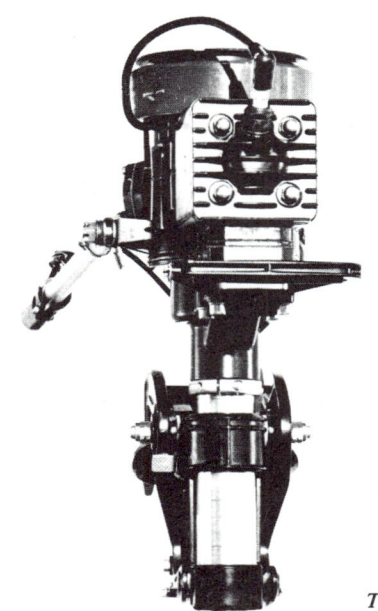

*The 6 h.p., 37-pounder from Fiat Nautica.*

Dear Editors:

Unusual features of all the Fiat Nautica motors are their light weight and the adjustable transom height—by means of sliding the motor on its stainless drive casing tube up or down in the transom mounting bracket, and locking a stainless steel collar at the required height. This feature also makes it possible to raise the motor vertically out of the water and lock it in position rather than tilt the motor when not in use. The motor also has a tilt up and lock angle of 70 degrees, which also stops the motor trailing in the water in its tilt position.

The range of motors includes shaft lengths of 23", 33", and 38", measured between the top of the mounting bracket and center of the prop. The motors are available with a fast and slow drive ratio of 2:1 and 3½:1, the fast version having through the prop exhaust. All motors have a one-piece solid state ignition unit (2 in the case of the twin cylinder models) which can be replaced in less than 5 minutes and require no timing setting after replacement. The 8 and 14 h.p. models have full F-N-R gears and all models have the capability of being rotated through 360 degrees to give forward, side or reverse full power thrust.

The motors use a simple fixed jet carburetor and very efficient gas flow design, which gives high horsepower with very good economy, i.e., 6 h.p. motor uses .58 U.S. gallon per hour at full r.p.m. of 5,000. All the range of motors swing a larger than average diameter and pitch propeller at lower r.p.m. than other well known outboard motors. The 14 h.p. model swings a 9" x 9" jet exhaust prop at 5,300 r.p.m. with a cubic capacity of 11.49", which is 1.22 h.p. per cubic inch. Comparisons with other outboard motor specifications indicate the Fiat Nautica motor to be highly efficient. The 14 h.p. model uses .79 gallon per hour at full r.p.m. All motors are water cooled.

The motor is constructed of military specification marine alloys with every fitting and fastening manufactured from military spec stainless steel. It can be taken apart and assembled with no special tools and in fact requires only 3 sizes of metric Allen wrenches, 2 standard metric wrenches, and a screwdriver. The whole range of motors utilizes interchange-

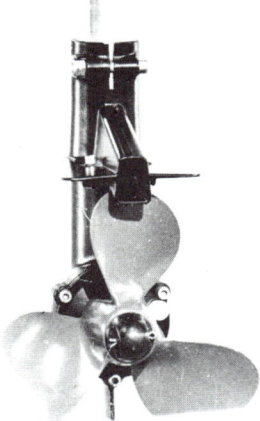

able parts, many of which fit the complete range of horsepowers, thus reducing spare parts inventory, etc.

Each unit is ideally suited, because of its versatility and light weight, to small fishing boats, dinghies, tenders, and sailboats up to 35'. The retail price includes a separate fuel tank of 3 and 4½ gallon capacity and options include gear and throttle accessories and a 5 amp generator. The motors have been tested under the most adverse conditions and have a reputation for being practically indestructible, quick and simple to service and repair, economical, easy starting and competitively priced.

—**Yan Cowlishaw
President
Voyageur Motors, Inc.**

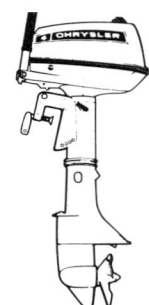

*The single-cylinder Chrysler outboard.*

Dear Editors:
Re: Long shaft outboard motors, pages 69, 70, of MC-4. You obviously are unaware of an excellent North American product. The small Chrysler outboards from 6 hp to 15 hp take a special 15-inch leg extension, which brings the shaft length to a bit over 30 inches (I think I measured 31½ inches). I have used an older model now for 5 years, and I am entirely satisfied. I use a single 13-hp motor to power a 33-foot Crowther trimaran. You are beginning to give a lot of foreign supply sources, but please do not neglect local products!

—Hubert E. Bing
**Coburg, Ontario, Canada**

---

Dear Editors:
Your Mr. Cheney (MC-6, p. 69) gets my attention. My own Seagull is a "Forty Plus," and pushes my 12-year-old Alberg Corinthian sloop (20 feet and close to 3,000 pounds) in cruising trim very well. The hull and motor are well matched, using the novel transom mount similar to Cape Dory Typhoons. This motor of mine is 12 years old; it and the boat look new. She starts first pull, and hasn't given trouble yet. I get 4½ knots or more, push well into heavy air or tide, etc. Most of the other guys around our cruising waters (Severn River area, Md.) expect this from Seagull and get it.

I've had a Johnson and two Evinrudes, also usually good reliable motors, but heavier and more complicated by far than my 3-horse Seagull. While I'm obviously satisfied, I wonder if Mr. Cheney might have a "well design" or mounting problem? Or, could be he got a lemon, but I doubt it. Sounds like a mismatched prop, outboard well, or something else. My old motor has the old-type water pump and never has had trouble from overheating. Runs inexpensively, too.

No manufacturer tries to build a bad product, but I've had nothing but trouble from a 4-horse late-model Evinrude that acted like Mr. Cheney's Seagull. I finally sold it in disgust, as he did his Seagull. When you get any good one, *hang onto it*. Our sailing club swears by 'em all, IF you have a good one, regardless of make almost.

Don't let one bad letter spoil the Seagull reputation. I don't know about the new ones, but the old ones were *gems*. I *invite* Mr. Cheney for a sail come Spring to see for himself.

—Charles L. Tringali
**Millersville, Maryland**

---

THE AMERICAN GIANT-CRAB.

Dear Editors:
Have enjoyed your *Mariner's Catalogs*. They rank now beside *National Fisherman* in my estimation.

I don't have all issues, so what I propose as a subject for investigation may have already been covered.

The subject is straight-line drive outboards or inboards, portable, which is what they are.

The British make one . . . a light-horsepower job, air-cooled, with a shaft eight or ten feet long that they claim is just the thing for waters cluttered with lily pads, etc. You just raise the shaft and clear the prop. The shaft breaks down for storage.

I see, to my surprise, in documentaries on Vietnam and its canals, numbers of boats being propelled by a much larger version of this same theme, made, I'd guess, in Japan.

And, suddenly, in a James Bond movie, here's this nifty hot rod version—a little V8 by the look of it—driving a far-out planing hull in a mad chase with another, similarly propelled boat.

When I've been called upon to deface the lovely stern of a sailboat with an outboard bracket, my thoughts have turned to this configuration; all it would need is a sort of big oarlock, and the height of the stern doesn't matter, you just change the angle you hold the thing at.

Or it could solve better the problems of catamaran owners to reach the water with power of some sort.

It's a mechanical yuloh!

Just thought I'd pass on my thinking—and what an interesting, off-beat but practical, and somewhat exotic subject it would make for future *Mariner's Catalogs*.

—Murray Osmond
Box 304
**Mastic, N.Y.**

P.S. The British version came to my notice when I contacted the importer of Seagulls, and he sent me a brochure from the manufacturer of this other somewhat outlandish rig; but I don't think it's so outlandish, now; in fact, I'd like to try one, but I'm married to three Seagulls and can't change. . . .

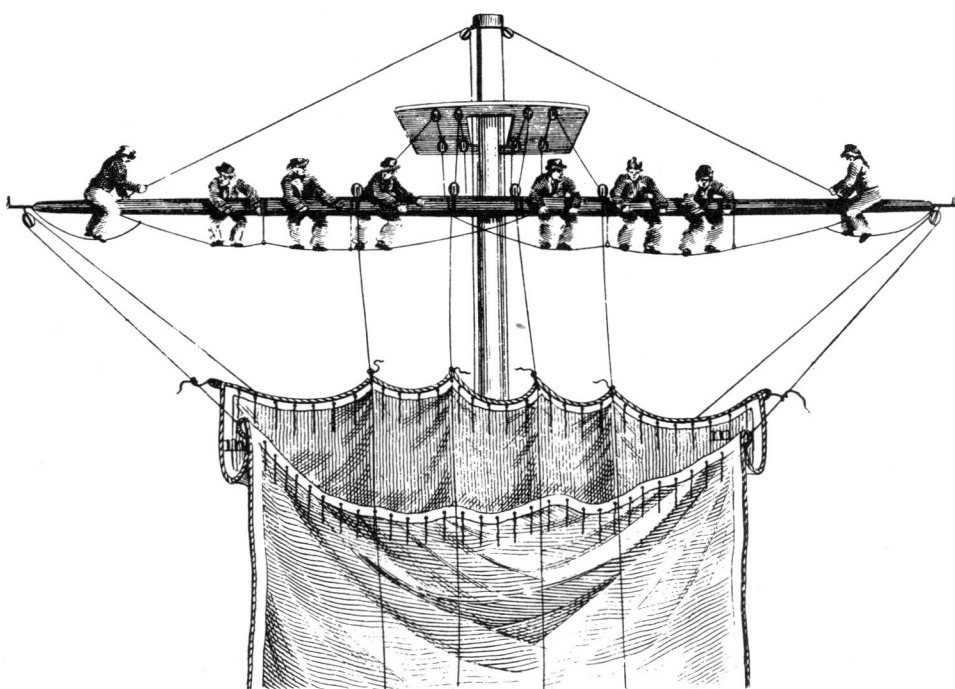

# Tophamper Happenings

*You all look so small down there.*

—Fred Brooks
from the masthead

A couple of volumes ago we listed a rigging gang in Wilmington, Delaware. Intrigued at the time, we had since wondered how they were getting on and so wrote to ask. They sent this good letter in return—not for publication, but just answering our note. However, the visions it conjures up are so vivid that we're sticking it in. Thanks, Nick.

Dear Editors:

The Rigging Gang has been up to some of the following more notable activities. The *Woody Guthrie*, which is a smaller version of *Clearwater*, received wire rigging and outfitting services and I was captain on her first sail. I cut the wire for the *Sojourner Truth*—the ferrocement version—but it has yet to be completed. I organized a rigging crew of volunteers for *Clearwater* and we wormed, tarred, parcelled, and served her shrouds. I replaced her headings, seizings, etc. Bent on sails and running gear for *Charlotte Ann* and two of us assisted in delivering her to Florida from New York.

Rigged *Omorca* on display (wire only) at the Wooden Boat Festival in Port Townsend, Washington. I was the rigging instructor for the Symposium and cut the rigging for this 38-foot-on-deck Culler Presto (schooner-ketch).

The *Western Union* was dismasted in a whopper with the ex-chief mate as acting master. The captain and owners insisted I not only re-rig the vessel but that I come up with my own version of the rig without changing Mr. Wittholz's sail area. They accepted full responsibility for the incident and made it clear that nothing from our shop gave way. So we got two large sticks from Oregon and new wire and I put in my own concept of the rig. This time I also did the running rigging instead of just being a consultant. Then I sailed on her as mate for three months doing finishing touches. The captain and owners are fully pleased and I feel much better knowing that they have made no compromises and everything is in fine order.

There has been the usual piecework: deadeyes, wire splicing, service, sail plans, etc., and rigging smaller or less known vessels.

On May 1, 1979, The Rigging Gang, formerly the St. Margaret Rigging Gang, will be five years old. In that time 1,600 wire splices, two miles of served cable, and 16,000 feet worth of seizing wire has left our lofts. I don't know how much total rigging, but it is a lot, maybe eight miles. The two miles of served cable does include the shrouds on *Clearwater* served by myself and volunteers. I don't know where all the seizing wire went, but I suppose most of it went toward seizing thimbles into oversized wire bights, turning up lower ends and serving headstay splices where sail hanks would cut marline. This still works out to about 2,000 miscellaneous seizings of all types and sizes.

—Nick Benton
The Rigging Gang
Wilmington, Delaware

*Left: A member of the Rigging Gang at work.*

## How Does it Work?

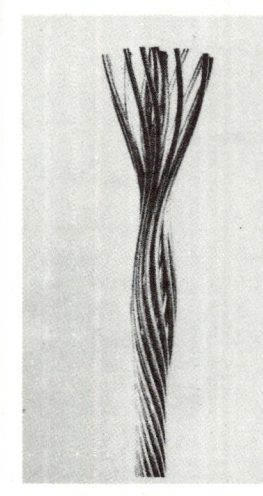

The Castlok terminal has been made possible by the advances of modern resin technology. The unlaid rope end is locked into a cast resin plug, which grips the entire surface of each separate wire. This provides enormous gripping surface rather than a number of pressure points (which tend to weaken the wire) as in most other terminals. The plug and chamber are conical, with a predetermined angle of taper, so that the harder the cable is pulled, the more tightly the wires are gripped. The 'coke bottle' shape of the unlaid wires resists any tendency to pull out by 'unscrewing' since the inner wires are spiralled oppositely to the outer wires. The result is the strongest, simplest to use, most durable terminal ever designed.

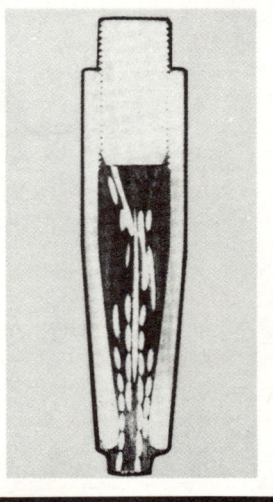

*From Castlok Marine.*

Castlok Marine seems to have developed a rigging terminal system that literally gets around the problems of corrosion and wire injury inside the terminal fitting by expanding the wire within the barrel and then filling the barrel with resin. Good idea! From:

**Castlok Marine**
**C. Sherman Johnson Co., Inc.**
**Norwich Rd., 82**
**East Haddam, Connecticut 06423**

No question that a lot of rigging fails at the terminal because of corrosion and crimping of the wire where it enters the barrel; but we've noticed that a lot of workmen in busy boatyards during the chaotic spring fitting-out aren't too particular about where they walk. With the spars and rigging of dozens of boats lying about, it is inevitable that the relatively heavy terminals will flop this way and that and often end up creating a sharp hairpin turn just above the fitting. One unconcerned boot can crimp this turn, fatiguing the wire, and so cause its failure within the season.—Eds.

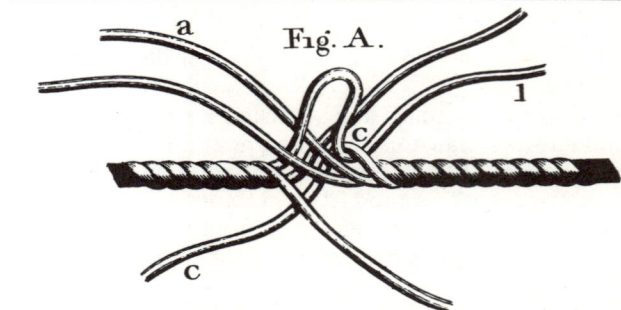

In England we found these electrical cutting devices for severing synthetic rope, webbing, and sheeting. The same sorts of products are available domestically, of course. We just wanted to be difficult. These are from:

**Lyteze Products Ltd.**
**113 Oxford Road**
**Clacton-on-Sea**
**Essex, England**

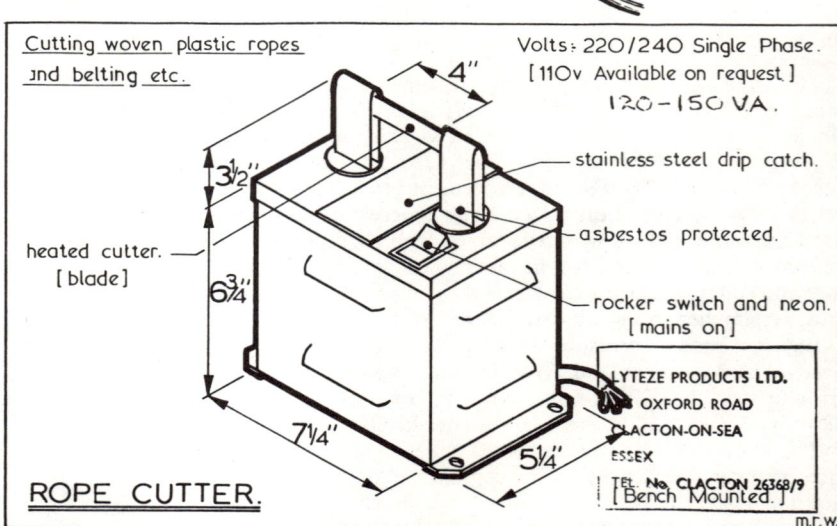

*Right: A veddy British cutter from Lyteze.*

*Knots and Ropework*
**by Eric C. Fry, photographs by Peter Wilson**
**Arco Books, New York**
**1977, illus., $8.95**

Many knot books have been reviewed and recommended in past *Mariner's Catalogs*, and picking the best from the lot is a difficult task to say the least. But this book deserves a place near the top of the list, if only because of the clarity of the photographs. Each knot, splice, and bend is shown being made in a step-by-step fashion, and you would have to be blind not to be able to figure out even the most complex one shown. This is not an encyclopedia of knots; rather, it's a book showing those most commonly used—30 knots, 19 splices, 7 decorative knots, and 5 wire splices.

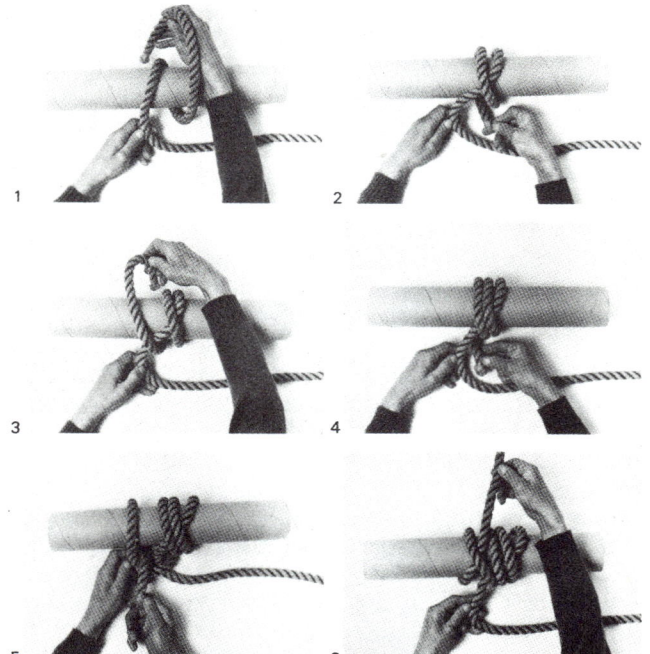

This is simply a clove hitch with two (or more) initial turns instead of one, laid back towards the standing part and over its own initial turn(s), thus jamming it, Figs 1 to 4. In the illustrations the tail end has been deliberately kept short to clearly show the lay of these initial turns, particularly in Fig 4, but in practice a longer tail end would be employed and indeed would be essential to complete the knot as may be seen in Fig 6.

As with the clove hitch this knot should be finished off with at least one half-hitch. It will withstand being hauled at right angles to its turns without sliding along the object to which it is tied, however smooth that object may be, provided it is hauled against the initial two or more turns. In Fig 6, it will only hold if hauled to the right.

When a rope or wire is hauled tight over a winch drum or capstan it is necessary to temporarily secure it whilst the end is removed from the drum and made fast permanently to bollards or the like. A short length of rope or light chain, called a stopper is used, one end being made fast to a deck fitting or even around the bollard itself and the other end made fast to the rope or wire in question. The wire is then slackened back until the load is taken by the stopper, when the wire is said to be stoppered off. A rolling hitch would be used to make the stopper fast, in such a case, whilst other uses of course depend on circumstances.

## 18 Rolling Hitch

*Above and left: From* Knots and Ropework.

Fred Brooks' outboard ran out of methane some two miles outside our cove the other day. His six chickens, while very enthusiastic producers of the stuff from which he makes his methane, just aren't up to the voracious appetite of the 15-year-old NoName machine, so poor Fred had to row his aluminum KumquatSport the whole distance to shore.

He said, however, that he didn't mind, and in fact had been planning a visit for some time, in order to show us his proposed *Mariner's Catalog* Official Boating Hat. It's an old bowler—an indifferent black-green-purple-in-some-lights affair—to which he has somehow managed to attach the visor of one of those billfishing caps. It's not the grotesque figment of a fevered imagination that you might suppose; we've grown to like it, and have unanimously adopted it. It is Official, and you are all urged to comply.

—Eds.

THE MARINER'S CATALOG OFFICIAL BOATING HAT.

## On Gaff Jaws . . .

I think many of the troubles with gaff jaws, leathered or not, are due to the fact that they don't fit properly, often being made by someone who really does not understand what goes on during use. Some observations on it:

Better do it the coaster way, using plenty of slush. Most people won't now slush a mast, but it lightens the work of making and taking in sail by half (assuming, of course, the rest of the gear is correct), saves much wear on mast and jaws, and is a good preservative for the stick. Many people consider slush "messy." I think it's good to go through life easily, without chafe and wear, even if a bit messy.

The tumbler in gaff jaws should stick out some from the horns, so it bears on the mast. Horns should be much eased on the top after edges where they bear on the mast. Simply imagining how they set, checking with a straightedge, or better, trying them to the mast in what's to be their sailing position will show where the trouble is. I think the horns of gaffs and booms are now often made too long, so that halyards and other lines hang up on them. Reaching two-thirds around the mast is quite enough; they will stay in place except when pressure is off them, and then the parrel line will hold them.

I find many modern-day gaff jaws are very awkward and poor in general shape, along with poor spar shape to boot. It now seems the traditional and best "engineered" way is often ignored or not understood. A boom and gaff for a more or less traditional rig are smallest in diameter next to the mast, fullest about where sheet or halyards are attached, and always a little bigger at the after ends than at the jaws. These not only work the best, they look by far the best. It seems now we

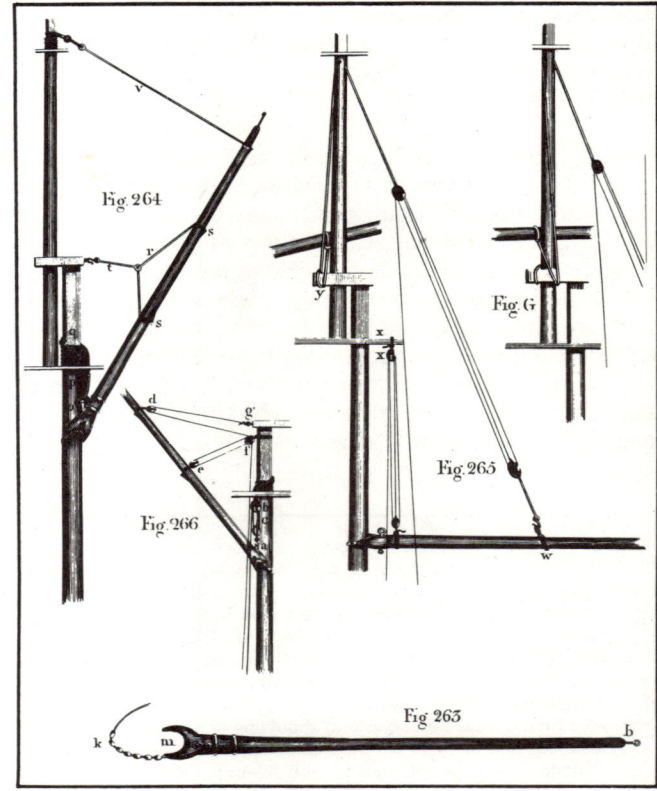

see a lot of spar-making done backward. However, the making of masts, spars, bowsprits, and jaws is another story.

—Pete Culler

---

*Arima Mast Steps.*

Dear Editors:

I just read in an article by Lin Pardey in *WoodenBoat* that Larry lined his hollow mast with aluminum foil before glue-up and the whole damned mast is now a go-to-hell radar reflector—much better than one of those reflectors that fall apart in the first blow. A ship skipper told him the boat gives out a signal as strong as an 80-footer.

—Brooks Townes

Up the down mastcase. Arima Mast Steps, from:

**Arima Mast Steps
262 Malvern Drive
Venice East, Florida 33595**

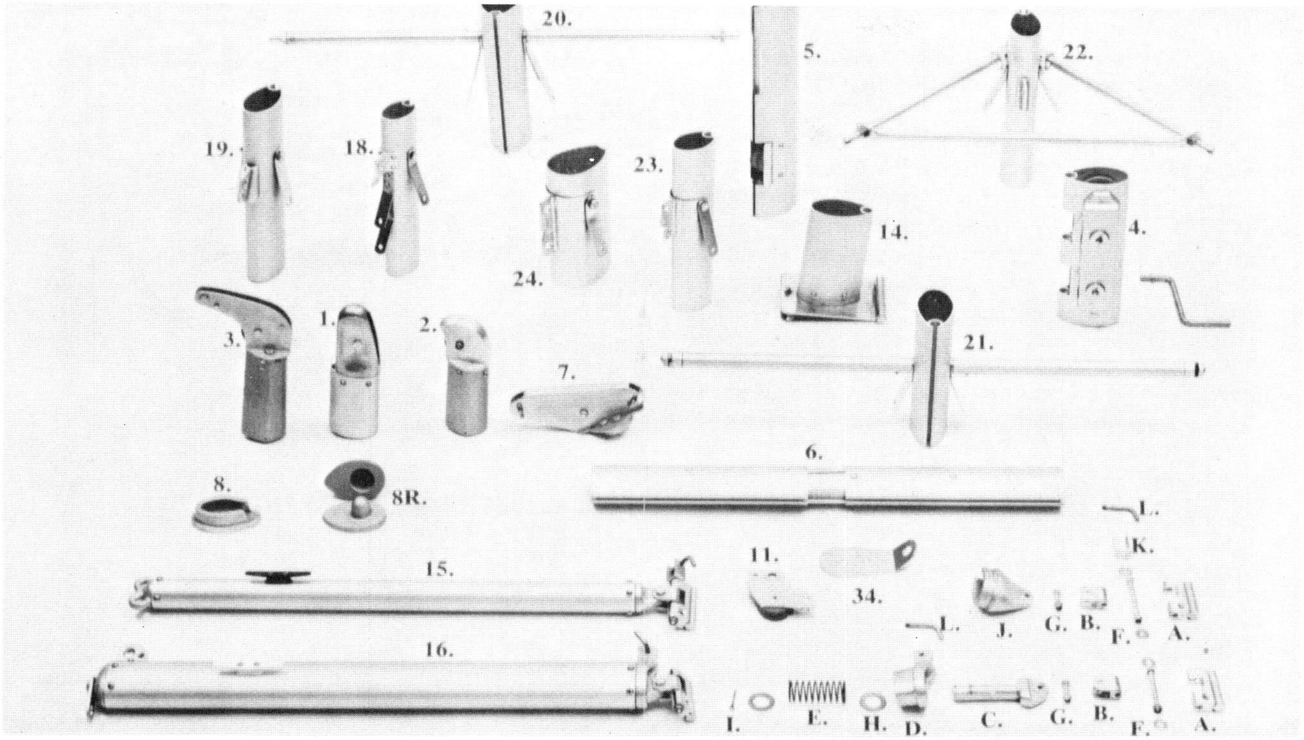

*Above: All kinds of metal rigging gear from the Zephyr Products catalog.*

What with this being Volume Seven and all, it really is time to be a little useful to those who want an aluminum spar of their own specification. Zephyr is a big outfitter with a host of blank stock and all the fittings for them. They're very well known.

**Zephyr Products Inc.
Wareham, Massachusetts 02571**

b & r has developed a system that in effect extends the rigging down into the boat, making it all one piece. It sounds like Hinduism, doesn't it? Perhaps, perhaps; but it is also very good sense in cases where designers or builders have pared away material to save weight, especially on racing craft where weight removal has become an addiction. Generally it has been against our own philosophy to "push" racing machine technology, but this patented system seems to us very thoughtful and, on further thinking, to open up all kinds of possibilities to the experimental home boatbuilder. With such a system as this, one could, with care, build a sailboat out of paper and varnish, and epoxy certainly. Contact:

**b & r mast & riggings
1121 Lewis Avenue
Sarasota, Florida 33577**

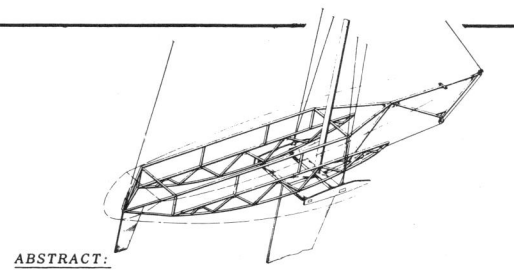

ABSTRACT:

A sailboat of the positive displacement type having a novel construction including transverse and longitudinal interior tubular structural frames for absorbing the loads from the mast including the rigging system and the fore and aft stays as well as the loads from the keel. The structural support frames may be prefabricated and are inserted in and attach to, a hull shell which because of the strength and load-absorbing capacity of the frames, may be made from a thin lightweight construction, for example, a balsa core sandwiched by Fiberglas skins. The hull shell is formed separately from the frames and its strength need only be sufficient for absorbing the forces of the sea since the stresses and strains from the aforementioned loads are absorbed substantially entirely by the internal support frames. The transverse support frame supports the mast with the shrouds being fastened through chain plates to opposite sides of this frame. In addition, the keel is fixed to the transverse frame. The fore and aft stays are fixed to the opposite ends of the longitudinal frame which resists bending about transverse axes. After the internal frames are inserted in and attached to the hull shell, the deck is installed and it may be supported by either the longitudinal frame or the hull shell but in either instance, no bulkheads are required.

*Above: The patented space frame from b & r.*

**Spritsails and Lugsails**
by John Leather
Charles Scribner's Sons, New York
390 pages, illus., glossary, index, 1979, $30

Perhaps the most common rigs on traditional small craft in the days of yore were the spritsail and lugsail, in all their variations. Why this was so is obvious: simplicity and economy. Interest in these rigs has revived recently, and we expect that even more will be generated by this book, which is a companion volume to *Gaff Rig*, also by Leather (see MC-3, page 21). The author provides the history and characteristics of the rigs on both sides of the Atlantic; because the author is an Englishman, however, the British Isles get the lion's share of the treatment.

*From* Spritsails and Lugsails.

## Sea Cloth

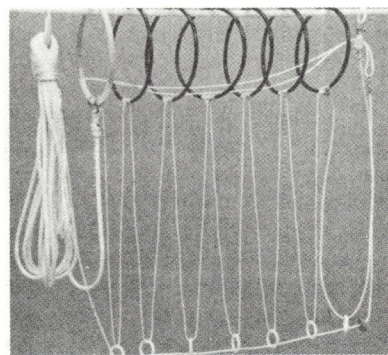
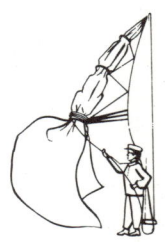

*Above and left: The Spinnaker Sally.*

*Left: The Zephyr.*

Spinnakers can be a lot of fun. At those times when you're shorthanded, though, thinking twice and not putting it up can save you one of those stupid heart-in-the-throat, screeching-and-hollering, nobody-talking-to-nobody situations the things can create for a small crew. But then, no one has any fun. (Ah, come on, skipper, you chicken er what?) So, here is the Spinnaker Sally, which can help out the small crew. You'll want to practice with it, of course, and take especially good care of it when stowing. It's from:

**The Spinnaker Sally
Box #413
Herndon, Virginia 22070**

In MC-6 we listed a cruising spinnaker made in Pennsylvania by David Bierig. This sail, cut full bunt in the luff and flat off the clew, has most of the pulling advantages of a regular spinnaker and most of the reaching and handling advantages of a genoa. Seems like a good idea. Wouldn't mind having one ourselves, in fact.

Now we hear that there is a similar sail being made and sold out of Costa Mesa, California. Called the Zephyr, information on it can be obtained from:

**Marshall Sails
629 Terminal Way, #13
Costa Mesa, California 92627**

> **MAIN/MIZZEN or JIB/GENOA/DRIFTER Kits**
> Your kit will contain:
> 1) A professionally lofted and presewn sail. Detail lines, cut out and patch lines are all marked on the sail.
> 2) Loose dacron cloth for the corner patches, luff tape, batten pockets are included plus all necessary machine and hand sewing thread.
> 3) Depending upon the type of sail, all hardware is included ie, sail slides, shackles, headboards, rivets, piston snaps, luff rope (that is presewn boltroping for easy installation), spur grommets and wooden battens. Everytning necessary to complete the sail, less the sewing machine and tools.
> 4) The kit contains step by step illustrated instructions using proven sailmaking techniques similar to what we use in our custom, sailmaking shop. The directions are easy to follow and leave nothing to chance. Instructions are not sold separately.

Halfway between starting from scratch and ordering someone else to build you a sail, there is a way to get the inconvenient lofting and panel-sewing done and then to do the labor-intensive finishing (edging, roping, cringles, etc.) yourself, saving big bucks. Cut & Stitch offers the service.

*Specifications from Cut & Stitch.*

**Cut & Stitch Sailkits**
P.O. Box 177
Sumner, Washington 98390

## Concordia's Sail-Tanning Recipe
### by John Gardner

For the strict traditionalist, whose vintage vessel must be authentic in all details, nothing short of cotton sails tanned to a rich, reddish brown will do.

And it is not just a matter of appearance. The distinctive russet hue is actually the by-product of a preservative process developed centuries ago in Europe by fishermen for treating nets as well as sail cloth.

The recipe which follows for barking nets or sails was acquired by Captain R.D. Culler for the Concordia Company of South Dartmouth, Mass., from F. E. Amero, manager, and John Sylvester, chief dipper, of the former Linen Thread Company of Gloucester, Mass. We are able to furnish our readers with this recipe through the generous permission of Waldo Howland of Concordia.

Howland informed us that this formula and the method of applying it was brought over from Brittany by yachtsman Bill Eaton, who recorded the process as he observed it being used by fishermen for tanning their nets. Howland also mentioned that while they had found at Concordia that the protection from tanning lasts longer than that derived from modern proprietary fungicides—which tend to leach out more readily—the tanning process will shrink the canvas duck, and that this should be taken into account in applying the tanning process to sails.

### EQUIPMENT NEEDED
—Two vats, either of wood or iron, shape unimportant, of such size as to take the material to be tanned without crowding.

—Above each vat, a pole or rack for hanging the net or sail to drain.

—A method of heating water in the vats to a boil. One of the vats is for tanning; the other, for setting. Any mixture herein referred to as heated should be at a good rolling boil. The method of heating is immaterial, so long as a vigorous boil is obtained. Iron vats may be heated externally by a wood fire or by an oil or gas flame directly applied. Wood vats will require steam coils. Once again we emphasize that a vigorous boil must be obtained.

After removal from the tanning vat, the material must remain on the draining rack for an hour or so, drying, to save as much of the tan as possible, as well as to prevent dilution of the setting solution, immersion in which follows. Likewise after removal from the setting vat, the material should drain thoroughly followed by drying in the sun and air, finally to be well washed in clean, fresh water. When dry, the sail or net is ready for use.

### INGREDIENTS
Cutch. American Dye Wood Co., Chester, Pa.

Bluestone, otherwise known as sulphated copper, or blue vitriol. Obtainable from any chemical supply house. These two items go in the tan vat.

*(continued on following page)*

(continued from previous page)

Bichromate of potassium is the preferred fixative, obtainable from the same source as the copper sulphate. The solution in the fixing vat should be tested with litmus paper, stirring well the while. If the paper shows RED, washing soda is added gradually until the paper just begins to turn blue. So long as the litmus paper shows RED, this indicates the presence of free chromic acid, which will destroy the net or sail.

Plain potash may be used as a fixer, but is to be handled with caution, because of its burning effect. No more than 1/20 pound to 100 gallons of water. Tested bichromate is probably the safest.

### MIXING FORMULA

To tan-bark 30 pounds of goods, either nets or sails, add 5 pounds of cutch and 1/8 pound of bluestone to 35 gallons of water in the tanning vat. Heat water to a boil, and dissolve the cutch and bluestone, stirring well. Then put in the goods and boil for two to three hours. Remove goods and drain thoroughly. If a deep barking is required, add two or three pounds more of cutch to the water, and when dissolved and boiling again, put the goods back in the vat and boil them for about another hour.

It will be seen that some judgment is required as to the amount of tanning needed to obtain the color desired. The proportions of cutch, bluestone and water should be maintained as already given to obtain a standard tanning solution, decreasing or increasing the amounts used to suit the amount of goods.

For the fixing solution, 12 ounces of bichromate of potassium are dissolved in 35 gallons of boiling water in the second vat, and tested with litmus as previously explained. An hour or two of soaking is followed by draining, drying, a thorough wash in clean water and final drying.

It will be noted that this is a rather easy, but time-consuming process, and that some degree of judgment is needed, as well as strict attention to directions.

The finished product is much protected from decay, has a rich, red-brown color, and is resistant to mildew, soiling and the absorption of water. Sails treated this way are nice to handle and have a long life. Like all things, the tan will give out in time, but there is no reason why the process cannot be repeated—at rather long intervals—as long as the nets or sails are sound. This will greatly prolong their life, as well as keep a sail looking well as long as it is used. Tanning is effective for linen, manila or cotton rope, also.

### CUTCH?

When I first read these directions, I must own I had never run across the word "cutch" before. After some searching in the library, I find it is an extract of vegetable origin, sometimes called catechu, used for dyeing and tanning, and is obtained from the wood and/or the bark of various foreign trees, including the mangrove of Borneo and the Philippines, and two species of acacia native to India. Possibly someone with a flair for experimenting might obtain satisfactory results using the barks of native oak or hemlock, both of which were much used in early times for tanning the best of leather.

As for boiling water in wooden vats, if steam coils are not easily available, another way is to connect a section of large-diameter copper tubing to the bottom of the vat, so that a circulation of water—from the vat through the tubing and back into the vat—is obtained, with enough of the tubing outside the vat for the flame of a plumber's torch to be safely applied to it. If properly installed, this device will keep water at a quick boil, once it has been heated, and with only a little flame.

As for vats, I should think that two large wooden barrels or casks would do nicely if such can be obtained today. But for ordinary amounts of material, two metal oildrums with the ends removed would probably serve well. They could even be set up on the beach and heated with a driftwood fire.

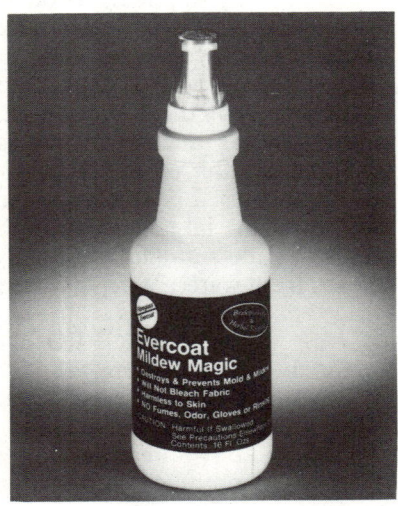

Folks with cotton sails often get into situations where they've come in from a fine old time and then find themselves having to bag up the sails wet or damp, knowing that they will not be returning to the boat for a couple of weeks. One feels guilty, but then, what can you do? For such situations, Mildew Magic could save the day, and the sails, from:

**Fibre Glass/Evercoat Co., Inc.**
**6600 Cornell Rd.**
**Cincinnati, Ohio 45242**

*Left: Mildew Magic from Fibre Glass/Evercoat.*

The Reads Sail Maker sewing machine is now distributed in this country. With both hand-powered and electric options, this machine has been the choice for several English long-distance racing efforts. It would seem to us that a hand-operated machine with heavy-duty and contemporary sewing capabilities would give anyone in limited-power situations the old raised-eyebrow syndrome. From:

**Cook Marine Products
P.O. Box 1133
Stamford, Connecticut 06904**

*All this and it only weighs 38 pounds.*

## The Skirt and I

**by Elsie A. Parry**

I was born in the middle of New York City (where the Pennsylvania R.R. Station sits, to be exact), but that didn't prevent me from handling a rowboat competently by the time I was 10 nor keep me from knowing how to tie (and use) a clove hitch and a running bowline. Much later my husband was to insist that I came into the world with salt water in my veins. Well, perhaps.... In any case, it's been good "blood!"

Boats and the sea came into my life early, and it was a case of love at first sight—and for life. Our 40-foot bridge deck cruiser *Frances* was my classroom for boatmanship and seamanship, with Father as an exacting but patient teacher. The things I learned how to do (and how not to do!) would make a sizable list. And they weren't all fun things by any means. I learned how to take a trick at the wheel (and how I loved *that!*), but I washed down decks, too; I boxed the compass and I polished brass and scraped down teak. Permission to row depended on how well I had worked in keeping the dinghy shipshape. The dinghy towline was my first serious responsibility, and Heaven forfend that I let it get caught in the propeller when *Frances* was being backed. I cleaned fish as well as caught and ate them . . . !

I look back with amusement at my pigtailed self of those long-gone days, when I was as lively as a cricket and as agile as a monkey. The amusement is occasioned by remembrance of my youthful boating get-up—a middy blouse and a SKIRT.

Pants, of course, were not respectable female attire 60 years ago, and as for shorts.... But I missed neither, and their absence certainly did nothing to cramp my seagoing style. I skipped nimbly in and out of rowboats, up and down companionways, into and out of hatches, across heaving decks—skirt and all. Hadn't I *always* worn a skirt on land, for goodness' sake—so why not at sea? If a woman could ride sidesaddle in a skirt, I could surely maneuver on *Frances* in one.

The skirts were mostly wide-wale cotton corduroy, washable, nonclinging, heavy enough to defeat the wind. Not really *maxi* but decidedly not *mini!* When I look at current feminine nautical fashions in all their brevity, I wonder just how any gal today could ever manage in my skirt.

Or how she would manage, if at all, in my swimming outfit. Swimming, of course, was a natural concomitant, enthusiastically pursued, of our boating activities. But in the early 1900s one swam in a *costume*, (continued on following page)

(continued from previous page)
complete with bloomered underdress, concealing overdress, stockings, and high, laced shoes. All that was lacking was a pair of white gloves. . . .

Because of my youth I was spared the shoes-and-stockings routine (to my dissatisfaction, be it said), but until Annette Kellerman, greatly daring, arrived on the aquatic horizon in a one-piece suit, we went thoroughly clad into the sea. My maternal grandmother added a straw hat to her ensemble. This was tied demurely under the chin and duplicated the kind worn by horses to shade their heads from the summer sun. In Grandmother's case, only the holes for the ears were lacking.

And in these improbable outfits we swam—indeed we did. I had had proper swimming lessons when I was six and my breaststroke, that hardy perennial, was not only competent, it had style. Grandmother's technique left little to be desired. She swam strongly; goodness, she had to, to keep herself as well as her costume afloat! Like myself in my boating skirt, she blithely refused to recognize limitations.

When, after a dozen blissful years, *Frances* went out of our lives for reasons beyond our control, her departure left a void. Summer was never to be quite the same again. But a love of boats and the sea is not thus readily cast off. In due course we filled the void amply, though not in identical fashion, with globe-girdling freighters of all sizes and under many flags. Here we found a different but fascinating sort of life on the water.

However, one thing remained the same—I still wore a SKIRT afloat!

With the rapidly enlarging assortment of sports clothing for ladies—pants, slacks, shorts, briefs, jeans—I might well have been expected to shift gears with relation to my own. But comfortable old habits are hard to break. The SKIRT and I had done a lot of nautical doing together. And continued to do so. . . . It and I floated down the Yukon in a rubber raft, went exploring on Bolivia's Lake Titicaca in a reed boat, ventured onto the Antarctic ice from a landing craft, landed on the island of Bali from a ship's lifeboat, sailed in a 49-foot ketch among the less frequented islands of the Caribbean, careered up and down the slanting decks of assorted freighters on a wide-flung collection of oceans, seas, and bays. The only fall I've ever had took place in Fiji when I was strolling sedately on a hotel sidewalk that gave way under my unsuspecting feet. . . .

No doubt a psychiatrist would smugly relate all the above to some deep-seated pattern of congenital idiocy and would thereby miss the point entirely. Actually I anticipated a now well-defined modern trend. To illustrate: A friend of mine, along with assorted relatives, recently attended the college graduation of a granddaughter. In the large audience only my friend and one other woman wore a hat. The former found herself being apologetic to a young grandson about her conspicuous headgear. "Never mind, Grandma," he comforted her, "you just do 'your thing!' "

All these many years I have been "doing my thing. . . !"

*Inflatable jacket from Henri-Lloyd.*

People who read boating publications are familiar with the Bacon & Associates ad symbol, the one with that incredibly patched sail on a Bahamian sloop. They have dealt in used sails for years and are much respected for the integrity of their service. Well, now they are offering the well-known Henri-Lloyd line of marine clothing from England. This line is probably the most diverse in the industry. A dozen configurations of foul weather gear are included and they are perhaps the last specialist firm in the business that still offers dress clothing expressly for the marine environment, including suits. From:

**Henri-Lloyd Division
Bacon & Associates
528 Second Street, P.O. Box 3150
Annapolis, Maryland 21403**

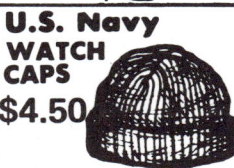

*Left: From the Ruvel Company catalog.*

I suppose that the young are still enamored of army-navy surplus stores, but anyone who remembers what they were like after World War II and into about the mid-fifties knows what a contemptible, mere shadowy vestige of former glory they now are. Who wants poorly made jeans and sweatsuits?! Whatever happened to the boxes and boxes of Neat Stuff?!

Apparently some smart cookies in Chicago went around and gathered it all up and put it one place and offer it out of a catalog. The Ruvel Company looks like army-navy stores used to look, and even their prices have that familiar and attractive ring. Here's a page of their clothing.

**Ruvel Company
3037 N. Clark Street
Chicago, Illinois 60657**

We found two things for renewing deck shoes: a product and a service. The product is Deck Shoe Renew Kit, by MDR, the well-known company that makes about a zillion marine-related goops and gorps for boat and engine appearance, maintenance, and efficiency.

**Marine Development & Research Corp.
116 Church Street
Freeport, New York 11520**

*Left: Ever tried smoked elk for your deck shoes?*

The deck-shoe service is Scotty's Incorporated, who sent this note.

Dear Editors:
We are in the business of resoling and reconditioning boat shoes. Sailors send us their worn-out deck shoes in the mail. We then proceed to put them in the best possible shape, which includes a set of new soles (known for their paper-thin grooves which assure a deck-grabbing action). We also refinish or shine the uppers, patch rips, etc. We then mail back usually via U.P.S. and charge the low price of $13.00. You'll have to agree that this is a lot cheaper than shelling out $40.00 for a new pair. Forty percent of our jobs are repeats or referrals, so we know that our customers are happy with our service.

—Scotty Harlan

**Scotty's Incorporated
1102 E. Las Olas Blvd.
Fort Lauderdale, Florida 33301**

What Currin-Greene says about its slipper is true. Fishermen like a shoe of this configuration because it works well just as is. Also, it slides into an oversized waderboot for added warmth while still allowing fast egress in case of going overboard. The Rainier Fishermen's Slipper, from:

**Currin-Greene Shoe Company
2932 First Ave.
Seattle, Washington 98121**

*Above: Pride of the Northwest—the Rainier Fishermen's Slipper.*

Among the various brands of deck shoe, Sebago offers one of the more reasonably priced lines in many moccasin, sneaker, and sandal forms. Most interesting, however, is that they are the U.S. distributors for Aigle seaboots, made in France. These are probably the best seaboots made.

*Left and below: From a Sebago catalog.*

## DOMESTIC MARINE SALES

| | | | | | | |
|---|---|---|---|---|---|---|
| California | John Miller<br>Seaport Marine<br>P.O. Box 465<br>Seal Beach, Cal. 90740 | | Maine<br>New Hampshire<br>Vermont<br>Massachusetts<br>Rhode Island | Peter Sutton<br>Peter R. Sutton Co., Inc.<br>69 Holter Street<br>Danvers, Mass. 01923<br>Mr. James Peirce<br>47 High Street<br>Topsfield, Mass. 01983 | Eastern<br>Pennsylvania<br>New Jersey<br>Maryland<br>Delaware<br>Washington D.C.<br>Eastern Virginia | Scooter Pierce<br>211-F Victor Parkway<br>Annapolis, Md. 21403 |
| Oregon<br>Washington | Jack Gale<br>4654-95th N.E.<br>Bellevue, Wash. 98004 | | New York<br>Connecticut<br>Pennsylvania<br>(Harrisburg<br>West) | John Thommen<br>130 Coe Ave. Apt. 56<br>East Haven, Conn. 06512 | Florida<br>North Carolina<br>South Carolina<br>Georgia<br>Mississippi<br>Louisiana | Larry Miller<br>4716 Shore Acres Blvd., N.E.<br>St. Petersburg, Fla. 33704 |

Look at this first-class duffle bag from:

**Port Canvas Company
Dock Square
Kennebunkport, Maine 04046**

*Right and below: The medium-size duffle from Port Canvas.*

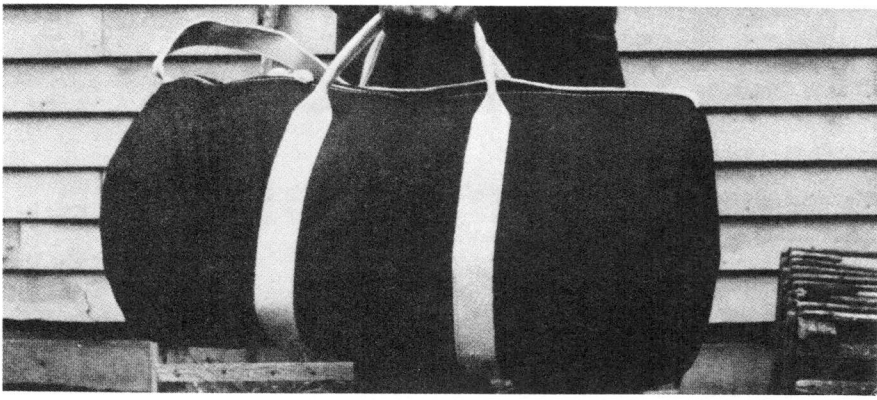

Ah, yes: the moon through the rigging, water gently lapping, the mast-truck scribing an arc through the crystal zenith. The Caribbean matrimonial hammock, from:

**Terry Stern
Dos Egnis Co.
22333 W. Pacific Coast
Malibu, California 90265**

*Right: What more could you ask?*

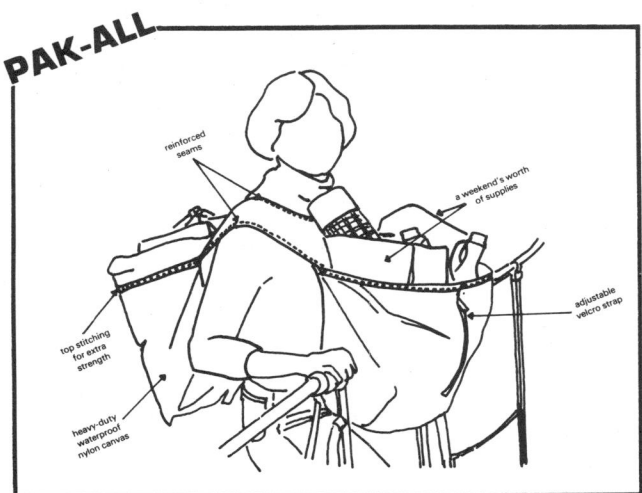

Getting provisions out to the boat can be a terrific pain in the neck. Any help is gratefully received, and we gratefully list Pak-All, from:

**The La Conner Company
34 Skokomish Way
La Conner, Washington 98257**

# Steering, Navigation, Electronic Sundries

Owners of Friendship sloops, catboats, and other craft congenitally prone to weather helm will be most interested in this article from Norman Benedict, a fulsome correspondent of the *Mariner's Catalog* and an enthusiastic retiree from the think-tanks of the aerospace industry.

## A Little Tab Will Do Ya

Boat rudders and airplane rudders operate identically. However, it is not unusual to see a boat helmsman braced rigidly across the cockpit resisting say, weather helm, at 7K. The airplane pilot obviously couldn't perform similar human resistance to yawing at 250K—so his rudder is equipped with trim or servo tabs that operate either automatically via built-in linkage or manually by a hand-operated wheel. In any case, tabs are located on trailing edges and are deflected *opposite* to desired rudder movement as a result of the moment arm distance from the rudder fulcrum. While developments in wind vane self-steering devices emphasize trim tab "unloading" of unwanted rudder forces, they can be used otherwise to overcome forces on very large rudders or to provide selective trimming for infinite or varying steering conditions.

In the sketch note that the trim tab control arm may be routed to the helmsman's hand for either port or starboard adjustment (A) and lodged in a holding hole, slot, or friction device. The main advantage of this is instant release for emergencies or occasionally rudder-tab system damage—a damaged trim tab contributes enormous unwanted directional forces. However, if the control arm or rod is *fixed* at some point (B) it will automatically actuate the tab to unload the rudder when turned in either direction. This is quite helpful in instances where rudder loadings are high, or in cases of fatigue, seasickness, or crew incapacitation for various reasons. Design safety is paramount in rudder tabs, and the best overall treatise on the subject is *Self-Steering for Sailing Craft*, by John S. Letcher, Jr. (International Marine Publishing Company, Camden, Maine).

—**Norman Benedict**

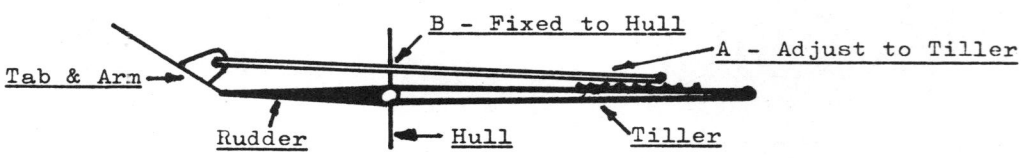

TOP VIEW OF TILLER-RUDDER-TAB STEERING

## A Safe Vest Pocket Tiller Holder

Just about anyone can conjure up a mechanical assemblage that will hold a tiller while underway—and just about everyone does. Unfortunately, it takes these would-be inventors time to discover that their baby: (1) is quite inflexible in operation, (2) is non-adjustable for wave conditions, (3) takes up a great amount of space both in and out of operation, and (4) cannot be disconnected instantly in emergencies.

I've found that the best tiller holder is a length of selected bungee cord about 24 inches longer than the distance between the cockpit seat sides that constitute the foot well. This elastic cord, which may vary in diameter between 1/8 inch and 1/2 inch, utilizes the same pre-formed wire hook ends provided for camping, etc., equipment tiedowns. It is hooked into port and starboard eyes, then wrapped around the tiller as near the outboard end as possible, with appropriate slack taken up by successive wraps. You'll find the subsequent elasticity quite adjustable for your boat and conditions, and by twisting the wrapped section like a motorcycle throttle, you can adjust the tiller for desired lee or weather helm. Mainly, in the event of emergencies or conditions necessitating wholly manual steering, you can wipe the wrapped cord instantly off the end of the tiller where it'll lie harmlessly on the cockpit sole. Then, you can detach it from the eyes and roll it up in your vest pocket. Can one ask for much more. . . ?

—**Norman Benedict**

---

Self-steering systems use the trim-tab principle all the time. We have listed various self-steering systems in earlier volumes, and here are a couple of others, showing the continuing development in these systems: the Navik from Chris Bock Instruments and the Sailomat (made in Sweden) from Scanmar.

**Chris Bock Instruments
2321 Washington Boulevard
Marina del Rey, California 90291**

**Scanmar Marine Products
298 Harbor Drive
Clipper Yacht Harbor
Sausalito, California 94965**

HOW THE NAVIK OPERATES:

1- THE BOAT CHANGES ITS COURSE
2- THE WIND VANE SWINGS AND
3- MOVES THE TRIM TAB
4- THE TRIM TAB DRIVES THE PADDLE CONNECTED TO THE TILLER BY MEANS OF 2 LINES
5- BOAT COMES BACK ON COURSE

*The Navik self-steering gear.*

*Below: The Sailomat.*

Cybernetics and late-night conversations amongst those with some venture capital and a desire to bring some changes in their lives continue to bring more and better USEFUL DEVICES (UDs) into the marketplace, e.g., these auto-piloting systems—two for tillermen, and two for the wheel, deedle deedle dee dee deal.

The Seacourse, in two sizes, from:

**EPSCO Marine
411 Providence Highway
Westwood, Massachusetts 02090**

*Below: From EPSCO Marine.*

The Coepilot, from:

**Coe Mfg. Co.
P.O. Box 463
Dana Point, California 92629**

*Below: Coe's "unhuman helmsman."*

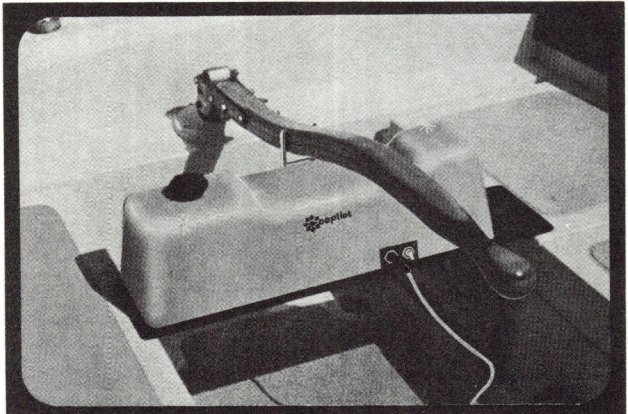

The Mate-B40, from the manufacturer at:

**Sharp & Company Ltd.
Richborough Hall
Sandwich, Kent, England**

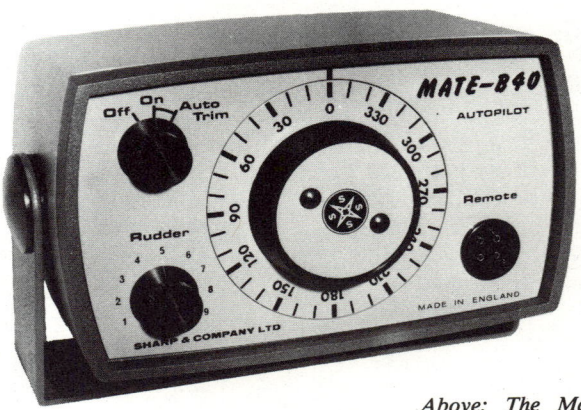

*Above: The Mate-B40.*

Or from their U.S. distributor, which also carries Sharp & Company's Seapilot model.

**International Marine Instruments
Signal Road
Stamford, Connecticut 06902**

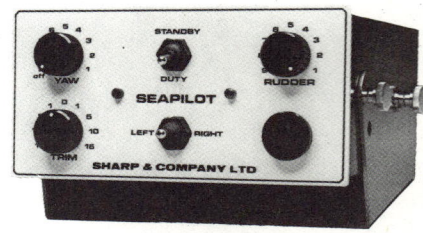

*Above: The Seapilot.*

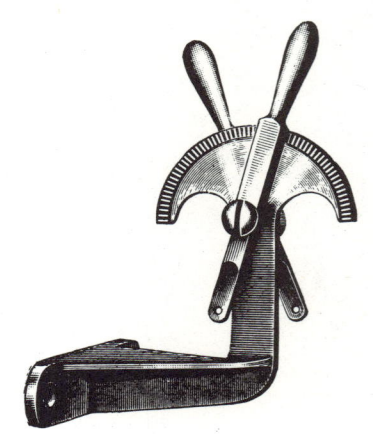

Most all of the inexpensive devices for determining speed through the water are unsatisfactory for one or another reasons. Even a proper log is a hassle in some situations, and they aren't inexpensive. So we have been matchstick and second-hand sailors, at least until we saw the Knotstick, priced to give it a try . . . from:

**Knotstick**
**P.O. Box 1947**
**Wilmington, Delaware 19899**

*Below: The Knotstick.*

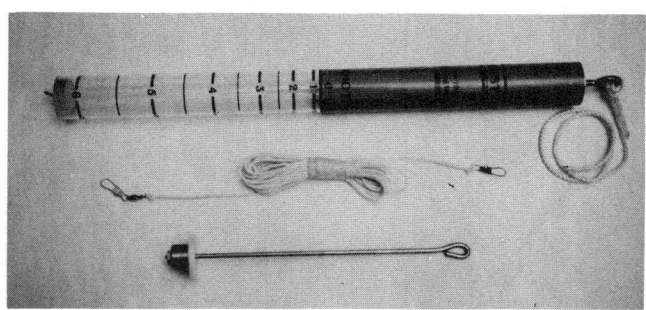

The Nightwriter, the perfect stocking-stuffer, from:

**Celestaire, Inc.**
**416 South Pershing**
**Wichita, Kansas 67218**

*Below: Light Makes Right.*

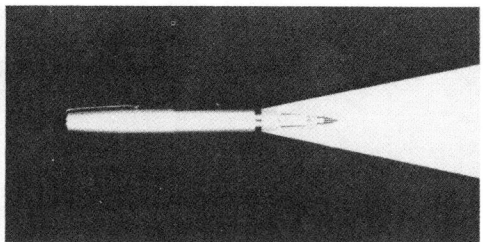

### NIGHTWRITER

Lights where you write! An absolute "must" for night celestial navigation. Aids in observing and recording sextant readings; times of observations; even computations or log entries late at night. This pen, powered by standard sized batteries, makes a perfect spare or emergency light source for boat or airplane, without being so bright as to destroy night vision. Comes with batteries and spare ink refill cartridge.

$6.95

Plath, an ancient and respected name in navigation equipment, now offers its own navigation calculator. It has a nice shape and looks as if extraneous stuff has been pared away from it. Several other brands that we have listed in the past have been (are) basically navigationalized general-use models.

**C. Plath**
**North American Division**
**4927 Calvert Road**
**College Park, Maryland 20740**

*Left: The Navicomp Navigation Computer.*

Chip technology and digital readouts have entered yet another marine problem-area: engine status monitoring systems. If there ever was a question (and there always has been a question) of "How's the mill doing?", the answer can now flash away before you continuously. For the well-to-do questioner and the poor-but-like-being-amazed, it's the Seamatic II Monitoring and Control Systems, from:

**Megasystems, Inc.**
**5909 West 130th Street**
**Cleveland, Ohio 44130**

*Below: Something for the Big Boys from the Big Boys.*

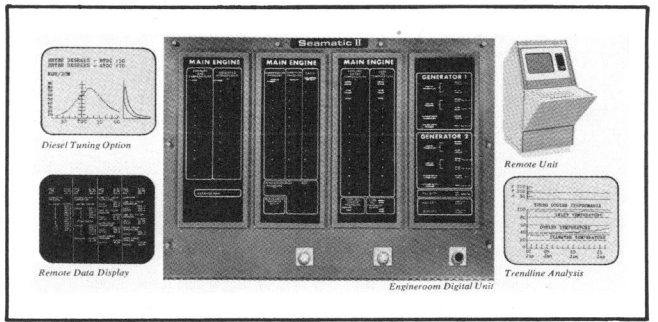

## Look! Up in the Sky! It's the . . .

Stars. Not too long ago, to study navigation was to study astronomy first. It is not by chance that *Dutton's Navigation and Piloting* was entitled *Navigation and Nautical Astronomy* in its first edition (1926). A student of navigation was expected to be able to step out of the charthouse door no matter where he might be on the face of the earth and pick out the constellations, planets, and stars, without the use of star-finding gadgets of any kind. Today's student of navigation, and many practicing navigators as well, not only can't name the heavenly bodies on sight, but also can't even figure out how to use their star finders without instructions written at the level of the average third-grader.

Why this situation obtains is difficult to imagine. To be sure, the importance of celestial navigation has decreased in recent years with the advent of electronic systems, such as Loran, Decca, and satellite methods, but most yachtsmen and small boatmen today still navigate by the stars when they go offshore. We suspect that the lack of interest in astronomy stems from the demystification of space. When you see men walking on the moon and robot probes flying by Jupiter, you no longer believe that Ursa Major is the Big Bear, or that Betelgeuse marks the right shoulder of Orion. All you know is that Arcturus, if you're lucky enough to find it, can help you find your position—that it might be part of a greater whole, or play a role in ancient mythology, is immaterial.

Watching the stars is fascinating; watching digital readouts is not. We suggest that the raven-haired Tahitian maiden who stands watch with you in the Macassar Straits will be far more impressed if you say, "Love of my life, allow me to point out the principal stars of Delphinus," than if you say, "Observe, my dear, the lovely shades of green on the Loran readout." (Women in the audience may, if they wish, replace "Tahitian maiden" with "Hawaiian stud.")

So we will become amateur astronomers. A certain amount of astronomical knowledge can be gained from the major navigation texts. Dutton's and Bowditch spring to mind. But to do it up right, an astronomy book is required. One that we have found especially helpful is described below.

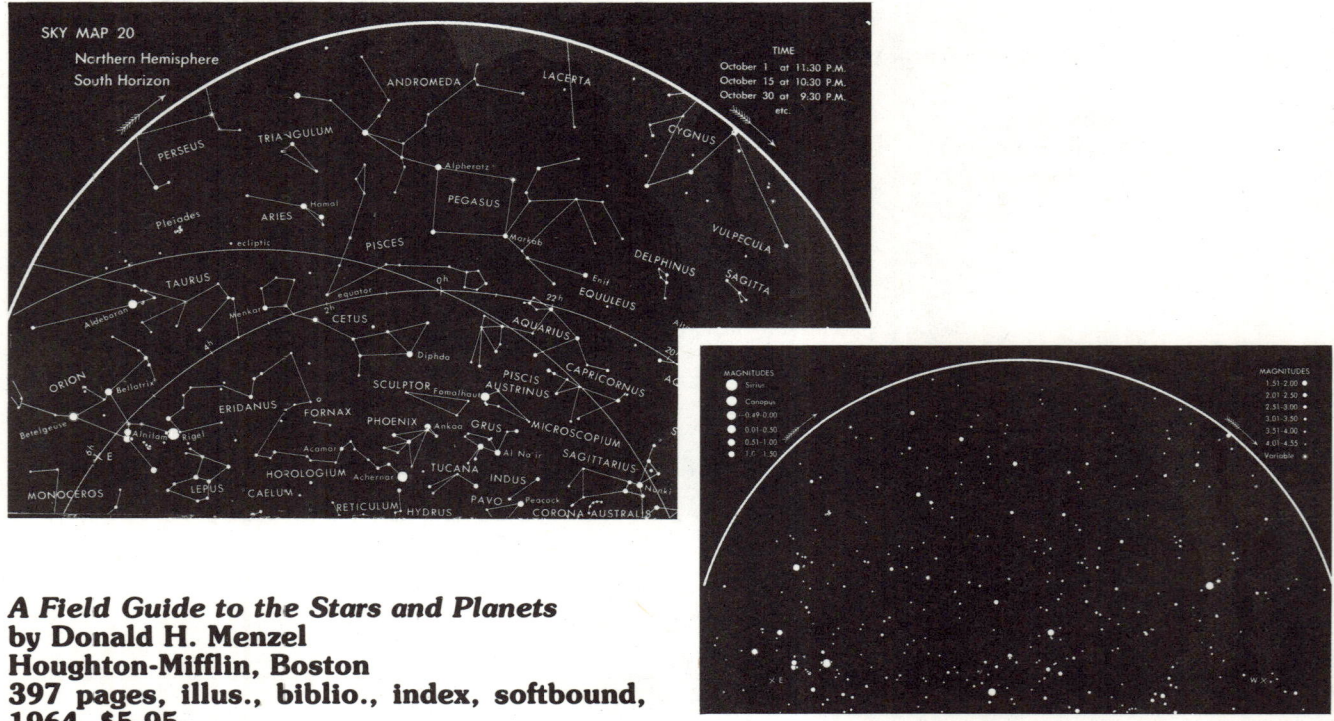

*Above and above left: From* A Field Guide to the Stars and Planets.

***A Field Guide to the Stars and Planets**
by Donald H. Menzel
**Houghton-Mifflin, Boston**
397 pages, illus., biblio., index, softbound, 1964, $5.95*

Number 15 in the excellent Peterson Field Guide Series, this handbook is about as clear and concise as you can get. Filled with stellar charts, diagrams, photographs, and tables, it helps you understand what you are looking at, whether you are observing with the naked eye or a telescope. With this in hand, you'll find yourself wandering around the yard on a clear night marveling at what you see.

Other fascinating objects are the variable stars, which alter in brilliancy over short periods. Betelgeux in Orion is one such object. Sometimes it far outshines Aldebaran, and has even been known to rival Rigel; at others it is little brighter than Aldebaran. The changes are real, and are due to alterations in the diameter of the star.

Betelgeux has no definite period, and its behaviour cannot be predicted with any accuracy, but other variables are as regular as clockwork. δ Cephei, a relatively inconspicuous star in the northern sky, changes between magnitudes 3·7 and 4·3 in a period of 5·37 days, and its magnitude for any moment may be forecast years in advance. Less reliable are the long-period variables, of which Mira (o Ceti) in the Whale is the most famous. At maximum Mira may attain the second magnitude; at minimum it sinks to below 9, so that even binoculars will not show it. The period is about 331 days, but is not constant, and may alter within relatively narrow limits.

*Above and right: From* The Observer's Book of Astronomy.

Another book of value to amateurs is:

**The Observer's Book of Astronomy
by Patrick Moore
Charles Scribner's Sons, New York
221 pages, illus., index, 1974 (rev. ed.), $2.95**

Number 32 of our favorite Observer's Series, this little book is not as detailed or comprehensive as the Field Guide opposite, but it is perfect for the person who wants a lot of knowledge in a compact volume. For that matter, forgo a case of beer and buy both.

### THE STAR CLOCK

The dial of the star clock is the zodiac, and the hour hand is your meridian, or north-south line. When the vernal equinox (Pisces) is due south, the star time is zero hours, and each 15° eastward indicates another hour. Taurus, for example, is 60° east of Pisces, and it indicates four hours star time.

The star clock and the sun clock shift against each other as the sun moves eastward among the stars. If you observe the stars at the same sun time, say 9 P.M., you will notice the stars shift slightly westward each night, toward the setting sun. In the course of a year, the stars make one more rotation than the sun, so the star clock rotates more rapidly, by about 1° per day, and the stars set 3 minutes 56 seconds earlier each night than they did the night before. This difference accumulates to one day in a year.

The star clock and the sun clock agree on September 21. At midnight, for example, both clocks read zero hours of the new day. To compute the difference between these clocks at a later date, add 3 minutes 56 seconds for each day that has elapsed, remembering that the star time is *ahead* of sun time.

A precise knowledge of star time is required by those who wish to compute the direction to point their telescope for a particular star, but you will not ordinarily need it. Instead, you may estimate sun time directly from the star clock using the star finder in this book. The method is simple and is described in the next section.

TABLE 1
STARS THAT RISE WITH THE SUN ON VARIOUS DATES

| STAR OR GROUP | CONSTELLATION | RISES WITH SUN (INVISIBLE) | RISES ONE HOUR BEFORE SUN |
|---|---|---|---|
| Alpha and Beta | Capricornus | Jan. 15 | Feb. 7 |
| Alpheratz | Pegasus | Feb. 1 | Mar. 1 |
| Circlet | Pisces | Feb. 20 | Mar. 20 |
|  | Triangulum | Mar. 18 | Apr. 16 |
| Pleiades | Taurus | May 16 | June 3 |
| Aldebaran | Taurus | June 7 | June 22 |
| Betelgeuse | Orion | July 2 | July 16 |
| Pollux | Gemini | July 10 | July 25 |
| Procyon | Canis Minor | July 27 | Aug. 9 |
| Sirius | Canis Major | Aug. 4 | Aug. 15 |
| Regulus | Leo | Aug. 21 | Sept. 2 |
| Denebola | Leo | Sept. 10 | Sept. 22 |
| Arcturus | Boötes | Oct. 7 | Oct. 20 |
| Spica | Virgo | Oct. 17 | Oct. 29 |
| Alpha | Libra | Nov. 6 | Nov. 19 |
| Albireo | Cygnus | Nov. 26 | Dec. 6 |
| Antares | Scorpius | Dec. 7 | Dec. 18 |
| Altair | Aquila | Dec. 15 | Dec. 27 |

No matter how proficient you become in observing the heavenly bodies, there will be times when a star finder will be indispensable. A marvelous one is:

**Whitney's Star Finder
by Charles A. Whitney
Alfred A. Knopf, New York
104 pages, illus., index, paperbound, plastic star locater, 1978, $5.95**

*Above: From* Whitney's Star Finder.

This is a book with an accompanying plastic wheel-type star locater. The text tells you how to observe the stars and use the wheel, and it has tables for planetary positions through 1981. It is intended for use in North America.

Two publications designed for navigators are:

***Brown's Nautical Star Chart (£1.20)***

and

***Brown's Star Atlas (£2.60)***
**Brown, Son & Ferguson
52 Darnley Street
Glasgow, Scotland**

The *Nautical Star Chart* is a big poster "for use any time in any part of the world, to find what stars are suitable for observation, their approximate altitudes and azimuths, or to identify an unknown star." On one side is a large chart for finding altitudes and azimuths. On the other side are seven smaller ones for identifying important stars. Instructions are included.

*Brown's Star Atlas* is a two-part book. Part 1 is a series of charts showing stellar positions. Part 2 is a short text, with practical problems, on using stars for navigation.

To keep up on developments in astronomy, a magazine subscription might be in order. A worthy publication is:

***Sky and Telescope***
**Sky Publishing Company
49 Bay State Road
Cambridge, Massachusetts 02238**

Scotcade is offering a beautiful, small, highly accurate Quartz Micro Alarm Clock. The problem is that for various reasons, it is not available in North America. Pick it up, or have it picked up in England for you, from:

**Scotcade, Ltd.
33-34 High Steet
Bridgnorth
Shropshire WV16 4HG, England**

*Above: Scotcade's Micro Alarm.*

Personal emergency strobes and rescue locator beacons are offered by:

**ACR Electronics Inc.
3901 North 29th Ave.
Hollywood, Florida 33020**

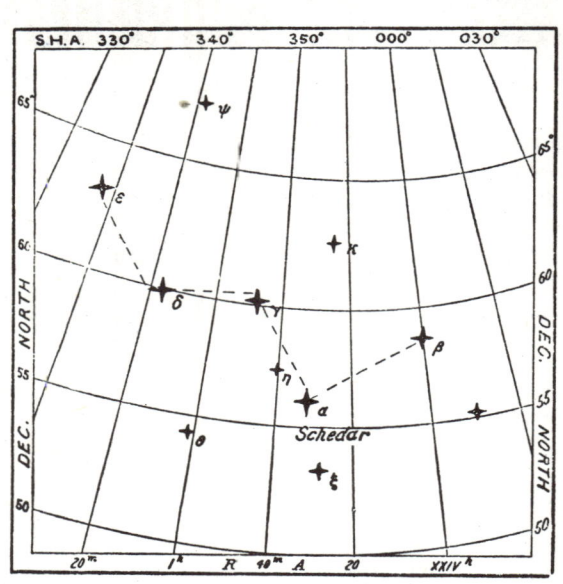

**CASSIOPEIA.**

On the opposite side of the Pole Star, but a little nearer to it than Ursa Major, is the smaller constellation CASSIOPEIA, also visible on all clear nights to observers in a higher North latitude than 45°. When URSA MAJOR is above the Pole Star, CASSIOPEIA is below it, and *vice versa*.

To obtain **a** view of these constellations as they appear when below the Pole, hold the small maps straight before you, facing North, instead of overhead.

*From* Brown's Star Atlas.

*Left: ACR's Rescue Lite.*

*Right: The 14-inch JABSCO searchlight.*

JABSCO, factors of all sorts of unusual marine fittings (mostly interior systems), offers electric control searchlights for pleasure craft.

**JABSCO Products
1485 Dale Way
Costa Mesa, California 92626**

Good ideas come from clear minds temporarily befuddled as they put two or more older ideas together into new ones. Here, for example, is an outboard self-steering gear of a configuration we usually associate with a wind vane (which it can also use) that in fact is activated by a compass, usually associated with totally electronic rigs.

**Browning Marine, Inc.
38 W. 306 Ferson Woods Drive
St. Charles, Illinois 60174**

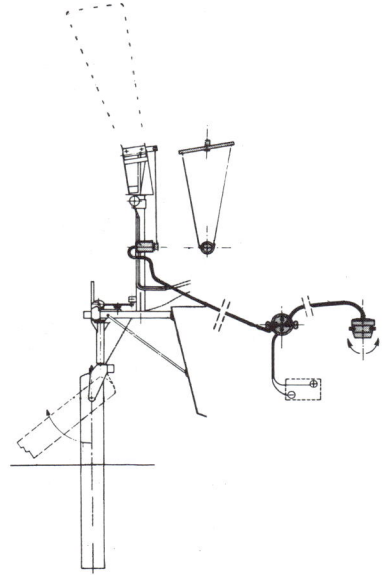

*Right: Browning Marine's Rube Goldbergian self-steering gear.*

Dear Editors:
Interest in self-steering gear seems to be on the uprise and we plan to return to the show circuit this year. Previously it was very much a case of answering a mass of questions from people who were convinced that they could build their own—as promised by a nine dollar book for under $15.00 (excluding cost of book) and who either wanted to pick one's brain or tell you that the concept was a ridiculous price or something.

I nearly got hysterical the other day on reading Hal Roth's (otherwise very excellent) latest book where he complained that if only importers would be content with 40% profit. . . . I would settle for much less and with currency fluctuations at times have settled for losses before now, but that's another story.

The compass course attachment is really great; it uses the power of the servo oar to move the helm—a very small electric 12-volt motor replaces the "vane"; current consumption is very small. It isn't, of course, just for running under power in no-wind conditions but also for running downwind at speed in, say, the Trans Pac type of situation where one is running downwind at high speeds and the apparent wind is constantly moving as one speeds up and down. By Trans Pac, I don't of course mean the race—the normal crewed one but cruising boat/solo boats, etc., running down the trade winds for distances.

—John Browning, President
Browning Marine, Inc.

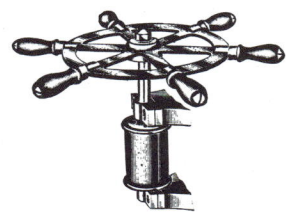

## Maps and Charts

Everything is collectible today, though some more than others. Hot items are antique maps and charts, whose market prices are rising rapidly. (For that matter, has anyone priced a common, modern, new nautical chart these days? We suspect a lot of outdated charts are still in use because of their high replacement costs.) Bona fide collectors seem to have their own sources and dealers; we found an interesting one in:

**Richard B. Arkway, Inc.
114 E. 61st St.
New York, N.Y. 10021**

Arkway publishes a neat catalog, which not only lists the maps and prints they have for sale, but also describes the maps in some detail and provides short passages on maps and mapmaking.

*Right: From the Arkway map and print catalog.*

If you're going to get into collecting maps and charts in a serious way, you had better know your stuff, because the field is filled with sharks and dilettantes. A good introductory book, aimed at both the historian and the collector, is:

***Maps and Map-Makers*
by R.V. Tooley
Crown Publishers, New York
140 pages, illus., biblio., index, 1978, $14.95**

*Right: From* Maps and Map-Makers.

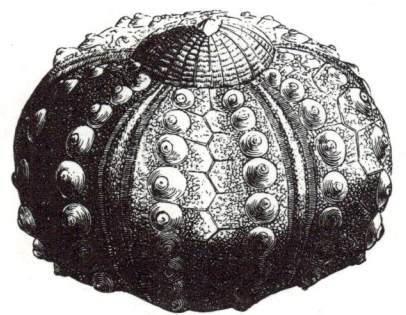

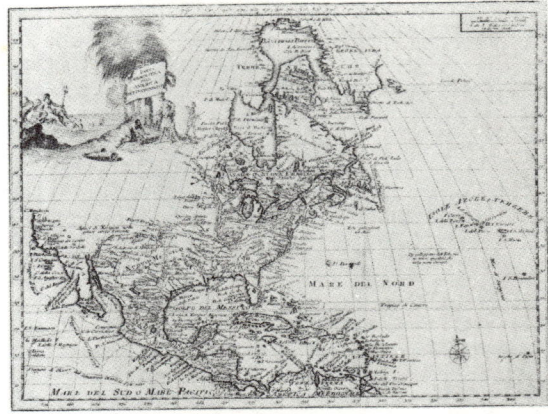

Item #21

21) **NORTH AMERICA
DE L'ISLE 1740**
Carta Geografica Dell'America Settentrionale (Venezia, C. Albrizzi Q. Girol, 1740). 12⅞" x 16½". Wide margins. Excellent condition. $150

*A pristine copy of De l'Isle's attractive map of North America adapted for "the Italian De l'Isle" atlas. This map is from the earlier edition published in 1740. Included are tracks of Cortez', Drake's and other significant voyages. The fine engraving is typical of Italian craftsmanship.*
Reference: Phillips. "Atlases," #594.

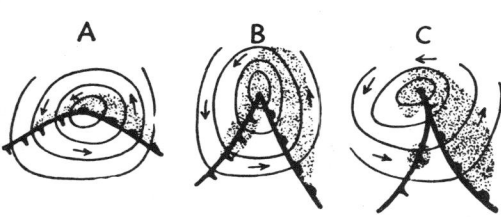

THREE STAGES IN THE DEVELOPMENT OF A DEPRESSION
(Shaded portion is the rain area)

One of the most familiar weather instruments, to be found in many households, is the ordinary aneroid barometer that hangs on the wall. It consists of a flat, round metal box that has been emptied of air. The atmosphere presses the top and bottom of the box towards one another, according to whether the pressure is high or low.

This is shown on the "clock" face of the barometer, that has a scale of readings in inches of mercury, ranging on most instruments from 28 inches to 31 inches. On the outer rim is a guide as to the weather to be expected at the different readings: "Stormy"—"Rain"—"Change"—"Fair"—"Very Dry."

Although the meteorologist requires instruments of greater precision, the aneroid barometer is sufficiently accurate for the average householder. Yet it is often subject to a good deal of scathing criticism and slander when, although the indicator points to "Very Dry" it may be raining outside, or when it points to "Rain," the sun is shining from a clear blue sky.

Many people become quite infuriated on such occasions; however, it is not the barometer that is at fault, but the householder, who has not taken the trouble to study the reasons for the behaviour of the barometer under certain conditions.

You must not assume that because the barometer is high it will be a fine day, or because it is low it will be rainy. The important thing to observe is whether it is rising or falling.

## The Observer's Book of Weather
### by Reginald M. Lester
### Charles Scribner's Sons, New York
### 152 pages, illus., index, 1964 (rev. ed.), $2.95

As past reviews in the *Mariner's Catalog* would suggest, we are great fans of the Observer's Series, which are little (literally) pocketbooks packed with information on specialized subjects. They don't make you an expert, but they do give you an *understanding*, which is critical for any future study you might undertake. *The Observer's Book of Weather* is in the finest tradition of the series; we might mention, though, that this is weather in general, not marine weather specifically.

*Left: From* The Observer's Book of Weather.

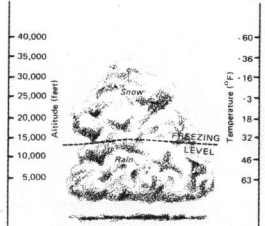

Stage I: *Cumulus clouds form when warm, moist air rises to the point where visible cloud droplets form. In the process, heat is released, which causes the cloud to grow even larger.*

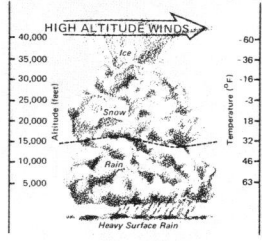

Stage II: *Rain and snow fall inside the cloud. But the strong updrafts in the cumulonimbus catch the raindrops and snowflakes and carry them upward again. Ice particles (hail) form in the cold uppermost reaches of the thunderhead. Heavy precipitation begins to fall out of the cloud; lightning and thunder begin.*

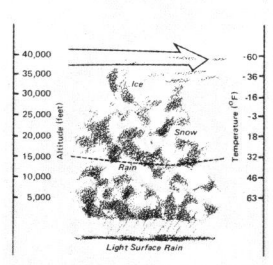

Stage III: *The downdraft of cold air that accompanies the precipitation signals the impending self destruction of the cumulonimbus. Updrafts within the cloud cease, and the storm's energy source is cut off. Precipitation weakens, then stops as the downdrafts cease.*

## The Whole Air Weather Guide
### by Walter F. Dabberdt
### Solstice Publications
### 1188 Laureles Dr., Los Altos, Cal.
### 64 pages, illus., glossary, index, paperbound, 1976, $3.50

Ever since Stewart Brand gave us *The Whole Earth Catalog* and made it work, a whole new way of titling books has evolved. Those who are easily jaded will slide right past books with ripped-off titles, but in at least this case, they will be missing out on a good thing.

*The Whole Air Weather Guide* is not a catalog. Instead, it is one of the best short introductions to the weather we have read. You can find many treatises on the weather that will tell you more, and many more that will tell you less, but for a short course about the atmosphere, this is top dog. You won't learn how to forecast or anything like that, but you will gain enough background knowledge to put the weatherman's report into the perspective it deserves.

*Left: From* The Whole Air Weather Guide.

# Sounds

*Illustration by Mike Rayhill.*

Gordon Lutz is a gentleman and scholar from New Jersey. With a lifetime of interest in film, he began a film distribution partnership. Another thing he did to disturb the neighbors is like music a lot. So he went out and got a couple of thousand albums (he doesn't move very often) and then listened to them.

## Down to the Sea in Chips

Being an Examination of the Revolution in Mobile Electronic Sound Reproduction and Music-making Equipment Wrought by Computer-Generated Synergetic Design Factors Manifesting a Corresponding Qualitative Improvement in Audio Performance,

With a Helpful Compendium of Consumer Advice on the Acquisition Thereof. . . .

or,

## How to Boogie 'til the Tide Floats Her Off

*by Gordon Lutz*

One advantage armchair mariners used to enjoy over their boated brethren and sistren, aside from most everyday creature comforts, was the chance to switch on their favorite recorded ditties. No longer is life so unfair. Even in the Stone Age of hi-fi technology (roughly 10 years ago) it was possible to indulge a taste for the undiminished splendor of the Siberian Symphony or perhaps The Flaming Hairies without venturing out of your recliner. But while we advise leaving your chaise ashore, bringing the sounds along on a cruise is now increasingly easy and satisfying.

Thank your car. As the breathless pace of refinement in home entertainment products approached escape velocity fired by miniaturization, and as autos became entertainment products themselves, the fully spec'd set of wheels naturally included ever fancier sound gear. Every large drug store now sells "car stereos." Today a mushrooming audio industry reaches out after the boat owner, too. Every dealer we talked to volunteered that he had just outfitted some guy's Hatteras for serious stereo merrymaking. You can customize or buy it off the rack, and now that the consumer electronic technocrats (them) have converged on newly identified markets (us), everything afloat can be rigged for a musical blast. Wiring up for this giggle may be no laughing matter, however. Competitive (?) discounting (plus trade-in allowances) lowers the cash requirement, but who'd have thought the day would come when you need to finance a box with a bank loan?

The International Brotherhood of Electronics Pushers, headquartered in Tokyo, has undermined our tolerance of tin can sound along with our balance of payments. Your spoiled correspondent spent an otherwise gorgeous weekend cruise off the Atlantic coast sharing the cockpit with a portable weather-band item that drifted in the vicinity of a succession of AM (Airwave Manure) stations. Research reveals we didn't have to put up with that. We could have fed our listening habit in a variety of snazzier fashions.

Cassette tapes are the niftiest things since sliced bread, and a damn sight more fun. They offer the only really portable medium for recordings, and considering you can handle them like poker chips, they are the only bet for stowing your own programming aboard—your choices when you want 'em, home-made or store bought. (Stay clear of any 8-track cartridge format junk; it was just that to begin with and it's now obsolete.) But cassettes are old news already. What may not be is that they have entered the era of world-class, big time hi-fi. Rampant R&D has made them a serious contender by overcoming earlier deficiencies inherent in slow tape speed (1 7/8 ips) and teeny track size. New computer-designed magnetic oxides are fast eliminating objectionable noise and limited dynamic range; the best cassette decks now compare favorably with fine reel-to-reel equipment (and are comparably priced).

*The* class act in this department is put on by Nakamichi Research, Inc., whose top-of-the-line "1000" 3-head studio deck is held in reverential awe by audiophiles. The heaviest entry in the mobile audio field is the breathtaking Nakamichi 250 cassette player. By extending the technology developed for their model 550 portable recorder (itself beyond the scope of our survey), they have come up with one righteous piece of gear. If you want to see an appreciative smile (or a squint of disbelief—depends on how you're dressed), drop by any plush audio showroom and ask for a demonstration. Try not to drool on the furniture because you won't believe what you hear, it's that good. It has built-in Dolby noise reduction, playback equalization for a choice of tape biases, fully automatic shutoff, balance and tone controls, a tape counter, accepts AC or 12-volt power and can be used as a pre-amp in a home system as well. The frequency response is ±3dB from 40 to 17,000 Hz, and the signal-to-noise ratio, thanks to the Dolby, is better than 62dB. And hey, it's classy looking!

The 250, priced at a mere $310, is a playback deck only; you cannot record tapes with it. For that added function you will need to step up to the Nakamichi 350, selling for $440. But chances are you've already got or are planning on buying a good home recorder capable of out-performing the recording section of the 350. It then makes better sense to stick to the 250's excellent playback characteristics for cruising enjoyment, and dub your collection of Git Tanner and the Skilletlickers onto tape at home. And if you're really up for the primo system, pack your cassettes into the hammered aluminum suitcase sold by Analog Digital Systems for carrying their superb 2002 amplifier/speakers (a pair), the Nakamichi 250 deck, and the ADS power converter for running these beauties off 120/220 house current where available. Around $800 will fix you up with the 250 and a pair of the 40w bi-amp'd ADS 2002s. The power pack for AC use runs $140, the aluminum carrying case is $90, and flush-mounting brackets are a few extra bucks if you want a permanent installation. Personally, I'd be delighted with that set-up strapped to a galvanized wash tub navigating my flooded basement.

For ADS speakers without amps, designated the L200/II or mobile version L200C with quick-disconnect surface mounting brackets, you're talking $112.50 each plus $5 for the bracket, as opposed to $470 for the pair of 2002s. The slightly larger L300C can go louder and deeper for $150 apiece. Their solid aluminum housings measure a minuscule 6¾ inches by 4⅓ inches by 4¾ inches for the L200, and 8½ inches by 5¾ inches by 5¾ inches for the L300, justifying ADS's "invisible sound" slogan. Braun makes an identical speaker for $5 more, but few dealers bother with them, since the components and appearance are the same.

It's hard to get interested in talking about less fantastic devices, but for those who have to settle—or can't tell the difference or don't honestly give a damn—there are alternatives. Taking loudspeakers first, you'll find a few others in the subcompact field. Most notable are the Visonik D (for David series) -5000, mobile version of their miniature (6¾ inches by 4⅛ inches by 4¼ inches) 2-way system costing $220 the pair. Another small system comes from AAL for $150 a pair, also in a practical aluminum cabinet of roughly the same size. Remember, these are not "car stereo" speakers, but miniature multispeaker systems designed for tight quarters and those opposed to electronic furniture.

You can, of course, sidestep the speaker issue by opting for headphones, but they suffice only if you're alone or are trying to be. A bunch of humans squatting around a cabin wearing private plastic headgear ain't a human way to get a shot of rhythm and blues. But if it turns you on, at least go for an open or semi-open design that will let you hear the Coast Guard hailing you topside while you're grooving to The Electric Jive Turkeys below. No phones stand up to anything less

*(continued on following page)*

*Left: The Nakamichi 250 cassette player.*

(continued from previous page)
than Tender Loving Care, and once an off-balancing swell sits you down on the pair you left lying on the bunk, their fi won't be so hi. Our choice for quality and durability are the Yamaha HP 1-A ($65) and its slightly lighter, less sensitive, and acoustically less efficient cousins, the HP-2 ($50) and HP-3 ($35).

*Yamaha HP-1A headphones.*

For a sound source, if you tend to look down your nose at house-brand, chain-store variety car stereo hardware (all of which, let's face it, can be mounted in a bulkhead as easily as in a dashboard), Pioneer makes a range of fine quality units incorporating radios and tape. Their KPX 9000 AM/FM/cassette player and KP 500 FM/cassette combo (about $270 and $212, respectively) can both be used with the customary car rigs or in tandem with their GM 40 "Stereo Main Amp" power booster ($75) or their Power Amplifier AD 320 ($70) to drive higher-rated speakers.

Blaupunkt gets from $700 to $1,200 for a series of first-rate AM/FM/shortwave/cassette decks (the Heidelberg, the Bamberg, and the Berlin), but more reasonably priced at $304 is their CR 2000-D AM/FM/cassette player with Dolby noise reduction. For $275 you can get the same beast without Dolby, the 2000, or for $350 they'll serve it with buttons (forever after known as digitals) instead of knobs, labeled perhaps prophetically the 2001. Honest. For an extra $150 you can pipe them through their BEA 100 equalizer/power amplifier that will drive up to four speakers independently, if you have boat enough to need them, and color the sound to suit your ear.

For years the battery-operated radio has been packed with the beer for excursions on land and water. Recent versions harbor more gimmicks than Harpo Marx's overcoat, with features that do everything but tell you your fly is undone. But even though some are hefty enough to provoke a hernia, they *are* portable. That's a distinct advantage if you prefer to take your toy with you on shore leave rather than abandon it for some pirate to confiscate in your absence. For the less paranoid, portability simply means you can play it anywhere, running on a stack of D cells or with the AC cord plugged into a household outlet.

These "boxes with the works" also have a cassette recording capability, so they are pretty self-contained, though you can add auxiliary speakers to hang in the head, and some have a pre-amp output for playing through home components. Microphones are separate extras or integrated into the unit for live taping, and you can copy from the built-in radio, too, of course. The most attractive choice here is the Aiwa TPR-920, going for $300. Features include a doo-dad called "Stereo-Wide," which, while playing, appears to separate the left and right channels by several feet instead of the several inches physically separating the front-panel speakers. It accepts external speakers ($120 a pair), gives a good and loud 3.6w per channel, will play a turntable through its phono input for taping records or just listening to them, and it's equipped with an automatic level limiter to avoid distortion when recording unpredictable loudness peaks. Twin whip antennas can be bypassed with an external hook-up for optimum FM reception, aided by a signal-strength meter. A choice of four models (H&G, C, F, SSH) assembles various combinations of FM, shortwave (1 or 2 bands) and so-called "medium wave" (AM) reception. And a bias equalization switch gives you a choice of two cassette tape oxides (there are three currently on the market).

*The Aiwa TPR-920 stereo radio-cassette recorder.*

The competition revolves around JVC's half-dozen models, listing from $85 to $350. Tops here, comparable with the Aiwa above, is their JVC 838 "Biphonic" Stereo Portable System featuring 4 speakers, 4w approximate output, built-in mikes, shortwave/AM/FM/cassette with bias EQ, line inputs and outputs, all powered by eight D cells or AC. The less sophisticated 636 is tagged $240. Next in line are Sanyo's 9977 at $230: AM/FM/cassette, 2-way speakers (also with wide-angle effect), bias EQ, line inputs/outputs; and the slimmed-down 9920 for $140. The Sanyos are very lightweight, using a lot of very breakable plastic.

Now if none of this suits your self-image or your cabin decor, there is yet a further possibility that is fun to suggest to pathological cases of audiophilia. First stop, Sears (yes, Sears) for a power inverter. Their current catalog (no pun intended) shows two, one delivering 500w, the other 200w of 110/220v AC current from your 12v system (priced $170 and $100, respectively). Naturally one could juice up anything from an electric toothpick to a vacuum cleaner thus, but if your person and quarters are spotless, or you care more about hearing some tunes, you can tap it to power your itsy-bitsy Mitsubishi line-up, a champagne-gold finished outfit they call their "Microcomponent Series." Take the specs for granted, they're state of the art. But dig the sizes: all four boxes measure 10⅝ inches across the front and 9¾ inches or less deep; the digital control preamplifier (M-P01, $370) and the quartz phase-locked loop synthesizer stereo tuner (M-F01, $340) are barely 2¾ inches high, while the 70w per channel power amp (M-A01, $500) stands 5⅛ inches and the dual-capstan drive cassette deck (M-T01, $560) only 5½ inches. Throw in some speakers and for a mere two grand you've got just about all you could ask for—more, in fact, than most mariners have use for in shipboard confines.

This brief survey of the field has not gone into much detail of specifications because they change faster than the weather and they don't tell you what anything sounds like. You have to judge that with your ears. We can only offer a subjective evaluation of how some pieces sound to us, and we experienced none of them in marine installations for which optimum output power, for one thing, will vary widely. High-quality goods dominate the market, though service and repair difficulties crop up regionally and seasonally. Spend time before spending money: listen, ask, compare, listen, ask, compare, etc. Prices have risen as much as 40 percent in three years, so we include them in round numbers with the caveat that we can't tell what you will find on the sales tag by the time you read this. Discounts run about 15 percent. An $800 list item should retail for $700 or under, a $360 one for roughly $300, so figure accordingly.

(continued on following page)

---

Dear Editors:

Course 'n I got this stuff on them unnerwater speakers you was all hot fer, but a mite too late to put in the piece proper, tho' I held it up long as I could. Leastwise it come at all 'n mebbe you can fix up a spot fer it if you've a mind. Or p'raps you'll find another place fer it altogether. But cast yer eye over page 8 o' the instructions, specially that last item under "Uses . . ."—I mean these fellas mean business!

—**Gordon Lutz**

*Left and right: Lubell Laboratories' underwater loudspeaker.*

```
        IV. USES OF LUBELL LABORATORIES UNDERWATER
               COMMUNICATION & RECALL SETS
```
These remarkable sets are a decade ahead of their time. Many engineers and scientists working in the field of underwater acoustics are still unaware of the feasibility of compressing the size of a low frequency transducer without reducing its efficiency; or of the feasibility of driving a piezoelectric transducer over a broad band of frequencies using simple audio amplifiers of both vacuum tube and transistor designs. A partial list of uses follows:

- Swimming Instruction
- Scuba Instruction
- Gunlap signal, competitive swimming
- False start signal competitive swimming
- Recall of scuba divers to excursion boat
- Recall of scuba divers to sunken habitat
- Paging of scuba divers at popular resorts (Sportsman's Lake)
- Making underwater movies
- Coordinating underwater work parties
- Coordinating underwater explorations
- Coordinating underwater treasure hunts
- Interrogation of suspicious or illegal divers by Coast Guard patrol boats or other jurisdictions
- Military uses
- Training of killer whales, dolphins and other species
- Repelling Beluga whales, sharks, and other species
- Dispelling congregated sea lions prior to setting off an atomic explosion.

(continued from previous page)

And a word on care: water and salt are relentless enemies of nearly everything human-made, and environmental resistance isn't a notable feature of the gear under review. Whenever possible, disconnect sensitive components and take them to shelter on dry land. And/or surround them with bags of silica gel from the hardware store to absorb moisture. Buy plenty, maybe even making your own custom-shaped muslin bags to sew it all up in. When discolored, the stuff can be dried out in an oven and re-used.

Now then, a thought for the crew that wants to play live music on board, lending a whole new meaning to the term "windjammers." We checked out electronic keyboards and found two manageable tabletop models, the Hohner Pianet T, weighing about 35 pounds ($415), and the Marlboro Piano, about 21 pounds ($325). Stashed in their carrying cases, they occupy roughly 3 feet by 1 foot by 6 inches, and for compact blowing room, hook into the pros' favorite practice amp known as the Pignose, a practical speaker unit giving maybe 5 or 10 watts out of a cabinet about 6 inches by 10 inches by 5 inches. It's $70 and only slightly bettered by the Dwarf Amp at $85.

Either will provide ample service for a jam session accompanied by flutes, harmonicas, whistles, guitars obviously, and our own preference, a grab-bag of affordable, portable hand drums, shakers, maracas, and other entertaining gadgets of the sort made by Latin Percussion, Inc., priced starting under $5. A dollar to P.O. Box 88, Palisades Park, New Jersey 07650, will get you a catalog. And just think about turning that peaceful cove into someplace all your own. Turn it up!

(Thanks to Robert Cox of Stuart's Audio in Raritan, New Jersey, for invaluable assistance in the preparation of this article.—G.L.)

## Bloogle

Ooooooh; we knew a girl from Idaho. Now doo do dido doo doo do do dooo. Get the Bloogle from:

Ray DiPietro
205 S. Central Ave.
Minoa, New York 13116

*What more can we say?*

Soniar offers a fascinating line of marine sound gear; a hailer/marine intercom and environmentally resistant amplifier, underwater speakers, and a gadget that turns your FM radio into a collision warning system. From:

Soniar Electronics Inc.
335 Riverside Drive
New York, N.Y. 10025

*Soniar's Mega-Hailer.*

**IT'S A HAILER...
IT'S AN INTERCOM...
IT'S A BOAT AMP...**

IT'S A MEGA-HAILER by Soniar Electronics, inventors of the Soniar 112. This hailer typifies the versatility inherent in all Soniar products. It is, first, a loud and clear hailer. Second, it has inputs for a variety of other electronic components. Third, it has special inputs that make it ideal as an amp for the Soniar 112 collision warning system, our Hydro-com (two-way surface-to-diver communication speaker/hydrophone) and our Soni-com underwater speaker. It has a special transmit-and-receive switch that permits two-way surface-to-diver communication when coupled with the Hydro-com unit mentioned above. The Mega-Hailer also features independent DC power source.

*Specifications:*

| | |
|---|---|
| Circuit | 4-TR Push-Pull Output |
| Output Power | 10W max., 6W 10% H.D. |
| Frequency Response | 40-16,000 Hz |
| Gain | 30mv for 6W output |
| Input impedance | About 50K ohms |
| Output impedance | 4, 8 & 16 ohms |
| Power Source | 8 size C batteries |
| Current Consump. | About 15 mA at no signal, 1.5A for max. output |
| Weight | 3 lb |
| Size | 5¼" x 6" x 8¼" |
| Made in the USA | |

# Interesting Boats

*"Boats are, after all, what boats are all about."*
—**Fred Brooks (in *Boats for the Republic*)**

Who ever heard of a boatshop where you can go and *shop* for a small wooden boat; where you can find choices in all manner of bronze fittings, boatbuilding tools, hard-to-find fastenings, books, and all kinds of the stuff we've talked about for years? The notion of one existing is ridiculous. There's one in Seattle.

We (Joe Bucek and I) have been active in Seattle's Traditional Wooden Boat Society for about a couple of years; after some thought and soul-searching last fall, we decided that we ought to go ahead and try to add a level of visibility to the efforts of the Puget Sound wooden boatbuilders and wooden boats in general. Thus The Wooden Boat Shop.

—**Land Washburn**

Photo by Marty Loken.

**The Wooden Boat Shop
1007 Northeast Boat Street
Seattle, Washington 98105**

Custom small craft & models:

**David Sweet, Boatbuilder
P.O. Box 178
Northeast Harbor, Maine 04662**

*One of David Sweet's lapstrake craft.*

I am primarily a custom builder, building any design in the traditional methods. I build my boats either lapstrake or smooth plank using cedar for planking, oak keels and frames, and local spruce for spars and oars. I also use natural crooks whenever possible. All craft are fastened with bronze and copper.

—**David Sweet**

**Sanford Boat Company, Inc.
Lower Pleasant Street
Nantucket, Massachusetts 02554**

Rather than develop a new design for our 26' sloop we felt it more sensible to choose a boat that had already proven its ability and desirability. In the past, as today, most designs were strongly influenced by the current fashions or rating rules which distorted their shapes away from the fastest and most seakindly ones. From time to time, though, boats have been designed with only the sea as a rule and pleasure of movement as a goal. Such was N.G. Herreshoff's Alerion, a boat which gave him and her subsequent owners a satisfaction that we seek to reproduce.

Herreshoff built her in 1912 for his personal use. He sailed her for 17 years until at age 81 he had a fainting spell in her and gave up sailing alone. He sold her to Charles Rockwell who in turn gave her to a cousin, Amory Skerry. Mr. Skerry wrote of her, "She is a sweet sailer and sweet to handle. . . . For twelve years Alerion was a beloved member of the Skerry family. Then the war came. . . ." After the war she went to Isaac Merriman. Francis Herreshoff reports that, "In a letter to me he said, 'I think she is one of the finest boats that was ever built,' and he should know because he has owned some of the best of them." Merriman willed her to his son who after a period of years gave her to the Mystic Seaport. The Seaport thought her important enough to have her completely refurbished, restored to her 1924 rig and put on permanent display. There she sits, admirable but frustrating to those who would sail her.

—Sanford Boat Co.

*Above and right: Sanford's Alerion, a classic built of cold-molded wood.*

*The Wood Marine 24.*

The Wood Marine 24, in red cedar strip over laminated fir:

**Boat Barn Inc.
P.O. Box 269
Coupeville, Washington 98239**

The boat is hand-crafted by myself and son and requires approximately one year from date of order to completion. Due to our location on Whidby Island, Washington, we mill over 90% of the materials used in our wooden boat.

—Richard C. Anderson
Boat Barn

Custom wood builders in the 30- to 38-foot range:

**Roberts & Adams
3816 Railway Ave.
Everett, Washington 98201**

We are a custom shop, doing mostly new construction, but also some repair on wooden boats. We generally work on boats in the 30'-38' range, but have handled down to 8', and may be starting a 40' boat soon if we find a design the customer likes. We have a small production run of 8' cold-molded sailing prams called the Serious Tender that is distributed by the Wooden Boat Shop in Seattle. Mostly, though, we do custom work for individuals. Our standards are only first yacht quality, and we care a great deal about what we do.

—Nancy Sosnove
Roberts & Adams

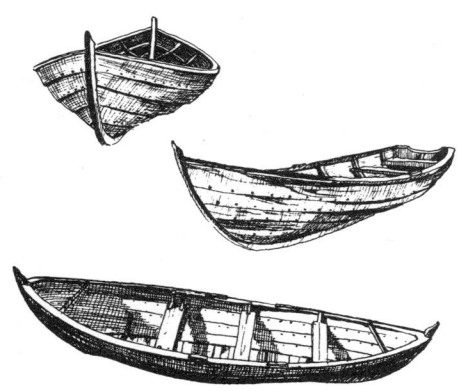

Faerings—graceful, ancient, enduring, beautiful:

**Faering Design
Chip Stulen, Boatbuilder
Route 1, Box 223
Suttons Bay, Michigan 49682**

The Bjorkedal faering depicts many of the same fine lines as her Viking predecessors. Her ample beam through the midships offers high load capacities without sacrificing efficient hull characteristics. The faering can be built as either the traditional double-ender or with a stern transom. The transom stern is set high enough so that she is still double-ended on the waterline. The boat's length ranges from 3.35m (11') to 6.09m (20') and its beam from 1.27m (50") to 1.77m (70"). Boats over 4.88m will be equipped with two rowing stations. The boats can also be fitted with simple free-standing sprit, gunter or gaff sailing rigs, all of which store easily in the boat and offer the owner the option of choosing between sail or oar while on the water.

The faering's planking is of Atlantic white cedar, the keel and stem pieces of white oak and the sawn frames of either white oak, locust, ash or spruce. The hull is copper riveted throughout. Spars and oars are constructed of solid Sitka spruce; the latter are carved in the traditional Norwegian manner, offering an aesthetically beautiful and efficient oar. Finished naturally with oil products, the real beauty of these craft comes alive.

—Chip Stulen

Plans of one hull for power *or* sail for the home builder:

**J.P. Hartog
Holland Marine Design
3510 Geary Blvd.
San Francisco, California 94118**

The boats were designed for home construction of plywood or planked skin and decks over easily available 2 x 4 framing with longitudinal battens.

The sportfishing version is strictly a displacement hull and requires only a relatively low h.p. motor. A version with a less raked transom is available for an outboard motor of up to 35 h.p.

—J.P. Hartog

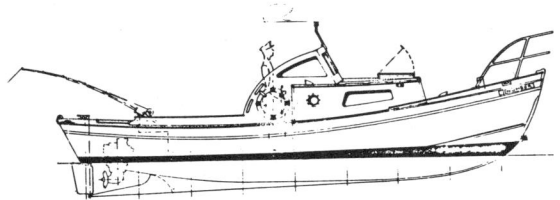

*Left: J.P. Hartog's adaptable hull design.*

*Above: Ben Ostlund's 24-footer "designed for general pottering about in Newport Beach, California."*

Plans for a neat little 24-foot tug:

**Ben Ostlund
P.O. Box 2206
Newport Beach, California 92663**

Plans for a round-bottomed surf boat:

**George E. Meese
194 Acton Rd.
Annapolis, Maryland 21403**

This sturdily built boat is designed to withstand the extremely rough waters of a pounding surf. With a total weight of 837 pounds, she rides easily and surely through strong currents and high waves.

The hull is typical round bilge construction. Steambent white oak frames are on a white oak keel and keelson. Planking is lapstrake white cedar.

Propulsion may be oars (3 pairs can be shipped) or with a 5 to 15 HP outboard motor.

—George E. Meese

*Below: George Meese's surf boat.*

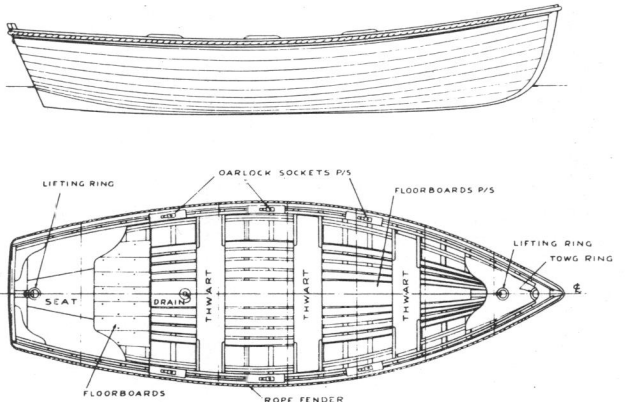

The North Atlantic 29 with junk rig:

**Designer:
Angus S. Primrose
Mercury Yacht Harbour
Hamble, Hampshire SO3 5HR
England**

**U.S. Builder:
Bounty Enterprises
15661 Producer Lane
Unit 1
Huntington Beach, California 92649**

*Below: The junk-rigged North Atlantic 29.*

Inside Steering Station. One of the most unique features is the inside steering station. It removes the helmsman from the elements: hot sun or foul weather. The port and starboard adjustable swing seats enable him to remain level in rough seas, or when the yacht is heeling. These two innovations reduce the "fatigue factor," long the enemy of ocean sailors. The Acrilan pram hoods, that swivel 360°, are directly over the swing seats and afford good visibility and protection. With the aft-led halyard, sheet and reefing downhauls, the yacht can be completely controlled from the inside, or the cockpit. Both the sheet and halyard are led through the deck to the station, and the slack is taken up on aluminum storage reels. In extreme conditions, the prams can be quickly removed and dog-down hurricane hatches secured. There are port and starboard opening ports, teak main hatch lid and cribboards.

—**North Atlantic 29 brochure**

*Left: The Lowell 12.*

Stock wood rowboats, tenders, skiffs, and sailboats:

**Lowell's Boat Shop
459 Main Street
Amesbury, Massachusetts 01913**

Of our three sailboats, the Lowell 12 is the smallest and cat rigged. The 14- and 16-footers are sloop rigged. We use a sliding gunter rig on the 12 but have altered it per the enclosed photo for better windward performance—a boom is optional.

The Lowell 12, 14, and 16 are all built with the WEST System™ now to reduce maintenance and make it easier (and drier to drysail them). A daggerboard is standard on the 12 and centerboards on the 14 and 16.

—Jim Odell
**Lowell's Boat Shop**

See it now. The Boy-in-the-Man, his dog, and Harmony, from:

**Harmony Boats
RFD
Vineyard Haven, Massachusetts 02568**

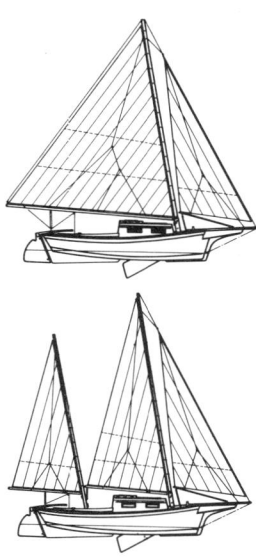

*Left: Rig options on the Oysterman 23.*

Oysterman 23, with scads of options:

**Menger Enterprises, Inc.
P.O. Box 141, 77 Cedar Street
Babylon, New York 11702**

The sloop is an accurate replica of a design by H.I. Chapelle (in wood). We have only lengthened the cabin and designed a ketch rig to break the large sail area up into 3 areas. The boat will sail itself by raising and lowering the centerboard to balance the sail area!

We are just this year starting to produce kits of both versions. Our kits A & B are very complete and include all necessary pieces to complete the boat except for sails.

—William M. Menger

*Below: The Oysterman 23 ketch-rigged version.*

|  | Bottom Length | Overall Length | Sheer | Rocker | Maximum Beam | Depth | Weight (Approx.) | Oar Lengths | Capacity in Pounds |
|---|---|---|---|---|---|---|---|---|---|
| LITTLE SISTER | 8' | 11' 3" | 8" | 2½" | 3' 10" | 1' 3" | 95 lbs | 6- 6½' | 800 |
| ADMIRAL'S DORY | 10' | 13' 7" | 10" | 4" | 4' 3" | 1' 4" | 190 lbs | 7½' | 1000 |
| BLACK ROCKS DORY | 11' | 14' 8" | 11" | 4" | 4'6" | 1' 4½" | 220 lbs | 8' | 1200 |
| LUNENBURG DORY | 12' | 15' 6" | 1' | 4" | 4' 8" | 1' 5¾" | 260 lbs | 8' | 1400 |
| HANDLINE DORY (single) | 13' | 17' | 1' 3" | 4½" | 4' 11" | 1' 7" | 325 lbs | 8½-9' | 1700 |
| BASTARD DORY | 14' | 18' 4" | 1' 5" | 5" | 5' 4" | 1' 10½" | 400 lbs | 9' | 2000 |
| TRAWL DORY (double) | 15' | 19' 9" | 1' 5" | 5½" | 5' 5" | 2' | 455 lbs | 9½' | 2400 |
| FISHMAKER'S DORY | 16' | 21' 1" | 1' 6½" | 6" | 6' 1" | 2' 1" | 535 lbs | 10' | 2900 |
| FORTUNE BAY DORY | 17' | 22' 2" | 1' 7½" | 6½" | 6' 4½" | 2' 2" | 700 lbs | 10' | 3500 |
| NEWFOUNDLAND DORY | 18' | 23' 1" | 1' 9" | 7" | 6' 8" | 2' 4" | 760 lbs | 10' | 4200 |
| SEINE DORY | 20' | 25' 9" | 1' 11½" | 8½" | 7' 1" | 2' 7" | 890 lbs | 10½-12' | 5400 |

*Right: From Atlantic Shipbuilding.*

Dories 11 to 30 feet. Here's the successor to W. Lawrence Allen Dory Builders:

**Atlantic Shipbuilding Co.**
**P.O. Box 1150**
**Lunenburg, Nova Scotia, Canada**

*Right: Crown Point's 30-footer.*

Sailing dories & skiffs in several sizes:

**Crown Point Marine**
**Rte. 3, Box 74**
**Wilmington, North Carolina 28403**

These boats are intended for the man who wants an inexpensive shallow draft weekender or limited cruising boat but also wants a seaworthy boat and one that behaves like a sailboat.

They are all well-balanced ketch rigs (sprit or gaff) and will sail with mainsail alone or jib and mizzen. They point well, come about quickly even in light airs, and sail as fast or faster than most cruisers their size.

With the great amount of flare in their sides they are unusually dry boats and give a smooth ride in rough waters.

We build three sizes—22', 26', and 30'. This is the length on deck and the overall length with bowsprit and rudder is 2 to 3 feet larger.

In order to keep costs down we keep our boats as simple as possible and finish the interior only as an extra at the request of the buyer.

All boats are similar in materials and design. They are plywood construction with 10-oz. fiberglass overall. The ports are fixed plexiglass.

—Crown Point Marine

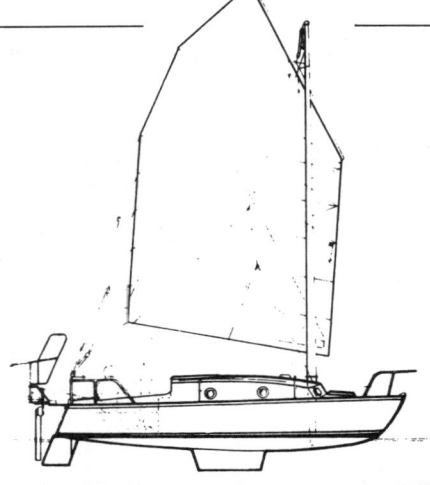

Kingfisher 20, roomy for size and Hasler junk rig option:

**Kingfisher Yachts**
**Westfield Engineering Ltd.**
**7 Cabot Lane**
**Creekmoor, Poole**
**Dorset BH17 7DA, England**

An 18' 4" sailing dory, bare hull to fully found:

**Beach Comber Boat Building
P.O. Box 338
Jensen Beach, Florida 33457**

The modern Beachcomber was designed with practicality in mind. The unique inboard motor well allows the outboard motor to tilt directly into the well while under sail or for beaching purposes. Her mahogany kick-up rudder and retractable centerboard allow her to be launched anywhere. She can be stepped and unstepped in a matter of minutes by one person. The spars can be stowed neatly inside the boat for easy trailability.
—**Beach Comber Boat Building**

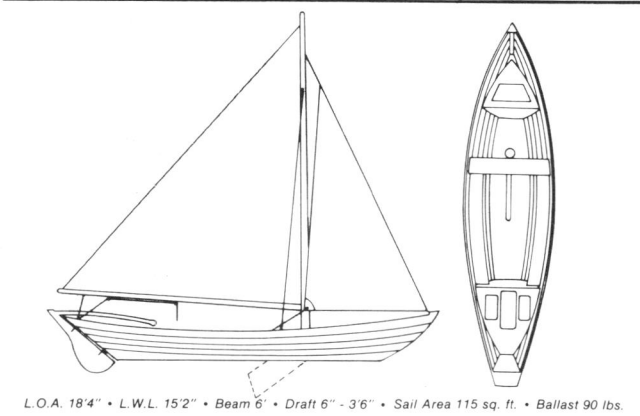

L.O.A. 18'4" • L.W.L. 15'2" • Beam 6' • Draft 6" - 3'6" • Sail Area 115 sq. ft. • Ballast 90 lbs.

*Above: The Beachcomber Dory.*

Ultralight rowing dory, the Cetacea:

**Bluebird Dories
945 Hope Ave.
Santa Barbara, California 93110**

- Unsurpassed beauty and strength of Bruynzeel African Mahogany hull that is handmade using Olympic class wood epoxy matrix construction which is further protected with five coats of Imron aircraft enamel.
- The spruce spoon oars are made to the same rugged standards as the hull.
- Cetacea is specifically designed for solo cartopping and launching.
- Her carbon fiber ribs enable Cetacea hulls to be nested together snugly on a small vehicle for group trips.
—**Bluebird Dories**

*Oh to be in California....*

From here on everything is fiberglass ('cept way later)

Lightfoot in glass, straight ahead and practical:

**Traditional Watercraft
P.O. Box 203
Indian Rocks Beach, Florida 33535**

The simple sprit rig would be hard to improve on for convenience. It features easily handled spars that can be stowed inside the boat. With no stays or shrouds and with sails furled on the masts, it takes only minutes to set up and be under sail, making trailering especially convenient. A mid-position mast step is provided for single sail use.
—**from a Traditional Watercraft brochure**

*Above: Traditional Watercraft's Lightfoot.*

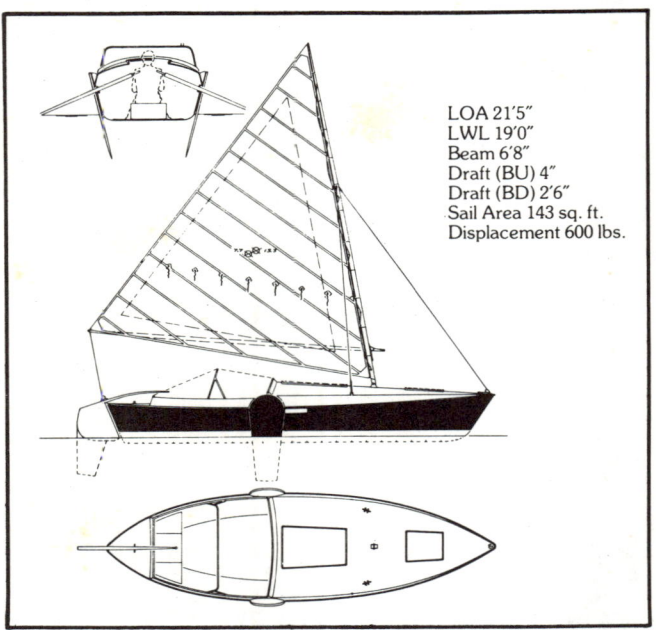

LOA 21'5"
LWL 19'0"
Beam 6'8"
Draft (BU) 4"
Draft (BD) 2'6"
Sail Area 143 sq. ft.
Displacement 600 lbs.

Dovekie, Bolger genius, and a price breakthrough of sorts.

**Edey & Duff
30 Harbor Road
Mattapoisett, Massachusetts 02739**

As to the rowing: I've rowed her as much as five miles in two hours without more effort than it would take to walk the same distance in the same time. (But the walker couldn't carry two or three other people while they rested; with a crew of three taking turns, *Dovekie* could be rowed something like twenty-five miles on a windless summer day.) She carries way well between strokes and is no trouble to keep straight. One man can't quite get her up to three knots even with a strong effort, but he can make useful progress against a stiff breeze by keeping his stroke short. Rowing downwind is apt to be more laborious than going into it, as the stern is blown around and demands hard pulling with both hands on the weather-side oar; a second person along to drop the rudder and steer is a great help at such a time.

It's illuminating to try to row her with the leeboards and rudder in the sailing position. There's a sensation as of trying to drag a parachute, and if the mast is left standing as well and there's the slightest breath of wind, she becomes quite helpless with a single oarsman.

—*Edey & Duff brochure*

---

Frances 26 and related larger craft, good-looking boats:

**Thomas D.C. Morris
Yacht Builders
Southwest Harbor, Maine 04679**

*Right: Two rig options in the 26-footer Frances, designed by C.W. Paine.*

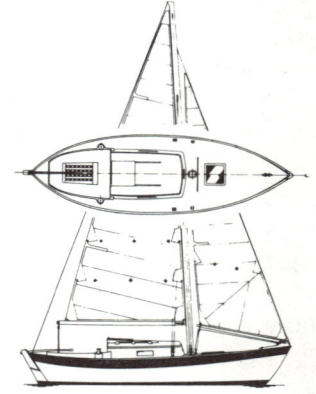 

l.o.a. 26'0" / l.w.l. 21'3" / beam 8'2"
draft 3'10" / displ. 6,800 lb.
ballast 3,500 lb. / 337 sq. ft. of sail

She's a double-ender.
Not as fast as a transom or counter stern, but not much slower, either, and the sea keeping qualities are so well known as not to require repeating here. Many hours were devoted to developing the hull shape, including the carving and gradual perfection of a half model. The entry is modeled quite sharp (the fastest racing yacht I ever designed of comparable size had an entry half angle of 22 degrees). The keel extension is carried right up to the "canoe body" of the hull with a very tight fairing radius. This allows the entire keel to act like a vertical wing and thus prevent leeway. The rig is tall and narrow, increasing the leading edge of the sails. These three factors make *Frances* a weatherly boat. She has quite a high freeboard. This is used fore and aft to provide 4-inch-high bulwarks around the forward and after decks. Now bulwarks have gone out of fashion on the racing boats, but once you sail with decent bulwarks as well as lifelines betwixt yourself and the hereafter, you won't go to sea again on a boat that is not so equipped. Amidships the high freeboard combined with a flush deck are responsible for all that lovely room belowdecks.

—*from a Morris brochure*

Bahama Sandpiper, personality in a cat ketch:

**C.W. Paine Yacht Design Co.
P.O. Box 763
Camden, Maine 04843**

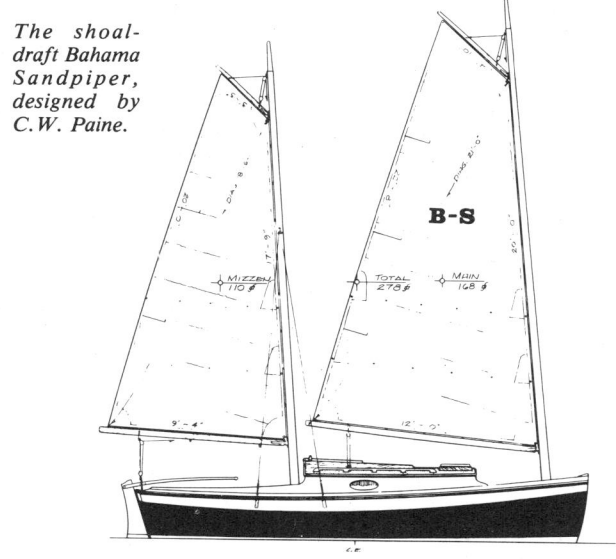

*The shoal-draft Bahama Sandpiper, designed by C.W. Paine.*

The whole idea of the Sandpiper was to develop a boat, other than the catboat, which could be sailed in only eighteen inches of water. I have found the boat to sail extremely well, and fast, in such conditions on a reach and run. Unexpectedly, I also discovered that the boat can be made to sail to windward (sideslipping to beat the band) and can even come about, with both the centerboard and rudder full up. I'm not saying she sails well in such eventualities, but she can be made to go to windward in eighteen inches of water, which opens up all sorts of possibilities for cruising.

—Chuck Paine

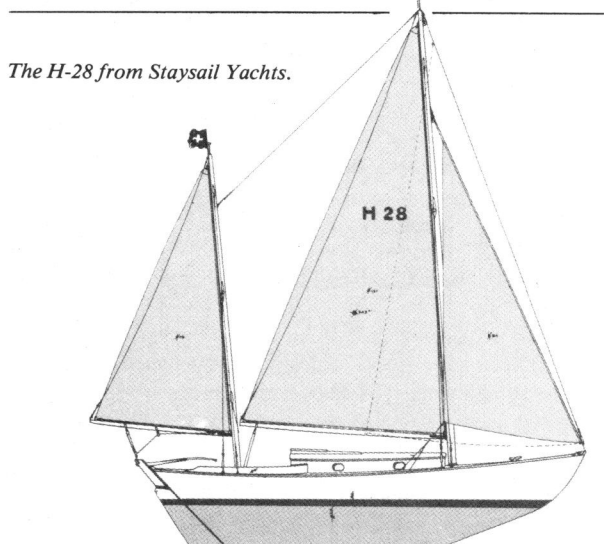

*The H-28 from Staysail Yachts.*

The H-28 in glass. L. Francis understood ketches better than anyone:

**Staysail Yachts Ltd.
East Shore Road
Huntington, New York 11743**

... 'tis then that the H-28 comes into view at her mooring, and as her white form is silhouetted against the opposite shore she seems beyond the realm of mere things—a mythical dream come true, the answer to a sailor's prayer.

—L. Francis Herreshoff

Nonsuch 30, room and simplicity:

**Hinterhoeller Yachts Ltd.
8 Keefer Road
St. Catharines
Ontario L2M 7N9, Canada**

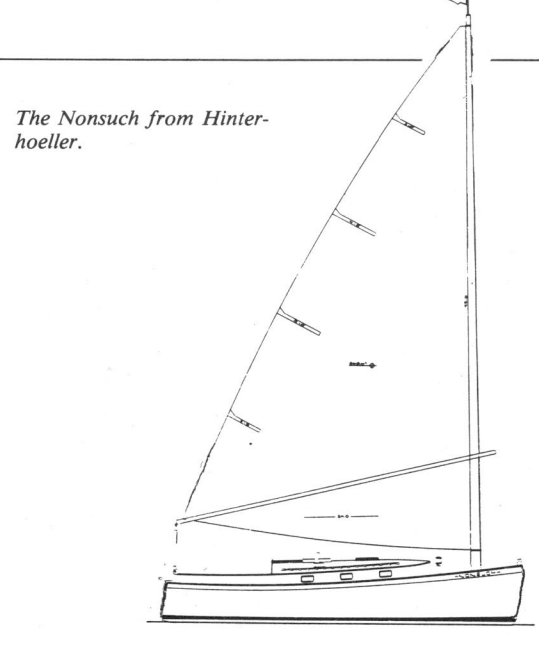

*The Nonsuch from Hinterhoeller.*

The most innovative aspect of the Nonsuch is the unstayed tapered aluminum mast and aluminum wishbone boom. The mast requires no shrouds or stays to support it, rather, it is through a deck stepped and pinned to a reinforced integral hull and deck structure and is free to bend as the wind blows. This may sound frightening to some traditionalists but as Gary Hoyt, who developed a similar concept on the "Freedom 40," said, "How long ago did they give up staying airplane wings?"

—Hinterhoeller Yachts brochure

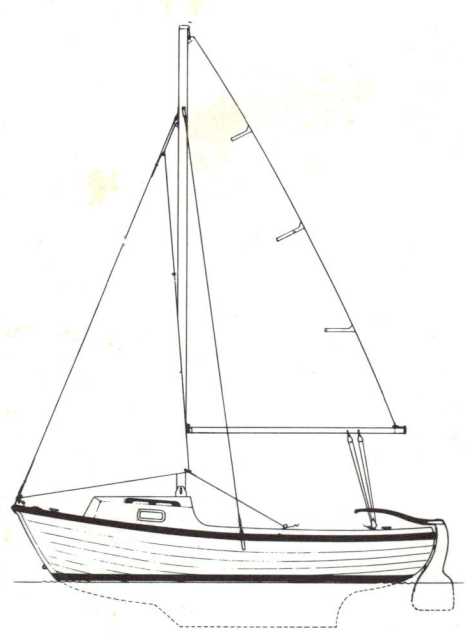

*Ted Hermann's Lazy Jack 32, designed by Ted Brewer.*

The Skipper Cuddy; small-time commercial fishing?

> **Southern Sails**
> **1780 Calumet St.**
> **Clearwater, Florida 33515**

Lazy Jack 32, wholesome and good kit options:

> **Ted Hermann's Boat Shop**
> **3631 Ocean Ave.**
> **Seaford Harbor, New York 11783**

Rowcat, gocat:

> **Art Javes Design, Ltd.**
> **1 Smith Street**
> **Norwalk, Connecticut 06851**

Why the schooner rig? Why not? It gives us what we want, divided rig, good balance under shortened sail, eliminating the need for those genoas and winches, the main mast is out of the business end of the boat, the cockpit area, and most important, it looks nice too.

Some wonder why schooners are not being built these days. One reason is that the various racing rules have put them at a disadvantage and, whether we like it or not, racing rules are the all-important factor in determining what the mass market buys. Another motivation is fashion. Sloops, catamarans, trimarans, reverse sheer, reverse transoms, fin keels, spade rudders, genoas, winches, and transom cockpits.

—Ted Hermann brochure

*The Rowcat from Art Javes.*

Two more inflatables. Surely we must have them all by now!

Barakuda line, five models:

> **Elco Marine Sales**
> **21912 Winnebago**
> **El Toro, California 92630**

The Angeviniere Bombards, 14 models for all purposes:

> **J.P. Hughes International, Inc.**
> **523 West Sixth Street**
> **Suite 361**
> **Los Angeles, California 90014**

SB SERIES

The SB series is designed for those with very little storage space but want a dinghy in a hurry. It comes complete with wood flooring, seats, bag, pump, and repair kit. The seats and flooring roll up in the boat so that this dinghy is just dumped out of the nylon bag and inflated by the foot bellows. Optional folding motor mount is available. ($49.95)

*The Bombard 3S.*

WESER SERIES

The Weser series is designed for those who require a little more room and stability from their boat. With a wide beam and special bow design, this sportboat gives the fisherman or partier all the room he requires. The Weser series comes complete with wood floorboards, inflatable keel, bag, pump, and repair kit.

*From Barakuda via Elco Marine.*

Dear Editors:

My observations of the Yuloh in China differ slightly in detail from what is shown in the *Mariner's Catalog*, Volume 3, p. 29.

(1) The eye in the loom for the lanyard was set in a pin some 6 inches long set at right angles to the loom.

(2) There was a wooden grip on the lanyard located about a foot below the eye.

In use, one hand was on the loom and the other on the handle. The pull was on both. At the end of the stroke, the pull on the lanyard handle was reversed immediately prior to reversing the pull on the loom. This action, of course, gave the blade the proper angle—no ifs, ands or buts.

My observations were primarily in Shanghai, where details in everything were probably different than in the north.

I can say that I've seen tiny Chinese women move a lighter with a load in excess of 20 tons, both with and against the river's current.

—Don McIver
Finksburg, Maryland

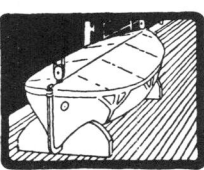

## The Case for the Cruising Trimaran
**by Jim Brown**
**International Marine Publishing Company**
**Camden, Maine**
**224 pages, illus., 1979, $17.50**

The man who is responsible for putting hundreds of people in their own cruising trimarans delivers his entire philosophy of multihull design and seamanship, and faces squarely the bane of the multihull—capsize.

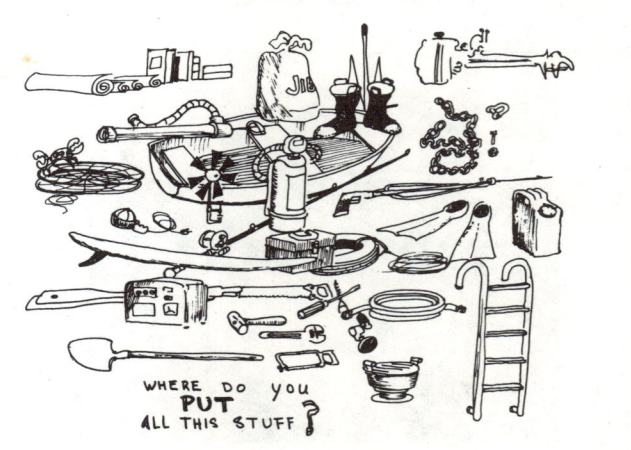

In theory, the stowage problem is easily solved by the multihull's extra hulls; but in fact, it is often compounded in designs that have standing headroom walkways in all hulls. This means that the majority of deep space (whether in the central or the outer hulls) is simply unavailable for the stowage of anything but air. It is used for the passage of people's feet. The displaced plunder usually gets heaped up in the wings, high above the waterline, where the superstructure must now be designed around it. The boat's windage and "roll center" are thereby elevated in the interest of floor space. Alternatively, or simultaneously, stowage articles are pushed out toward the ends of the vehicle where they are hard to reach, and where their weight amplifies gyration and degrades the steering properties—especially downwind steering in survival weather. A lofty mast and large sailplan further compound this dangerous progression. This unscientific approach to multihull design is simply not well suited to serious seafaring.

Now, let's face the greatest stowage problem of all: where to put the dinghy? The usual solution nowadays is to settle for an inflatable dinghy. And yet, to commute around the harbor in a rubber boat, you need a small outboard motor, since rowing the "bladder boats" any distance is a herculean job. And that's what the dinghy is for: to commute around the harbor, often against the wind and chop, hauling fuel, ice, groceries, laundry, water, and people, sometimes over considerable distances.

*From* The Case for the Cruising Trimaran.

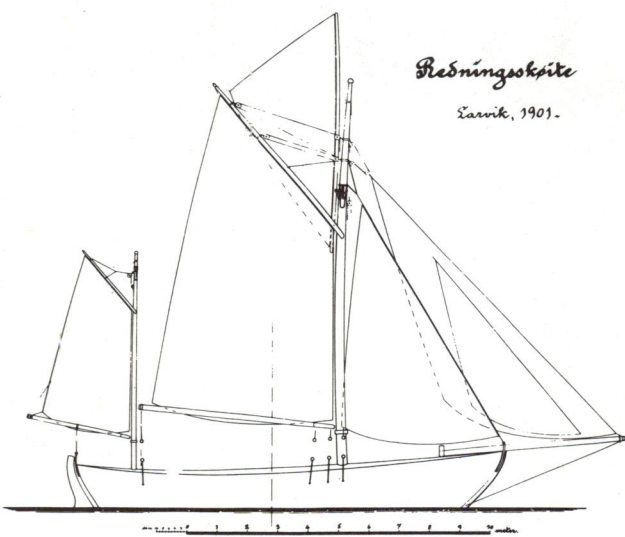

*From* Colin Archer and the Seaworthy Double-Ender.

## Colin Archer and the Seaworthy Double-Ender
**by John Leather**
**International Marine Publishing Company**
**Camden, Maine**
**176 pages, illus., index, 1979, $17.50**

A history and analysis of Colin Archer's legendary redningsskoites, pilot boats, polar ships, and yachts, and the craft that were patterned after Archer's classic style.

*The key to the Spray's sailing ability was to take advantage of a good slant. This photograph gives a view of the robustness of her rig.*

*From* The Spray.

## The Spray: Building and Sailing a Replica of Joshua Slocum's Famous Vessel
**by R.D. Culler**
**International Marine Publishing Company**
**Camden, Maine**
**144 pages, illus., 1978, $9.95**

In his last book, Pete Culler tells about the boat he built and lived aboard for over 20 years, and in the process reveals much about the simple life and answers the critics of the *Spray*'s design.

Uffa was always ready to prove his theories correct with a practical demonstration. *Vigilant* was such an extreme example of light displacement that the "Q" Class refused to allow her to race with them in the Solent, yet he sailed her to Sweden and back in a summer of strong winds. He made many friends in the Baltic countries and did a lecture tour there one winter. Very different to the *Vigilant* trip was the voyage from Norway to Cowes in the Falmouth Quay Punt *Twilight*, finding out how this heavy-displacement type behaved while running down across the North Sea in a series of northerly gales. Six Metres were invariably treated as day boats; but Uffa, who could always be relied on to do the unexpected, sailed *Lintie* from Cowes to the Whitaker Beacon, at the mouth of the River Crouch, in 21 hours. His experience in every kind of craft was as wide as can well be imagined, and this was invaluable, for a designer.

*From* Best of Uffa.

**Best of Uffa: 50 Great Yacht Designs from the Uffa Fox Books**
**edited by Guy Cole**
**International Marine Publishing Company**
**Camden, Maine**
**160 pages, illus., 1978, $15**

An anthology of classic designs, with complete plans and design commentary by one of the 20th century's great masters.

## Motorsailers

There was a time in the not-so-recent past when the boating press devoted considerable space to debating the merits and demerits of motorsailers, those neither-fish-nor-fowl craft that are so tempting to people who seek the best of two worlds. The argument seems to have died away lately, perhaps after some sage or other declared authoritatively that motorsailers make poor motorboats and worse sailboats. That could very well be true, but then again, they are still being built and no one has yet been able to prove that they are any worse than some of the stock auxiliaries that are sold today for "mom, dad, all the little kiddies, and the family dog." That's a lame argument for mediocrity, of course, much like the argument made by the spokesman for the last Republican administration in defense of mediocrity on the Federal bench, yet it does make sense to conclude that if you are going to have a lousy boat, you might as well have a lousy boat you can be comfortable on.

Dag Pike, an experienced boatman, makes a reasoned argument for the motorsailer:

**Motorsailers**
**by Dag Pike**
**David McKay Company, New York**
**224 pages, illus., 1976, $12.50**

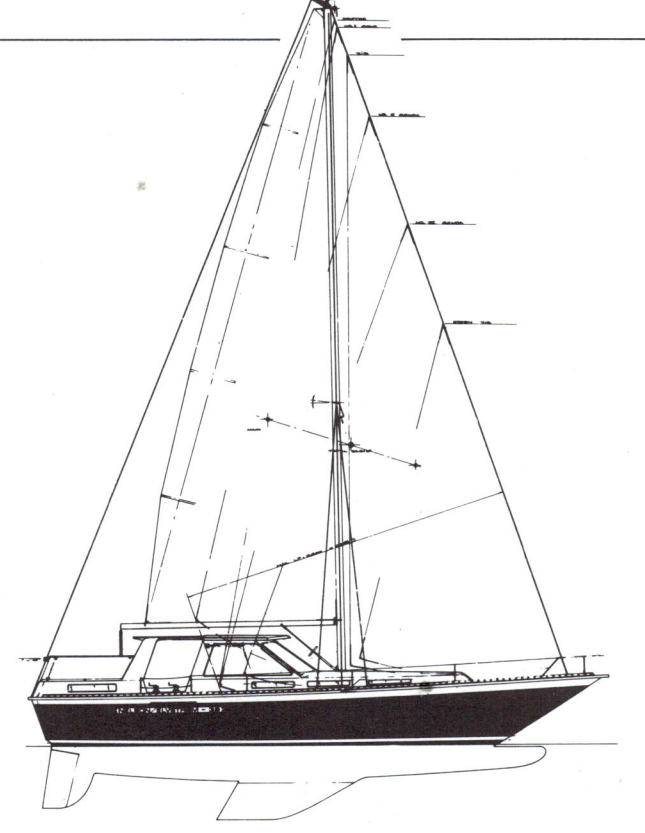

*From* Motorsailers.

*From* Hydrofoil Options.

## The AYRS Strikes Again

The Amateur Yacht Research Society in England is still going strong, doing what it does best—looking into the more technical, sometimes esoteric design problems surrounding modern sailing yachts. Their journal is a veritable goldmine of ongoing research results and advanced speculation, and their publications, many of which stress various applications of aerodynamics and hydrodynamics, are filled with the more-than-the-usual. We sometimes get lost in some of the theories and ideas AYRS publications present, but we're always impressed by the sheer desire of the authors to try to find answers to questions most others haven't even gotten around to asking.

Two new AYRS publications have crossed our desk, and, as expected, these booklets are filled with information for the curious:

***Hydrofoil Options***
**80 pages, illus., 1978, $4.00**

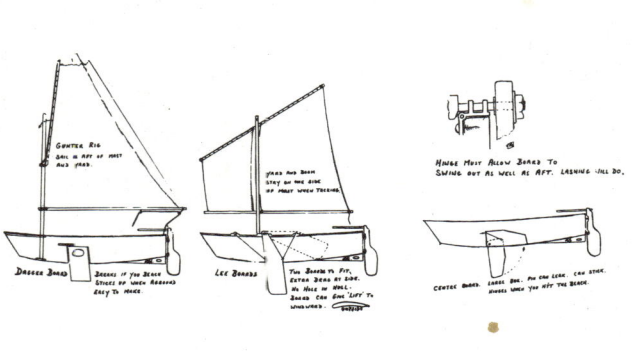

*Above and right: From* Yacht Tenders and Boats.

If you can accept that your tender does not need to fold into a bag, it is possible to have a proper rigid-bottom boat with inflatable sides. When stowed on deck the sides can be deflated leaving the bottom with a total depth of about 9 ins. A prototype of such a tender was shown at the 1976 Southampton Boat Show, and was available at the Players Speed Trials at Portland where a number of A.Y.R.S. members took the opportunity to try her. This boat started as a smaller version of the "Force Four" and is called "Force Three." Force Four is a speedboat for water-skiing and runabout, with a speed of over 20 knots, pushed by an outboard of 25 to 40 horsepower. From the same stable, the 'Force Three' has a rigid bottom and inflatable sides, and the makers claim that she is "designed to row, power, sail or waterski" and also that she is 'car-toppable.' Unfortunately, the ability to waterski comes under the heading "numerous secondary tasks a tender may be used for" and the ideal shape for water-skiing is not the best for sailing. An engine large enough for water-skiing becomes unreliable when working for long periods within the five or six knots speed limit reasonably imposed in most harbours to prevent just such tearaways imposing noise and wash on others. There is also the problem of lifting the larger engine on and off the parent yacht and providing the petrol.

and

***Yacht Tenders and Boats***
**64 pages, illus., 1977, $3.00**

Each book is essentially a forum, where members present ideas, which are then responded to by other readers. It's much like being in the middle of a seminar or a technical debate.

**Amateur Yacht Research Society
Hermitage, Newbury
Berkshire, England
Annual membership is $15.00**

## Home on the Waves

There's a difference between a houseboat and a boat that you live on. The latter is a conventional craft that is intended to put to sea on occasion when the mood strikes; the former is a house that floats, period.

Houseboats have always been around and have always had romantic symbolism—remember the one in James Fenimore Cooper's *The Last of the Mohicans*?—but it is only lately that they have become "in" in the sense that jogging, cross-country skiing, and, yes, wooden boats have become "in." Be that as it may, there's something about a houseboat....

Two books have been published recently that explore the mystique of the waterhome:

*Above: From* Houseboat. *Right: From* Waterhouses.

***Houseboat***
**by Ben Dennis and Betsy Case**
**Smuggler's Cove Publishing**
**107 West John St., Seattle, Wash.**
**1977, paperbound, $9.95**

and

***Waterhouses: The Romantic Alternative***
**by Ferenc Maté**
**Albatross Publishing House**
**Vancouver, B.C., Canada**
**1977, $14.95**

Both are filled with gorgeous color photography and limited text. Of the two, we prefer *Houseboat* for its essay on the history of houseboats and its awesome presentation. Both will make you wish you owned a houseboat; neither will tell you how.

"PERISHABLE FREIGHT NOT TAKEN."

## The Symposium Book
**Chiodi Advertising & Publishing Co.**
**North Quincy, Mass. 02171**
**270 pages, illus., paperbound, 1977, $16.50**

If monohulls had something to prove, you would see articles published with titles like "Monohulls—Are They Safe?", you would hear arguments rage in the Club about whether to stress self-righting ability or knockdown prevention, and you would hear about such events as the World Monohull Symposium. Monohulls have nothing to prove, but multihulls, for a variety of reasons, do. You've read the articles, listened to the arguments, and heard about the Symposium, which was held in Toronto in 1976. We have zero experience in multihulls, so will neither make an attempt to analyze the arguments nor offer solutions to the nagging questions.

We will, however, recommend *The Symposium Book,* which is a transcription of the World Multihull Symposium. The Symposium brought together this generation's greatest minds on multihulls—D.H. Clarke, Jim Brown, Rudy Choy, Norman Cross, Lock Crowther, Robert B. Harris, Edward B. Horstman, Derek H. Kelsall, J. Rod Macalpine-Downie, Hugo Myers, Richard Newick, Tom Roland, Andrew Simpson, and James Wharram.

The transcription, by the way, is verbatim, so along with the wheat you get a hefty amount of chaff, some in the form of half-finished sentences and impossible thoughts, others in the form of announcements and banter: "I have two short announcements. Movies will be shown in this room at 7 o'clock . . . The designer's forums start at 4 o'clock and the parlor numbers for each designer are posted at the Boutique."

**HORSTMAN:** I guess we'll put it this way. You buy an airplane and it's a 4-seat airplane and it has certain specifications and you're not to overload it. If you overload it, you're in danger. You buy a trimaran or a catamaran and it has the designer's weight limitations on it. The Coast Guard makes every manufacturer put those crazy things on there, which are not really crazy, they are there to protect the person that buys the boat. You find some individuals that overload conventional boats also and this detracts from their performance.

What I think we're all saying on this panel is that you can't overload a boat, and then go out to sea and be safe in it. And, yes, we as designers have that feeling for your safety. I know people that have bought and built a 27'9" with intentions of later building a 38-footer. Then when I went down to look at it, here they put a dog house on it this high, and said: "Well, I guess I couldn't afford the 38-footer, so I decided to get the same accommodations as a 38-footer." This boat is going to be overloaded. We are saying, that if you buy a boat, and it is placarded and safe for a certain number of pounds, that's it. Speed and other things are built into the hull, but multihulls main forte is performance, and with a certain load carrying capability...and that's just an inherent feature.

*Above: From* The Symposium Book.

## "You Are First"
### The Story of Olin and Rod Stephens of Sparkman & Stephens
**by Francis S. Kinney**
**Dodd, Mead, New York**
**327 pages, illus., index, 1978, $17.95**

*Dorade,* Blue Jay class, Lightning class, *Stormy Weather, Palawan, Baruna, Bolero, Finisterre,* the DUKW, Shields class, *Figaro, Columbia, Vim, Constellation, Intrepid, Courageous* . . . well, you get the point. This book tells all in very flattering terms, which you would expect since the author works for Sparkman & Stephens. We found the text difficult at times—probably caused by the overuse of a tape recorder. Yet for a detailed look at the Stephens brothers and their domination of American yachting for decades, there's no place else to turn.

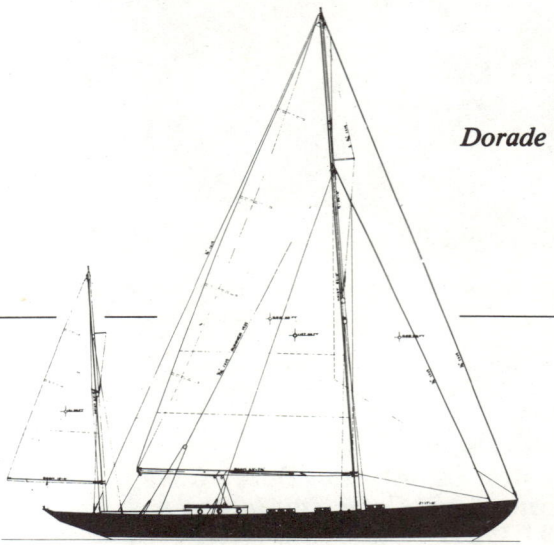

*Dorade*

What goes on in the S & S brokerage office is a different activity from the happenings at the firm's design office, where I work. Now both are together at 79 Madison Avenue, which is at 28th Street in New York City. I had a chat with Bob Garland about the brokerage aspect. He is the top yacht broker at S & S, and I wondered roughly what was the total yearly value of the boats he himself handled when buying, selling, and chartering for his clientele.

"Probably something over $3 million worth of yachts a year," he told me.

Then I asked, "Do you find that when there's an America's Cup Race you get more clients?"

"Well, I think there's a general heightening of interest in yachting," he replied, "and it's more apparent in the chartering of yachts during the summer, and a little more purchase and sale of boats going on. It's a big show, particularly the final trials, which seem to create more interest for knowledgeable yachtsmen than the Cup races themselves."

*Right: From* "You Are First."

*Power Yachts*
**by Rosemary and Colin Mudie
Granada Publishing
St. Albans, Herts., England
286 pages, illus., index, 1977,  £15**

Considering the prevailing attitudes about powerboats and the people who own them—that they are outrageous machines operated by incompetent speed freaks who don't have the brains to learn how to sail—few serious books are written and published on powerboats. Partners in their own yacht design business, the Mudies fortunately were undeterred by these attitudes and have written what has to be considered the powerboatman's guidebook. They discuss all aspects of power yachts, including construction, naval architecture and design, displacement and planing craft, engines, electrics, and such. The chapter entitled "Edge of Performance," while short, is worth the price of the book.

*Left, below, and bottom: From* Power Yachts.

### The Dancing Boat

All marine vehicles dance on the waters. Large ships move with an elephantine movement which only becomes impressive or even attractive in heavy seas. Small craft have movements varying from the ponderous through the graceful as far as the frenetic. But all have this individual quality of movement of a largely rhythmic character to make them dance with the largely rhythmic movement of the sea. Even a racing power boat doing its ridiculous belly-flops in rough water is responding to the sea with its own particular qualities of movement.

Human and animal dancers have muscles all over their bodies to influence their natural movements while boats have only the prop thrust and the incitement of the sea. Their quality of motion is therefore almost completely dependent on the distribution of weights within the volume of the vessel modified by the hydrodynamic values of the underbody form and the aerodynamics of the top.

Set a boat rolling in flat water and she will roll to a constant period like any other pendulum. The rolling is damped by the movement of the hull in the water, and the speed of damping depends on skin friction, keels, bilge keels and so on, plus the effect of the hull form. The rate at which, and the amount the hull has to be lifted and lowered bodily as it rolls up and down on its bilges can obviously have a big damping effect or, in some cases, if it should match the period of the hull weights, can reinforce the rolling. There is the occasional boat in most anchorages which is a real roller and which mysteriously keeps at it even in flat water. This phenomenon is more common to sailing boats than motor boats but illustrates the effect of hull shape on movement other than that of moving forward.

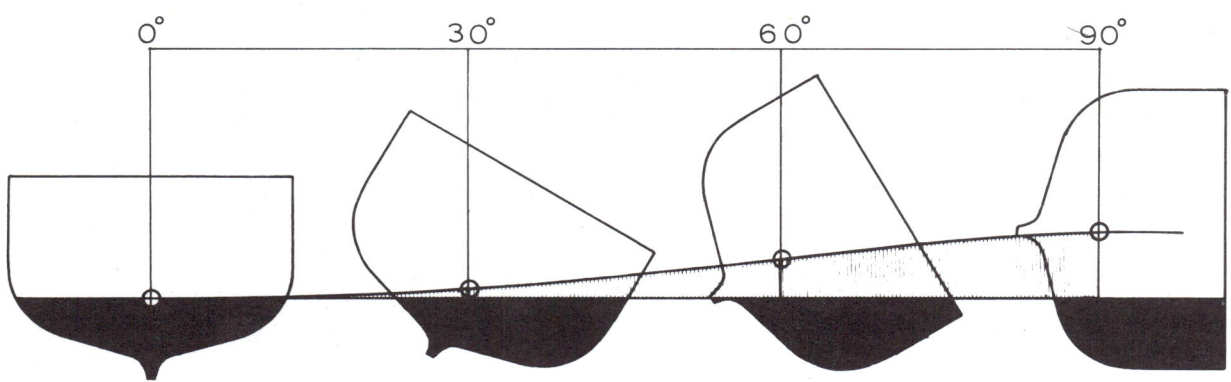

*Fig. 128  Many hulls have to be lifted bodily in the water when rolling, greatly increasing the energy need.*

# Canoes

As the cost and availability of clear cedar plankstock and canvas grapple with one another in a mutual deathgrip, epoxy-reinforced wood strip construction, the WEST™ system or its related kin, is slowly taking over the wood canoe business. We looked around with some diligence to discover a planked canoe factor that we had not yet listed, and didn't find one. So here are some more strippers:

Seven classy and classic models, including Rushton models offered nowhere else, plus four kits, from:

**The Bear Mountain Canoe Company**
**Bear Mountain**
**R.R.1**
**Powassan, Ontario**
**Canada P0H 1Z0**

We build longitudinal wood strip canoes combining traditional techniques and style with sophisticated space age engineering materials. Visually, they are reminiscent of the luxurious old timers like Rushton, Stephens, Walter Dean Lakefield, etc., yet their strength and durability would have to be rated with the toughest wilderness canoes available.

The hull is a high strength to weight ratio epoxy/fabric-wood-epoxy/fabric sandwich referred to as a "monocoque" structure. A monocoque structure gains its strength from the composite sandwich "skin" of the hull itself and does not require frames or ribbing. Our canoes are trimmed with black cherry and selected hardwoods, the seats are cane filled and brass is used for fastenings, stem bands and name plates engraved with your choice of inscription. We build all of our boats to order, and encourage input from our customers. We hope this initial involvement will begin a long love affair with their boat and that they will care for it with the same affection that built it.

—Bear Mountain Canoe Co.

*The 16-foot Rushton Ugo from Bear Mountain.*

Custom designs, from:

**Steve Redmond
4 Howard Street
Burlington, Vermont 05401**

**About our canoes:** The combination of western red cedar and a flexible glass and resin system yields a fiberglass sandwich canoe which combines the virtues of extreme light weight, toughness, and classic good looks. The fiberglassing schedule for these canoes calls for up to six layers of cloth in high stress areas. Maintenance consists of a once a year varnishing simply to remove a season's scratches and restore that first class finish. The simple maintenance of these canoes made possible by their glass sandwich construction will insure a lifetime of service, and incidentally, a high resale value.

Custom design services can provide a canoe tailored to the individual, while our presently expanding line of stock models provides an economical alternative for the average canoeist. All stock boats are high performance hulls, as compared with the usual run of recreational canoes, sacrificing some beam and initial stability for superior handling, speed and ability.

—**Steve Redmond**

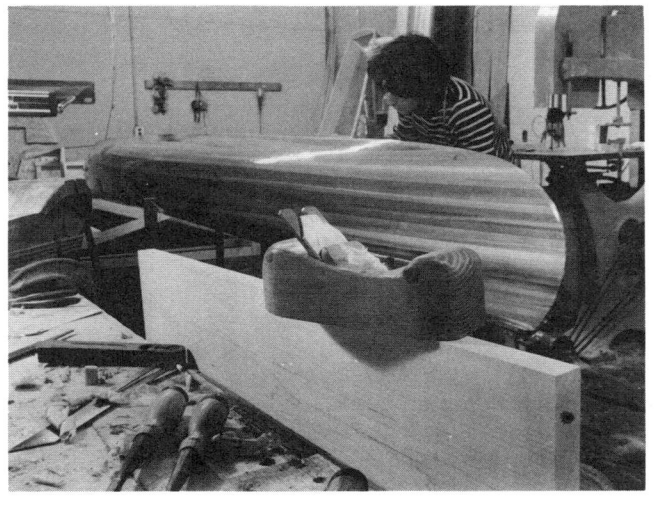

*Above: Steve Redmond's 16-foot tandem RT-16, a 50-pounder.*

A 16-foot 60-pounder, from:

**Cedar Creek Canoes
Bog Road
North Lebanon, Maine 04027**

The strong, lightweight ribless hull is cold molded by the WEST-System™*. Two ⅛" thick cross laminations of the highest grade vertical grain Western red cedar veneers are epoxy bonded under a vacuum process. The application of two coats of epoxy resin to both the inside and outside saturates all the surfaces of the wood, accomplishing the following:

1) The moisture level of the wood is held to a very low and constant level.
2) Strength and stiffness of the wood are greatly increased.

*(Wood Epoxy Saturation Technique)

—**Cedar Creek Canoes**

*Below: Cedar Creek's 16-footer.*

A one-man shop producing one-man Rob Roys:

**Pacific Boats
Route 3
Box 3378
Yelm, Washington 98597**

### Rob Roy Cruising Canoe

*Hull*—cold-molded of Western red cedar, using the WEST™ system. 3 layers of ⅛" coated inside and out with resin and finished with 2 coats of varnish. 1st and 3rd layer fore and aft.
*Deck*—3 layers of cedar with last layer fore and aft in laid deck pattern . . . coated with resin and 2 coats of varnish.
*Paddle*—made of Douglas fir in either right hand or left hand configuration. Double spoon blades. 8'3" long. . . Optional.

—**Pacific Boats**

*Below: The Rob Roy from Pacific Boats.*

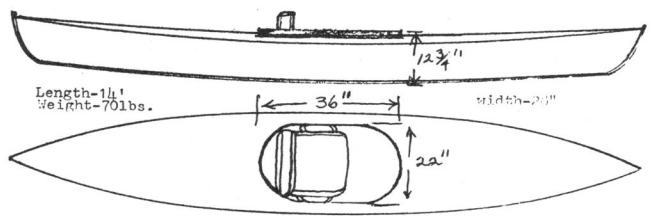

It is quite apparent that Old Town has been reading the mail. If you've a mind to do some strip building yourself, but are timid about the hassle for materials, Old Town now offers a *Canoe-in-a-Box*, for under $500. From:

**Old Town Canoe Company
Old Town, Maine 04468**

*Top and below: From Old Town.*

### CANOE-IN-A-BOX

To satisfy the growing interest in do-it-yourself canoe building, Old Town has developed a cedar strip wood canoe kit...the "CANOE-IN-A-BOX".

The only items the builder must furnish are some basic tools, a strong back frame and wooden forms cut from our paper patterns.

Everything is included in the kit; pre-cut cedar strips, resin, glass, glue, seats, decks, thwarts, etc. There are lots of plans for canoes but the problem for a canoe kit builder has always been where to buy quality wood. Old Town has solved this by using its many years of wood-buying knowledge to get the best cedar for our kit.

The wood we use is vertical straight grain western red cedar of the same selected high quality the famous Old Town wood canoes are made.

CANOE-IN-A-BOX KIT includes:
56 - 18 foot western red cedar strips
1 - bow and 1 - stern caned seats
1 - thwart
8 - dowel spacers
2 - decks
2 - sitka spruce inrails
2 - mahogany outrails
6 - ash strips
3 - gallons resin
1 - gallon glue
1 - gallon acetone
2 - 30" x 18' 6 oz. fiberglass cloth
2 - 60" x 18' 6 oz. fiberglass cloth
6 - 5" x 5' bias cloth
1 - pint wood sealer
1 - quart urethane varnish hardener
plastic strapping
brushes
rollers
nuts, bolts, washers, screws
complete instructions

We had not heard of many canoes or kayaks on the market in foam-sandwich construction until we found the 6-H line, herewith for those who prefer the method, from:

**6-H Products Ltd.
80 Hickson Ave.
Kingston, Ontario K7K 2N6
Canada**

*The decked Micmac from 6-H.*

*Above: The Mansfield Canoe from Stowe.*

Stowe has an interesting wrinkle in its fiberglass canoes, or two actually. First, the insides of their canoes are reinforced with ribs, no doubt providing added strength in addition to some visual legitimacy. They also build a 12-foot *boat* with the same construction technique. At a hundred pounds, there is not much that can compete with it.

**Stowe Canoe Company
Stowe, Vermont 05672**

*Canoe Design and Construction*
**by Alan Byde
Transatlantic Arts
Levittown, New York
176 pages, illus., index, 1975, $10.75**

We reviewed this book in MC-4, page 23, and gave it high marks. It was published by Pelham Books in England, and since then Transatlantic Arts has taken over American distribution. If you're interested in fiberglass canoe and kayak building, get it from them.

*Left: From* Canoe Design and Construction.

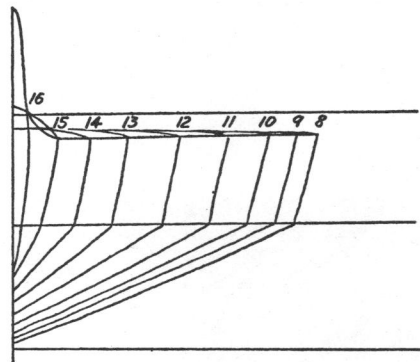

John Jacob is a guy whose business is selling canoe and kayak building plans. He has lots of them, and they look terrific. His brochure may be obtained thus:

**Jacob Design
Newport Boat Plans
4 Battery Street
Newport, Rhode Island 02840**

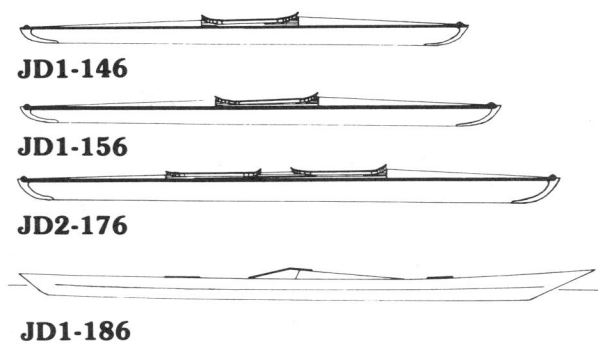

*Right: John Jacob's touring kayak designs.*

**The Big Drops: Ten Legendary Rapids
by Robert O. Collins and Roderick Nash
Sierra Club Books, San Francisco
256 pages, illus., maps, biblio., index, 1978, $18.50**

Taking small craft over thundering rapids and through foaming whirlpools takes some kind of brazenness and is a sport that is sometimes incomprehensible to a blue-water sailor. To the latter, it is not unlike intentionally sailing into the eye of a hurricane for the sheer hell of it, or navigating through New York harbor at midnight with the lights off and the lookout blindfolded. Traversing heavy white water in a canoe, boat, raft, or kayak is closer in spirit to downhill racing or ice climbing than it is to sailing or cruising, and because of that, it attracts the exhibitionist that lurks deep within our psyches. "I took a kayak through Hell's Half Mile" turns their heads ever so more quickly than, "We waited for slack water and slipped over the bar."

Fast water has a way of becoming slow water—you can blame the Corps of Engineers and hydroelectric developers for that—and the Sierra Club, the group of archetypal conservationists and environmentalists, works hard to at least stall things. *The Big Drops* is a weapon in their arsenal, a method of telling us what we have and, by inference, what we are likely to lose. History, geography, over- and understatement—they have used it all to make a monument to 10 stretches of North America that turn river runners' legs to soggy pasta. The book will do one of two things to you: make you a tireless water conservationist or a tither in favor of the Corps of Engineers to rid us of crazy exhibitionists.

A major river like the Snake magnetizes dam builders. In 1941 a group of engineers ran Hells Canyon on a business trip. Asked by reporters if they had experienced any "thrills" on the trip, their spokesman coolly replied, "We were impressed by the rapids rather than thrilled." What did thrill the engineers was the abundance of dam sites in the canyon. In the ensuing years some in the upper gorge were utilized: for Brownlee Dam (1958), Oxbow Dam (1961), and Hells Canyon Dam (1967). Drowned under reservoirs were most of the original Big Drops of Hells Canyon, including Buck Creek Rapid. Indeed, only eighty-five miles of free-flowing river remained after the dam builders finished their work. Then, seizing on a Federal Power Commission recommendation that more dams in Hells be authorized, utility companies made plans to complete the taming of the Snake. If these plans had been implemented, Granite Creek Rapid would have gone the way of Buck Creek and the others. But a 1967 Supreme Court decision, spearheaded by a longtime friend of wilderness, Justice William O. Douglas, forced reconsideration. The Court simply asked if the Federal Power Commission had considered the option of building no more dams at all on the Snake, and sent the case back for further study.

*Above: From* The Big Drops.

Dear Editors:

You ought to check out the Northwest River Supply catalog (214 N. Main, P.O. Box 9243, Moscow, Idaho 83843): 12 river-running rafts, accessories, pumps, 10' oars, manganese *or* silicon bronze oarlocks, oarlock stands, waterproof bags, wet suits and everything else you can think of for river running. This is probably the last occupation going where you can earn a living pulling a pair of oars so the "state of art" comments are pretty interesting: John Gardner would not be happy with nylon rope "leathering" or hose clamp "buttons" I'm sure, but it seems to be the popular western way. Sorry I can't furnish a copy of the catalog.

—P.F. Jacobs
FPO Seattle, Washington

# Ice Boats

Several correspondents have written to ask about ice boats; how come we never say anything about ice boats? I don't know; it's hard to design space for a berth maybe? The cooking is poor? They're a drag in July? They scare the yabadabadooy out of me? Actually, a friend of ours has one of the old 19th-century models that has big, long outriggers up forward and weighs about a thousand pounds. With the old kind like her you can put a dozen people aboard and skitter along very nicely, with the ¾-inch-thick skate irons barking and scrintching pleasantly.... Fun, and your heart stays out of your throat. You have to make one of these yourself. For the more modern, forward-steering zippers there are perhaps a dozen well-known models, either complete or in kit form. Here are three:

The Arrow is a big and growing class iceboat with championship regattas held under the auspices of the National Iceboat Authority. Cockpit is open.

**Arrow Iceboats
P.O. Box 126
Mt. Clemens, Michigan 48043**

*The two-seater Arrow. Sail area is 80 square feet.*

A bit larger and with a closed cockpit is the Nite, from:

**S & R Marine
501 Hickory Street
Pewaukee, Wisconsin 53072**

*The Nite weighs in at 260 pounds. Sail area is 67 square feet.*

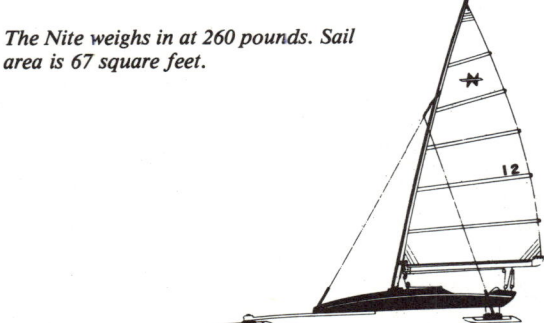

A bit smaller and less costly, the Skimmer 45, from:

**Lockley Recreational Products Division
310 Grove Street
New Castle, Pennsylvania 16103**

*Lockley's Skimmer.*

## Real Men

On northern lakes in the winter, and on some tidal estuaries, too, you'll sometimes see people staring at holes in the ice. These people are engaged in one of the last macho sports around—ice fishing, an unorganized yet highly ritualistic method of proving to all who care about such things that they are Real Men. Ice fishing is hardly what you would call fast paced, yet it takes a tremendous amount of endurance to keep from freezing before the fish do. As you can imagine under the circumstances, booze is a large part of the game, not to mention other ingenious ways of staying warm, such as catalytic hand warmers, heated chair cushions, and newspapers stuffed in boots.

If we were to become ice-fishing cultists (though not too likely; we do our drinking in the local saloon), our guide would be:

*Ice Fishing*
**by Gene Little
Contemporary Books, Chicago, Ill.
186 pages, illus., index, 1975, paperbound, $4.95**

*Right: From Ice Fishing.*

Staying warm, finding bait, using lures, cutting holes in ice, spearfishing, where to go, etc.

Joe Upton has fished both West and East Coasts in various boats for numerous species with all kinds of gear. This year he's taking a crack at East Coast groundfish with automatic jiglines. We asked him why and he said on account of the girls(?). Anyway, his *Alaska Blues*, a book describing his experiences in the salmon fisheries in Southwestern Alaska, is wonderful (see review in MC-6, p. 120).

*Above: Hand troller in evening fog, Point Baker, Alaska. (Joe Upton)*

## Skiff Trolling
### by Joe Upton

My friend Byron built his boat right from scratch for hand trolling. He built it at his folks' house in Seattle one winter; his only design criteria were that it be trailerable so he could get it on the ferry to Alaska, he had to be able to haul halibut over the side, and it had to be cheap and easy to build. It's just a big pram, but *big*, 16 feet long with an easy 6 feet of beam. Oak skids on the bottom, so he could go up on a beach, and a 16-hp Briggs and Stratton for power, a couple of belts and sheaves for the reduction gear.

One spring I was at Port Protection, buying some grub at the trading post there, when he came in from the outside coast. He'd been following the fish and camping on the beach for a month or so. That "skiff" of his was just about overflowing with stuff, but he still had almost two feet of freeboard. He had a Sportyak, all his

*Two hand trollers at the float, Point Baker. (Joe Upton)*

camping gear, a couple of boxes of food, fishing gear—salmon and halibut—plus at least 500 pounds of old rail wheels for ballast, all in a 16-footer! He was sitting there at the tiller he carved; in front of him were two old army packs full of dirty clothes and crumpled-up charts.

(continued on following page)

*Hand trollers' laundry day, Port Protection. (Joe Upton)*

(continued from previous page)

He told me he fished the outside—Cape Ulitka, Granite Point, etc.—with the big boys. That's the ocean out there, big and mean. He said once he swamped, got in a rip, and a queer one came right over the rails and pretty much filled him, killed the engine. He figured that was it, she was going down for sure, when out of nowhere a big troller appeared, threw him a line, and started steaming easy, so his skiff would stay on top. He threw over his ballast and bailed like crazy. Lucky. Said he had looked around just a moment before it all happened, hadn't been another boat in sight.

But Byron's unusual—my mother used to call him "iron men and wooden ships." Most of the skiff trolling is right around Point Baker or a few other spots in southeastern Alaska; there aren't too many who go outside like that now. Years ago there were little camps up and down the coast where the skiff fishermen used to camp on the beach for weeks at a time, going after the kings in the spring and the silvers in the summer, selling their fish to little buying scows anchored up in the coves, maybe even with a shower too, if they were lucky. But those days are gone now—in a few places you can still see the ruins of the old shacks but that's about it—the regulations have changed so much now that skiff trollers aren't even allowed to go most places on the outside.

But still, for a little summertime low overhead fishery, skiff fishing/hand trolling's hard to beat, especially with salmon prices so high. There is no cheaper way to get into the salmon business—especially if a guy is a scrounger. Around the Point there, you can get away with a 14-foot boat and a 10-horse outboard, or even less. Your fishing gear consists of a "gurdy," some stainless wire, a lead, and a bunch of leaders, snaps, and lures or hooks. Half the gurdies are just plywood reels, a hand crank made out of pipe fittings, and a brake out of a leather strap.

Our fleet there consists of everything from Boston Whalers with twin Mercs on down to plywood creations held together with roofing tar and good luck. A few of the old Davis skiffs are still around too—40 years old or older—beautiful boats built specifically for the skiff fishery in the Thirties and earlier. Point Baker was a big center then for skiffs—they didn't even fish outside then—just trolled in the harbor—rowing! I've seen

*Skiff troller hauling gear. (Joe Upton)*

*Above: "Flea," oldest hand troller at Point Baker. (Joe Upton)*

With a narrow entrance and the trees almost meeting overhead, opening up to a lake-like bay, it's a fine spot to lie. Occasionally the fish will be running on the far side of the straits or in among the islands—there's an old homestead there with a grassy field sloping down to the cove, another good place to camp and fish.

Hand trolling has been the fastest-growing salmon fishery for the last few years; it still remains the only salmon fishery that an individual may enter without purchasing a "limited entry" permit for the going price of many tens of thousands of dollars. Many of the larger power trollers are seeking to reduce the numbers of hand trollers that they see as a threat to their livelihood.

Still, in a fishing industry that is becoming increasingly capital- and technology-intensive, hand trolling for salmon in small boats in southeastern Alaska is a refreshing change. Few boats even have sounders; at Point Baker, the best fishing area is less than a mile away from the bar that floats on huge logs in the middle of the harbor. Yet, due to the high prices fishermen now receive for their fish, the skiff fishery is very much a viable fishery economically.

And even if it weren't, how can you beat tying up your skiff, selling your fish for cash, strolling down the dock, and stepping into the bar with the big sign over the counter—"Point Baker—Where the fishing gets interesting"?

*Below: Fifty-four pound king salmon landed from a skiff. (Joe Upton)*

faded pictures of the harbor in those days with several men visible in their Davis skiffs—standing up, facing forward, and rowing.

For a long time it slowly faded out; for a while Flea, an older man, was the only one left, going out each summer day in a tired old boat when the tide turned. Then young Byron came, then a few others, the price of fish took a big jump, and now it's not unusual to see 30 or more skiffs out there when the silvers are running, in August. If the fish are running down at Hole on the Wall, some boats will lay up for the night there, camp.

# Models and Modeling

"The real shipping magnate of the yachting world."

*Index of Model Periodicals*
**1971 through 1975
by Paul Cardwell, Jr.
The Scarecrow Press, Metuchen, New Jersey 08840
789 pages, 1977, $27.50**

A book for the real enthusiast and for libraries. This index is very weak on marine and nautical modeling, and is of interest here primarily because it has strong sections on tools and shop techniques that can, of course, be applied to one's own purposes.

*Below: From* Index of Model Periodicals.

Magazines indexed:
*AFV G2, Aeromodeller, Air Enthusiast/Air International, Airfix Magazine, American Aircraft Modeler, Armies & Weapons, Aviation News, Flying Models, Fusilier, IPMS Magazine, IPMS Quarterly, Military Modelling, Model Airplane News, Model Boats, Model Railroader, Modelworld, NMRA Bulletin, Narrow Gauge and Short Line Gazette, PAM [Plastic Aircraft Modeller] News, RC Sportsman, Radio Control Modeler, Railroad Model Craftsman, Random Thoughts, Replica in Scale, Scale Models, Sword & Lance, World War 2 Journal.*

Whenever possible we like to locate competition for the would-be Only Ones. Here's the Precision Petite you may want to consider along with the Dremel. PP also makes an interesting plastic welder.

**Precision Petite Ltd.
119a High Street
Teddington
Middlesex TW11 8HG, England**

*Above: The Precision Petite welder and drill.*

Sometimes you just forget to list the obvious. Oh, well, better late than never. X-Acto carries on in its limitless way, with a full line of modeling tools; someone with whom to grow, as have others before.

**X-ACTO**
**45-35 Van Dam Street**
**Long Island City, N.Y. 11101**
**Catalog is $1.00**

*X-Acto's stripper.*

People who are seriously interested in small-scale tooling should have the Cal-Lab catalog at hand. Micro-machine tools, screws, pins, locks, washers, etc.

**Caltronic Laboratory**
**461 S. Cochran Ave.**
**Box 36356**
**Los Angeles, California 90036**

"Hardsteel" tools employ friction drilling to drill, countersink, counterbore, and ream hardened steel, eliminating need to anneal before drilling. The straight flute design employs three bearing surfaces with chip clearance grooves. The drill cuts only on the bearing surfaces, not the sides. Bearing surfaces are maintained by grinding the drill tip to a simple pyramid point. In addition to sizes shown below, Black Drill will supply from stock drills from No. 52 to 1-inch, number and letter. Other sizes to 2½-inch to order. Complete selection of mm sizes also available.

*From the Caltronic Laboratory catalog.*

Listed previously in another context, the GLHS also offers plans for ship modelers, including plans for the *Edmund Fitzgerald* of modern-day tragedy and balladeering.

**The Great Lakes Historical Society**
**480 Main Street**
**Vermilion, Ohio 44089**

## Interesting Kit Sources

One aspect of nautical enthusiasm, and certainly much of marine modeling, that is a little disturbing is the tendency to be nostalgic, to pay attention only to the past as against the present, to think of the past as somehow better. The truth of it is, of course, that those who experienced the past as the present thought it all a big drag and would have peddled their grandmothers to enjoy our maritime conveniences.

The usual—and frankly a little prurient—way in which model kit companies respond to this is to produce clippers and schooners on the one hand and Formula RC blastmobiles on the other. So it is rather nice when a company comes out with a line of model kits in wood of the real modern-day marine craft that do the world's real work. Sterling is offering such a line, here represented by their *Caltex Lumba-Lumba*, an S&S-designed marine petro personnel carrier operating out of Singapore.

**Sterling Models Inc.**
**Sterling Building**
**3620 "G" Street**
**Philadelphia, Pennsylvania 19134**

*The Caltex Lumba-Lumba, with an overall length of 38½ inches.*

We know of no other source of Chinese junk kits than:

Ship Models, Inc.
Route 2, Box 307
Sultan, Washington 98294.

As is evident from this illustration, these models have been simplified in many respects. But, they are all wood—even the sails—a fun curiosity, surely. Kit for this one is $62, $200 all built.

NYLET offers five class RC sail model racing kits that look to be slippery fine sailers. They're English, so you may want to check with domestic rules to see whether there is a class here in which you can race one of the limey hulls. On the other hand, and come to think of it, don't. If you like it, buy it and sail it. Be the only one with a boat like yours. Beat their socks off.

NYLET Ltd.
118-122 Station Road
Fordingbridge, Hampshire, England

And for you who want the thrills, spills, and chills without spending your salad days in a truss and dialysis machine, RC and model power train technology hold no candle but for size to the real thing. Hulls, engines, mounts, trimtabs, dual rudders, redundant systems—everything is now available in configurations that leave little to the imagination. Amazing.

From England there is a full line of hulls and accessories:

S.H.G. Marine
Unit C4
Stafford Park 2
Telford, Salop, England

*Below: An offshore racer from S.H.G.*

Dozens of hulls from:

Model Exports Ltd.
320 St. John Street
London EC1V 4NT, England

*Left: From the Model Exports Ltd. catalog.*

*Remember, that postage is very high these days. (How can you forget?) Be sure to include a return post coupon when corresponding abroad.*

Slick, yachty things from:

**Stratos Models
19 Earsham Street
Bungay, Suffolk, England**

*Below: A 34-incher from Stratos.*

And believe that the Swedes shall not be left behind either. The Brandt gear is almost spooky.

**Brandts Hobby
Smedjegatan 28
552 40 Jönköping, Sweden**

*Below: Realism from Brandts Hobby.*

**Happiness is model boating.**

You can even start your model's engine from where you stand now, with Lectra-Starter, from:

**Eastcraft Specialty Products
709 Longboat Ave.
Beachwood, New Jersey 08722**

*Eastcraft also offers the Sea Tiger, a larger displacement mill for larger displacement boats.*

Many times we have listed sources of steam engines and fittings, but stock hulls for them are not so common, and it's fun to be able to list one as nice as *Diana*. The cast propeller made for her is really a piece of jewelry. Nice going, Steamfitter!

**The Steamfitter
R.D. 3, Box 326
Chestertown, Maryland 21620**

*Below: The cast propeller for the model of Westy Farmer's* Diana.

## Breeches Buoy

You get a little funny sometimes. Cuckoo. Hootier than a barn full of owls, etcetera. You have to be around boat-nuts, really. When you consider how many things there are that most people would not dream of being able to afford, and then see them plunge into boating or, rather, out of boats they have purchased, it helps to be a little peculiar yourself, not so much for any understanding it might provide, but for the Fellowship.

Take marine model shows: For twenty dollars' worth of materials and a very inexpensive array of simple tools, one can spend several hundreds of hours fabricating a model of any ship or craft that ever floated, or that would have if it existed. It is a way of taking out the frustrations of not inheriting a chain of department stores. (Of course, if you spent the same amount of time pumping gas or clamming, you could buy the bloody real thing.) Anyway, people who do this sort of thing exist in great numbers and, once in a while, get together under sundry auspices and have model shows wherein they display their compulsive skills and wares.

Here is a three-speed coffee-grinder winch a quarter-inch high that really works. Over there is a suit of sails hand woven from a spider's web to provide authentic scale-size stitching. Two booths away is a ¾-inch-scale rowboat rowed by a model mechanical man with scale dandruff and rumors that his marriage is in jeopardy. And so on.

The day of the show passes slowly, the judges moving from display to display, the craftsmen milling about, mumbling over their fellows' sins of omission and sharing, carefully even-steven, secret techniques. Through this skillful haze an awestruck public passes, including children who cannot imagine possessing such wonderful toys.

I cannot help myself. I've tried and tried to cast off this awful curseful thought, but cannot. Like wanting to shout something Truly Weird between movements at a symphony orchestra concert, I have this nagging desire to submit a well-done piece to one of these modeling shows and, drawing fellow entrants into technical conversation, hold up the exquisite little preciousness as if to make a point, and crush it into a mangled maelstrom of terrific pocket lint. The sheer glory of it....

Another fun thing to do would be to plank a whale. There would be nothing to it, really. You wait for a whale to come ashore, bury it in an anthill until the tissues are gone, and then bolt on planks bow to stern around the ribcage. Then you can flip it over and go shrimping, sterndragging, or even gunkholing. With the right attitude, it would be a cheap and easy whaleboat.

—GP

About once a year Louis Davison adds to their list of Waterline Shipmodelers' Planbook Series. This year it's U.S. Submarines, from:

**Louis Davison**
**3531 Milford**
**Pensacola, Florida 32506**

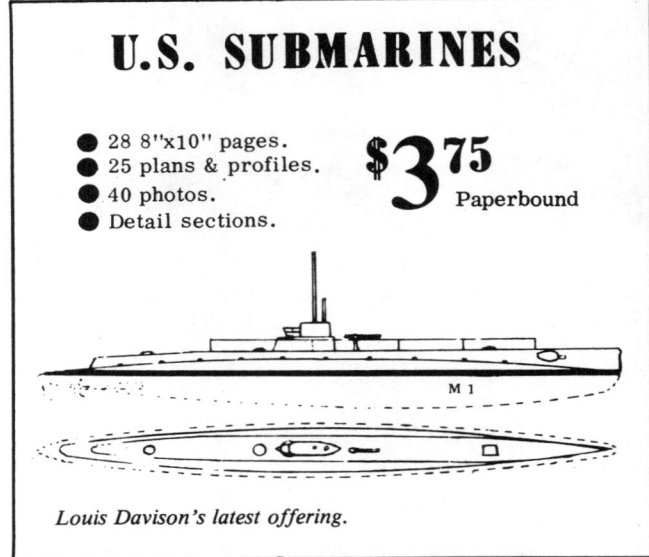

*Louis Davison's latest offering.*

Finally, we've gone right to a source, the printer, of the list of working drawings of Harold A. Underhill. There are two sections, power craft and sailing ships.

**Bassett-Lowke Ltd.**
**Kingswell Street**
**Northampton, NN1 1PS, England**

*From the Bassett-Lowke catalog.*

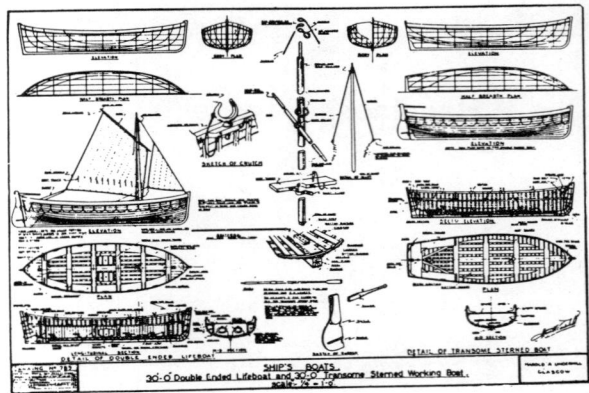

This English outfit is offering a line of navy ship kits that lie halfway between the fully built-up model and the carved hull method. British destroyers, frigates, corvettes, minesweepers, and other types are offered. They look to be good ones for the intermediate-level craftsman. From:

> Woodcraft
> Back Greenwell Street
> Darlington, Durham DL1 5DJ
> England

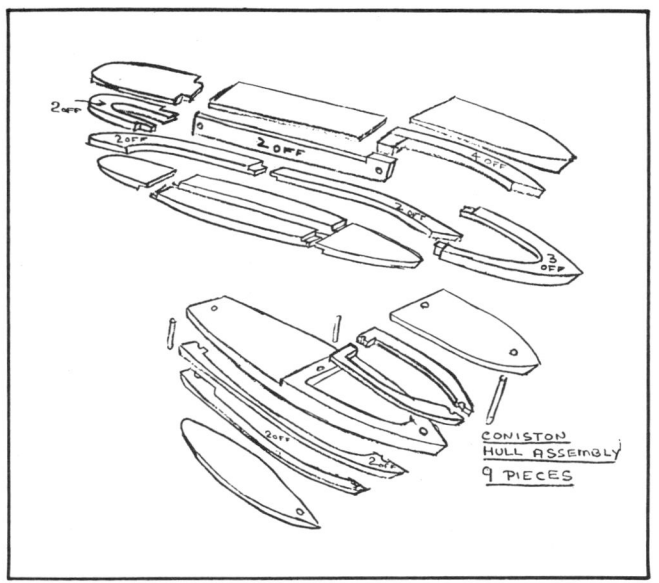

*Kits from Woodcraft.*

***Building Model Ships from Scratch***
**by Kent Porter**
**Tab Books**
**Blue Ridge Summit, Pennsylvania 17214**
**368 pages, paperbound, 1977, $7.95**

Most books on modeling ships and boats introduce the subject with some 10 or 20 pages on "the easy method," that is, building up the hull using waterline lifts and then sanding to fair lines. They then merrily graduate to "the real thing" and devote the remainder of the book to the regular construction techniques that signal the "real" model builder.

We are not entirely convinced that a better afterlife awaits the frame-and-plank builder over the lift builder, and this 368-page book begins and ends generally assuming the use of the lift system, which is perfectly acceptable in the company of people who don't have a little leprechaun to go below in the model and bring back a report of the truth. There is a chapter on the frame-and-plank method, however. While the drawings are not a draftsman's *tour de force*, there are lots of them and they show good detail omitted by other well-known texts on the subject. The book offers good value.

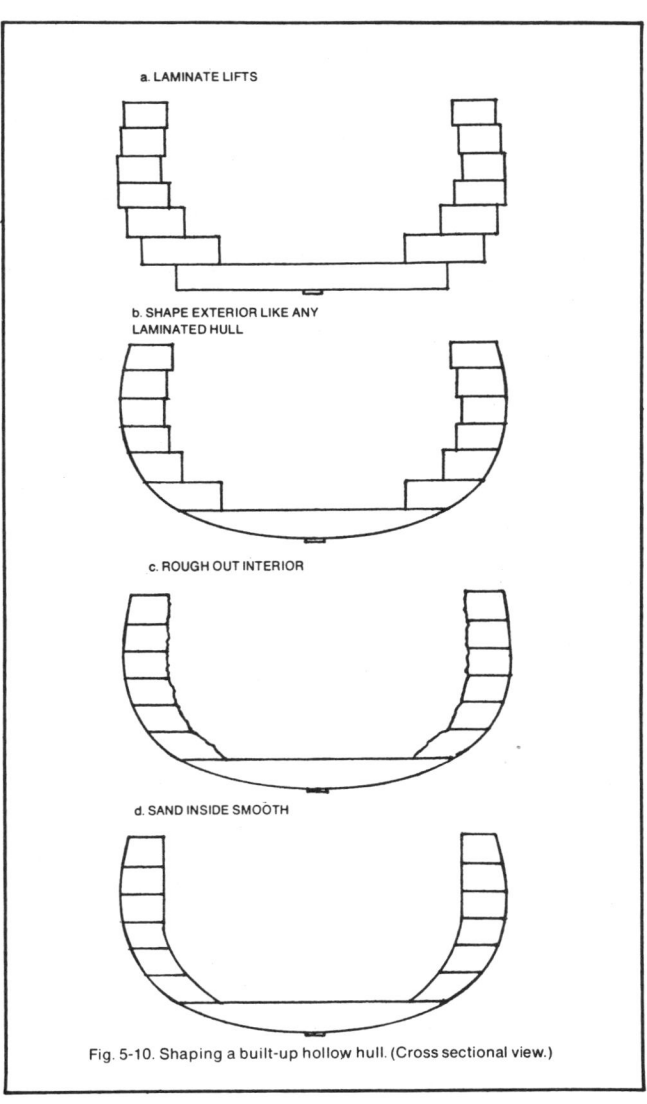

Fig. 5-10. Shaping a built-up hollow hull. (Cross sectional view.)

*From* Building Model Ships from Scratch.

# Shoreside Structures, not to mention moorings

THE HARBOURMASTER.

Somewhere between the barefoot kid walking a half-mile through the puckerbrush to the edge of the salt marsh where he keeps his simple punt hidden in the esparto grass, drags it across the mud and slips it into the stream and so to adventure, and the executive who drives to the 2,000-boat marina in his other car to find Pier 87 where, a half-mile out on the docks, he boards his twin-52, there must be something like moderation possible. Of course there is; and here are some thises and thats for such 'longshore places.

## Boat Handling Stuff

There are very few small boatyards left that have not run out of storage room right at the yard. More and more they are having to contract for room on vacant lands in the area. For those yards not sufficiently capitalized for a large travel hoist and whose local police department is clamping down on dragging cradled boats over public roads, Hydrahoist may be just the ticket; various models from:

**Marine & Yacht Services
Lake City, Minnesota 55041**

*Hydrahoist's boat trailer.*

Shoreside elevators and powered davits in several configurations are offered by:

**Mechanical Methods Co.
3400 S. Federal Hwy.
Fort Lauderdale, Florida 33316**

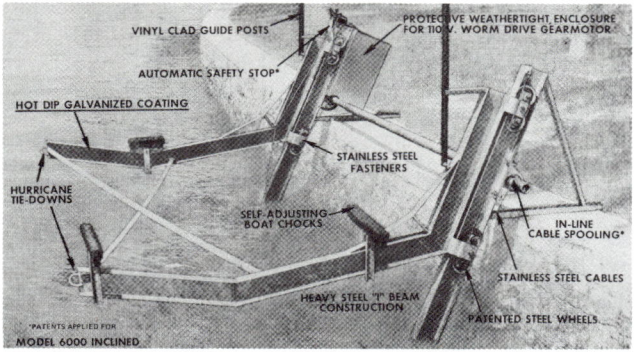

*Bottoms up from Mechanical Methods.*

If you've ever poked around in large warehouses with overhead cranes and observed what a convenience they are, and wondered whether anyone offers small and medium ones that would work in a boatyard or indoor storage facility, so have we. Found one in the Mini-Crane Kits offered by:

**DEMAG Material Handling Corp.
29201 Aurora Road
Solon, Ohio 44139**

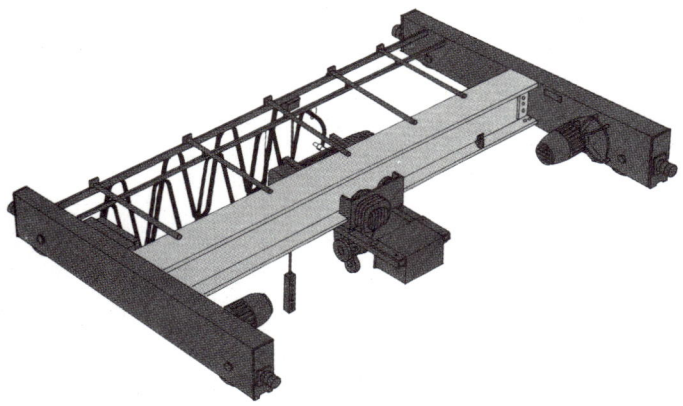

**Kit Selection Table**

| Kit No. | Capacity (lbs.) | Hoist Model | Lift (ft.) | Lift Speed (FPM) | Hoist H.P. | Hoist Trolley Speed (FPM) | Hoist Trolley H.P. | Trolley Flange Width Adjustment | Shipping Weight |
|---|---|---|---|---|---|---|---|---|---|
| MCK-2 | 2,000 | EKPL82 4/1 | 18 | 20 | 2.5 | 56 | .25 | 6-1/2,8,10 | 1,350 lbs. |
| MCK-4 | 4,000 | EKPL84 4/1 | 18 | 20 | 2.5 | 56 | .25 | 6-1/2,8,10 | 1,350 lbs. |
| MCK-6 | 6,000 | EKPL168 4/1 | 18 | 16 | 4 | 56 | .25 | 8,10,12 | 1,500 lbs. |
| MCK-10 | 10,000 | EKP210G8H11L 4/1 | 18 | 16 | 6.5 | 56 | .75 | 10,11-1/2, 12 | 2,000 lbs. |

*Mini-Cranes from DEMAG.*

And a more modest and reasonably priced setup is offered by:

**Hartsell Boat Hoist Mfg. Co.
Airport Rd., Rt. 4
Box 546A
Rockingham, North Carolina 28379**

*The Mighty Midget from Hartsell.*

If you have in mind the fabrication of your own rig, but are looking for a source of those powerful hoist slings to hook onto it, Minderman has them. They also have a classy-looking boatyard carrier.

**Minderman Marine Mfg. Co.
215 Buckeye Blvd.
Box 269
Port Clinton, Ohio 43452**

*Minderman's boatyard carrier.*

## A Few Dock, Wharf, & Float Things

If oil drums and plastic foam bats don't appeal, SuperCraft carries linear polyethylene floats in round or square section, also dock modulars, brackets, leveling jacks, even slides and diving boards.

**SuperCraft Products**
**R.R.1, Box 56A**
**Center Harbor, New Hampshire 03226**

*Make your own with help from Super-Craft.*

And a heavy-duty line is distributed by Marine Docks, which also has begun a newsletter about docking called *Marine Dock Lines*, from:

**Marine Docks**
**Box 70**
**West River Road**
**Waterloo, New York 13165**

Would you believe a 48-foot-long Boat House for $2,250? You wouldn't? Shame. No doubt that at press time prices will be a bit higher, but Loretex, another reinforced plastic fabric, makes it possible, from:

**York Marine**
**P.O. Box 204**
**Yarmouth, Maine 04096**

Paging through *Boats & Harbors* not long ago, we came to an ad for portable bridge pontoons. In a fit of panic at the thought that some lonely reader was pining away for not being able to find one, we got the scoop. Tell your friends. We think they're neat. Wish we had a bridge to cross. Wouldn't burn it after crossing, either. From:

**Southeastern Equipment Company, Inc.**
**P.O. Box 5438**
**Augusta, Georgia 30906**

*Bridge pontoon from Southeastern Equipment.*

For the po' folk who have to step down to the dock, we mention this nonfederally supported aid, the Accommodation Boarding Ladder, from:

**Don Allen, Inc.**
**So. Pacific Ave.**
**San Pedro, California 90731**

*Don Allen's ladder.*

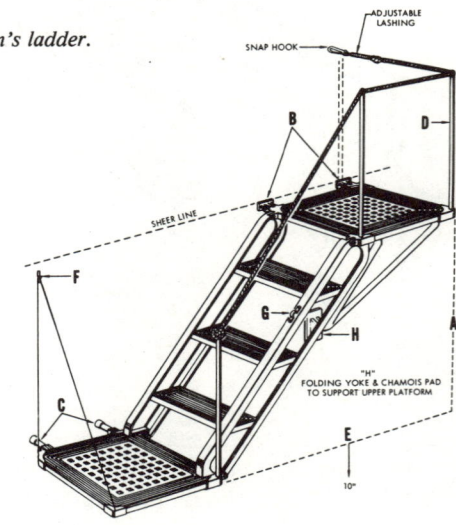

Sailing Specialties is one of those venture outfits that offers such a range of clever things marine that it is hard to figure out where to place them: companionway screens, helmsman seats, cockpit tables, and other unique items. However, we'll place them here because of the plastic piling caps they offer. From:

**Sailing Specialties, Inc.
P.O. Box 527
Lexington Park, Maryland 20653**

The Stamford Packaging Company has improved two things: the strength and resilience of polyethylene plastic through woven reinforcement, and the old rock-and-string trick with tie-downs. Size for size against tarps, it looks to be about a half to a third of the price, from:

**Stamford Packaging Co.
P.O. Box 3091
Stamford, Connecticut 06905**

*The classiest pilings around, from Sailing Specialties.*

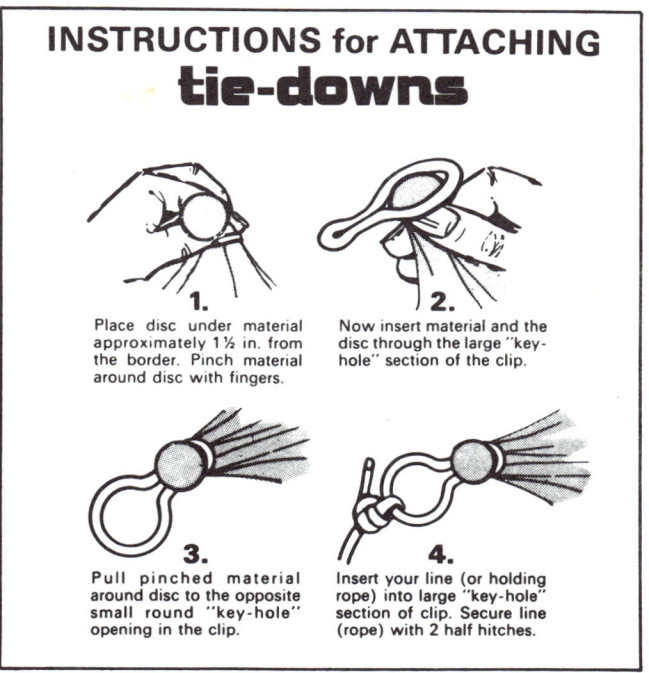

*Stamford's tie-downs.*

## A Small-Craft Mooring System

### by Pete Culler

I have a mooring system when I use a small craft directly off a protected beach; obviously, it cannot suit all shores, exposed or not, but for the place I use it, it has worked fine for many years. I use a 35-pound stock anchor because that's what I have; in most harbor bottoms, a modest mushroom or a fair-size Navy anchor would do just as well. I suggest it be considerably bigger than you think your small craft (such as a sailing skiff or dory) would need. It can be quite awkward and rusty; you only put it down and take it up once a year. The idea is to have something the boat can't move under any conditions. Fast to this anchor is a chain pendant about a fathom or so long; depending on your location, you may want it longer. Mine is overly heavy because I happen to have ½-inch chain somewhat rusted. Shackled to it is an iron bail or big ring, again ½-inch diameter, squeezed hot around a large round thimble about 3 inches diameter. This big thimble is essential; small ones choke with weed, small stones, and shells. What you can get away with is a matter of what kind of bottom you have.

Once hauled out, the boat is in about a fathom of water. The length of line required to accomplish this, at this particular location and range of tide, is about 250 feet. This is rove through the big thimble and the ends are bent to each other and stopped. Attached to this bend is a ½-inch pendant about 9 feet long, ending in a float buoy with a piston-type bronze snaphook, large for the job. It needs to be the pattern that can't come open itself, like the kind used on large racing boat spinnakers. In fact, the whole of the line is castoff Dacron, the main haulout being ⅝-inch stuff from a large racing craft. Whether you like synthetic line or not (and for some things I hate it), for continuous underwater use, this secondhand Dacron has given nine years of wonderful service. I've renewed the short ½-inch pendant a

*(continued on following page)*

*(continued from previous page)* couple of times, for it, being more or less upright in the water, grows weed and barnacles. The long haulout, being on the bottom and dragging in the sand, grows very little. To cut the fouling of the lighter pendant, I parcel it with synthetic sail-cloth strips marled down with synthetic net twine. Then I copper paint it, a custom of a big yacht harbor near here. This makes for very long-lived pendants, even though they foul up in spite of the paint. Oh yes, my bronze snapshackle is of the swivel type, and I must say that its service has been excellent, having been made by a well-known yacht hardware outfit no longer in business. It is doing work it was not intended for, although the loads on it are far lighter than when it was racing.

What it amounts to is an endless line, with pendant and buoy, leading to an offshore anchor. The idea is rather like those clothes lines you see strung between buildings in a city. I take the shore end to a piling just because it's there; a stake can be put down if needed. I have a mark on my line so I don't get turns in it; if they do get in, a bit of common sense will get them out. This is a most successful rig. The boat hauled out is out to the chain, and when she gets to jumping heavily, this chain takes up the jerks. My Swampscott used this setup for years, and she's a nervous type, prone (as all dories are) to much dancing and thrashing on occasion. The haulout was easy on her. My present wherry, although far more sophisticated than the dory, is very staid in her movements on the mooring and very full of go underway. She's easy on herself and the mooring. Both boats have a dory strap—tarred and served where it chafes—that goes through holes back of the stem, with a thimble seized in for the snaphook. The whole setup is about as unchafeable and strong as you can get. I never worry for the craft in the most violent weather. They can swamp out, but stuff is lashed in, so they can't get away unless—and this is a risk in any mooring—some other craft or wreckage drives into them.

This mooring setup does not suit all locations. Each has its problems, things you have to work out to suit the location. It's simply one way of doing it where the method fits.

---

**The Timber Framing Book**
**by Stewart Elliott and Eugenie Wallas**
**Housesmiths Press**
**P.O. Box 416**
**York, Maine 03909**
**170 pages, illus., 1977, paperbound, $9.95**

Barring your ability to purchase an old church or train station, the prospect of inhabiting a truly *sound* building with anything like durability and lasting value is receding with calamitous speed. The overpriced roughage you get from the lumber companies would be laughable if the situation it creates were not so serious. Two-by-fours are 1½" by 3½"; if you can find a straight one, take it to the local school so the kids can tell *their* grandchildren that they saw one once.

Timber framing, known as post-and-beam construction in some parts, is an ancient and wonderful construction technique. It is strong, stable, gives big spans for boatshops and storage buildings, saves on wood used and certainly on fastenings. With proper planning, one person can potter away on his (her) own for a few weeks working up all the joints and—with plenty of potato salad, beer, and friends—the building can go up in a day. Your building will still be there when your neighbor's stud-framed building will have been reduced to a cellarhole twice over.

This book takes you through the whole process from timber selection to topping out, with all the options along the way. It's terrific.

*From* The Timber Framing Book.

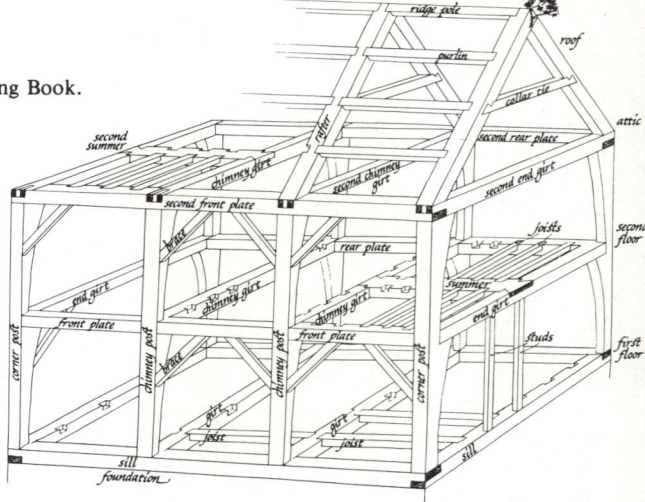

## Fussing Around With Stuff Stuff

Lowery manufactures their own, and distributes other factors' gear for hoisting, towing, and binding most anything in most any industry. We like the hoists and Prosafe binders by Ratcliff, and the strap load binder by:

**Lowery Bros., Inc.
6100 Fourth Street
P.O. Box 650
Marrero, Louisiana 70072**

*Right and below: All kinds of stuff from Lowery.*

People who are building a boat in steel or erecting a building in some sheeting material will be interested in the unique lifting clamps that have been developed by Merrill. Working on a cam-friction principle, they are positive and rugged and can be that hard-to-find other guy, from:

**Campbell Chain Company
3990 E. Market St.
P.O. Box 3056
York, Pennsylvania 17402**

*Below: Clamps from Campbell Chain.*

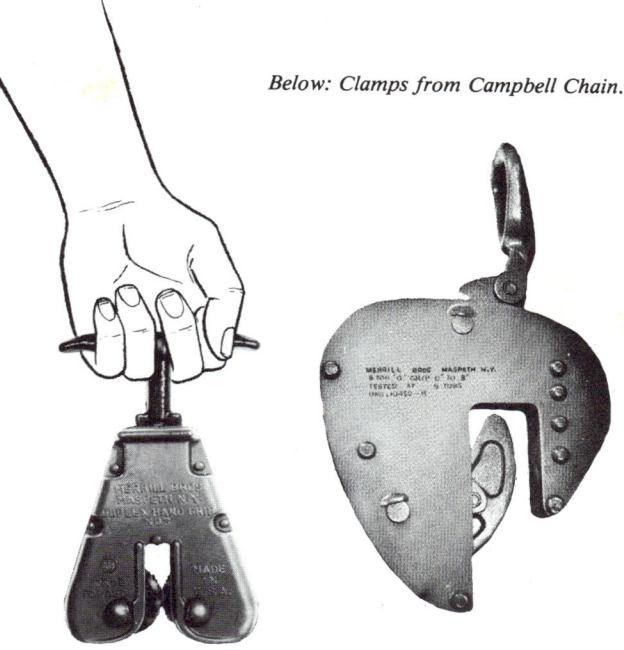

Here's a little block from the Crosby Group. Just being funny, but their Western blocks *are* tough and practical—and come in sizes less inappropriate.

**The Crosby Group
(sales offices nationwide)**

Here are some cable cross-sections from a Bridon American brochure. Blink blink.

**Bridon American
c/o A.A. Michael
365 Dalziel Rd.
Linden, New Jersey 07036**

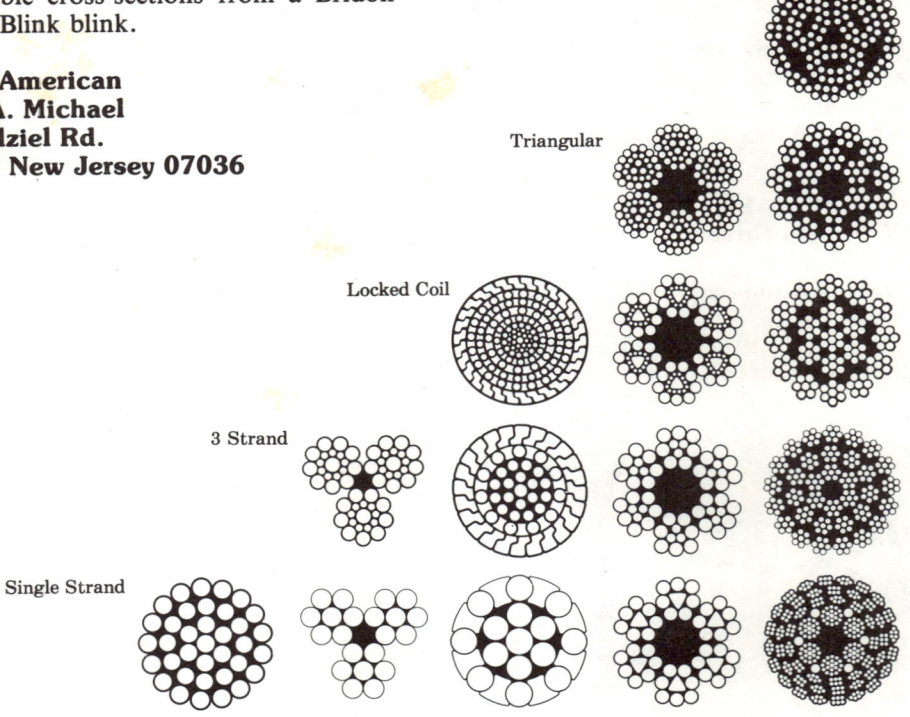

---

Ice Eater is an electrically driven, temperature-started water circulator for installation under docks or boats to keep them ice-free, from:

**The Power House
2682 West Patapsco Ave.
Baltimore, Maryland 21230**

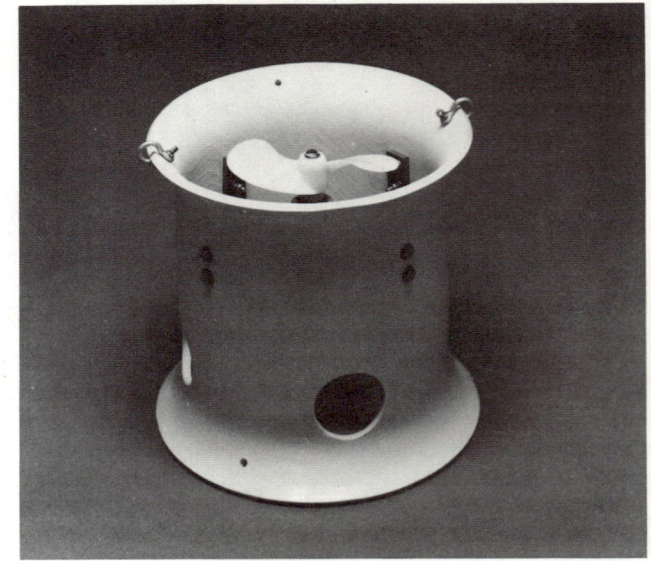

*Churn it up.*

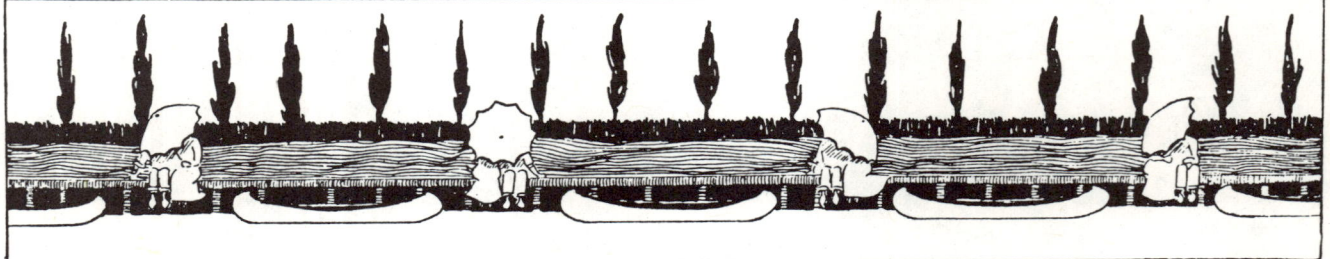

# Books and Things

## Hail Britannia

You have to admire the British. When they attack a subject—regardless of its obscurity—their thoroughness is mind-boggling. When an Englishman gets involved in modeling, for instance, he gets *involved*. All you have to do is pick up an English modeling magazine to understand this. English amateur model-makers have jobs to make money like everyone else, but they don't sleep. Rather, they stay up all night making working deck winches to scale and writing Letters to the Editor. Those who aren't modeling could very well be studying ship recognition.

That's right, identifying ships, the marine buff's version of bird watching. In England there's an organization called the Ship Recognition Corps, which is a volunteer, civilian force supported by the Ministry of Defence. Members are trained as a back-up group to take over when electronic ship recognition methods fail. They're coast watchers, so to speak.

The director of the Ship Recognition Corps is Lt. Cmdr. E.C. Talbot-Booth, RNR, who in the 1930s developed a systematic method for visually identifying ships according to certain categorized characteristics. He has written a multi-volume work using his system; ship-recognition enthusiasts, who are legion in Britain, swear by it:

*Right: From* Talbot-Booth's Merchant Ships, *Volume 1.*

***Talbot-Booth's Merchant Ships***
**Volumes 1 & 2, £12 each**
**Marinart/Kogan Page**
**Pillory Gate Wharf**
**Sandwich, Kent, England**

Volume 3 will be published next year. Every six months a supplement is issued to bring the information up to date.

MFFM  H
**23. GUNUNG DJATI.** Ia/Ge 1936; P; 17900; 176 x 8 (578 x 27); TSM; 17; Ex EMPIRE ORWELL 1959; Ex EMPIRE DOON 1949; Ex PRETORIA 1945.

MFFM  H
**25. PRINCESS MARGUERITE.** Ca/Br 1949; P; 5900; 114 x 4.6 (375 x 15); TSD-E; 23½; Sister **PRINCESS PATRICIA.**

For particulars on the Ship Recognition Corps, write:

> The Director
> Ship Recognition Corps
> Ashburnham, Torrens Drive
> Harbledown
> Canterbury, Kent, England

Then there's the Englishman I met last summer. Charles V. Waine is a fellow so consumed with his subject that he is driven to do everything himself. An avid ship buff, he wrote a book called *Steam Coasters and Short Sea Traders*. He did the drawings himself, with such exquisite draftsmanship that they have to rank up there with the best of L.F. Herreshoff's work. Waine was so dissatisfied with the quality of other publishers' work that he decided to publish the book himself. And finding printing quality low as well, he set up his own press in his garage (gay-raj in English English), and learned to operate it himself. The resulting book is a monument to amateur ingenuity and craftsmanship. The typesetting leaves something to be desired, but the illustrations, especially the color ones, are fantastic.

**Steam Coasters and Short Sea Traders**
**by Charles V. Waine, Ph.D.**
**Waine Research**
**Beamish Lane**
**Albrighton, Wolverhampton, England**
**152 pages, illus., index, 1976, £7.95**

Mr. Waine tells us that the first two printings are sold out, and he does not intend to reprint the book unless demand picks up. In the meantime, for those who appreciate marine books of the highest order, he has published a new book:

**The Complete Book of Canal & River Navigations**
**by Edward W. Paget-Tomlinson**
**Waine Research (address above)**
**361 pages, extensive biblio., glossary, illus., £13.50**

Once again the drawings are by Waine, and the printing quality as good as before.

*Below: From* The Complete Book of Canal & River Navigations.

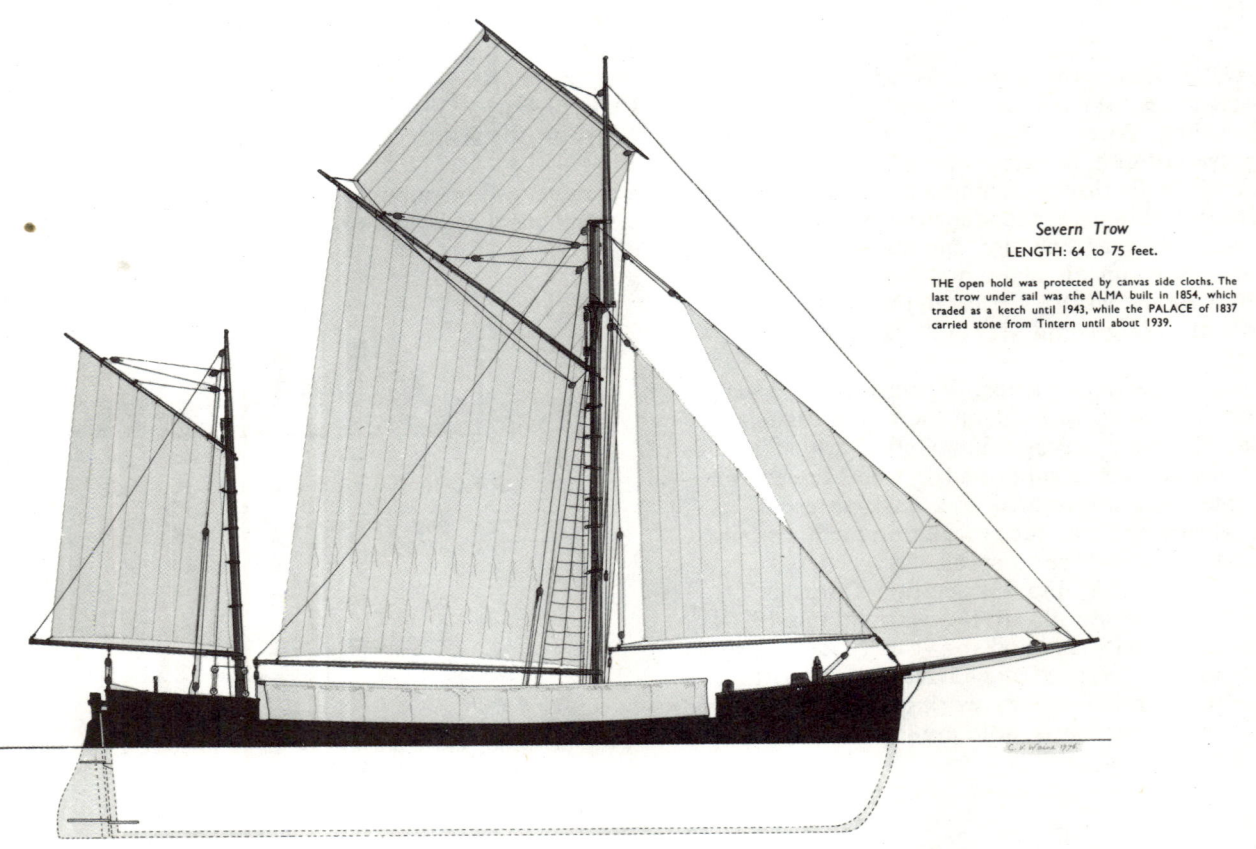

**Severn Trow**
LENGTH: 64 to 75 feet.

THE open hold was protected by canvas side cloths. The last trow under sail was the ALMA built in 1854, which traded as a ketch until 1943, while the PALACE of 1837 carried stone from Tintern until about 1939.

## Her Majesty's Stationery Office

Like the U.S. government, the British government publishes thousands of books, booklets, monographs, charts, etc., many of which are of value to marine enthusiasts. Finding out what they have to offer is another thing again. In response to our query, they told us that HMSO catalogs can be seen at all British consulates and embassies worldwide. In addition, two organizations act as HMSO distributors in the United States:

**Pendragon House of Connecticut**
**Box 255**
**Old Mystic, Connecticut 06372**
and
**Pendragon House**
**2595 East Bayshore Road**
**Palo Alto, California 94303**

The home office is:

**Her Majesty's Stationery Office**
**Atlantic House**
**Holborn Viaduct**
**London, England**

Orders should be sent to:

**The Government Bookshop**
**P.O. Box 569**
**London, England**

"The real shipping magnate of the yachting world."

For those who wish to keep up with the publishing of Her Majesty's Stationery Office, daily, monthly, and yearly catalogs are available:

(For information on similar services available from the U.S. Government Printing Office, see "The U.S. Government as an Information Source" in MC-1, page 127.)

**Daily List.** Every day, except Saturdays, Sundays and public holidays, a list of publications issued is produced and posted to subscribers. The list of Statutory Instruments prescribed under Section 3(1) of the Statutory Instruments Act, 1946, is published as a part of the Daily List. This Service is of value to all who must ascertain immediately what is being published by the Government from day to day.
*Annual Subscription inclusive of postage — £22.50*
*Extra copy to same address — £6*
The Daily List is also posted in weekly batches, a cheaper arrangement which will meet the needs of many subscribers.
*Annual Subscriptions inclusive of postage — £10*
*Extra set to same address — £6*

**Monthly Catalogue.** The monthly catalogue includes a loose inset with short descriptions of important publications and is fully indexed. The catalogue is of special value to librarians, many of whom regard it as indispensable for Reference Libraries and for use in selecting material for permanent accessions.
*Annual Subscriptions inclusive of postage—£3.85*

**Annual Catalogue.** 1975. (0 11 700309 3) 700g £1.80. The annual catalogue comprises a fully indexed bibliography of all Government Publications issued in the year except Statutory Instruments. Pagination is consecutive for five years so that five catalogues may be bound together as one consolidated edition. A consolidated index is issued every five years; the most recent edition covers the years 1966-70. 280g £1.05

## National Maritime Museum Publications

The only gripe we have about England's National Maritime Museum is that it is over there, not here. It is a vital, vibrant institution that could teach a thing or two to American maritime museums. The British may well have lost their preeminent maritime strength, but they haven't forgotten their heritage. As proof, we present a truly impressive list of publications available from the National Maritime Museum. They can be ordered from:

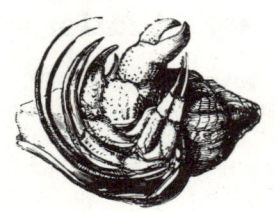

National Maritime Museum
Greenwich
London, England SE109NF
(prices are as of 1978)

### National Maritime Museum

| Monographs | | Cost | P&P UK | Abroad |
|---|---|---|---|---|
| 1. | Aspects of the History of Wooden Shipbuilding Symposium 1969 | 25p | 32p | 40p |
| 2. | The Opening of the Pacific—Image and Reality Symposium 1970 | 25p | 42p | 55p |
| 3. | China Station 1859-64, The Reminiscences of Walter White Symposium 1972 | 30p | 42p | 62p |
| 4. | Plymouth's Ships of War by Lt Commander K V Burns 1972 | 50p | 66p | 96p |
| 5. | Problems of Ship Management and Operation 1870-1900 Symposium 1971 | 25p | 42p | 40p |
| 6. | Three Major Ancient Boat Finds in Britain Symposium 1971 | 25p | 34p | 62p |
| 7. | The Irrawady Flotilla Company by Captain H J Chubb 1973 | 50p | 98p | £1.30 |
| 8. | China and the Red Barbarians Symposium 1972 | 25p | 32p | 40p |
| 9. | The Second World War in the Pacific Symposium 1972 | 25p | 42p | 40p |
| 10. | The Birth of Navigational Science by E G Forbes 1974 | 30p | 34p | 62p |
| 11. | The Gokstad Faering Part I by S McGrail 1974 Part II by E McKee 1974   for both parts | 40p | 45p | 62p |
| 12. | Problems of Medicine at Sea Symposium 1973 | 25p | 42p | 40p |
| 13. | The Cattewater Wreck Interim Report 1973 | 25p | 42p | 40p |
| 14. | Inshore Fishing Craft of the Southern Baltic by W Rudolph 1974 | 25p | 32p | 40p |
| 15. | The Boats of Men of War by Commander W E May 1974 | 30p | 34p | 62p |
| 16. | Problems of the Conservation of Waterlogged Wood by W A Oddy 1975 | 50p | 66p | 96p |
| 17. | The Elizabethan Navy and the Armada of Spain by D W Waters 1975 | 35p | 42p | 62p |
| 18. | Navigation in the Days of Captain Cook by Professor E G R Taylor 1975 | 25p | 32p | 55p |
| 19. | Science and the Techniques of Navigation in the Renaissance by D W Waters 1976 | £1.00 | 34p | 62p |
| 20. | Ship Registers of the Port of Hayle by G Farr 1975 | £2.50 | 66p | 96p |
| 21. | Matthew Flinders by Rear Admiral G S Ritchie 1975 | 25p | 32p | 40p |
| 22. | Shipbuilding in North Devon by G Farr 1976 | £1.05 | 38p | 62p |
| 23. | The North Ferriby Boats by E V Wright 1976 | £2.00 | 42p | 62p |
| 24. | The Last Log of the Schooner Isabella by C H Ward-Jackson 1976 | £1.00 | 34p | 62p |
| 25. | The Westcotts and their Times by I D Merry 1977 | £4.00 | 66p | 96p |
| 26. | The Chinese Maritime Customs: An International Service 1854-1950 by B Foster Hall 1977 | £1.00 | 34p | 62p |
| 27. | Shipbuilding in the Port of Bristol by G Farr 1977 | £1.05 | 65p | 68p |
| 28. | Sundials on Walls by C St J H Daniel 1978 | £2.00 | 36p | 40p |
| 29. | Naval Policy between the Wars by Captain S W Roskill 1978 | £1.00 | 36p | 40p |
| 30. | North East Coast Cobles by E McKee 1978 | £2.50 | 36p | 40p |
| 31. | Scottish Inshore Fishing Vessels by A Noble (edited by E McKee) | £2.50 | | |
| 32. | The Hardanger Faering by O H Wicksteed | £1.50 | | |

**Books by Trustees and members of staff (past and present)**

| | | Retail Price |
|---|---|---|
| E.01 | Archaeology of the Boat by Basil Greenhill | £8.50 |
| E.02 | Child o' War by Garfield and Proctor | £1.25 |
| E.03 | Coastal Trade by Basil Greenhill and Lionel Willis | £30.00 |
| E.04 | Collier Brigs and their Sailors by Sir Walter Runciman | £3.80 |
| E.05 | Francis Place and the Greenwich Observatory by Derek Howse | £9.00 |
| E.06 | Greenwich Observatory — set of 3 Vols. | £25.00 |
| E.07 | Greenwich Observatory — Vol. III by Derek Howse | £12.00 |
| E.08 | Guide to the Manuscripts in the National Maritime Museum by R J B Knight | £12.50 |
| E.09 | Maritime Struggle for India by Ayland and Archibald | 30p |
| E.10 | Merchant Schooners by Basil Greenhill - Vol 1 | £3.00 |
| | Merchant Schooners by Basil Greenhill - Vol 2 | £3.00 |
| E.11 | Metal Fighting Ships in the Royal Navy by E H H Archibald | £7.80 |
| E.12 | Out of Appledore by W J Slade | £1.00 |
| E.13 | Quayside Camera by Basil Greenhill | £3.75 |
| E.14 | Rutters of the Sea by D W Waters | £25.40 |
| E.15 | Sea Charts by D Howse and M Sanderson | £6.50 |
| E.16 | Sources and Techniques in Boat Archaeology by S McGrail | £6.00 |
| E.17 | Swords for Sea Service by Cmdr W E May and P G W Annis | £8.00 |
| E.18 | Tompion Clocks at Greenwich by Derek Howse | 60p |
| E.19 | Victorian and Edwardian Navy from old photographs by J Fabb and A P McGowan | £4.45 |
| E.20 | Victorian and Edwardian Sailing Ships from old photographs by Basil Greenhill and Ann Giffard | £4.25 |
| E.21 | Victorian Maritime Album (limp) by Basil Greenhill | £2.95 |
| E.22 | Voyaging with the Wind by Alan Villiers | 75p |
| E.23 | Way of a Ship by Alan Villiers | £3.50 |
| E.24 | Westcountry Coasting Ketches by W J Slade and Basil Greenhill | £4.20 |
| E.25 | Westcountrymen in Prince Edward Island by Basil Greenhill and Ann Giffard | £3.15 |
| E.26 | Wooden Fighting Ships in the Royal Navy by E H H Archibald | £7.50 |

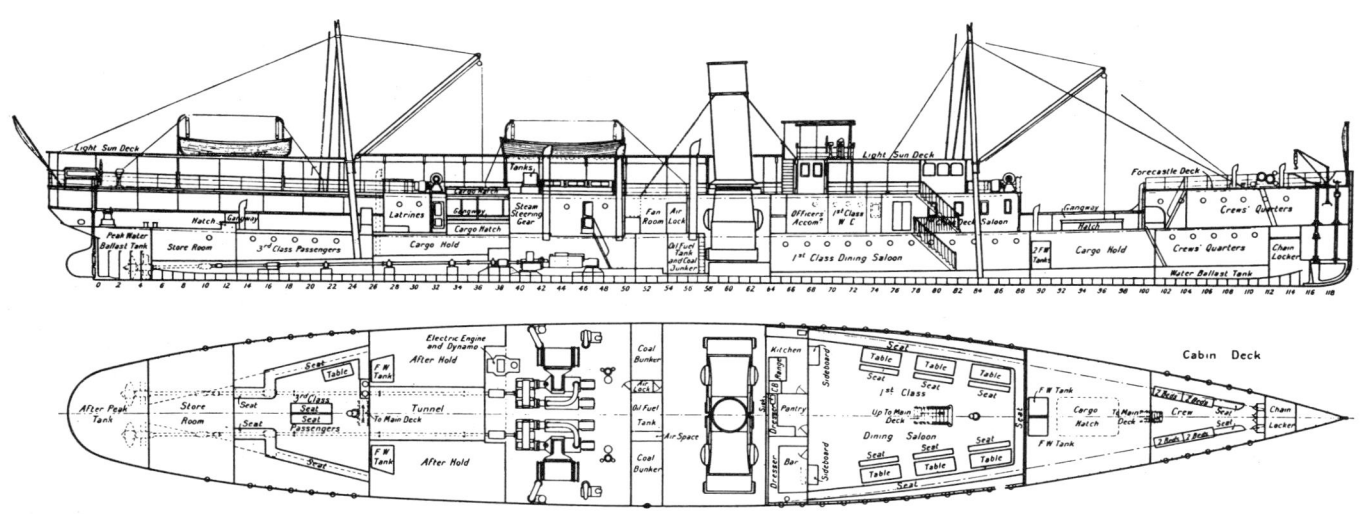

INBOARD PROFILE AND DECK PLAN OF TURBINE STEAMERS CURZON, HARDINGE AND ELGIN

The NMM's Archives Department, by the way, has an eight-page questionnaire of great value to oral historians, both amateur and professional. It is a list of questions to ask retired seafarers about their lives, and enables interviewers to structure an interview to gain the best results for future historians. We got our copy from:

**Alan Piersall
Head of Archives Department
National Maritime Museum
Greenwich
London, England SE109NF**

63 St-MALC - L'Avant Port et le Quai de Dinan

## Consider the Postcard

The first cousin of the collector of ships on stamps (see MC-4, page 139) is the collector of ships on postcards. There are more of them (both collectors and postcards) than you think, and 50-year-old cards that sold for two for a nickel a few years ago now sell for 50 cents each and upward. Like collectors of everything else, postcard lovers are a strange breed, given to such eccentric behavior as subspecialization and compulsive trading.

Correct us if we're wrong, but we have been unable to find a periodical devoted to postcard collecting in the United States. We did find one in good old England:

*Postcard Collectors Gazette*
**36 Asmuns Hill
London, England
£7/yr. U.K.
£15/yr. outside U.K. surface mail
£25/yr. outside U.K. airmail**

The real value of the magazine is in the advertisements, which include some dealers in the U.S. and which indicate some interest in marine topics. The articles are fairly shallow, primarily because most postcard collectors are more interested in the cards themselves than in the pictures on the cards or the subjects they portray.

## MARITIME COLLECTING

As I am often asked how to set up a Maritime Collection in this day and age, I thought it would be of interest to give some ideas on the subject.

Since we used to be the most important maritime nation in the world, it should not be too difficult to think back to various family links with the sea of yesteryear, e.g. Naval, Merchant, Lifeboat Service, Sailing, etc. etc., for a source of inspiration, and proceed from there. However, one must be careful not to "spread one's net too wide", if one has a lot of nautical links with the past, as I have!

Even those who cannot trace any direct links with the sea, need not despair, though the first thing to decide is the financial outlay available, as like all collecting interests, it can be either very expensive, or alternatively can be set up for a very modest sum!

A glance through the various catalogue columns under the many possible shipping headings (ADVERTISING, BUILDINGS, DISASTERS, RAILWAYS, SHIPPING, CANALS) will begin to give a guid to the scope available.

For those fortunate enough to live near to one of our Maritime Museums, and particularly Greenwich, a visit will surely bring back a flood of memories of the sea. Libraries can also be a useful source of information and particularly the larger ones, which have a Marine Dept., and perhaps have copies of old Editions of Lloyd's Register of Shipping. Now a brief run-through the various categories.
**Advertising (Shipping).** As will be noticed, Poster Types, which are very rare these days, and include some beautiful specimens by various Publishers, are quire expensive, whereas Company Publicity types involve a more modest outlay.
**Buildings.** These are three types as listed under this heading in the I.P.M. Catalogue (though maybe it would be less confusing if all types were listed under Shipping), i.e. Bridges, Lighthouses and Piers, though even to some extent Memorials could be included.

Lighthouses are a fascinating subject, and it is possible to obtain a Marine Chart of all the U.K. Lighthouses, with the names, locations, and characteristics plotted on it, and mark off your cards on the Chart as you get them. Piers, likewise, are very interesting, and one only has to think back to the fire on Southend Pier, and destruction of Morecambe, and Margate Piers to realise they are today a "dieing breed", whereas in the Edwardian era they were both a "status symbol" and a "hive of activity". These postcard subjects involve only a modest financial outlay.
**Bays and Harbours.** Another interesting and yet inexpensive subject. Until one gets a decent collection together of these items, one is apt to overlook how many beautiful bays and harbours we have in the U.K. from Lands End to John of Groats, East and West, Isle-of-Man, and across the Irish Sea. With this as with other subjects it can be stimulating to collect "Ancient and Modern" and make comparisons! I nearly forgot to mention various other Islands:- Channel Isles, Isle-of-Wight, Orkneys, Hebrides, Anglesey and many more.
**Shipping (Naval).** A past and/or present link with the Navy all helps. From there it is necessary to decide whether to collect all types, from Battleships down to Destroyers, though remember that the smaller the Ships generally the cheaper the cards become. This postcard category can be extended to include other items, e.g. naval personnel docks, establishments, etc.

*From the* Postcard Collectors Gazette.

## Dictionaries

Discovered two more interesting nautical dictionaries, both from Great Britain. The first is from our friends in Scotland:

**Dictionary of Nautical Words and Terms**
**by C. W. T. Layton**
**Brown, Son & Ferguson**
**52 Darnley St., Glasgow, Scotland**
**392 pages, 1967 (2nd ed.), £12.60.**

An expensive book for its size and scope (British book prices seem to be rising faster than ours), it's still worth attention. With over 8,000 definitions, it was compiled by a master mariner "to embody in one volume the words and terms used by seamen in connection with their work." Definitions are short and to the point. British definitions, of course, obtain.

"Monkey Poop. Low poop. Sometimes applied to a deck above an after cabin."
—from *Dictionary of Nautical Words and Terms*

*The Boat-Owner's Practical Dictionary*
**by Denny Desoutter**
**Hollis & Carter, London**
**Dist. by Transatlantic Arts, Levittown, N.Y.**
**247 pages, illus., 1978, $10.95**

By the editor of *Practical Boat Owner* magazine, with over 1,500 definitions. Less of a formal dictionary; more of a chatty, sometimes light, exposition on the concerns of modern English sailors.

"Hove-to. In English, 'hove' is the past tense and past participle of the verb 'to heave.' It retains those functions when in the compound verb to Heave-to. Thus: 'Please heave-to.' 'I have hove-to.' 'That boat over there is hove-to as well.' 'We were both hove-to yesterday afternoon.' It ought to be clear enough, but not to some people it ain't: hence my lengthy examples. Personally I rather fancy 'I have hoven-to' for the past tense. Either is permissible, but the older 'hoven' pleases me."
—from *The Boat-Owner's Practical Dictionary*

*The Visual Encyclopedia of Nautical Terms Under Sail*
**Crown Publishers, New York**
**354 pages, 1978, illus., $15.95**

Visual it is; an encyclopedia it's not. We'll call it an illustrated dictionary. This is a British book, though the publisher doesn't make much effort to make that clear, so some of the terms once again have to be measured against one's knowledge of their American counterparts. Why can't an American publisher and an American author team up on a book like this?* The definitions are short and straightforward, but it's their organization that makes things difficult. Instead of alphabetical organization, the definitions are grouped topically (though thankfully alphabetized within topics). Topics are varied and wide-ranging—methods of expressing position, steering a course, types of boats, construction of ropes, mast fittings and parts, etc. For us dullards, there's a complete index of the terms defined, which is our recommended entry into the book unless you're just browsing. The illustrations, especially the old cuts, are first rate.

*We are.—Publisher.

*Below: From* The Visual Encyclopedia of Nautical Terms Under Sail.

**Back board.** Board in a boat's stern just forward of the TRANSOM (01.01) and against which the COXSWAIN (10.02) leans when steering.

**Bank.** Collective term for the oars along one side of a boat when they are manned. Ancient craft such as biremes and triremes carried two and three banks or tiers of oars respectively.

**Becket rowlock.** Short length of rope securing an oar between thole pins. A feature of boats working from beaches where the breakers alongshore were liable to jerk the oars from between the THOLE PINS (09.02).

**Benches.** Curved seats in a boat's stern. Traditionally the place for ship's officers, guests and other important persons.

**Bent timbers.** The frames or ribs of a boat.

**Bilge piece,** or **bilge rail.** Fore and aft timber fitted outside the BILGE (03.10) and recessed with hand-grips to enable the crew to remain with the boat if it is capsized.

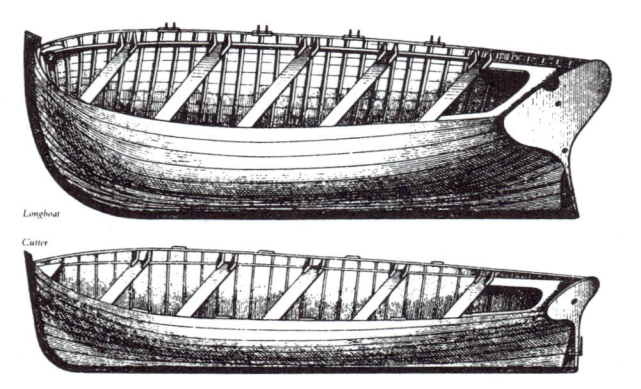

*Longboat*

*Cutter*

> ONE THAT GOT AWAY
>
> In Forest Land Co. v Black, (SC 1950) 216 SC 255, 57 SE 2d 420, Forest owned a tract of land near Columbia and subdivided and sold out residential lots around its private 152 acre lake. The buyers' deeds provided that the use of the lake was subject to Forest's rules which might provide for closed seasons for hunting and fishing and reasonably restrict the use of certain kinds of boats and motors and other kinds of craft.
>
> Black, an owner, bought a 60 hp Chris Craft and used it on the lake for a few weeks after which Forest promulgated a rule that: "No motor boat is to be operated on the lake at any time", and sought to enjoin Black's use of the boat. One of Forest's witnesses had never seen the boat, another testified as to its objectionable use. Black's testified to the contrary, that it was operated at 15 mph or less, without objectionable noise or excessive wave height, and there was no shore line erosion.
>
> The court held that the deed from Forest created an easement by express grant for operation of motorboats on the lake subject to a right of reasonable restriction of use. This did not mean "prohibit" which could have been stated in the deed restrictions if that had been intended. Therefore, Forest's rules had not the right to prohibit use. The owner of the land over which the easement was granted might restrain excessive or unwarranted use of the easement, but here there was a failure of proof.

*Right: From* Small Boat Law.

**Small Boat Law**
by Herbert L. Markow
order from:
Herbert L. Markow
Box 011451
Miami, Florida 33101
1977, $19.95

Given the huge number of small boats afloat today and the incredible amount of difficulties they can get into, you would expect the legal profession to be full of specialists in small boat law. It is not. There *are* many admiralty lawyers, whose main concern is shipping, but the nature of their business makes them unprepared to deal with legal questions involving pleasure boats. So if you and your boat get into legal trouble—perhaps a question of liability, or theft, or taxation—your lawyer may very well have as little knowledge of the subject as you do.

This book is an attempt by a lawyer to assemble as much material on small boat law as possible. We are not qualified to pass on the veracity or usefulness of the material, but the author, besides practicing small boat law, teaches a course on the subject at Miami-Dade Community College. The text is easily understood by the layman and will provide a rich source of leads to precedent cases for lawyers.

By the way, the author tells us that a second printing of the book is due soon, and the price will rise dramatically. Check for the most recent price before you order.

**Marine Careers, Selected Papers**
edited by Bernard L. Gordon
Book & Tackle Shop
Watch Hill, Rhode Island
42 pages, illus., paper, 1974, $1.00

The physical appearance of this publication isn't much, but it's worthy material for those seeking marine careers. Four of the collected papers were presented at the Marine Careers Conferences at Northeastern and Boston Universities. The subjects: Professional careers in marine science with the federal government; Marine science government publications to aid teachers and students; Oceanography programs for teachers; Marine geological research and potentials; Today's youth in tomorrow's sea.

The Book & Tackle Shop didn't say anything about postage, but at the ridiculously low price for this publication, and for the obvious service they are performing, we suggest that it is only fair that you send 50 cents or so for postage and handling.

Which reminds us of our old refrain: Many of the people and companies listed in the *Mariner's Catalog* do what they do as a service or a hobby. Very few are getting rich on such obscure material or goods. Inquiries should be real, not idle, and the ways should be greased by including a stamped, self-addressed envelope or a little change for postage and handling. Besides, you'll be a better person for it.

## Great Lakes Newsletters

Bowling Green State University in Ohio publishes a unique newsletter covering the goings-on on the Great Lakes. Published weekly from March to December and biweekly in January and February, *Lake Log Chips* is for shipping enthusiasts and businessmen. The February 10, 1979, issue, for instance, discussed recent books published about the lakes, reported on ice difficulties encountered by various ships, listed ships laid up for the winter, and reported on the deaths of several people involved in lakes shipping.

*Lake Log Chips*
**Fifth Floor, University Library**
**Bowling Green State University**
**Bowling Green, Ohio 43403**
**$12/yr., 1st class mail U.S.; $6/yr., 2nd class U.S.**
**$8/yr., 2nd class Canada**

---

```
Short Entries - Toledo's Valley Camp Stores Company, the city's
  major ship supplier, was destroyed in a fire on Christmas Day.
  The next day, however, the company was back in business, oper-
  ating out of an office on Oak Street.  Deliveries to the ships
  laying up at Toledo were continued almost without delay.    *
  In December, Lykes Brothers Steamship Company scheduled its first
  calls at Quebec and Valleyfield.  Earlier in the season, Lykes
  vessels made their first stops at the ports of Duluth, Thunder
  Bay, and Port Alfred.    *  Cleveland's Midwest Container Services,
  Inc., began offering a new container service on December 1.
  The new service, designated "LCL (Less than Container Load)
  Express," is tailored for companies exporting goods from Ohio
  and Michigan.  The service links inland shippers with ports on
  the lakes, making it easier for them to use water instead of
  land transportation.    *  The Port of Montreal has announced
  that it soon will have a new container terminal in operation.
  The new facility will be located on a ten-acre parcel just
  below the Racine Terminal and it will have one berth and a
  roll-on/roll-off ramp.  A port spokesman also announced that
  another eleven acres will be added to the Racine Terminal and
  that more lines will begin using it soon.
```

*From* Lake Log Chips.

Another news publication on the Great Lakes is *Earthbeats,* the joint project of the University of Wisconsin's Institute for Environmental Studies and the Sea Grant College Program. A recent issue, printed in newspaper format, had articles on the Great Lakes shoreline, a voyage to the bottom of Lake Michigan, an elementary introduction to Great Lakes ships, a lakes crossword puzzle, and a short description of the art of fish printing.

*Earthbeats*
**Communications Office**
**Sea Grant College Program**
**University of Wisconsin**
**1800 University Avenue**
**Madison, Wisconsin 53706**

## Steamship Buffs Take Note

Dear Editors:
We deal totally with items related to ocean liners and steamships. Many times the steamship buff has only a very limited number of books and information available in local book stores. What we attempt to do is to offer as many publications that are in print (and some out of print) that are related to this subject. Many items are not obtainable in stores, as sometimes printings are very limited and with some items we purchase them overseas for sale here in the U.S.

We offer quick service and we try to update our catalog about 3 times a year. For readers of your publication, if they mention your name we will send them our current catalog free of charge.

—George C. Devol

**Fairtek Corporation**
**Box 104**
**Stamford, Conn. 06904**

They carry books with titles like *Great Passenger Liners of the World*, *The Good Ships of Newport News*, *Lives of the Liners*, *God Save the Queen*, the *Old Bay Line*, *Victory Ships and Tankers*, *Loss of the Titanic*, and the *History of Ships*.

—Eds.

## Another Boating Magazine?

Does the boating world need another magazine? Most definitely not if such a publication is a "consumer" mag with so-called boat tests, expositions on how to tie a bowline, and boat show issues filled with advertising copy fronting as editorial material. We have enough of those already, thanks. But yes if it is a sensible, straightforward magazine dedicated to the true interests of its readers. Most especially yes if it dedicates its coverage to small craft, power and sail, built of all materials. We have it:

**The Small Boat Journal**
**21 Elm Street**
**Camden, Maine 04843**
**Published monthly, $12/year**

*The SMALL BOAT Journal*

The pilot issue (March 1979) is an interesting magazine—not exciting, mind you, in the sense that the genesis of *Wooden Boat* was exciting—but a solid alternative to the slicks, which it makes no attempt to ape. *The Small Boat Journal* has *National Fisherman* tracks all over it, which is as to be expected, since it is a sister to NF.

Overall, I like SBJ, but I do have a bone to pick with the review in it by John Gardner of Mark White's new book, *Building the St. Pierre Dory*. Now, I would be the last to call into question John Gardner's boatbuilding ability or judgment, or his experience that enables him to criticize the work of others, but I do fail to see the logic in his basic criticism of White's book. Right at the beginning of the review, Gardner states that the St. Pierre dory is the perfect boat for amateurs to build, because it is capable of being modified to a great degree without destroying the effectiveness of the craft. Yet he then goes on to take White to task for modifying the boat and strip-building it with very heavy scantlings. Nowhere does he indicate he understands why White built the boat heavy (for use in Alaska during all seasons) and nowhere does he acknowledge that White wrote the book to describe how he built the boat, not how he wants everybody else to build it.

Especially difficult to understand is Gardner's extremely unfair generalization at the end of the review that: "Too many boatbuilding books these days are coming out of the libraries instead of the boatshops. Too many are being written by the readers of other writers' books, some of which were written by readers of other writers' books." I'm at a loss on that. To which books is he referring? To White's? If so, he didn't read the same book I read.

*The Mariner's Catalog* has published some critical reviews of books in the past. We like to think they are logical and fair.

—PHS

## A Professional Society

The world is filled with professional societies—you know, the American Potato Institute, the Society for Political Ethnography, the American Medical Association, the National Soybean Council, that type of organization. Most are thinly disguised lobbying groups dedicated to obtaining publicity and preferential legislation for asphalt paving contractors and the makers of lefthanded widgets (which are going out of business because of unfair foreign competition and should be protected by suitable tariffs, of course). They are generally mistrusted by most of us, with the exception of politicians looking for campaign funds and newspaper editors looking for copy and not caring where it comes from.

Some are true "professional" professional societies, though. By this we mean they look beyond their own self-interests and examine how they fit into the greater scheme of things. These organizations tend to be dedicated to self-improvement instead of self-publication and have as a result gained the respect not only of those within their professions but also of those without.

We have immense respect for the United States Naval Institute, which is a professional, private organization for Naval, Coast Guard, and Marine officers. Though the vast majority of the membership is serving on active duty, and though the president is by tradition always the Chief of Naval Operations, the Institute has managed to stake out its own neutral territory without undue influence from the Defense Department. Through its monthly magazine, the *Proceedings*, its annual publication, the *Naval Review*, and its scores of books and monographs, the Institute encourages the continuing education of its members and associates so they will be aware of trends within and without their profession and will not be afraid to engage in the necessary dialog to gain sane policies. (This has not been wholly successful, however; how can one explain away the building of multi-billion-dollar sitting-duck aircraft carriers?)

The Institute is truly interested in improvement through open debate, and if you don't believe it (and there is no reason why you should), take a look at any issue of the Naval Institute *Proceedings*. In it, you might find a lieutenant arguing that unionization of enlisted men is the road to better personnel relations, a captain suggesting that some naval bases in the Pacific are no longer necessary even though in his official capacity he is supposed to believe that they are, and a chief petty officer describing the hazards of shipboard maintenance procedures on fleet minesweepers. Take a look at some of the recent books published, from *Weather for the Mariner* to *Division Officers Guide*, from the *Art of Knotting and Splicing* to the *Battle of Trafalgar*, from the *Ships and Aircraft of the U.S. Fleet* to *Victorian and Edwardian Sailing Ships*, from *Dutton's Navigation and Piloting* to *Naval Policy Between the Wars*. If the sea services take the wrong course, it won't be because of the lack of education and introspection.

You don't have to be a naval officer to join the Institute. Membership is open to everyone, and if you truly care about what goes on in the ocean, you are well advised to join. You will discover a level of nautical experience substantially different from gentlemanly yachting.

**United States Naval Institute
Annapolis, Maryland 21402
Annual membership, $15
Book catalog available on request**

---

**United States Naval Institute**
June 1979
Volume 105/6/916

# Proceedings

### Articles

**SALT and the Navy** — 28
To most Americans, MAD is a magazine and MIRV is the first name of a talk-show host. But SALTalkers—both U. S. and Soviet—know that the U. S. Navy is both MAD and MIRV.
*By Lieutenant James L. George, USN (Ret.)*

**The Drift Toward the Draft** — 38
The All-Volunteer Force's worst enemies won't call it a total failure, and its firmest friends won't call it an unqualified success. Isn't that what was being said about the Draft when they abolished it in 1973?
*By Lieutenant Colonel Henry J. Sage, USMC*

**The All-Volunteer Force in 1798** — 45
Back in the days when 74 men were crammed into a 56-foot vessel, there were more deaths from "an old sore leg," "the fleux," and "mysterious fevers" than from enemy action.
*By Lieutenant Daniel W. Wood, USCGR*

**Andrew Irwin McKee: Naval Constructor** — 49
No man did more than he to make the pig-boat safe for her crew, a scourge to her enemies, and the sleepless sentry she has become today. But his talents were by no means limited to submarines.
*By Commander John D. Alden, USN (Ret.)*

**Countering Soviet Imperialism** — 58
Soviet hegemony over Eurafrica can best be thwarted by naval forces which are capable of controlling the seas, thrusting Marines onto hostile shores, and supporting them as long as necessary.
*By Colonel Joseph E. Hopkins, USMC, and Lieutenant Colonel W. R. Warren, USMC*

**Warships Should Look Warlike** — 66
Warships between wars, like middle linebackers between plays, ought to ooze intimidation. For some reason, our modern ships don't look menacing. Soviet warships do.
*By Lieutenant John C. Roach, USNR, and Herbert A. Meier*

**Cover**
To be effective against Soviet expansion, our amphibious forces must be both capable and ubiquitous, as posited in the article beginning on page 58. In this painting by Dante H. Bertoni, a CH-53 Sea Stallion is seen on board the USS *New Orleans* (LPH-11), in Subic Bay in the Philippines. (Courtesy of Navy Combat Art Collection.)
U.S. Naval Institute *Proceedings* (ISSN 0041-798X)

**Departments**
| | |
|---|---|
| Secretary's Notes | 17 |
| Comment and Discussion | 21 & 82 |
| Old Navy | 77 |
| Leadership Forum | 80 |
| Nobody asked me, but . . . | 94 |
| Book Reviews | 97 |
| Books of Interest to the Professional | 103 |
| Professional Notes | 105 |
| The U.S. Navy: Cruisers and Destroyers | 121 |
| Notebook | 123 |

*The opinions or assertions in the articles are the personal ones of the authors and are not to be construed as official. They do not necessarily reflect the views of either the Navy Department or the U. S. Naval Institute.*

*Proceedings is published monthly by U. S. Naval Institute, Annapolis, Md. 21402. Second-class postage paid at Annapolis, Md. and at additional mailing offices. Memberships/Subscriptions $15.00 one year U.S.A. Copyright © 1979 U. S. Naval Institute.*

The involvement of blacks with the menhaden fisheries began in 1868. That was the year old Elijah Reed, a Yankee entrepreneur, moved the operation of his menhaden boats from the Gulf of Maine to Chesapeake Bay. Finding lots of fish, he also sent south the processing equipment, boilers, and pressers that extract the oils. After Elijah's death his children carried on the work and the settlement became known as Reedsville. The move south was a lucky one, for in 1879 a shift in the water temperature of the northern waters made the menhaden disappear from the New England coast for nearly one hundred years. This drove most of the Yankee fishermen out of the menhaden fisheries and made room for the Virginia blacks, who have dominated the crew lists ever since.

In the nineteenth and early twentieth centuries the captains, engineers, "pilots," and mates were all whites, but gradually many of these jobs were opened to blacks. On the *Tideland* only Captain Edwards, descendant from a long line of whaling captains, and Kenneth Payne, pilot, were not members of the Afro-American comunities in Mathews County, Virginia.

Thus the coincidence of a shift of water temperature, the availability of a labor force of strong, active men, and the end of the Civil War and slavery combined to open a new field to black seamen and fishermen. Strength was needed by those who manned the purse-seine boats. The strongest fisherman dropped the three-hundred-pound "tom." (Today the "tom" weighs seven hundred pounds but is hoisted with a power winch.) Sixteen men on each boat were needed as "bunt-pullers" to tighten the net around the fish. They also manned the oars, two men to an oar. Two "seine men" let out the net and two "ringmen" watched for snarls. The captain or mate acting as boat steerer completed the boat crew. Pilot, engineers, and cook stayed aboard the mother ship and brought it alongside the boats to hoist the fish from the net. Until the 1930's the seine boats were still propelled by oars and the nets were tightened by hand. Steam drove the ships and powered the donkey engines that hoisted the fish from net to hold. Today gasoline and diesel engines have made some of the work easier, but the nets still have to have bulges pulled straight by muscle power and the edges fastened to the side of the ship by the crew climbing along the bulwarks. Strong, active, skilled men are still needed.

## The Sea is White, Right?

Like nearly every other endeavor, it's very easy to get the idea that only white men go to sea; to be sure, we reassure ourselves, black men do too to a certain extent, but only in dugout canoes and other such "native" craft. *The Nigger of the Narcissus* notwithstanding, nautical literature is not-so-strangely devoid of the contributions of blacks. We welcome, then, at least one attempt to straighten out the record:

***Black Men of the Sea*** 
**by Michael Cohn and Michael K. H. Platzer** 
Dodd, Mead, New York 
158 pages, illus., glossary, biblio., 1978, $8.95

A very short book, which only skims the surface, but on the other hand it serves well to raise a consciousness or two, and the bibliography and an appendix entitled "Where to See the Black Maritime Heritage" point the way toward the realization that the sea is, indeed, black and white.

*Left: From* Black Men of the Sea.

One maritime industry manned heavily by blacks is the menhaden fishery. Our friend John Frye has written a comprehensive book on the pogie business:

### The Men All Singing: The Story of Menhaden Fishing
**by John Frye**
**The Donning Company, Virginia Beach, Va.**
**242 pages, illus., index, biblio., 1978, $14.95**

Only lovers of striped bass fishing, fish oil, and fish meal pay much attention to the lowly menhaden, but the menhaden fishery has been and continues to be one of the largest on the eastern seaboard. This book is at once a history of menhaden fishing and a social history of the people involved. The cod, herring, salmon, striped bass, et al., have gotten their books. It is time for the menhaden. Frye has done a bang-up job.

```
         SONGS FROM THE JOHN O

   (Shouting and chatter)
Chanteyman:
   I left my baby standin' in the back
      door cryin'.
         Honey, don't go!
Fishermen:
   Lawd, Lawd, don't go!
   (Shouting and chatter)
Chanteyman:
   I'd go home but ain't got no money!
Fishermen: (drawing words out)
   Lawd, Lawd, ain't got no money!
   (Shouting and chatter)
Chanteyman:
   To pay my way____!
Fishermen:
   Lawd, Lawd, to pa-ay my wa-ay!
   (Shouting and chatter)
Chanteyman:
   Yes, I'm gonna row here few days
      longer,
         Then I'm goin' back home!
   (Here they got the net up and the
   singing stopped, the chattering
   resumed.)

   A second heavy set:
Chanteyman:
   I got a muley on the mountain, called
      him Jerry,
         Bring him down!
Fishermen:
   Lawd, Lawd, bring him down!
   (Shouting and chatter)
Chanteyman:
   If I go get him, who in the world goin' to
      ride him?
         Gonna ride him myself!
   (Here two or three men might shout,
   "Go get him, I'll ride him!")
Fishermen:
   Lawd, lawd, gonna ride him myself!
      Gonna ride him to____!
   (Shouting and chatter)
```

```
Chanteyman:
   Go and bring me old bad Lazarus!
      Bring him dead or alive!
Fishermen:
   Dead or ali-i-ve!
   (Shouting and chatter)
Chanteyman:
   Found old Lazarus down between
      two mountains!
Fishermen:
   Lawd, lawd, 'tween two mountains!

   A third set:
   (Shouting and chatter)
Chanteyman:
   We're goin' home but got no ready
      made money!
Fishermen:
   One more dollar and a quarter!
   (Shouting and chatter)
Chanteyman:
   Gonna make one more dollar and a
      quarter,
         Then I'm goin' back home!
Fishermen:
   One more dollar and a quarter!
   A fourth set (here another of the three
or four chanteymen in Captain Lowry's crew
started the singing.)
   (Shouting and chatter)
Chanteyman:
   Birmingham Road!
Fishermen:
   Lawd, Lawd, Birmingham Road!

   A fifth set:
   (Shouting and chatter)
Chanteyman:
   My little woman shakes like jelly all
      over!
Fishermen:
   From the hips on down!
   (Shouting and chatter)
Chanteyman:
   My little woman shakes like jelly over
      over!
```

```
Fishermen:
   From the hips on down!
   A sixth set:
   (Shouting and chatter)
Chanteyman:
   Bitin' spider, goin' round bitin' every-
      body!
         But he didn't bite me!
Fishermen:
   Lawd, Lawd, don't bite me!
   A seventh, especially heavy and to be
lost if impossible to raise:
Chanteyman:
   All the weight's on the mate's boat!
Fishermen:
   Hey, hey, honey!
   (Shouting and chatter)
Chanteyman:
   We gonna save them if we can!
Fishermen:
   Hey, hey, honey!
   (Shouting and chatter)
Chanteyman:
   She's long and she's tall!
Fishermen:
   Hey, hey, honey! Long and tall!
   (Shouting and chatter)
Chanteyman:
   Want to see her____!
Fishermen:
   Hey, hey, honey!
Chanteyman:
   I have a girl in Baltimore!
      Hey, hey, honey!
Fishermen:
   Streetcar runs right by her door!
      Hey, hey, honey!
   (This last verse was not on the
recording but was recalled by another
fisherman who had heard the "Hey, hey,
honey" refrain many times on other boats.)
   The men were an hour and a half to two
hours completing the set, and the John O
could head for Wildwood only well after dark.
```

*Above and left: From* The Men All Singing.

## Used-Book Dealers

Further to our listings in past *Mariner's Catalogs*, we have found a few more dealers in used nautical books who sell their wares through the mail:

**The Sailor's Bookshop
4208 South 16th St.
Arlington, Virginia 22204**

The part-time hobby of Bill Bolger, Phil Bolger's nephew, this mail-order business features books of all types from naval to marine, from cruising to racing. The catalog is updated periodically and lacks annotation other than bibliographical details, including the condition of the books. Prices are fairly reasonable.

**Christopher Hinchliffe, Books
815½ Bank St.
Ottawa, Canada**

A new operation, Mr. Hinchliffe's first catalog is entitled "The Sea and its Islands." Much history, both naval and maritime, some yachting, some literature. Prices are moderate, and about a third of the book listings are briefly annotated.

**History Book Shop
2 The Broadway
Friern Barnet Road
London, England**

Besides carrying books on all fields of history, the History Book Shop sub-specializes in naval and maritime history. A catalog is published periodically. It is well annotated and the prices are moderate to medium-high. We've seen some difficult-to-find books on their list at extremely fair prices.

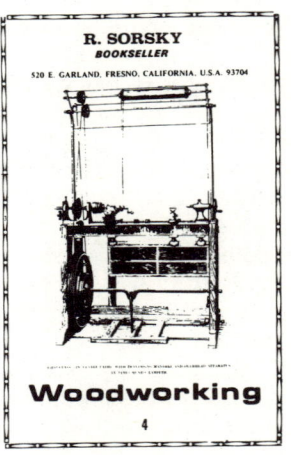

**R. Sorsky, Bookseller
520 E. Garland
Fresno, California 93704**

Sorsky specializes in books on woodworking, which makes his shop a rare find. His catalog number 4, for instance, lists 425 used books on all aspects of woodworking. Some of the listings are briefly annotated; prices are fair.

## Books for the Merchant Mariner

Boosters of the Big Apple always cite the availability of something for everybody in New York City. We're inclined to believe them after discovering the Maritime Bookshop, which is a sub-sub-specialist carrying only "maritime law and technical books for the shipping and export trade." They have a wide range of titles for merchant mariners and admiralty lawyers. They sell through the mail and publish a catalog, which is updated periodically. They will also special order on request.

**Maritime Bookshop
24 Beaver Street
New York, N.Y. 10004**

## London Bookshops

All marine bookworms naturally love bookshops, and most have their favorite haunts where they browse and occasionally buy. Four of mine are in London. I can seldom resist visiting at least one of these purveyors of rare and second-hand marine books when I visit there:

**Francis Edwards Ltd.
83 Marylebone High Street
London W1M 4AL, England**

**Norman Storey
3 Cecil Court
Charing Cross Road
London, England**

**Maggs Brothers
Berkeley Square
London, England**

**J. D. Potter
145 Minories
London, EC3 1NH, England**

For the devotee of maritime history, a visit to Francis Edwards is like the tourist entering St. Paul's Cathedral. A dignified hush pervades and ministering assistants converse in muted tones. The galleried walls hold thousands of books (not all marine) and provide an excellent selection covering warships, merchant ships, yachting, shipbuilding, and general maritime history.

Storey and Maggs Brothers offer similar delights, and all are accustomed to sending books to the ends of the earth, and frequently produce catalogs.

In the maritime part of the city of London, near the Tower, the old, established firm of J. D. Potter continues to offer and dispatch thousands of books and charts from their modern premises. Potter's is one of the oldest chart and marine book businesses in the world, but deals only in items currently in print. They can send any of their vast stock anywhere in the world.

—John Leather

## American Canals

Most of the material we have carried on canals in past *Catalogs* has been on European waterways, which is not surprising, since they have more of them and their tradition is stronger. But there *are* operating canals in the United States and there were even more in the not-too-distant past. Interest in them is picking up.

Two dealers in canal books and memorabilia are:

**William J. McKelvey, Jr.
98 Waldo Avenue
Bloomfield, New Jersey 07003**

Among the new books McKelvey carries are *Tales the Boatmen Told* ($12.95); *Champlain to Chesapeake: A Canal Era Pictorial Cruise* ($25); *The Delaware & Raritan Canal: A Pictorial History* ($14); *Delaware Canal Journal* ($10.50); *Canals Along the Lower Susquehanna* ($5); *Canal Children on the Chesapeake and Ohio, Pennsylvania and New York Canals* ($3); and *Snubbing Thro' Jersey* ($2.50). He also has on hand other publications and mementos of American canals.

**Canal Press, Inc.
39 West Springettsbury Ave.
York, Pennsylvania 17403**

The Canal Press says they feature "major publications on America's historic canals; used books, paper, antiques, etc. with a canal theme; consulting services to canal restorations; lectures and other program services; American Canal Research Center and Museum."

Below and on page 154 are a couple of books on American canals we have enjoyed recently.

*Canal Boatmen: My Life on Upstate Waterways*
**by Richard Garrity
Syracuse University Press, Syracuse, New York
222 pages, illus., 1977, $11.95**

The reminiscences of a canalman who worked on the Erie Canal and the New York Barge Canal System from 1905 until 1970. The writing isn't particularly notable, but the portrayal of canal life in upstate New York makes the book most worthwhile.

*From* Canal Boatmen.

*From:* Canal Days in America.

**Canal Days in America: The History and Romance of Old Towpaths and Waterways
by Harry Sinclair Drago
Clarkson N. Potter, New York
311 pages, illus., index, biblio., 1972, $10**

A history of the major American canals of the past, this book is an interesting introduction to canal lore. If you aren't hooked on canals by the end of the book, you have a heart and soul of concrete.

## The Mouth of the South

You can count on your fingers the yachtsmen who have gained fame beyond their field—Chichester, Mosbacher, Rose, Turner, a few others. All of them became well known as much for their courageousness and flamboyance as for their accomplishments. Ted Turner, it seems, became famous for all three. You have to admire a man who can be humiliatingly defeated in one *America*'s Cup season (1974, in the contender *Mariner*) and come out the supreme winner in the next (1977, in *Courageous*); a man who can take a tiny communications business and turn it into an empire; a man who can buy a major league baseball franchise and sit in the stands at games and chew tobacco and spit into a paper cup. Here is a man who obviously wants recognition and adulation, yet who will say almost anything that pops into his mind, even if it means being blackballed by the *America*'s Cup Selection Committee.

Roger Vaughan has written a penetrating biography of Ted Turner in the best tradition of what was once

called the "new" journalism. It's a book that is impossible to put down, regardless of your feelings about the *America*'s Cup, modern yachting, or Ted Turner himself. You might not come away liking Turner, but you will certainly appreciate him, and you will gain a better understanding of the reasons why the United States has yet to lose the Cup.

**Ted Turner: The Man Behind the Mouth
by Roger Vaughan
Sail Books, Boston
230 pages, 1978, $10.95**

## More Magazines for Mariners
### by Roger C. Taylor

The following pages present a sequel, obviously, to a section in *The Mariner's Catalog*, Volume 3, that was called "Magazines for Mariners."

In introductory remarks to that listing of about 100 marine periodicals, I estimated that there were probably some 500 such periodicals being published in English. If anything, I would now increase that estimate. At any rate, here are another half a hundred marine periodicals that I have learned about or that have started publication since that original listing in 1975.

I should repeat my caution about the tendency of magazine publishers to increase their subscription rates and change their addresses.

As far as I know, nearly all of the periodicals originally listed are still going. Here are three that aren't:

*Maritime History*. This English quarterly was listed as a promising fledgling in 1975. Since then, it has stopped publication, started up again under new ownership, and now, at least temporarily, stopped again. I don't want to report its death prematurely, but it has certainly been suffering mightily. It's needed, and I hope it recovers.

*Rudder*. The grand old *Rudder* fell into a modern, slick style under Fawcett Publications. CBS bought *Sea*, bought Fawcett, dumped the *Rudder* subscribers into the pot, and now publishes *Sea* "combined with *Rudder*." The combined-with-*Rudder* part is in extremely small type. Alas, *Rudder* is no more.

*The Yachtsman's Wife*. This one died, apparently from natural causes, despite its sexist title.

I can report a couple of name changes:

*East Coast Digest* is now called *Coast and Country*. The subscription has been increased to $12.00. Happily, nothing else about this fine British magazine (including its address—Crown Quay, Sittingbourne, Kent, England) has changed.

*South Street Reporter* is now called *Seaport* and has an exceedingly handsome new format. Still quarterly. Annual membership in the Friends of South Street (which gets you the magazine) increased to $15.00. Address changed to South Street Seaport Museum, 203 Front Street, New York, NY 10038.

And now, here's an alphabetical listing of more magazines for mariners:

*Angler*. Angler Publications, Box 4206, Stockton, CA 95204. Bi-monthly. An attractive sportfishing magazine, mostly freshwater, but some salt. Good color photographs. Combination of how-to articles with fishing tales.

*Australian Boating*. Leisure Boating and Speedway Magazines Pty. Ltd., Box 319, Avalon Beach, NSW 2107, Australia. Monthly. A rather slim one with the usual mix of practical stuff and cruising stories aimed at the relatively inexperienced small boat sailor and motorboat person.

*Boating Industry*. Whitney Communications Corporation, Magazine Division, New York City. Subscriptions to 639 Marine Blvd., Marion, OH 43302. Fifteen times per year. $15.00. Aimed at people who make their living in the pleasure boating business. Sales forecasts, distributors, dealer analysis, "product" quality, the market, boat shows, etc.

*Canadian Fisherman and Ocean Science*. Muir Publishing Company, Gardenvale, Que. H0A 1B0, Canada. Bi-monthly. A trade journal covering commercial fishing, fish processing, fish farming, and oceanography.

*Canadian Yachting*. 3 Church Street, Suite 201, Toronto, Ont. M5E 1M2 Canada. Monthly. Cruising, racing, sail, power, practical articles and yarns. Fairly sophisticated. Well above average. Was *Pacific Yachting* until 1977.

### canoe

*Canoe*. Voyager Publications, Inc., 131 E. Murray St., Fort Wayne, IN 46803. Bi-monthly. $7.50. Freshwater canoeing. Racing, cruising, whitewater, still water. Includes canoe, kayak, and camping accessories guide periodically. "Official magazine of the American Canoe Association."

### THE CHESAPEAKE BOATMAN

*The Chesapeake Boatman*. Whitney Publications, Inc., 222 Severn Avenue, Annapolis, MD 21403. Monthly. $9.00. Mostly cruising, mostly sail, mostly Chesapeake Bay. A good magazine mix. Tabloid newspaper format.

*Fairplay*. The *Financial Times*, London, England. U.S. office: Suite 2105, 75 Rockefeller Plaza, New York, NY 10019. Weekly. A trade journal for international shipping. World shipping news. Ports, shipbuilding, marine insurance, maritime law, finance, markets, ship sales, people in the industry. "Published weekly since 1883." This one has a well-deserved good reputation.

*Fine Woodworking*. The Taunton Press, 52 Church Hill Rd., Box 355, Newton, CT 06470. Bi-monthly. $12.00. Not marine, but of obvious interest to boatbuilders. Extremely high quality as to content and magazine design and printing. Covers wood, tools, joinery, finishing, turning, shaping, carving, and on and on. Outstanding.

## FISHERIES
### A Bulletin of the American Fisheries Society

*Fisheries*. The American Fisheries Society, 5410 Grosvenor Lane, Bethesda, MD 20014. Bi-monthly. "A bulletin of the American Fisheries Society, the oldest and largest professional society representing fisheries scientists." Resource management, the environment, pollution, American Fisheries Society news, legislation, and so forth.

## FISHING WORLD

*Fishing World*. Allsport Publishing Corp., 51 Atlantic Avenue, Floral Park, NY 11001. Bi-monthly. A slick sportfishing magazine covering both fresh and salt water. Stories, tactics, and gear.

## GEARTEST

*Geartest*. 13-14 Homewell, Havant, Hampshire PO9 1EF, England. Quarterly. $20.00, airmailed to U.S. An experienced, international editorial committee evaluates boat gear and fittings both from a common-sense seamanship point of view and from a highly technical point of view and reports the results. *Geartest* carries no advertising. (See *Mariner's Catalog*, Volume 5, page 98.)

*The Great Lakes Fisherman*. Nan-C Publications, Port Stanley, Ont. N0L 2A0, Canada. Monthly. Covers commercial fishing with emphasis on bygone days, boats, and fishermen. Keeps you up to date on current news too, though. This is a small magazine on newsprint. In a way, it's kind of a tiny *National Fisherman* for the Great Lakes.

*Harbour & Shipping*. Progress Publishing Co. Ltd., C310 Marine Bldg., 355 Burrard St., Vancouver, B.C. V6C 2G6, Canada. Monthly. $18.00. A merchant marine trade journal emphasizing the Pacific Northwest. Includes vessel plans. Nicely done.

*The International Journal of Nautical Archaeology and Underwater Exploration*. Academic Press, London, England. U.S. office: Academic Press, Inc., 111 Fifth Avenue, New York, NY 10003. Quarterly. $33.50 airfreighted to U.S. A new, excellent, scholarly journal emphasizing the results of digs in terms of new knowledge of old vessels, gear, and usage. Many detailed photographs, diagrams, and vessel plans. Handsome. Everything you'd hope such a journal would be.

## THE LIFEBOAT
### THE JOURNAL OF THE RNLI

*The Lifeboat*. Royal National Lifeboat Institution, West Quay Rd., Poole, Dorset BH15 1HZ, England. Quarterly. This is the journal of the RNLI. A section called Lifeboat Services gives the details of lifeboat operations during the quarter. This, of course, makes fascinating reading. The journal also serves as a "house organ" for the RNLI. Includes material on lifeboat design and construction.

*Lines & Offsets*. Traditional Wooden Boat Society, Box 10190, Bainbridge Island, WA 98110. This is the Society's "journal." A typewritten sheet that is a combination of articles about traditional wooden boats and newsletter for the Society.

## Marine Business

*Marine Business*. United Marine Publishing, Inc., 38 Commercial Wharf, Boston, MA 02110. Monthly. $20.00. From the people who bring you *Sail* and *Motorboat*, this is a new trade magazine for the boating industry. Management, profit, merchandising, news of the industry, inventory financing, cutting floor plan costs, pricing, the hard sell.

## Marine Equipment News

*Marine Equipment News*. Symcon Publishing Co., Box 1800, San Pedro, CA 90733. Bi-monthly. A slim trade magazine covering technical developments in merchant shipping.

*The Marine Observer*. Her Majesty's Stationery Office, 49 High Holborn, London WC1V 6HB, England. Quarterly. A journal of maritime meteorology. The Marine Observer's Log section contains observations made at sea by ships' officers describing a wide range of unusual phenomena in sea and sky. Articles cover freak waves, ship routing, ice conditions, and so forth.

*Mariner's Exchange.* Suite 2845, 45 Rockefeller Plaza, New York, NY 10020. Bi-monthly. Advertising of boats and gear, together with the usual classified ad categories. Building from 32 pages, containing mostly individual ads for boats for sale by their owners. No editorial.

*Nautical Quarterly.* 141 Lexington Avenue, New York, NY 10016. $35.00. Published to "express perfectly the aesthetics, technology, heritage, and pure pleasure of boats and the marine environment." That's a big word, "perfectly." *Nautical Quarterly* comes very close. Editorial content is first rate. Photographs (most in color), plans, and printing quality have to be seen to be believed. Large, square format. Each issue comes in its own slipcase. This is relatively new. The first eight issues are available at $15.00 each. (There have been rumors—and even a fancy promotional brochure—concerning the birth of a similar publication to be called the *Maritime Quarterly* coming out of Mystic, Connecticut [no connection to the Mystic Seaport, though], but this event has yet to occur.)

*Maritime Wales.* Gwynedd Archives Service, County Offices, Caernarfon, Gwynedd, United Kingdom. A new journal of maritime history that looks just fine.(Now, I hope we don't jinx the thing the way we did *Maritime History* by saying that.) Shipping and trade, sail and steam, fishing vessel and yacht. Substantial and nicely put together.

# NAVAL ENGINEERS JOURNAL

*Naval Engineer's Journal.* The American Society of Naval Engineers, Inc., Suite 807, Continental Bldg., 1012 14th Street, N.W., Washington, D.C. 20005. Bi-monthly. A technical journal on the design and construction of naval vessels and their components.

*New England Offshore.* Offshore Publications, Inc., 572 Washington St., Wellesley, MA 02181. Monthly except December. $4.95. Coastwise and boating news and articles. A bit slim.

*Ocean World.* Box 8819, Washington, D.C. 20003. Bi-monthly. $18.00. A handsome new one "to explore the beauty, challenge and complexity of . . . saltwater." Oceanography, sea law, ocean mining, sea creatures, shipping, commercial fishing. A mix of beautiful color art with facts about the sea.

*Norlantis.* Box 3175, Saxonville Station, MA 01701. Building to seven issues per year from February through October ("we publish when the water isn't frozen"). $2.25. This is the "journal of the North Atlantic underworld." Covers diving, underwater gear, marine biology, shipwrecks, underwater photography, oil drilling, etc. "If it's underwater, we're interested in it." Tabloid newspaper.

# powerboat

*Powerboat.* Nordco Publishing, Inc., 15917 Strathern St., Van Nuys, CA 91406. Speed, speed, and more speed. Covers high-performance motorboats and powerboat racing.

*Rod Crafters Journal.* 14 Chippewa Dr., Allentown, PA 18104. Bi-monthly. A little one that tells all about making your own fishing rods.

# SAFETY AT SEA
## International

*Safety at Sea International.* Includes the Nautical Institute supplement. Fuel and Metallurgical Journals Ltd., Queen's Way House, 2 Queen's Way, Redhill, Surrey RH1 1QS, England. Monthly. "Devoted . . . to the promotion of safety in the design, construction and operation of shipping." Firefighting aboard ship; salvage operations; collisions, founderings, strandings, and their resulting inquiries; operating shipboard equipment safely; pollution prevention; safe ship handling; ice patrol; and so forth.

## The Sailorman

*The Sailorman.* The Polynesian Catamaran Association, 42 Park Hill, Carshalton, Surrey, England. A sharing of ideas about catamaran design, construction, rigging, and sailing. Includes cruising yarns. Tight-budget format.

## Seaway Review — The Voice of The Lakes®

*Seaway Review.* The Lesstrang Publishing Group, 3750 Nixon Rd., Ann Arbor, MI 48105. Quarterly. A handsome trade journal for Great Lakes shipping.

## segeln

*Segeln.* Verlag Für Wassersport GmbH, Postfach 2769, 2350 Neumünster 1, West Germany. Monthly. A German-language magazine on racing and cruising under sail.

## Ships monthly

*Ships Monthly.* Waterway Productions Ltd., Kottingham House, Dale St., Burton-on-Trent, Staffordshire DE14 3TD, England. Good coverage of ships in descriptive text and photographs. Sail, steam, diesel, nuclear power, men-of-war, freighters, tankers, liners, towboats, fishing vessels, old and new. Good stuff here.

*The Small Boat Journal.* Published by *National Fisherman*, 21 Elm St., Camden, ME 04843. Monthly. $12.00. This is a brand new one, published right upstairs. All kinds of small boat coverage: sail, oar, power; work and pleasure; old and new; wood, fiberglass, aluminum, steel, or whatever else can be used to build boats. Small craft have been covered to some extent in other publications such as *National Fisherman* and *WoodenBoat*, but now they will have a magazine all their own. High time.

*Telescope.* Dossin Great Lakes Museum, Belle Isle, Detroit, MI 48207. Bi-monthly. $7.00. A nice little journal of Great Lakes maritime history. One feature is an almost day-by-day journal of Great Lakes and seaway news. Indexed.

## UOMO MARE

*Uomo Mare.* Edizioni Conde Nast (sound familiar?), Piazza Castello 27, 20121 Milano, Italy. Bi-monthly. A huge, colorful, very glossy battle plan of the way the Italians are attacking the water in swift, swept-back powerboats and swift, swept-back sailboats. Text is, naturally, Italian; the salient points are translated in the back into English and German. This is what the American slick yachting magazines are trying to do, but somehow fail to achieve, so, from the people who bring you *Vogue*, *House and Garden*, *Mademoiselle*, and *Glamour*, here is *Uomo Mare*.

## Water Spectrum

*Water Spectrum.* Department of the Army, Office of the Chief of Engineers, Washington, D.C. 20314. Quarterly. $5.50. A handsome magazine about waterways past, present, and future, "management" of the coast, and various projects that involve the U.S. Army Corps of Engineers. Sort of a house organ subsidized by the Army Engineers. Why is this magazine being published?

*The Waterman's Gazette.* Maryland Watermen's Association, Inc., 48 Maryland Ave., Annapolis, MD 21401. Monthly. A newspaper on commercial fishing on Chesapeake Bay.

## WATERWAYS WORLD

*Waterways World.* Waterway Productions Ltd., Kottingham House, Dale St., Burton-on-Trent, Staffordshire DE14 3TD, England. Monthly. Everything you always wanted to know and may not have known whom to ask about cruising in the inland waterways of the United Kingdom. Includes historical pieces.

*Wood Worker.* Model & Allied Publications Ltd., Box 35, Bridge St., Hemel Hempstead, Hertfordshire 1HP 1EE, England. (U.S. distributor: Eastern News Distributors, Inc., 155 W. 15th St., New York, NY 10011.) Monthly. Not maritime, and, in fact, quite oriented to furniture, and probably chiefly valuable to the boatbuilder for methods and ads for tools.

*Yacht Racing/Cruising.* North American Publishing Co., 401 N. Broad St., Philadelphia, PA 19108. (Editorial headquarters in Darien, CT.) Ten times per year. $15.00. This used to be just *Yacht Racing*, the */Cruising* having been added with the January, 1978, issue. Before that it was *One-Design Yachtsman*. Still plenty of emphasis on racing.

# At Sea

That little ribbon of land called the shoreline that surrounds us has become something of a bone of contention in these latter days. In our local waters the children of the Depression and World War II begin to arrive earlier in the spring and leave later in the autumn as they are able to devote more of their time to fluffing prospective terrestrial pillows on which to lay the heads of their salad days. It is an understandable, even sympathetic thing to do, but a little too proprietary sometimes.

Generally it is thought that the land ends at the mean high water line, and that below this fuzzy line lies territory that belongs to the people of the United States—US. Everyone *without* a place on the shore knows this, the clarity of it being subject to some loss of focus upon signing a purchase and sales agreement. Occasionally it's funny. A friend of ours had some mechanical difficulty with his outboard and temporarily beached his boat on a half-tide rock 25 yards off the shore so as to work on her a bit. By and by, a querulous voice is heard from the shore, an irate rusticating elder with a stick(!) allowing as how he was most displeased with this trespass on his half-tide rock.

The details of the ensuing Anglo-Saxon verbal exchange are neither here nor there; the funny part occurs some five or six hours later when our friend arrives back in harbor after a day's fishing to find a yacht on his mooring. It's the half-tide rock owner having cocktails with friends. Funny, right?

Another funny thing going on lately is that there is a mainland surveying outfit specializing in shore properties that has given up using steel tape to measure distances along the shore. They have switched over to a chain, which they drape along the high-tide line *exactly*, over rocks and logs and piles of seaweed, and so on. They then measure the chain used. Funny, funny.

It's going on all over. On the next page is a letter copy we received recently, censored of the relevant names. The writer is a nautical fellow with words for the mayor of a well-known southern port town.

Dear Sir:

My family and I *were* going to sail to Blank from our home in Sarasota. We *had* planned to anchor in the protected waters at the Blank anchorage.

Here in Sarasota, prohibitive costs prevent the docking of our boat at a commercial marina. Instead, we have our boat permanently docked in a sheltered cove a few miles from our house.

When in Blank we had planned to live on the boat, at anchor, for several days while purchasing supplies for the continuation of our cruise.

A recent article in *Sail* magazine pointed out that the anchorage was closed to prevent "undesirables" from living on their boats at the Blank anchorage. I suppose the next thing will be to close off certain neighborhoods just because there are "undesirables" living in them. If *something* had to be done because these "undesirables" were a threat to Life, Limb and Property in Blank, it seems to me that it would benefit both the citizens of Blank and the general boating public to have banned living on board a boat for more than a specified length of time. This way people who are not wealthy but own boats would have a place to keep their boats, and cruising sailors, who don't want to stay at an expensive marina, would have a place to stop, rest and reprovision their boats.

An ordinance such as the one prohibiting anchoring within three hundred feet of the city's shoreline and prohibiting the leaving of dinghies on the beach is tantamount to burning down the barn to get rid of the rats.

In many northern states large moorings are provided by the government and rented to boaters, rather than banning permanent anchoring at a particular area. Instead of banning permanent anchorage at the Blank anchorage, the City of Blank should construct permanent moorings at such protected areas. By renting these moorings for a nominal fee, the City could then control their use.

Anchoring a boat in a safe area where it does not interfere with navigation in a designated channel is a right as old as seafaring itself. It is a gross injustice that sets a frightening and dangerous precedent for the City of Blank to make illegal this ancient, traditional, maritime right. *Who gave you the right to close the ocean?*

Sincerely,
John Boat

*Below: From* Identifying and Evaluating Aesthetic Elements of the Landscape.

> CHAPTER I
>
> INTRODUCTION
>
> Concern about deterioration of the physical environment has been accompanied by an increase in public awareness of the impacts of resource development on existing levels of visual or aesthetic quality in the landscape. It is the intention of this report to discuss the evolution of the importance of aesthetic value of the landscape in environmental management, and to trace the theoretical basis for methods of assessing the visual quality of landscape resources. The major focus of this document, however, will be upon the synthesis of current information and relevant concepts in aesthetic research, environmental psychology, and planning, into a new technique for the assessment of visual quality of landscape resources, with particular reference to the study and evaluation of the visual quality of the coastal environment.

As the bones of shoreline contention increase in number and intensity, government raises its Keynesian head and participates in the issues of what is valuable on the shore and what portion of it remains for the pleasure of the public. But public moneys have to be spent scientifically, the rightness of decisions proved, concepts developed, jargon created, and measurements taken. After all, just because *you* think a view is lovely, doesn't mean it *is* lovely. It could just be nice, or even gorgeous. Anyway, a science of Evaluation of Aesthetic Elements of the Landscape is being developed so that lawmakers can make comparative judgments, As you can imagine, it is a very baroque sort of process. If you would like to take a crack at how it is done, a couple of fellows at the University of Southern California have created a growing body of literature on the subject which can be secured from:

**Sea Grant Office
University of Southern California
University Park
Los Angeles, California 90007**

*Identifying and Evaluating Aesthetic Elements of the Landscape: . . .*
by James O.S. Gollub

*The Public View of the Coast: Toward Aesthetic Indicators for Coastal Planning and Management,*
by Tridib Banerjee & James Gollub

*Who Values What?: Audience Reaction to Coastal Scenery,*
by Tridib Banerjee

*Rocks and Minerals*
**by Joel Arem**
**Bantam Books, New York**
**paperbound, 1973, $2.25**

A dangerous subject this. It brings out fits of moralizing verging at times on towering indignation. Not to be interested in stamps or milk glass is understandable, forgivable. I will share your cup of disinterest. But the earth, the stuff of our being? May schools without required general science taught by good teachers well-grounded in the earth sciences be denied forever a place on the earth they ignore! May there someday be a decent book on mineralogy and geomorphology of practical use for beach-walkers!

This book, the one for kids by Golden Books, and the Peterson Field Guide are about the only things available on the subject and, useful as they can be in some situations, they fall short of our needs. The authors are academicians as well as mineralogical enthusiasts. This means, first of all, that never in a million years will the crystals you are concerned with look anything like the classic museum samples they use for illustration. Second, the mineralogists have the most childish drawings and explanations of how rocks are formed, and the structural geologists simply rattle off the mineral characteristics of their formations.

All we want is something that talks about what we have in hand here and there, now and again, at the beach. This book is okay, even good, but it still ain't *it*. If there's a publishing geologist reading this out there, take your next sabbatical at the beach.

*Right: From* Rocks and Minerals.

### IGNEOUS ROCKS

Igneous rocks form in conditions of high temperature and sometimes high pressure as well. They are therefore composed almost exclusively of silicates, and chiefly those with high melting points. **Intrusive** igneous rocks cool and crystallize deep within the earth or amid other types of rocks at shallower depths. Their textures are generally coarse due to slow cooling. **Extrusive** rocks form by the rapid cooling of molten material ejected onto the earth's surface. Extrusive rocks are therefore fine grained or glassy, due to very rapid cooling.

This overall classification of igneous rocks is based on texture and cooling history rather than composition. Therefore, every intrusive rock has a compositionally identical counterpart among the extrusive rocks. The general appearance of an igneous rock is largely determined by the type of minerals it contains. Amphiboles, pyroxenes, micas, and olivine are frequently dark colored, and rocks rich in them are called *mafic, basic,* or *melanocratic* (from the Greek word *melanos*, meaning "black"). These dark minerals are collectively termed *ferromagnesians* because they tend to be rich in iron and magnesium. Rocks containing abundant quartz and feldspar are light colored, and termed *felsic, acidic,* or *leucocratic* (from the Greek word *leukos*, meaning "white"). *Ultrabasic* or *ultramafic* rocks are very dark and usually consist wholly of olivine, with perhaps some pyroxene.

### Igneous Formations

A **formation** is a rock mass that can be described as a unit. It may consist of one rock type or several types that are considered together for geologic reasons. Formations may also be recognized because they are somehow unique and stand out from surrounding rocks. Intrusive igneous rock formations are known in all parts of the earth.

**Batholiths** are very large intrusions, sometimes extending over 100,000 square miles. They cut across pre-existing rock layers and are thus called *discordant plutons;* a pluton is any igneous rock formed below the surface of the earth. The Greek word *bathos* means "deep," and batholiths increase in size downward. Their slow cooling leads to uniform and moderate grain size; the chief rock in most cooled batholiths is granite. Batholiths form from magma chambers that feed most volcanic activity, and they are associated with many types of ore deposits. They often form the cores of mountain ranges, such as the Sierra Nevada of California.

A **laccolith** is an intrusion formed when magma is forced into overlying rocks, pushing them up into a dome shape. The base of a laccolith is usually parallel to the rock beds below it, but the top is in the

---

*Underwater: The Northern Lakes*
**by Douglas R. Stamm**
**University of Wisconsin Press**
**Madison, Wisconsin**
**116 pages, illus., biblio., paperbound, 1977, $7.95**

We've seen scores of books showing life under the sea—so many, in fact, that they have all run together and new ones hardly elicit a yawn. Our senses were revived by this one, however, because the location has changed. Instead of focusing his camera on Bahamian coral reefs, the author chose common lakes in northern climes. Things are indeed different down there. . . .

VERY NEW HAND (On lookout and sighting red, white and green lights of steamer ahead)—PLAZE, SOR, THERE'S A DRUG SCHTOOR RIGHT AHEAD, SOOR

*Detail of the World Ocean Floor Panorama.*

There comes a point where superlatives turn back on themselves, where their use in all the hype culture has programed us to turn off rather than on to what is being described in such glowing terms. And so, when we come to describe the WORLD OCEAN FLOOR PANORAMA as the most fantastic, splendiferous, incredible orgy of science and color ever to be placed on a confined two-dimensional surface, one is bound to treat it much as one would the guy who lies in wait in the showroom as you stand at the parts counter—with reticence and incredulity. But it happens to be true.

### World Ocean Floor Panorama

*World Ocean Floor Panorama by Bruce C. Heezen and Marie Tharp (1977) was painted by Herr Heinrich Berann in Innsbruck, Austria, and depicts physiography of the sea floor as compiled and synthesized from more than five million miles of precision soundings and profiler records from Lamont Geological Observatory (New York) and many other countries. Supporting evidence from other disciplines such as magnetics, earthquakes, bottom photographs, cores, deep drill holes, and dredges aided in the interpretation of the sea floor topography. The panorama is at a scale of 1:23,000,000 and a dimension of 44" x 72". It is in full color and laminated. Price: $40.00 each, $30.00 each for ten or more. Also available is a 24" x 38" size in paper finishes of laminated or kimdura, with or without grid. Price: $20.00 each, $18.00 each for ten or more. Quantity discount prices available upon request. Shipping and handling extra.*

**Marie Tharp
Oceanographic Cartographer
1 Washington Avenue
South Nyack, New York 10960**

Having listed kites and various baubles in the past, we would probably be remiss to exclude jigsaw puzzles with nautical themes. Koplow makes a series of them, a possible savior during that third day of wind and rain beating your cruise to mushy pulp. From:

**Koplow Games
Box 965
Hull, Massachusetts 02045**

*Top and below: Nautical puzzles from Koplow Games.*

**An Orchestration of Marine-Related Organizations and their Literature:**

The North American Society for Oceanic History has a new address:

**NASOH
c/o Clark G. Reynolds
Humanities USMMA
Kings Point, N.Y. 11024**

**World Ship Society
c/o General Secretary
35 Wickham Way
Hayward's Heath
West Sussex RH16 1UJ, England**

*A Sociable Society*

A most important function of any society is to be sociable, and so local Branches of the World Ship Society have been formed wherever enthusiasts are thick on the ground. The activities of branches are as diverse as the ideas of their committees: an Australian Branch has its own publishing company, whilst many branches duplicate their own newsletters and magazines with articles and news of local interest. The Port of New York Branch recently chartered the *Queen Elizabeth 2,* whilst inland branches in England have been known to cruise on canal narrow boats. All branches, however, provide a friendly atmosphere in which members can meet ashore and afloat to visit, look at or just talk about the subjects of their abiding interest.

*Who Joins?*

The answer is simple—virtually anyone interested in ships. Some members are at school, others are retired. There are members at sea, whilst others work in shipping offices. Many well-known authorities on ships and shipping find membership invaluable. The majority of members, however, are enthusiasts pure and simple, and are content to read, talk about and look at ships.

Membership of the World Ship Society is available to anyone for £5 sterling a year. Anyone requiring further details is invited to send 13p in stamps, or 4 international reply coupons, for a brochure and a current copy of *Marine News* to Dept MC, 9 Crowley Road, Timperley, Altrincham, Cheshire WA15 7ST, England. Any other enquiries about the Society should be sent to the General Secretary, 35 Wickham Way, Hayward's Heath, West Sussex RH16 1UJ, England.

—World Ship Society

**Gaffers Society
1139 Greenwood
Victoria, B.C. V9A 5L9, Canada**

The Gaffers are a loose-knit group of gaff-rigged sailboat owners mainly in the vicinity of Victoria, B.C., although our membership extends into Puget Sound and across to Vancouver. We have no constitution, no rules or regulations, no dues, etc. We put out a Newsletter every so often and we sponsor 3-4 events each year. The 3 main attractions are: 1. The Annual Gaff Rig Race off Sidney, B.C. 2. The Armchair Cruising Series (slides and lies about past cruises). 3. In co-sponsorship of the Annual Classic Boat Festival, Inner Harbour, Victoria, B.C., Labour Day Weekend.

We are not open to sending our Newsletter all over the continent as it is of benefit only to those who can make use of the Club activities, and because the Newsletter is not a subscription but is only supported by donations.

—Gaffers Society

**Seven Seas Cruising Association
P.O. Box 38
Placida, Florida 33946**

The SEVEN SEAS CRUISING ASSOCIATION was formed in March 1952 at Coronado, California, by a group of people living aboard six sea-going sailboats. Their idea was one of merging together for the purpose of sharing cruising experiences through the medium of a monthly Bulletin ($10/year for 12 issues). It is now a world-wide association of cruising folk who live aboard and cruise their own sailing craft.

—S.S.C.A.

**The Corinthians
Membership Committee
c/o Andrew R. Hutson
7 Sunset Drive
Summit, New Jersey 07901**

THE CORINTHIANS is a non-commercial membership association of amateur yachtsmen. Its primary objectives are to promote sailing, to encourage good fellowship among yachtsmen afloat and ashore, and to serve as a "clearing house" between non-boat owning amateur sailors and boat owners needing occasional hands for cruising and racing. The organization is equally concerned with both the beginner and the expert sailor.

—The Corinthians

Most all of the national news magazines have published articles on the Dynaship Corporation's efforts to create modern (and competitive) wind-driven cargo ships. But the next week comes along and the Human Interest editors must come up with something else to talk about, letting the windships recede into the minds of subscribers to become "something they read somewhere." But Dynaship continues, and their address is:

**Dynaship Corporation
81 Encina Avenue
Palo Alto, California 94301**

Teachers(!), do you know about the National Marine Education Association? Well, you should, because 400,000,000 years ago *all* our ancestors were fish, and the kids ought to be told. It's:

**National Marine Education Association
c/o VIMS—Sea Grant
Marine Education Center
Gloucester Point, Virginia 23062**

And while you are writing off to NMEA, you might check out a nice pamphlet on the subject from the Delaware Sea Grant:

*The Need for Marine and Aquatic Education*
**by Harold L. Goodwin and James G. Schaadt
University of Delaware Sea Grant
College of Marine Studies
Newark, Delaware 19711
Free**

*Right: From* The Need for Marine and Aquatic Education.

## Course Outline

1. Boating Nomenclature — Glossary of Terms
2. Small Boat Design & Classification, Origin of Small Craft Design, Fundamentals of Small Boat Design, Classification of Types
3. Fundamentals of Boat Building, Plans & Blueprints, Lofting
4. Boat Building Material, Wood Identification, & Characteristics, Plywood, Fastenings & Glues, Spar & Rigging Material, Ropes & Knots, Marine Hardware, Wood Preservatives
5. The Back-bone — Setting Up — Right Side Up — Upside Down
6. Framing, Planking & Decking Methods — Lapstrake — Carvel
7. Flat Bottom Hull Construction
8. V-Bottom Hull Construction
9. Round Bottom Construction
10. Fiber Glass R. P.
11. Lofting
12. Interior Joinery Work
13. Installation of Engines, Tanks, Steering & Control Systems, Shafts, Pumps, Plumbing & Electrical
14. Associated Yard Work
15. Final Review
16. Cost Control, Inventory & Purchasing, Labor Records, Estimating, Foremanship & Training, Customer Relations

During the course of instruction, the student will be involved with construction of various projects including restoration work, joiner work, and research work.

P. O. Box 371
Norfolk, Virginia 23501
804/627-7266

*Left: Brochure from The Norfolk School of Boatbuilding.*

**The Norfolk School of Boatbuilding
P.O. Box 371, Pier B, Foot of Brooke Avenue
Norfolk, Virginia 23510**

Dear Editors:

The Norfolk School of Boatbuilding is operated by Nautical Adventures, Inc., a non-profit parent corporation. Tuition for the 12-month program is $225.00 per month (each month) or $250.00 per month if the student needs tools.

The first 12-15 weeks of student time is divided among an academic boatbuilding class, a conventional shop class in the afternoon, and student projects designed to familiarize the student in the appropriate technologies and gradually break him in to actual boat construction.

The remaining time (once basic principles and skills are mastered) is directed at gaining specific knowledge by working on the construction of as many different kinds of craft as possible: glass, cold-molded, plywood, lapstrake, carvel, strip-planked. We even joke about building our own paper boat on our cold-molded frame.

—**Nick Benton**

A rich man has a dog. Etc. Etc. There are numerous breeds of dogs that have been bred especially for their affinities for and competence around the water. So we thought that we would lead a series of stuff on water dogs with the:

**Portuguese Water Dog Club of America**
**c/o Diana H. Metcalf**
**243 Cheswold Lane**
**Haverford, Pennsylvania 19041**

## Learning to Sail

If you haven't learned already, you can wing it on your own or go to school. For the latter, the American Sailing Council has a free listing of sailing schools in the U.S.:

*Where to Learn to Sail*
**American Sailing Council**
**Box 5555, Grand Central Station**
**New York, N.Y. 10017**

---

*Underwater Engineering*
by Ron Goodfellow
**Petroleum Publishing Co., Tulsa, Okla.**
**155 pages, illus., 1977, $11.95**

There's a lot of activity going on under the sea in the name of industry and defense. The last decade or two has seen technology give us capabilities unheard of before; as a result, undersea research, mining, oil-drilling, and what-have-you have become commonplace. This book is an introduction to underwater engineering and has such chapter headings as diving technology, inspection and maintenance, underwater vehicles, underwater power sources, and subsea oil production. If you've ever wondered how pipelines are laid under the sea floor, this is your book.

*Below and below right: From* Underwater Engineering.

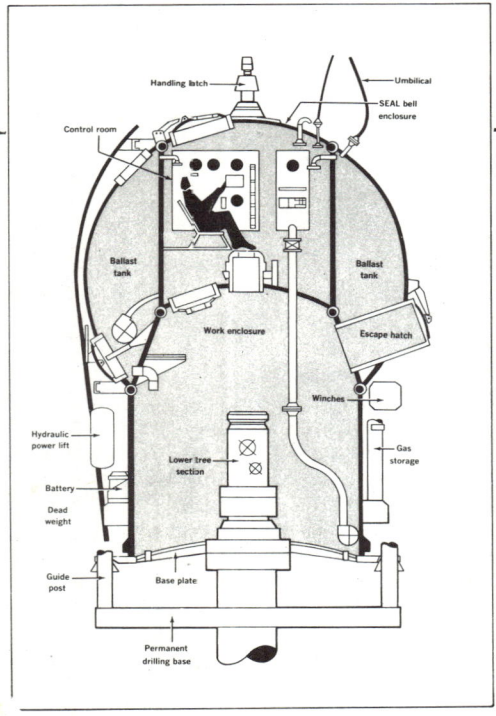

FOR political; economic and logistical reasons man is searching farther and farther afield to assure his supply of oil and gas. Initially, this involved exploration and production in the shallow coastal waters; now exploration is moving further offshore and into deeper water.

The traditional approach of building man-made steel islands proves uneconomic in water depths exceeding 200-300 meters. Structure costs rise exponentially with increasing water depth.

The new approach locates production equipment on the seabed, making the facility less dependent on a fixed surface piercing structure. While the exact amount of equipment to be located at the mudline is currently subject to a number of restraints, two clearly independent philosophies are apparent with regard to system intervention. As with the exploration of outer space where manned and unmanned techniques are employed, so in the exploitation of the sea (inner space) using subsea equipment.

Where manned access is employed, the philosophy is based on the concept that one should not fight the subsea environment, but instead isolate man, and where necessary, equipment from it. Transportation between the surface and the seabed is by a service capsule or diving bell. Other developing systems rely heavily on remote intervention for installation and maintenance using robots or surface controlled handling tools and guide-line systems. Between these extremes systems are developing which provide for manned backup if required to supplement remote intervention techniques.

Thank the stars that all that foolishness about sharks is beginning to dissipate into the obscurity it deserves. We've always wanted to see a horror movie based on ELBOWS, so we hated JAWS from the beginning. They don't want to play our game, then we won't play any game at all, so there.

But, sharkwise, really interesting work is being undertaken by the Shark Tagging Program. This interagency program is dedicated to basic research on the life-cycle, movements, and behavior of sharks. A very interesting feature of the program is that it actively recruits the participation of citizens, both to tag sharks they should happen to catch and to report any tagged sharks they may capture. Thousands of sharks have participated. How about you?

**Shark Tagging Program
Northeast Fisheries Center
Narragansett Laboratory
South Ferry Road
Narragansett, Rhode Island 02882**

*Below: From* The Shark Tagger, *newsletter of the Cooperative Shark Tagging Program.*

SUMMARY OF SHARKS AND TELEOSTS TAGGED
JAN.-DEC. 1978

| SPECIES | TAGGED BY FISHERMEN (SPORT & COMM.) | BIOLOGISTS (NMFS & OTHERS) | TOTALS |
|---|---|---|---|
| **SHARKS** | | | |
| Blue shark | 2,237 | 488 | 2,725 |
| Sandbar shark | 609 | 30 | 639 |
| Dusky shark | 279 | 2 | 281 |
| Mako shark | 83 | 22 | 105 |
| Scalloped hammerhead | 116 | 33 | 149 |
| Smooth hammerhead | 8 | - | 8 |
| Great hammerhead | 9 | - | 9 |
| Bonnethead | 30 | - | 30 |
| Hammerhead (unident.) | 38 | - | 38 |
| Blacktip shark (Small Blk. tip) | 84 | - | 84 |
| Spinner shark (Large Blk. tip) | 11 | - | 11 |
| Blacktip (unident.) | 14 | - | 14 |
| Bull shark | 16 | - | 16 |
| Reef shark | 15 | - | 15 |
| Atlantic sharpnose shark | 62 | - | 62 |
| Lemon shark | 15 | - | 15 |
| Nurse shark | 20 | - | 20 |
| Silky shark | 82 | 5 | 87 |
| Blacknose shark | 22 | - | 22 |
| Tiger shark | 56 | 3 | 59 |
| Night shark | 1 | - | 1 |
| Oceanic whitetip shark | 19 | - | 19 |
| Sand tiger shark | 21 | - | 21 |
| Thresher shark | 7 | 4 | 11 |
| Smooth dogfish | 10 | - | 10 |
| Spiny dogfish | 5 | - | 5 |
| Finetooth shark | 4 | - | 4 |
| Basking shark | 3 | - | 3 |
| White shark | 1 | - | 1 |
| Carcharhinid shark (unident.) | 12 | - | 12 |
| Other sharks* | 28 | - | 28 |
| Total Sharks | 3,917 | 587 | 4,504 |
| **TELEOSTS** | | | |
| Swordfish | 48 | 5 | 53 |
| Tunas | 11 | 3 | 14 |
| Billfish | 32 | - | 32 |
| Misc. Teleosts | 3 | 2 | 5 |
| Total Teleosts | 94 | 10 | 104 |
| GRAND TOTAL | 4,011 | 597 | 4,608 |

*Includes species reported simply as "shark".

### Splicing Broken Rods

This is the most exacting job you'll encounter on the list of repairs that are practical for the amateur. It's really not a hard job, but it does take some time and some careful measuring and sanding. It's a useful technique to learn, though, because it's the same method that you can use to update metal-ferruled rods and lighten them as well as improve their action by converting them to self-ferruled rods.

The one special tool that I've found almost indispensible in carrying out either this repair or the conversion is a warding file. This kind of file has one or more toothless sides, and makes filing an accurate right-angled joint easy and fast. A warding file, with a smooth face at right angles to a cutting face, enables you to file a true right angle, since the smooth or safe face rides along on the work without deepening the cut while the toothed face forms the angle. Machine shops still use warding files; so do newspapers that have Linotypes in the printing shop. If you can't find a warding file, you can make one by grinding the teeth off one of the narrow edges of a regular file. It's not a tool you'll need often, but it does make the job of splicing or plugging a fiberglass rod a lot easier.

Besides a file, the only tool you'll need is a saw. On the materials list, you'll need a section of a solid fiberglass rod of a diameter just a bit smaller than the inner diameter of the section of hollow rod you'll be splicing, epoxy glue, fine sandpaper, and a pencil. You'll also need a bit of patience. You can probably find a used solid fiberglass rod in a secondhand store, perhaps in a tackle shop. Discount houses usually have a bin full of solid glass rods at very low prices—a dollar or so.

*From* The Care and Repair of Fishing Tackle.

### The Care and Repair of Fishing Tackle
by Mel Marshall
**Winchester Press, Tulsa, Okla.
237 pages, illus., index, 1976, $10**

If every fisherman took the concepts of this book to heart, the fishing tackle industry would go the way of chlorophyll toothpaste manufacturers: they would either clean up their act or cease business. That most fishing tackle sold today is shoddy and worthless goes without saying. That the business is in the grip of consumer hucksterism is even obvious to non-fishermen.

*The Care and Repair of Fishing Tackle* teaches you how to get off the bankrupt fishing gear cycle—you know, buy, use, break, throw away, buy, etc.—and do something for yourself, rather than for the Nation's economy, for a change. The author tells you how to make moderately good tackle better, and how to make it last. He also gives you something to do between fishing seasons other than idle away the time slathering over still more tackle catalogs filled with stuff you don't need at prices you can't afford.

### Tales of an Old Ocean
by Tjeerd van Andel
**W.W. Norton, New York
176 pages, illus., index, 1978, $8.95**

To make a sweepingly unfair generalization, scientists have a communications problem. They go out and learn eminently interesting things and fail miserably in telling the rest of the world about them. We want to know, indeed we do, but who can understand what they're trying to say? Books by scientists for laymen are usually hopeless, boring tracts, devoid of meaning except to other scientists. *Tales of an Old Ocean*, subtitled "exploring the deep-sea world of the geologist and oceanographer," is an exception. The author clearly is in love with his work (he's an oceanographer) and he is sympathetic to his audience. He puts oceanography and marine geology in perspective and relates it all in an easy style that makes his book a hard-to-put-downer. We especially enjoyed the chapter on plate tectonics and continental drift.

"A quotation from an author whose name I have never known keeps coming to mind, 'And after the party they all went home and wrote books.' Perhaps it would have been better if they had gone to bed."
—Tjeerd van Andel

We're glad he stayed up.
—Eds.

The trouble with dingdang bureaucracies is that they are so persistent. The bloody things just lie there like a Dali watch until you get over your mad about their proposed leash on you; and then, when you go away to continue your life, they just go ahead with their proposed leashing. It's the old Tar-Baby syndrome.

Some of the most irksome propositions pending during the past decade are those having to do with boating pollution laws. The whole thing has been a stupid scam from beginning to end. Any mariner with a digestive system ought perhaps to look into one of the few voices that remains between dinner and Washington.

**Boating Pollution Control Committee
402 Main Street
Port Washington, N.Y. 11050**

Dear Editors:

Your recent letter requesting information on the Boating Pollution Control Committee opens up a Pandora's Box. As an Ad-Hoc committee, it was formed in June 1971 to rally interest and support of boatmen to attend the EPA hearing in New York on standards and performance of the Federal Water Pollution Control Act of April 1970. We expected to win the fight, but we are still at it 8 years later with a few victories under our belt.

Membership consists of affiliated yacht clubs and squadrons as well as a thousand or so individual members, all of whom contribute from $10 to $100 donations, not annually, but whenever funds are needed. Also, working with other boating groups, we have specialized in and have been in the forefront of the effort at Federal and State levels. A few years ago, together with Donald Danilek, I appeared before the Congressional Public Works Committee representing over a million boatmen nationally.

—**Judah Richards, Chairman
Boating Pollution Control Committee**

## What Have You

Having brought the lubber's craft to sea, we'll now bring the nautical ashore. Two out of three places we wrote looking for rowing machines told us that they were discontinued. Here's one that is not, the $159.95 Rowing Machine, from:

**Hammacher Schlemmer
147 East 57th Street
New York, N.Y. 10022**

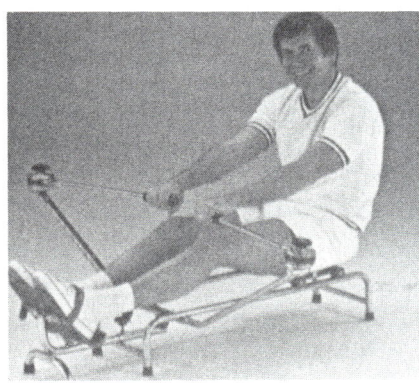

*From a Hammacher Schlemmer catalog.*

Alienate your lovers and friends. Pipe them over the side with really nice bosun's pipes in various (cheap to expensive) metals, from:

**Seamaid House
141 Dogwood St.
Fairhaven, Massachusetts 02719**

They also offer nice bell lanyards.

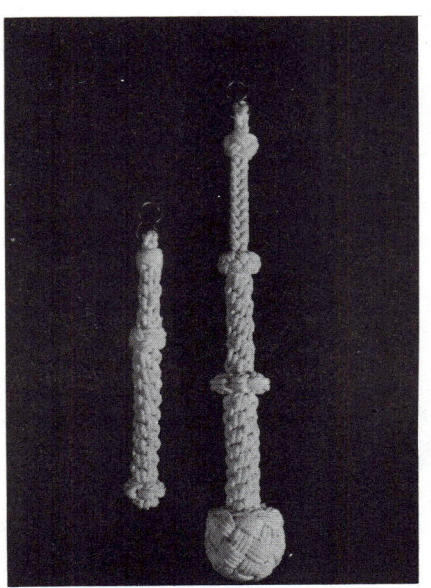

*Good stuff from Seamaid House.*

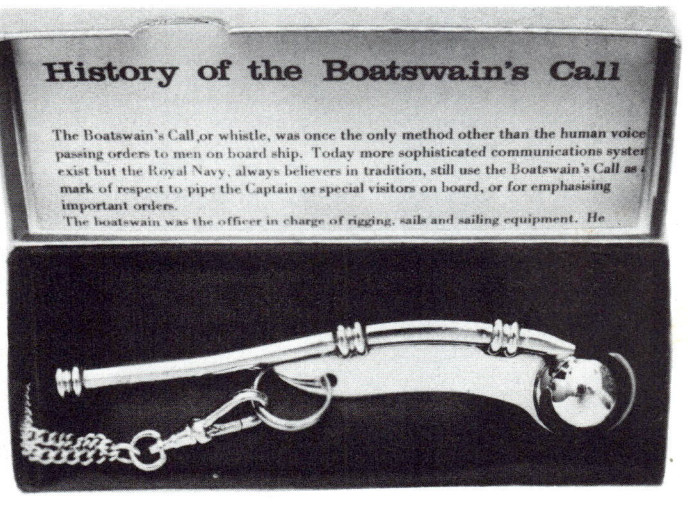

Riverine readers with a throb for towboats may want to pine away over a towboat desk set, $39.95, from:

**Stringham Ranch
Belgrade, Missouri 63622**

*The Nelson Spencer in miniature from Stringham Ranch.*

Here's a floating fish light. Since these were installed on the Great Barrier Reef, fish vandalism has decreased 82 percent, from:

**Fore and Aft
12055 Seminole Blvd.
Largo, Florida 33540**

*From the Fore and Aft catalog:*

### SPACE AGE FLOATING FISH LIGHT

Attracts crappie, white bass, flounder and other species. Ultra modern construction techniques used for durability and long life. Lamp is sealed in urethane foam and encased in a tough plastic shell to withstand rough handling. It is functional, attractive and of the highest quality. 12 volt light has low battery drain of only 3 amps yet has a powerful penetrating beam. Two models both with 10 feet of cord.

**DESIGNED TO FLOAT WITH THE LENS SLIGHTLY BELOW THE WATERS SURFACE FOR DEEPER LIGHT PENETRATION.**

Dear Editors:

As most people concerned with boats have probably found out, Army surplus cartridge boxes provide an excellent container for any rustable items. Well, for the sea-going photographer, better protection than most is provided by these boxes because of their watertightness.

It is quite simple to convert a cartridge box into a camera case by using the Styrofoam packing that comes with new cameras. I find I have room for two lenses, one camera body, six rolls of film and several large filters. If the rubber gasket around the lid of the box is not perfect, try a little Vaseline or silicone sealant.

Keep up the good work.

—John H. Betts
Champaign, Illinois

The bikini of the generators, AquaBug, from:

**AquaBug International, Inc.
100 Merrick Road
Rockville Centre, New York 11570**

*Below: The AquaBug.*

Want to see a neat fish-cleaning knife, especially good for keeping the roe intact when opening the fish? No? Too bad, you're going to anyway... Virginia Sea Grant came up with it.

*Right: Using Virginia Sea Grant's roe knife.*

 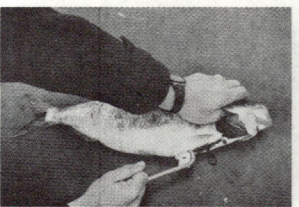 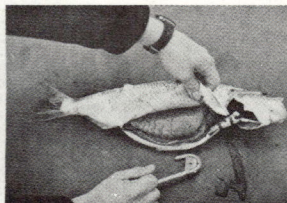

***How to Make and Mend Cast Nets***
**by Ted Dahlem
Great Outdoors Publishing Co.
4747 28th St. North, St. Petersburg, Fla.
72 pages, illus., paperbound, 1978 (rev. ed.), $1.50**

Cast nets are what the name implies: they're cast from shore to cover and encircle a small school of fish. They are simple, cheap, easy to use, and effective. So, too, is this book. The author tells you how to make a net using various methods (and in the process also tells you how to make a hammock) and then provides instructions on how to use it. Included with the book is a netting needle and mesh-size gauge. You provide the line and the desire. This is our kind of book.

Other interesting titles (which we have not seen) from Great Outdoors Publishing Company are:

***How to Smoke Seafood* by Ted Dahlem ($1.50)
*How to Cook Your Catch* by Rube Allyn ($1.50)
*How to Fish for Snook* by Earl Downey ($1.50)
*How to Fish for Bass* by A. Paul Smith ($1.50)**

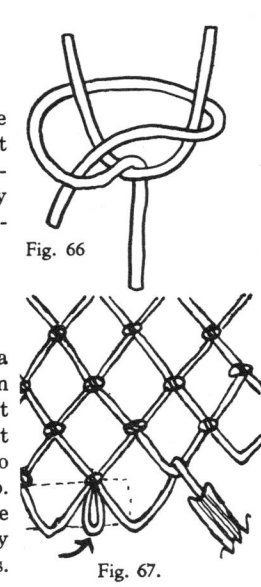

Figure 66
SHEET BEND
This knot is properly called the mesh knot because it is the knot used to tie netting. It is also frequently called a half hitch by many fishermen who are not particularly interested in proper names.

Figure 67
WIDENER
This knot is sometimes called a spacer because when it is tied, an extra space or mesh is created. It is made by going up to a knot before tying, instead of going to the next open (knotless) loop. Each time a widener is made, the number of meshes is increased by one. Paddle shown by dotted lines.

*Above: From* How to Make and Mend Cast Nets.

It is hard to describe to people who have not lived with a weathervane the virtues of these riders of the upper air. Once you have one around the place, other places seem incomplete, uniform, the roof naked where no weathervane can be found staring into the teeth of it. We found a place making these traditional codfish:

**Early American Workshop
Port Sanilac, Michigan 48469**

*Below: An all-copper cod from the Early American Workshop catalog.*

Not ordinarily an advocate of the posh appointment, the *Mariner's Catalog* would, in fact, look quite nice on one of these tables from:

**Emerson Sales, Inc.
19 Doncaster Road
Lynnfield, Massachusetts 01940**

*Below: Elegance from Emerson.*

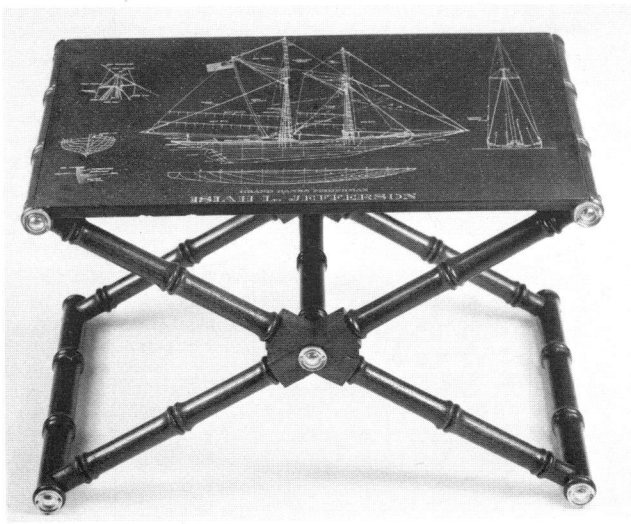

## OH BOY OH BOY OH BOY OH BOY OH BOY!

Every year three or four publishers spring for *their* diving-for-treasure-probing-the-mysteries-of-the-past book, and every year three or four go out of print. Wreck diving and underwater archaeology are compelling subjects and so such books have become *trade* items, with the lack of quality control that implies.

But it is changing, for it appears that the world has become large enough to support: (1) an American Institute of Nautical Archaeology, (2) a graduate program in Nautical Archaeology (leading to a masters degree) and (3) an *International Journal of Nautical Archaeology and Underwater Exploration*. This is great news, for as such things do their work, the public consciousness is increased and a better-informed readership is created. The Institute and the degree program are at:

>  **Nautical Archaeology
>  Texas A & M University
>  College Station, Texas 77843**

"... a fat feast of a publication, with something for everyone, happily unencumbered by chronological or geographical limits ... The Council for Nautical Archaeology must be congratulated for producing a very necessary journal ..." — Antiquaries Journal

"One excellent feature ... is the inclusion of an 'International Newsletter' giving brief progress reports on underwater archaeological sites. The scope of these reports and their number indicate the world-wide interest in marine archaeology. It has long been realised that a need existed for a journal to bring all such material under one cover." — Sea Frontiers

The themes of this journal are seas, ships, cargoes, sailors of the past: subjects which have excited interest throughout history. The *Journal* keeps readers abreast of the latest exploration, discoveries and technical innovations. Studies on ancient ships, harbours, artifacts and cargoes, whether from excavation or documentary sources, will furnish new material for the naval architect, the historian and the archaeologist. The material produced by underwater archaeology is often in excellent condition, and can usually be precisely dated. Thus it is of great value to archaeologists and historians of all periods, especially as much of the material, because of its perishable nature, is seldom if ever found in excavations on land.

Those interested in trade routes and the transport of merchandise will find much stimulating data. For the prehistorian, the discovery of submerged sites and caves can shed light on ancient sealevels in remote periods.

For scientists, papers relating archaeology to geology, ecology and oceanography will indicate the close association of these disciplines.

*Above: From* The International Journal of Nautical Archaeology.

The *International Journal of Nautical Archaeology* is a quarterly, $33.50 a year, and may be subscribed to via:

> **Academic Press, Inc.
> 111 Fifth Ave.
> New York, N.Y. 10003**

## AMERICAN INSTITUTE OF NAUTICAL ARCHAEOLOGY

new branch of archaeology—nautical archaeology— came into being in the late 1950's. Prior to that time, objects of historical interest had been raised from seas, rivers and lakes by sport divers or as chance finds of fishermen. The decade of the 1960's was devoted to development of techniques for the scientific study of undersea archaeological remains. George F. Bass and Michael L. Katzev pioneered this effort with excavations of Bronze Age, Greek, Roman and Byzantine shipwrecks.

In 1973, the American Institute of Nautical Archaeology was founded as a non-profit, scientific/educational organization. AINA's purpose is to gather knowledge of man's past as left in the physical remains of his maritime activities and disseminate this information through scientific and popular publications, seminars and lectures.

Initially, AINA staff members concentrated efforts in the Mediterranean and Aegean seas. An enlarged staff has allowed the institute to become active on four continents, studying ship remains covering a range of 3,300 years.

AINA supports a variety of related endeavors, ranging from research in the treatment of waterlogged wood, to the study of past sea-level changes, to the excavation of harbor towns.

*Diving for Treasure*
**by Peter Throckmorton**
**The Viking Press, A Studio Book**
**New York, N.Y.**
**illus., 1977, $10.95**

The author is one of the most respected names in marine archaeology, not only because his scientific work is so well executed, but also because of the fine work he has done to make underwater archaeology a subject of popular concern, always a necessary step in getting support for these difficult, expensive, and often dangerous projects.

This book is not Throckmorton's most technically complete, nor does it in any way "cover" the field. It is a coffeetable or library browsing book that introduces the history and development of marine archaeology. It talks about wrecks in general, then numerous specific wrecks and the particular problems that each presented to the investigators. It inventories developments in techniques, talks about how politics rears its ugly head in archaeological matters, and, of course, presents superb photography above the water as well as below. It would make a nice gift for a young adult casting about for something in which to become interested.

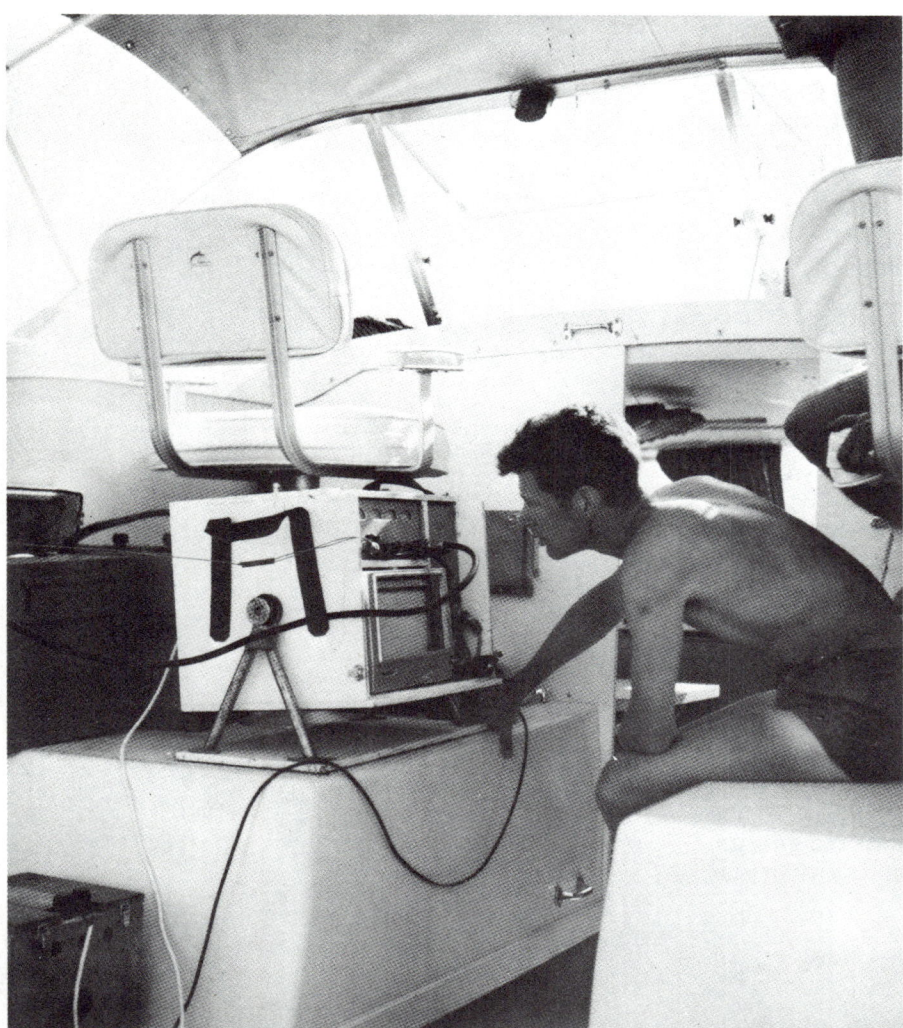

*Left: From* Diving for Treasure.

*The Charter Game: How to Make Money Sailing Your Own Boat*
**by Ross Norgrove**
**International Marine Publishing Company**
**Camden, Maine**
**224 pages, illus., 1978, $15**

The author has been in the chartering business for nearly 20 years in the Pacific and the Caribbean; he relates the who, what, when, where, why, and how much.

## Hooks

We're constantly on the lookout for the unusual, partly to titillate our readers and partly to keep ourselves from going insane from the usual. Not so strangely, the offbeat and unusual many times turns out to be the most interesting:

*A History of the Fish Hook*
**and the story of Mustad, the hook maker
by Hans Jurgen Hurum
Adam & Charles Black, London, England
148 pages, illus., 1977, £ 4.50**

Our amusement turned to amazement after cracking the covers. This is as fine a popular treatment of an obscure subject as you'll ever see—history, uses, manufacturing techniques, theory, the works. We've run across collectors of just about everything; surely there's a bundle of fishhook collectors out there who just have to own this book to round out the library. All others will find it plain, unadulterated good reading.

*Below: From* A History of the Fish Hook.

Lost Arts

. . . Another is the hook maker profession. A long time has passed since the profession went into a decline, and may now be regarded as having died out completely. But at one time it had considerable influence in this city.

The older citizens of Bergen may remember the hookmaker stalls on various centrally located street corners, and on the Hanseatic Wharves. Different types of hooks were sold, and these were both solid and good, whether the dimensions were large or small.

However, foreign – especially English – factories, through Norwegian wholesale distributors, began to swamp the fishery districts with hooks. And Norwegian manufacturers joined in, so that in a short time, the Masters here in this city had a hard nut to crack in trying to compete. As this could not succeed, the Master Angle-makers had to give up.

The old *Lloyd's Register* has gone independent in recent times and, with the proliferation of stock fiberglass boats, does not make the highly variable and interesting reading that it once made. Still, lots of the old girls are still in there, and it is in a great tradition. It's $40 a year these days.

*The North American Yacht Register*
**Livingston Marine Services, Inc.
17 Battery Place
New York, N.Y. 10004**

Once you've broken the shackles of the tackle manufacturers, you'll quickly discover that you can build your own tackle, better in every way than most of what you can buy, for a fraction of the cost. Some time back, in MC-3, page 158, we recommended just that and suggested *Fiberglass Rod Building* by Dale Clemens as your guide. Those who received The Call will be ecstatic to learn that Clemens tells even more in his latest book.

*Advanced Custom Rod Building*
**by Dale P. Clemens**
**Winchester Press, Tulsa, Okla.**
**354 pages, illus., index, 1978, $14.95**

*Below From* Advanced Custom Rod Building.

### NONPERMANENT BONDS

Rod ferrules may wear in time and have to be replaced. Therefore a thermoplastic glue such as ferrule cement is generally used. It is not the strongest type, but when the metal ferrules are heated the glue will melt and the parts can be disassembled. If the parts become loose in use, repair is simple. The application of heat alone will often redistribute the cement, forming a good bond again. If that does not work, heat and disassemble. Scrape away the old glue and melt the end of a stick of cement and quickly smear it on the blank. Heat the ferrule section and the glue on the blank, and quickly assemble while hot. Once again heat the ferrule after it is on the blank to distribute the cement evenly inside the joint. If you carry a stick of ferrule cement in your tackle box or vest, these repairs are easily made in the field.

For years ferrule cement was also used on tip-tops, since in time they grooved and had to be replaced. Today, with aluminum-oxide ceramics, grooving is practically nonexistent. Replacement is largely limited to damaged tip-tops. The ceramic rings are mounted inside a plastic shock-absorbing ring. Too much heat applied to the tip-top tube will be conducted to the plastic ring, causing it to melt. The ring becomes loose and either then or later pops out. If ferrule cement is preferred, care must be taken to use only minimal heat. To keep the ring assembly cool, it helps to hold it in a wet cloth.

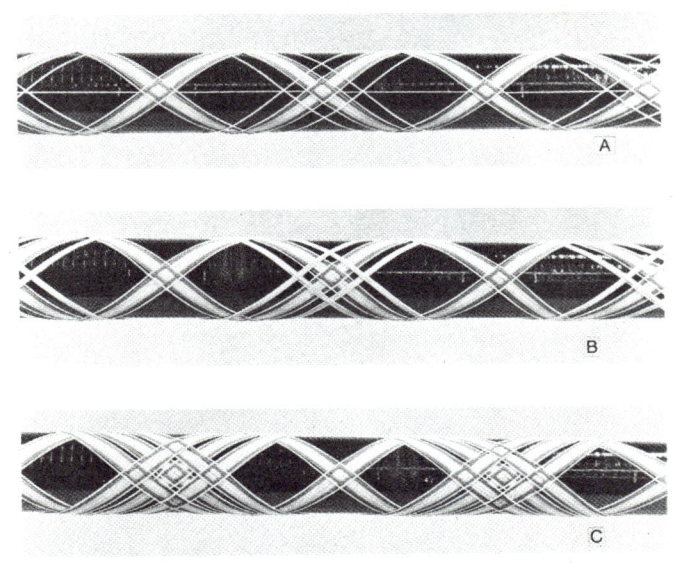

Diamonds surrounding diamonds. A: Small double diamonds completed. Alignment thread and two center threads in place. B: Alignment thread removed and center bands of surrounding diamonds made. C: Completed wrap.

*The Atlantic Ocean*
**by Charles H. Cotter**
**Brown, Son & Ferguson**
**Glasgow, Scotland**
**164 pages, 1974, £3.75**

The vastness of the Atlantic—13,000 miles north to south, almost 30 percent of the earth's water surface—would seem to require a monumental book. How many pages would you expect? 500? 1,000? 9,000? That an author could do justice to the world's premier ocean in a mere 164 pages seems impossible, yet apparently is not. To be sure, we would like to know more, but Cotter provides an entirely satisfactory introduction to an ocean whose importance and influence can hardly be measured. *The Atlantic Ocean* is a barebones book, to be read by those who seek a further understanding of the Atlantic but need to start somewhere. The greatest disappointment, then, is the lack of a bibliography to direct us onward.

The Arctic Ocean is described by oceanographers as a *mediterranean* sea. This type of sea is a large division of the hydrosphere which, like the classical Mediterranean (which is the type example) is almost landlocked. The waters of the Arctic Ocean are almost hemmed in to the south by the Atlantic islands which lie between Europe and North America, and by the two principal coastlines of northern Canada and northern U.S.S.R., which meet at the shallow and narrow Bering Strait which separates Alaska from Soviet Asia.

The Arctic Ocean, because of its unique physico-oceanographical character, is often considered, even by oceanographers, as a unit separate and distinct from the Atlantic. This does not mean that the waters of the Arctic seas are independent of those of the Atlantic or the Pacific, and it is useful to keep in mind that the world-ocean is physically indivisible. In other words no oceanic water-body is completely independent of other such bodies.

Because of the irregularities in the boundaries between continents and oceans it becomes convenient, and indeed necessary, to sub-divide the major oceanic divisions of the hydrosphere into smaller units such as seas, gulfs, bays and sounds.

*Above: From* The Atlantic Ocean.

**Clearwater
112 Market Street
Poughkeepsie, N.Y. 12601**

Dear Editors:

After having read 5 issues of *The Mariner's Catalog* and not seen *Clearwater* mentioned once, I feel it my duty to add to your knowledge of boats for once.

*Clearwater* has been turning people on to wind sailing and off to pollution since she left the ways of the Gamage yard in 1969. 76' on deck, 106' LOA, and carrying over 4,000 square feet of sail, she is believed to be the largest sloop in existence.

—J.J. Smith
North Wales, Pennsylvania

Dear Editors:

Your fifth volume of *The Mariner's Catalog* is a good one as usual, *except* for the fact that you let pass without comment an obnoxious instruction by the National Scuba Training Council to their members "... to support only retail store/schools that require certification cards for air-fill and rentals." (MC-5, p. 179)

Given the fact that you repeatedly carp about over-regulation of, for instance, small boat building, I find it highly inconsistent of you to laud an organization which out of obvious self-interest, both monetary and egotistic, attempts to impose its own narrow control over access to materials in a given field. What would you say if a group of established professional boatbuilders attempted through economic pressure to force the vendors of lumber and marine materials and equipment to sell only to boatbuilders who were "certified" by that group of professionals?

There are many competent people who have spent years studying and teaching themselves a given craft. This writer, for example, has spent over 10 years doing such—having studied, designed, built and repaired boats, managed a full-service marina, personally formulated and applied over 3 tons of epoxy resins in marine applications, and so on, all without having been "certified" by industry professionals. So too, this writer knows a diver of some 12 years experience who is both knowledgeable and experienced, but who happens not to be "certified." Are you going to tell me that it is all right to deny me the materials of my craft and/or to deny that diver the materials of his?

My work and my experience speak for themselves (references are available to any prospective client who requests them); and no organizational "certification" or lack thereof makes me any more or less competent, just as neither "certification" nor the lack of it makes that diver any more or less competent. Certification of whatever form in whatever field is merely a guide and possible convenience for a naive consumer market; it ought never to be elevated to the status of a necessary precondition to practice (medicine notwithstanding), for when it is, craft becomes cult. An organization may have the right to "certify" its members and to *recommend* that only its members be retained by the public for given services. Moreover, that organization may have the right to seek vigorous prosecution of incompetents who cause damage after representing themselves as experts. But no organization ought to have the right to monopolize the practice of a given craft, whether by means of lobbied legislation or economic extortion.

For highly independent and individualistic people, you certainly seem to have missed the point on this one.

—P.L. Friedman
**MPM Marine Enterprises Ltd.
Port Stanley, Ont., Canada**

**The Best of Sail Cruising**
edited by Anne Madden
Sail Books
38 Commercial Wharf, Boston
280 pages, illus., 1977, $11.95

Salted among the pages of *Sail* magazine, between the hopelessly repetitive articles on bareboating in the Grenadines and the advertising that more often than not shows, to quote a memorable quote, "some floozy wearing nothing, holding a stern bearing," are some truly informative practical and technical pieces. To *Sail*'s credit, they have taken the best of these and put them into an anthology of writings by some well-known modern observers like Ted Brewer, Jerry Cartwright, Larry Pardey, John Letcher, and Dag Pike. The subjects covered are: choosing a sailboat, sails and rigging, navigation, safety, tips and ideas, methods, and improvements. It's an excellent book for its type, with the exception of the lack of an index, which it could use.

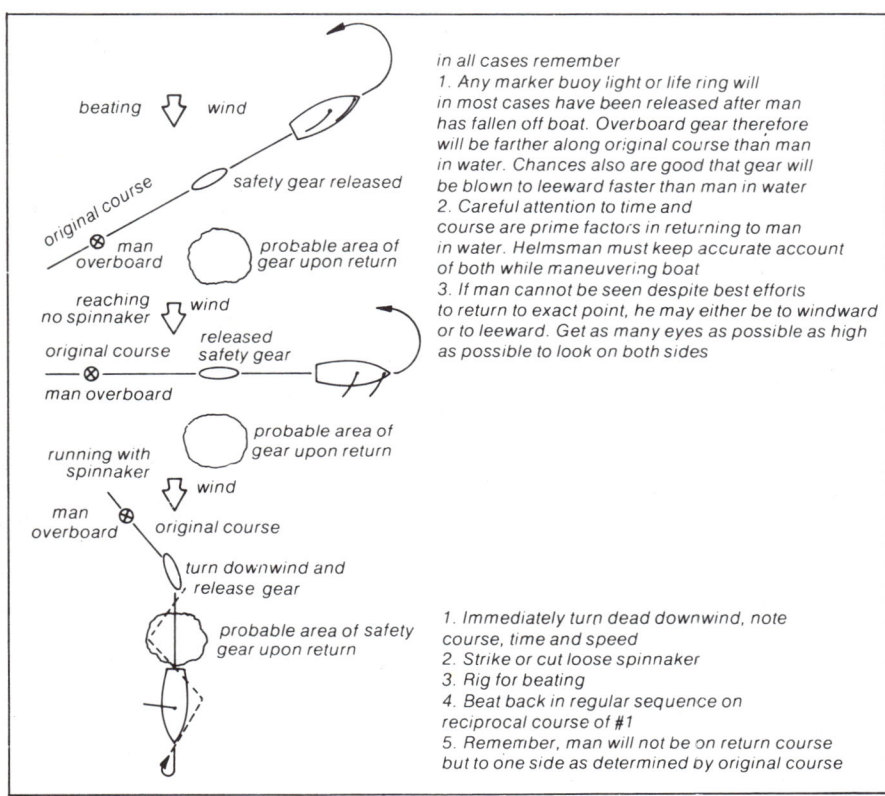

*Left: From* The Best of Sail Cruising.

We were sitting on the porch one day, when a car drove in. Out jumps a very pleasant couple. Hi, there, we're from California and really like *The Mariner's Catalog*. Oh yeah, great. Have a beer. Oh no, thanks. I just want to give you a copy of my limerick book. So we have this limerick book to list, see. And we bet no other marine book ever listed a limerick book before. It's:

**Limericks for Sail Watchers**
by Margaret G. Hindes
Academy Press
Nicasio, California 94946
72 pages, paperbound, 1974

*Right: From* Limericks for Sail Watchers.

A fellow whose name was Ray
lost the gaskets and oars in the bay.
They forgave him for that
but to windward he spat,
so they drowned him and called it a day.

A timid fellow named Price
is very correct and precise,
he coils all his lines,
his binnacle shines,
but he's only been sailing twice.

***The New Glenans Sailing Manual***
**translated by James MacGibbon and Stanley Caldwell**
**Sail Books, Boston, Mass.**
**Dist. by W.W. Norton, New York**
**782 pages, illus., index, 1978, $24.95**

The Glenans Sea Center in France is noted for the thoroughness of its how-to-sail training, and its first coursebook, published a number of years ago and translated into English, gained an enthusiastic audience in this country. This is a newly revised edition of the original book—bigger, better, and as you would expect, more expensive. But compared to other expensive sailing books, and other less expensive ones as well, this one is tops. It is a virtual encyclopedia of modern-day sailing, at least as practiced by the French, and, unlike most sailing books, which concentrate on one level of accomplishment—beginner, novice, or expert—it is intended to remain by your side throughout your sailing career. It's not without its problems, however, the greatest being that no attempt was made to Americanize or deFrenchify(?) the text during translation. Rather, we have a hybrid, since the main translation was by an Englishman for an English audience. So references to government publications, weather forecasting sources, navigation notices, and a number of other things can be very confusing unless you keep the origin of the book firmly in mind. Still and all, if you are using a book to learn how to sail, or perhaps supplementing your field instruction with a book, you will be hard pressed to come up with a better one in any language.

*Below: From* The New Glenans Sailing Manual.

### Making a ship's log

*The float.* Use a piece of 8mm plywood, a small wedge of timber and a piece of lead sheeting for making the float illustrated in the diagram. The lead weight must be just heavy enough to make it float upright, just breaking the surface.

The span consists of two lengths of line, 3–4mm in diameter and 80cm long and a clothes peg. Tie a figure of eight knot in the middle of one length and a loop at one end. Tie the other end to the hole in the piece of wood at the upper corner of the float. Fix the other length of line in the spring of the clothes peg with figure of eight knots on either side of the spring. Attach the other ends of this line to the lower corners of the float. All you have to do now is to clip the peg to the upper line in front of the figure of eight knot (to stop it slipping back). You now have a detachable span. Its three lines should be of equal length. This is a convenient arrangement when the log is pulled in: just shake the line, the peg opens, the float turns edge-on to the water and offers no resistance.

*The Line.* Use a plaited line 2–3mm in diameter and at least 70m long (if you expect to make 8 knots). To attach the line to the span, make a large loop at the end, big enough to go over the float. Pass it through the small loop at the end of the span, drop it over the float and pull tight.

Tie a series of figure of eight knots along the line, the first about 10m from the float. Theoretically the interval between knots should be 7.71, but in practice, as the boat is slowed a little by the log, 7.50m is more practical. Tie small pieces of different coloured materials in the figure of eight knots that can be easily recognised. Flake the line into a bucket attached to the stern.

If you have no such materials, the log can be made even more simply by attaching a bottle to the lead line, filled with just enough water to let it just float. In this case the knots should be spaced at 7m intervals to allow for the drag of the bottle

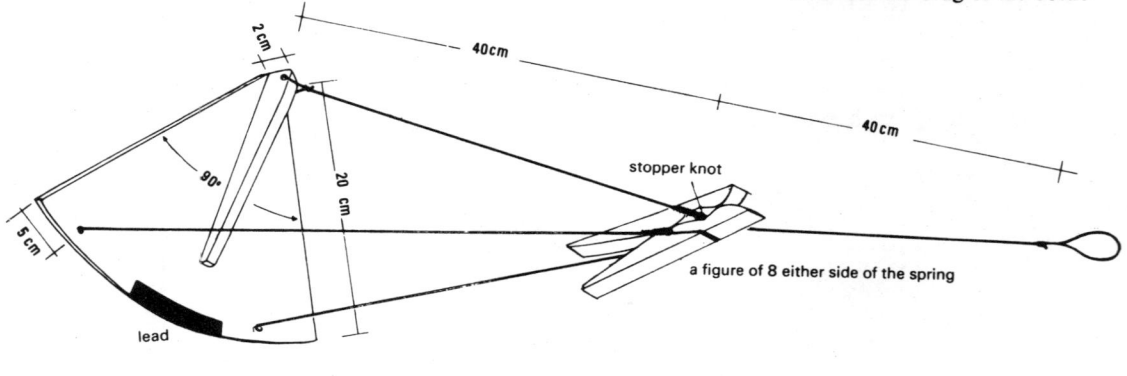

## An Update

**Cruising Information Center
Peabody Museum
East India Square
Salem, Massachusetts 01970**

Dear Editors:

You may be interested to learn that since its incorporation in 1974 this organization has assembled a collection of 1500 or more charts covering cruising areas throughout the world with both large and small scale charts. In addition we maintain a file of "port information" that describes anchorages, places where supplies can be secured and, with limitations, regulations regarding customs, immigration and appropriate special conditions governing visiting yachtsmen.

We are prepared to supply yachtsmen with plans for voyages in the Atlantic, cruising in European waters and within feasible limits, parts of the African coasts. We have supplied plans for voyages along northern South America, around the Caribbean, across the Pacific, cruising among the South Pacific islands, Indonesia and the Indian Ocean to Zanzibar, Suez and so on.

Our funds are limited, we are a "charitable, non-profit corporation" and cannot afford to advertise. However, perhaps your readers would be interested to know that we have distributed some one hundred cruise plans and can provide more. Because each cruise differs, these are compiled to answer specific requests. The cost of these plans varies with the details requested.

—Frederick Johnson
Director
Cruising Information Center

The National Association of Engine and Boat Manufacturers now offers a Boating Speakers Bureau. Here's the pitch. You get your group together and they'll send a speaker to talk about one or another of (to date) seven topics, your choice, with slides, movies, and so on. Arrangements are made six weeks in advance. For information, write:

**Boating Speakers Bureau
NAEBM
P.O. Box 5555
Grand Central Station
New York, N.Y. 10017**

*Below: From a Boating Speakers Bureau brochure.*

### HOW TO ORDER NAEBM'S BOATING SPEAKERS BUREAU PROGRAMS

NAEBM's Boating Speakers Bureau was designed to entertain and inform the public about recreational boating through a variety of programs presented to community groups, environmental organizations and boat clubs countrywide. Representatives of the boating industry in 46 geographical centers have volunteered to present the half-hour programs and answer questions from the group. The five color films and a slide show on sailing focus on environmental concerns, the many ways people enjoy boating today and boating's economic impact on society. Each of the informative and "non-commercial" programs is available at no cost through the boating trade association in an effort to bring a better understanding of the sport to the more than 48 million Americans who enjoy boating every year and to those who would like to learn more about boating.

1. Select a program and set a date for presentation at least four to six weeks in advance. Write or call NAEBM with request and provide a telephone number where the program chairman or organization's representative can be reached, along with an address and a little about the group.

2. NAEBM will contact a qualified speaker within the area.

3. The program chairman will receive a written confirmation with speaker's name and telephone number.

4. The speaker will provide the 16 mm color film (about 15 minutes running time) or color slides from NAEBM's distributor. Your organization provides the projection equipment. The speaker will get in touch with the program chairman to discuss arrangements and specific details to assure a smooth presentation.

5. The boating representative will be glad to answer questions and talk about boating with members of your group. Enjoy!

Tedium became our new enemy. Once or twice we glimpsed enough sun to make it worthwhile to hang the sleeping bags in the rigging and to try to dry out our clothes. But usually the weather was too foggy or too damp for any success. And it was so cold that the next migrant to land on *Brendan*, another water pipit, also failed to survive the night and perished. To pass the time, there was a shipboard craze for fancy rope work, and *Brendan*'s rigging sprouted complicated knots and splices, intricate lashings, and every item that could possibly be embellished with a Turk's head was duly decorated. To add to the boredom, there was an increasing sense of remoteness brought about by our limited horizon, which seldom exceeded three or four miles because of constant fog. Often the fog banks closed in so thickly that we could see no more than fifty yards in front of the vessel, and it was impossible to distinguish the line between air and sea, so that *Brendan* seemed to be suspended in a muzzy grey bowl. The only consolation was that there was very little chance of being run down by a ship. These were desolate waters, crossed only by an occasional fishing boat on its way between North American and the Greenland fishing grounds. Nor were there many coast stations either, and so *Brendan* gradually fell into a gap in the communications network.

*From* The Brendan Voyage.

### The Brendan Voyage
### by Tim Severin
### McGraw-Hill, New York
### 292 pages, illus., 1978, $12.95

We followed with our usual jaundiced eye the news reports of the voyage of the leather boat *Brendan* across the Atlantic from Ireland to Newfoundland, and, as expected, we greeted the publication of the *Brendan*'s story with our knee-jerk feigned indifference. After all, we're Educated Men, and our reputation for being free from the influence of hucksterism must be preserved at all costs. We know—as you do, we're sure—that leather boats can't float in seawater for very long, and even if they could, does it really (yawn) matter?

Much to our surprise, however, a friend (whose judgment we trust) told us he read *The Brendan Voyage* and loved it. Since we're always ready to join a bandwagon, provided it's a good one, we suspended our Good Judgment temporarily and read the book, too. Our friend was right. It's an excellent book, with a story well told and a hint of heroism in today's unheroic age. And leather boats *do* stay afloat.

If you have commercial marine interests, you are probably qualified to get on the mailing list to receive the *Mariners Weather Log,* NOAA's weather journal that rounds up the month's weather and its effects on ships and traffic. Fascinating always, horrific often, from:

**Environmental Data and Information Service, D762
Page Building One
Room 400
Washington, D.C. 20235**

Meanwhile, both Virginia and Wendy had reached typhoon strength and were tracking northwestward. Several Japanese ships, including the KUNIMISAN, NICHIJU, and HAMPTON MARU, battled 40- to 55-kn winds in 20-ft seas along Wendy's path. Wendy had come to life in the northern Philippine Sea and passed through the Ryukyus on the 28th. Maximum winds reached 75 kn near her center. On the 28th the PRESIDENT MADISON discovered 35-kn winds and 17-ft seas about 330 mi west of the eye. On the 29th the PRESIDENT FILLMORE was 240 mi east of the eye with 42-kn gales, 21-ft seas, and 26-ft swells. Presidential ships were bracketing the storm. The 12,299-ton Cypriot-registered ALAMAR ran aground at 33.5°N, 126.9°E, on the 31st.

Virginia's winds ranged from 65 to 70 kn as she approached Tokyo on the 31st. For several days prior to this the VOLNA, JUJO MARU, and ARIAKE 1 battled 30- to 50-kn winds in 20-ft swells generated by Virginia. Virginia brushed Honshu on August 1 as she recurved toward the east-northeast. The following day she was weakening rapidly. This same day she recurved toward the east-northeast. The PRESIDENT JOHNSON (fig. 34) (38°N, 143°W) was nearing Yokohama at 1800 on the 1st, when the storm passed southeast of her. The winds were only 20 kn and the seas 16 ft, but the pressure plunged to 980 mb. The following day she was weakening rapildy. This same day saw Wendy, now a tropical storm, recurve northeastward and move over Kyushu. There was little damage from either storm, but the warm flow triggered by Wendy combined with a foehn wind and touched off a heat wave across western Honshu. Temperatures were driven into the upper 90's (°F) and even to 100°F in some places.

Casualties--Fog was the culprit this month. On the 3d the 998-ton CHIYO MARU No. 11 and the newly built 19,364-ton Greek OINOUSSIAN VIRTUE collided in fog off Shodoshima. The CHIYO MARU was heavily damaged. The Canadian supply vessel ARCTIC PELLY reported at Tuktoyaktuk (Beaufort Sea in the Mackenzie River Delta) with freezing damage.

The two Korean vessels TOSONG and FLOWER collided in dense fog near 35.1°N, 129.3°E. The 13,255-ton Greek-registered STAR K. (fig. 35) and the 15,024-ton Singapore-registered TAIWAN PHOENIX (fig. 36) collided 600 mi south of Kodiak on the 19th, apparently in fog. The USCGC JARVIS was in the vicinity and standing by. Both ships were towed to the West Coast, the STAR K. stern first.

The American tanker GAINES MILL, which capsized off Kaohsiung in typhoon Thelma (July 25, 1977) while being towed to be scrapped, was refloated on July 22, 1978, almost a year later.

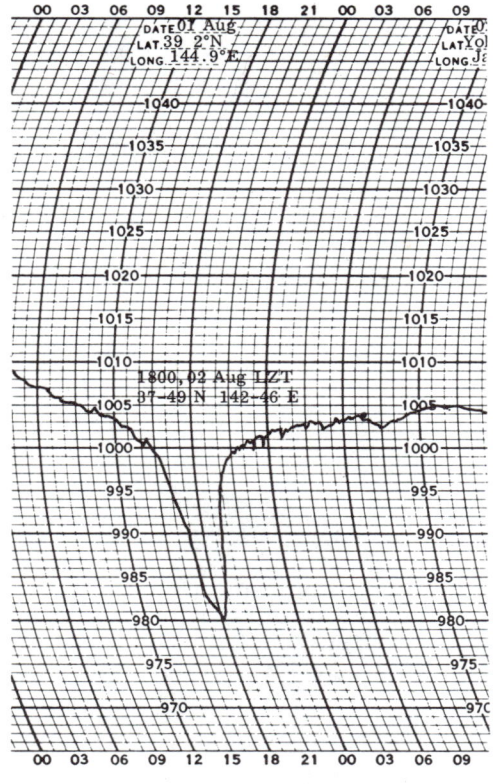

Figure 34.--Barogram of PRESIDENT JOHNSON.

Figure 35.--A view of the bow of the STAR K. U.S. Coast Guard Photo.

Figure 36.--A similar view of the bow of the TAIWAN PHOENIX. U.S. Coast Guard Photo.

*From the* Mariners Weather Log.

"GOOD-BYE, GOOD-BYE!"

# Index

Abbeon Cal, Inc., 28
Academic Press, Inc., 172
ACR Electronics Inc., 92
Adams, Andrew, Development Corp., 50
Adler/Barbour Yacht Services, 52
*Advanced Custom Rod Building,* 175
Adzes, 19
A.G.A. Correa, 47
Aigle seaboots, 84
*Alaska Blues,* 123
Allen, Don, Inc., 134
Allen, W. Lawrence, Dory Builders, 106
Allied Resin Corporation, 11
Allyn, Rube, 171
Aluminum, 8-9
The Amateur Yacht Research Society, 114
American Canal Research Center and Museum, 153
American Crafts Council, 32
The American Fisheries Society, 156
American Institute of Nautical Archaeology, 172
American Sailing Council, 166
The American Society of Naval Engineers, Inc., 157
Amherst Wood Working, 30
Amplifiers, 100
Analog Digital Systems, 97
Anchoring, 159-160
Andene Sales Associates, 56
Anderson, Eric A., 29
Andrew Adams Development Corp., 50
Angler, 155
Annis, P.G.W., 143
Antifouling, 42
Antique engines, 60-61
AquaBug International, Inc., 170
Archaeology, 143, 156, 172-173

*Archaeology of the Boat,* 143
Archer, Colin, 112
Archibald, E.H.H., 143
Arem, Joel, 161
Arima Mast Steps, 76
Arkway, Richard B., Inc., 94
Arrow Iceboats, 122
*The Art of Japanese Joinery,* 21
*Art of Knotting and Splicing,* 149
*Aspects of the History of Wooden Shipbuilding,* 142
Aspin, Terry, 48
*H.M.S. Association,* 48
Astro Chemical Company, Inc., 11
Astronomy, 90-92
Atlanta Cutlery Corp., 26
*The Atlantic Ocean,* 175
Atlantic Shipbuilding Co., 106
Atlas Marine Products, 39
Atomic engines, 58
*Australian Boating,* 155
Auto-piloting systems, 88
Auxiliary engines, 68
Axes, 32
Ayres Screw and Nut Shop, 5

*The Backyard Foundry,* 48
Bacon & Associates, 82
b & r mast & riggings, 77
Bailers, 54
Bandsaws. *See* Saws
Banerjee, Tridib, 160
Barney, Richard W., 27
Bass fishing, 171
Bassett-Lowke Ltd., 130
*Battle of Trafalgar,* 149

Beach Comber Boat Building, 107
Beacons, rescue, 92
The Bear Mountain Canoe Company, 118
Beckson Manufacturing, Inc., 51
Bells, 50
*The Best of Sail Cruising,* 177
*Best of Uffa: 50 Great Yacht Designs from the Uffa Fox Books,* 113
*Bibliography: Wood,* 32
Bierig, David, 78
*The Big Drops: Ten Legendary Rapids,* 121
Bilge pumps, 48, 51
Binders, 137
Bingham, Bruce, 35
Biotox, 42
*The Birth of Navigational Science,* 142
Black & Decker Inc., 12
*Black Men of the Sea,* 150
Blades. *See* Saws
Blagden, David, 49
Blandford, Percy, 40–41
Blaupunkt sound systems, 98
Block Bond, 32
Blocks, for hoisting, 137
Blocks, polishing, 26
Bloogles, 100
Bluebird Dories, 107
Boarding ladders, 134
Boat Barn, Inc., 102
Boatbuilding, 4–38, 43–45, 66–68, 137, 142; plywood, 66–68; steel, 137; wooden, 142. *See also* Boats
*Boatbuilding in Aluminium Alloy,* 9
*Boat Data Book,* 36
Boat design, 30
Boat houses, 134, 136
*Boating Industry,* 155
Boating Pollution Control Committee, 169
Boating Speakers Bureau, 179
Boat maintenance, 39–45
*The Boat-Owner's Practical Dictionary,* 145
Boats, 13, 37–38, 41, 43–45, 101–122, 126–138, 142, 155, 157, 180; canoes, 38, 118–121, 155; catamarans, 157; dinghies, 41; dories, 37, 106–107; faerings, 43–45, 103, 142; fiberglass, 107–110; fishing, 103, 110, 142; houseboats, 115; ice boats, 122; inflatables, 111; kayaks, 38, 120–121; kits, 38, 110, 118, 120, 122, 127–128; leather, 180; models, 13, 126–131; motorsailers, 113; multihulls, 112, 116, 157; plans, 103–104; powerboats, 117, 157; rafts, 121; rowboats, 105; sportfishing, 103; storage, 132–138; surfboats, 104; trimarans, 112; tugboats, 104; wooden, 101–107
*The Boats of Men of War,* 142
Boat storage, 132–138
Boat Study Workshops, 4
Boat trailer accessories, 52
Boatyard storage equipment, 132–138
Bock, Chris, Instruments, 87
Bolger, Phil, 37
Book dealers, 152–153
*The Book of the Unimat,* 13
Boots. *See* Shoes
Bosun's pipes, 169
Bounty Enterprises, 104
Boye, David, 27
Brady, George S., 37
Brandts Hobby, 129
*The Brendan Voyage,* 180
Bridon American, 138
Briggs & Stratton engines, 62
Briggs Marine, 50
Bristol Caulking Cotton, 5
British government publications, 141
Brooks, Fred, 46, 51, 55, 73, 75, 101
Brosius, Jack, 38
Browning Marine Inc., 93

Brown, Jim, 112
*Brown's Nautical Star Chart,* 92
*Brown's Star Atlas,* 92
Bryant and May, 51
Buckets, 46–48
The Buckingham Tool Co., 16
*Build and Sail Your Own Boat,* 38
*Building and Repairing Canoes and Kayaks,* 38
*Building Model Ships from Scratch,* 131
*Building the St. Pierre Dory,* 37, 148
Burns, K.V., 142
Byde, Alan, 120

C.T. (London) Ltd., 10
Cable, 138
Calculators for navigation, 89
Caldwell, Stanley, 178
Caltronic Laboratory, 127
Campbell Chain Company, 137
*Canadian Fisherman and Ocean Science,* 155
*Canadian Yachting,* 155
*Canal Boatmen: My Life on Upstate Waterways,* 153
*Canal Children on the Chesapeake and Ohio, Pennsylvania and New York Canals,* 153
*Canal Days in America: The History and Romance of Old Towpaths and Waterways,* 154
Canal Press, Inc., 153
*Canals Along the Lower Susquehanna,* 153
Canals, 140, 153–154; navigation, 140
*Canoe* magazine, 155
*Canoe Design and Construction,* 120
Canoes, 38, 118–121, 155; kits, 118, 120; plans, 121
Cardwell, Paul, Jr., 126
*The Care and Repair of Fishing Tackle,* 168
Careers in marine science, 146
Carving, 23
Case, Betsy, 115
*The Case for the Cruising Trimaran,* 112
Cassette players, 96–100
Castlok Marine, 74
Catamarans, 157
*The Cattewater Wreck,* 142
Caulking, 5, 7; guns, 7
Cedar Creek Canoes, 119
Celestaire, Inc., 56, 89
*C-Flex Construction Manual,* 11
Chainsaw mills, 32
*Champlain to Chesapeake: A Canal Era Pictorial Cruise,* 153
*The Charter Game: How to Make Money Sailing Your Own Boat,* 173
Charts, 48, 94, 143, 179; dividers, 48
*The Chesapeake Boatman,* 155
*Child o' War,* 143
*China and the Red Barbarians,* 142
*China Station: 1859-64, The Reminiscences of Walter White,* 142
*The Chinese Maritime Customs: An International Service, 1854-1950,* 142
Chip Stulen, Boatbuilder, 43–45, 103
Chopper Industries, 32
Chris Bock Instruments, 87
Christopher Hinchliffe, Books, 152
Chrysler outboard engines, 72
Chubb, H.J., 142
Clamcleats, 53
Clamps, lifting, 137
Clark, Fred, 22
Clauser, Henry R., 37
*Clearwater,* 176
Cleats, 52–53
Clemens, Dale P., 175
Clinometers, 49
Clinton engines, 66
Clocks, 92

Clothing, 81–84
Coastal management, 160
*Coastal Trade*, 143
*Coast and Country*, 155
Coe Mfg. Co., 88
Coepilot auto-piloting system, 88
Cohn, Michael, 150
Cole, Guy, 113
*Colin Archer and the Seaworthy Double-Ender*, 112
*Collier Brigs and Their Sailors*, 143
Collins, Robert O., 121
*The Complete Book of Canal & River Navigations*, 140
Conover Woodcraft Specialties, 26
Conversion units, low-current, 51
Cooke, Francis B., 49
Cooking, 171
Cook Marine Products, 81
Cooling engines, 40
*The Cooper and His Trade*, 26
Coopering, 26, 46–47
Cooper, James Fenimore, 115
The Corinthians, 164
Corp Brothers Inc., 55
Cotter, Charles H., 175
The Crosby Group, 137
Crown Point Marine, 106
Cruising Information Center, 179
Culler, R.D. (Pete), 6–7, 14–17, 24–25, 46–47, 57–58, 76, 112, 135–136
Cummins, Lyle, 61
Currin-Greene Shoe Company, 84
Cut & Stitch Sailkits, 79

Dabberdt, Walter F., 95
Dado heads, 17
Dahlem, Ted, 171
Dahl, Norman, 38
Dana Marine Laboratories, 42
Daniel, C. St. J.H., 142
Davey and Co., 49
David Sweet, Boatbuilder, 101
Davison, Louis, 130
Deck Shoe Renew Kit, 83
Deks Olje, 40
*The Delaware & Raritan Canal: A Pictorial History*, 153
*Delaware Canal Journal*, 153
DEMAG Material Handling Corp., 133
Dennis, Ben, 115
*Design and Aesthetics in Wood*, 29
Design, boat, 30
Desoutter, Denny, 145
Detco Marine, 7
*Dictionary of Nautical Words and Terms*, 145
Diesel engines, 58
*Dinghy Sails*, 41
DiPietro, Ray, 100
Diving, scuba, 176
*Diving for Treasure*, 173
*Division Officers Guide*, 149
Docks, 134–135
Dogs, 166
*Dome Notes*, 12
Don Allen, Inc., 134
Dories, 37, 106–107
Dossin Great Lakes Museum, 158
Dowels, 6–7
Downey, Earl, 171
Drago, Harry S., 154
Dress. *See* Clothing
Drills, 22
Duffle bags, 85
*Dutton's Navigation and Piloting*, 90, 149
Dynaship Corporation, 164

Earle, George F., 29
Early American Workshop, 171
Earphones, 97–98
*Earthbeats*, 147
*East Coast Digest*, 155
Eastcraft Specialty Products, 129
Edey & Duff, 108
Education, 164–166, 178
Edwards, Francis, Ltd., 153
Elco Marine Sales, 111
*The Elizabethan Navy and the Armada of Spain*, 142
Elliott, Steward, 136
Elvström-USA, Inc., 48
Emerson Sales, Inc., 171
*Encyclopedia of Small Craft Maintenance*, 40
Engineering, 166
Engines, 40, 50, 57–72, 89, 129; antique, 60–61; auxiliary, 68; diesel 58; gas, 60–62, 70; installation, 57–58; model, 129; mounts, 50; noise, 63–65; outboard, 50, 63–65, 69, 71–72; portable, 72; status monitoring systems, 89
*Engines for Sailboats*, 68
Environmental Data and Information Service, 181
Epoxybond Cure-Rot, 39
EPSCO Marine, 88

Faering Design, 103
Faerings, 43–45, 103, 142
Fair Price Tool Company, 22
Faire Harbour Ltd., 55
*Fairplay*, 155
Fairtek Corporation, 147
Farr, G., 142
Fastenings, 5–7
*Ferro-Cement Design, Techniques and Application*, 35
Fiat Nautica engines, 71
Fiberglass, 10–11, 38, 107–110, 175; boats, 107–110; laminating rollers, 10; resins, 11; rod building, 157, 175
*Fiberglass Rod Building*, 175
Fibre Glass/Evercoat Company, Inc., 11, 80
*A Field Guide to the Stars and Planets*, 90
*Fine Woodworking*, 33, 156
*Fine Woodworking Techniques*, 33
Finishes, 31, 40, 42; wood, 31
Finlaysen Forge and Foundry, 54
*Fisheries*, 156
Fish hooks, 174
Fishing, 103, 110, 122–125, 142, 151, 155–157, 168, 171, 174–175; bass, 171; boats, 103, 110, 142; hooks, 174; icefishing, 122; menhaden, 151; nets, 171; tackle, 157, 168, 174–175; trolling, 123–125
*Fishing World*, 156
Fish lights, 170
Fish oil, 41
*Fitting Out Ferrocement Hulls*, 35
Fittings, marine, 48
Flinders, Matthew, 142
Floats, 134–135
Foam, urethane, 12
Foods, freeze-dried, 56
Forbes, E.G., 142
Fore and Aft, 170
Fox, Uffa, 113
Francis Edwards Ltd., 153
*Francis Place and the Greenwich Observatory*, 143
Frog Tool Co., 19
Frye, John, 151
Fry, Eric C., 75

Gaffers Society, 164
Gaff jaws, 76
*Gaff Rig*, 78
Galleys, 55–56
Galvanizing compounds, 8

Games, 163
Gardner, John, 79–80, 148
Garrity, Richard, 153
*Gas Engine Guide*, 61
*The Gas Engine Magazine*, 60
Gas engines, 60–62
*Gas Engine Troubles and Installation*, 61
Gear, 46–56; belowdecks, 55–56
*Geartest*, 156
General and Maritime Trading, 50
General Propulsion, 58
Generators, 170
Geology, 161
Gibbia, S.W., 31
Giffard, Ann, 143
Gil Marine, 66
Gimlets, 22
Glenans Sea Center, 178
*God Save the Queen*, 147
*The Gokstad Faering*, 142
Gollub, James O.S., 160
Goodfellow, Ron, 166
*The Good Ships of Newport News*, 147
Goodwin, Harold L., 165
Gordon, Bernard L., 146
Gougeon Brothers, Inc., 22
Government, 50, 141; publications, 141; surplus, 50
The Government Bookshop, 141
Graf, Rudolf F., 18
Grease, waterproof, 39
*The Great Lakes Fisherman*, 156
The Great Lakes Historical Society, 127
*Great Passenger Liners of the World*, 147
Greenhill, Basil, 143
Greenlee Tool Co., 22
Green-lites matches, 51
*Greenwich Observatory*, 143
Gronicals, 54
Gronickers, 54
Gronicles, 54
Gronnackers, 54
*Guide to the Manuscripts in the National Maritime Museum*, 143
*The Gun Digest Book of Knives*, 27

Haft, Jay Stuart, 48
Hafting tools, 24–25
Hall, B. Foster, 142
Hammacher Schlemmer, 169
Hammocks, 85
Handles, 22, 24–25; for tools, 24–25
Hand tools. *See* Tools
*Harbour & Shipping*, 156
*The Hardanger Faering*, 142
Harken Yacht Fittings, 53
Harmony Boats, 105
Harra, John, Wood & Supply Co., 17
J. P. Hartog, 103
Hartsell Boat Hoist Mfg. Co., 133
Harvey, Michael, 35
Headphones, 97–98
Heaters, water, 5
Heezen, Bruce C., 162
Henri-Lloyd marine clothing, 82
Her Majesty's Stationery Office, 141
Ted Hermann's Boat Shop, 110
Hinchliffe, Christopher, Books, 152
Hindes, Margaret G., 177
Hinterhoeller Yachts Ltd., 109
History Book Shop, 152
*History of Ships*, 147
*A History of the Fish Hook*, 174
Hjersman, Peter, 12

Hoists, 132, 137
Holland Marine Design, 103
Holt, Jack, 38
Holywell Development Corp., 52
Hooks, fish, 174
Hornblower Marine Scientific, 49
Horsley, John E., 12
*Houseboat*, 115
*How to Cook Your Catch*, 171
*How to Fish for Bass*, 171
*How to Fish for Snook*, 171
*How to Make and Mend Cast Nets*, 171
*How to Make Knives*, 27
*How to Smoke Seafood*, 171
Howard-Williams, Jeremy, 41
Howse, Derek, 143
Hughes, B.R., 27
Hughes, J.P., International, Inc., 111
Hurum, Hans Jurgen, 174
Hydrahoists, 132
*Hydrofoil Options*, 114

Ice boats, 122
Iceboxes, 51
Ice Eaters, 138
*Ice Fishing*, 122
*Identifying and Evaluating Aesthetic Elements of the Landscape*, 160
IDTV Enterprises, 38
*Index of Model Periodicals, 1971 through 1975*, 126
Indiana Mills and Manufacturing Co., 52
Inflatables, 111
*Inshore Fishing Craft of the Southern Baltic*, 142
Installation of engines, 57–58
*Instant Boats*, 37
Instruments, musical, 100
Insulation, 12
Intercoms, 100
*Internal Fire*, 61
*The International Journal of Nautical Archaeology and Underwater Exploration*, 156, 172
International Marine Instruments, 88
*The Irrawady Flotilla Company*, 142

JABSCO Products, 93
Jacob Design, 121
Art Javes Design, Ltd., 110
Jaws, gaff, 76
Jay, F. Scott, & Co., 30
Jay Stuart Haft, 48
Jet propulsion, 70
Jigsaw puzzles, 163
John Harra Wood & Supply Co., 17
Joinery, 6–7, 21. *See also* Fastenings
Jointer knives. *See* Knives
J.P. Hughes International, Inc., 111
Junks, model kits, 128

Kayaks, 38, 120–121; plans, 121
Kennedy, Barry, 11
Kilby, Kenneth, 26
Kingfisher Yachts, 106
Kinney, Francis S., 116
Kits, 38, 110, 118–120, 122, 127–128, 131; canoe, 118, 120; ice boats, 122; models, 127–128, 131
Knight, R.J.B., 143
Knives, 14–17, 22, 27, 170; making, 27; sharpening, 14–17
Knots, 75, 149
*Knots and Ropework*, 75
Knotstick, 89
Koghlane's Waterproof Matches, 51
Koplow Games, 163
L.D. Kreitz Inc., 13

The La Conner Company, 85
Ladders, boarding, 134
Laidlaw-Dickson, D.J., 13
*Lake Log Chips*, 147
Laminating rollers, 10
Lamps, navigation, 49
Lapstrake boatbuilding, 37, 45
*Lapstrake Boatbuilding*, 37
*The Last Log of the Schooner Isabella*, 142
*The Last of the Mohicans*, 115
Latin Percussion Inc., 100
Law, maritime, 146, 152
Layton, C.W.T., 145
Leather boats, 180
Leather, John, 78, 112
Leroy, David, 38, 50
Lester, Reginald M., 95
Letcher, John S., Jr., 86
*Lettering Design*, 35
Lewis, Jack, 27
*The Lifeboat*, 156
Lights, 92-93, 170; search, 93; strobe, 92; fish, 170
*Limericks for Sail Watchers*, 177
*Lines & Offsets*, 156
Lipke, Paul, 43-45
Liquid Galvanize, 8
Little, Gene, 122
*Lives of the Liners*, 147
Livingston Marine Services, Inc., 174
*Lloyd's Register*, 174
Lockley Recreational Products Division, 122
*Loss of the Titanic*, 147
Louis Davison, 130
Loveless, Robert W., 27
Lowell's Boat Shop, 105
Lowery Bros., Inc., 137
Luggage, 85
Lugsails, 78
Lumber. *See* Wood
Lyteze Products, Ltd., 74

MacGibbon, James, 178
Madden, Anne, 177
Maggs Brothers, 153
Maintenance, 39-45
*The Making of Tools*, 23
Makita saws, 17
*The Mallet*, 23
*Maps and Map-Makers*, 94
Marco, 69
Marine archaeology, 143, 156, 172-173
*Marine Business*, 156
*Marine Careers, Selected Papers*, 146
Marine Construction and Design Co., 69
Marine Development & Research Corp., 83
*Marine Dock Lines*, 134
Marine Docks, 134
*Marine Equipment News*, 156
Marine News, 163
*The Marine Observer*, 156
*Marine Refrigeration for the Do It Yourself Sailor*, 56
*Mariner's Exchange*, 157
*Mariners Weather Log*, 181
Marine Yacht Services, 132
Maritime Bookshop, 152
*Maritime History*, 155, 157
*Maritime Quarterly*, 157
*Maritime Struggle for India*, 143
*Maritime Wales*, 157
Markow, Herbert L., 146
Marshall, Mel, 168
Marshall Sails, 78

Maryland Watermen's Association Inc., 158
Masts, 77
Mast steps, 76
Matches, 51
Maté, Ferenc, 115
Mate-B40 auto-piloting system, 88
*Materials Handbook*, 37
*Matthew Flinders*, 142
May, W.E., 142-143
McGrail, S., 142-143
McKee, E., 142
McKelvey, William J., Jr., 153
Mechanical Methods Co., 133
Medalist-Universal Motors, 58
Medicine, 142
Meese, George E., 104
Megasystems, Inc., 89
*The Men All Singing: The Story of Menhaden Fishing*, 151
Menger Enterprises Inc., 105
Menhaden fishing, 151
Menzel, Donald H., 90
*Merchant Schooners*, 143
Merry, I.D., 142
*Metal Fighting Ships in the Royal Navy*, 143
Midland Safety Systems, 52
Mildew Magic, 80
Miller, Conrad, 68
Mills, chainsaw, 32
Minderman Marine Mfg. Co., 133
Mischke, Virgil, 59
Model Exports Ltd., 128
Modelmaking, 13, 126-131; engines, 129; exhibitions, 130; kits, 127-128, 131; plans, 127; propellers, 129; tools, 13, 127
*The Modern Blacksmith*, 23
*Modern Sailmaking*, 40-41
Moore, Patrick, 91
Mooring systems, 135-136
Morris, Thomas D.C., 108
Motors. *See* Engines
*Motorsailers*, 113
Mountain House, 56
Mounts for engines, 50
Mudie, Colin, 117
Mudie, Rosemary, 117
Multihulls, 112, 116, 157; catamarans, 157; trimarans, 112
Museums, 23, 142, 153, 155, 158
Music systems, 96-100; instruments, 100
Mustad fishhooks, 174

NAEBM, 179
Nakamichi Research Inc., 97
Nameboards, 35
Nash, Roderick, 121
National Association of Engine and Boat Manufacturers (NAEBM), 179
National Carvers Museum Foundation, 23
*National Carvers Review*, 23
National Marine Education Association, 164
National Maritime Museum, 142-144
National Scuba Training Council, 176
*The Nature and Aesthetics of Design*, 30
*The Nature and Art of Workmanship*, 30
Nautical Adventures Inc., 165
*Nautical Quarterly*, 157
Naval Engineers, American Society of, 157
*Naval Engineer's Journal*, 157
Naval Institute, U.S., 148-149
*Naval Policy Between the Wars*, 142, 149
*Naval Review*, 148
Navigation, 48-49, 86-95, 140, 142-143, 149, 179; calculators, 89; charts, 48, 94, 143, 179; lamps, 49

*Navigation and Nautical Astronomy*, 90
*Navigation in the Days of Captain Cook*, 142
Navik self-steering system, 87
Navy ship model kits, 131
*The Need for Marine and Aquatic Education*, 165
Nets, 171
*New England Offshore*, 157
*The New Glenans Sailing Manual*, 178
Nicolson, Ian, 36
*The Nigger of the Narcissus*, 150
Nightwriter, 89
NOAA, 181
Noble, A., 142
Noise, from engines, 63–65
The Norfolk School of Boatbuilding, 165
Norgrove, Ross, 173
*Norlantis*, 157
The North American Society for Oceanic History, 163
The North American Yacht Register, 174
*North East Coast Cobles*, 142
*The North Ferriby Boats*, 142
Northeast Fisheries Center, 167
Northwest River Supply, 121
Nuts. *See* Fastenings
NYLET Ltd., 128

The Oak Cleat and Canvas Bucket Company, 48
Oar holders, 52
*The Observer's Book of Astronomy*, 91
*The Observer's Book of Weather*, 95
Oceanography, 161–162, 168
*Ocean World*, 157
Oddy, W.A., 142
*Old Bay Line*, 147
Old Town Canoe Company, 120
*One-Design Yachtsman*, 158
Opahl Absorber, 48
*The Opening of the Pacific—Image and Reality*, 142
Oregon Freeze Dry Foods, Inc., 56
Ostlund, Ben, 104
Otner-Botner, 19
*The Outboard Book*, 69
Outboard engines, 50, 63–65, 69, 71–72; engine mounts, 50
*The Outdoorsman's Guide to Government Surplus*, 50
Outjet, 70
*Out of Appledore*, 143

Pacific Boats, 119
*Pacific Yachting*, 155
Paget-Tomlinson, Edward W., 140
C.W. Paine Yacht Design Co., 109
Paint, 42
Pak-Alls, 85
Pansy Mark V stove, 55
Parallel rules, 49
Payson, Harold H., 37
Pendragon House, 141
Pendragon House of Connecticut, 141
Pike, Dag, 113
Piling caps, 135
Piloting: piloting systems, 88. *See also* Navigation
Pioneer sound systems, 98
Pipes, bosun's, 169
Place, Francis, 143
Planes, 14–17, 19–20, 25; sharpening, 14–17
Plans, 103–104, 121, 127; canoe, 121; kayak, 121; models, 127
C. Plath, 89
R.C. Plath Co., 52
Platzer, Michael K.H., 150
*Plymouth's Ships of War*, 142

Polishing blocks, 26
Pollution, 169
The Polynesian Catamaran Association, 157
Pontoons, 134
Portable engines, 72
Portalign Tool Corp., 22
Port Canvas Company, 85
Porter, Kent, 131
Portuguese Water Dog Club of America, 166
*Postcard Collectors Gazette*, 144
Potter, J.D., 153
*Powerboat*, 157
Powerboats, 117, 157
Power drives, 16
The Power House, 138
Power tools. *See* Tools
*Power Yachts*, 117
Precision Drill Guide, 22
Precision Petite Ltd., 126
Primrose, Angus S., 104
*Problems of Medicine at Sea*, 142
*Problems of Ship Management and Operation 1870–1900*, 142
*Problems of the Conservation of Waterlogged Wood*, 142
*Proceedings*, 148
Propellers, model, 129
*The Public View of the Coast: Toward Aesthetic Indicators for Coastal Planning and Management*, 160
Pumps, bilge, 48, 51
Purette water systems, 56
Puzzles, jigsaw, 163
Pye, David, 30

Quartz Micro Alarm Clocks, 92
*Quayside Camera*, 143

Radar reflectors, 76
Rafts, 121
Rainier Fishermen's Slippers, 84
Rapids, guide to, 121
Ratcliff binders, 137
Rathbun, J.B., 61
Ray DiPietro, 100
Reads Sail Maker sewing machine, 81
*The Recycling, Use & Repair of Tools*, 23
Red Wing Motor Co., 59
Redmond, Steve, 119
Reefing systems, 53
Reflectors, radar, 76
Refrigeration, 51–52, 56
Resins, 11
Richard B. Arkway, Inc., 94
The Ridge Tool Company, 16
Rigging, 68, 73–81
The Rigging Gang, 73
Ritchie, G.S., 142
Rivers, 121, 140; navigating, 140; running, 121
Roberts & Adams, 102
*Rocks and Minerals*, 161
Rod building, 157, 175
*Rod Crafters Journal*, 157
Roskill, S.W., 142
Ross Chemical Products Company, 8
Rot, cures for, 39
Rowboats, 105
Rowing machines, 169
Royal National Lifeboat Institution, 156
*Rudder*, 155
Rudders, 86
Rudolph, W., 142
Rules, parallel, 49
Runciman, Walter, 143

*Rutters of the Sea*, 143
Ruval Company, 83

*Safety at Sea International*, 157
*Sail*, 177
Sailing manuals, 178
Sailing schools, 166, 178
Sailing Specialties, 135
Sailmaking, 40, 41, 81
Sailomat self-steering system, 87
Sailor Boy Products, Inc., 56
*The Sailorman*, 157
The Sailor's Bookshop, 152
Sails, 40, 41, 78, 81; kits, 79; sailmaking, 40, 41, 81; tanning, 79–80
Sanders, 20
Sanderson, M., 143
S & R Marine, 122
Sanford Boat Company Inc., 102
Saws, 14–17, 25; blades, 14–17; handles, 25; sharpening, 14–17
Scanmar Marine Products, 87
Scarffer, 22
Schaadt, James G., 165
Schaefer Marine Inc., 53
Schools, 165–166, 178; boatbuilding, 165; sailing, 166, 178
Schweiss, Paul, 43–45
*Science and the Techniques of Navigation in the Renaissance*, 142
Scotcade Ltd., 92
*Scottish Inshore Fishing Vessels*, 142
Scotty's Incorporated, 84
Screws. *See* Fastenings
Scrub planes, 19
Scuba diving, 176
Sculpture Associates Ltd., Inc., 19
*Sea*, 155
*Sea Charts*, 143
Seacourse auto-piloting system, 88
Seafood, smoking, 171
Seagull engines, 72
Seamaid House, 169
Seamatic II Monitoring and Control Systems, 89
*Seaport*, 155
Searchlights, 92–93
*Seaway Review*, 158
Sebago shoes, 84
*The Second World War in the Pacific*, 142
Security Caulking Cotton, 5
Seemann Plastics, 11
*Segeln*, 158
Seike, Kiyosi, 21
*Self-Steering for Sailing Craft*, 86
Self-steering systems, 86–87, 93
Seven Seas Cruising Association, 164
Severin, Tim, 180
Sewing machines for sailmaking, 81
Shark Tagging Program, 167
Sharp & Company Ltd., 88
Sheet stoppers, 53
S.H.G. Marine, 128
*Shipbuilding in North Devon*, 142
*Shipbuilding in the Port of Bristol*, 142
Ship Models, Inc., 128
The Ship Recognition Corps, 139–140
*Ship Registers of the Port of Hayle*, 142
*Ships and Aircraft of the U.S. Fleet*, 149
Ship's bells, 50
*Ships Monthly*, 158
Shoes, 83–84
Shoreline, 159–161
Side thrusters, 69–70
Simmons, Walter J., 37
Sims, Ernest H., 9

Singlehanded cruising, 49, 53
*Single-Handed Cruising*, 49
6-H Products Ltd., 120
*Skiffs and Schooners*, 24, 57
*Sky and Telescope*, 92
Slade, W.J., 143
Slippers. *See* Shoes
Slocum, Joshua, 112
*The Small Boat Journal*, 148, 158
*Small Boat Law*, 146
*Small Gasoline Engines*, 62
Smith, A. Paul, 171
Smith, Art, 56
Smoking seafood, 171
Snap-Ease, 50
Sneve-Nysether, 53
Snook fishing, 171
Snow & Nealley Co., 32
*Snubbing Thro' Jersey*, 153
Solar stills, 56
Soniar Electronics Inc., 100
R. Sorsky, Bookseller, 152
Sound systems, 96–100
*Sources and Techniques in Boat Archaeology*, 143
Southeastern Equipment Company, Inc., 134
Southern California, University of, 160
Southern Sails, 110
*South Street Reporter*, 155
South Street Seaport Museum, 155
Sparkman & Stephens, 116
Spars, 77
Spartan Marine Products, Inc., 50
Speakers bureau, 179
Speakers, sound, 96–100; underwater, 99–100
Speck, Ray, 43–45
Speed determining devices, 89
Sperber Tool Works Inc., 32
Spinnaker Sally, 78
Sportfishing, 103, 155, 168, 174–175
*The Spray: Building and Sailing a Replica of Joshua Slocum's Famous Vessel*, 112
*Spritsails and Lugsails*, 78
Stamford Packaging Co., 135
Stamm, Douglas R., 161
Stars, 90–92
Status monitoring systems for engines, 89
Staysail Yachts, Ltd., 109
Steamboxes, 5
*Steam Coasters and Short Sea Traders*, 140
The Steamfitter, 129
Steamships, 147
Steering. *See* Navigation
Stemgas Publishing Co., 60–61
*Step-by-Step Knifemaking*, 27
Stephens, Olin, 116
Stephens, Rod, 116
Stephenson, George E., 62
Steps, 76
Sterling Hardware—Marine Division, 50
Sterling Models Inc., 127
Stern, Terry, 85
Stills, solar, 56
Stokes Marine Supply Inc., 59
Storage of boats, 132–138
Storey, Norman, 153
Stoves, 55
Stowe Canoe Company, 120
Stratos Models, 129
Stringham Ranch, 170
Stulen, Chip, Boatbuilder, 43–45, 103
Submarines, model, 130

*Sundials on Walls*, 142
Super Craft Products, 134
Surfboat plans, 104
Surplus, government, 50
Sweet, David, Boatbuilder, 101
*Swords for Sea Service*, 143
*The Symposium Book*, 116

Tables, 13, 171; folding extension, 13
Tackle for fishing, 157, 168, 174–175
Talbot-Booth, E.C., 139
*Talbot-Booth's Merchant Ships*, 139
*Tales of an Old Ocean*, 168
*Tales the Boatmen Told*, 153
Tanning sails, 79–80
Taylor, E.G.R., 142
*Ted Turner: The Man Behind the Mouth*, 154
Telescope, 158
Termalene Marine Division, 39
Termites, 42
Tharp, Marie, 162
Thermometers, 49
*Three Major Ancient Boat Finds in Britain*, 142
Throckmorton, Peter, 173
Tie-downs, 52
Tiller holders, 87
*The Timber Framing Book*, 136
*Tompion Clocks at Greenwich*, 143
*The Tool Catalog*, 26
Tooley, R.V., 94
Tools, 12–20, 22–28, 32, 127; modeling, 13, 127; power, 18; sharpening, 14–17
*Tools of the Maritime Trades*, 12
Towboats, 170
Towing lines, 52
Traditional Watercraft, 107
Traditional Wooden Boat Society, 101, 156
Trimarans, 112
Trolling, 123–125
Trunneling, 6–7
Tucker, Robert, 35
Tuckgammons, 46
Tugboat plans, 104
Tung Woo navigation lamps, 49
Turner, Ted, 154
Twin-Tow lines, 52

Underhill, Harold A., 130
*Underwater Engineering*, 166
*Underwater: The Northern Lakes*, 161
Unicorn Universal Woods Ltd., 30
Unimat, 13
U.S. Government Printing Office, 141
United States Naval Institute, 148–149
*U.S. Submarines*, 130
*Uomo Mare*, 158
Upton, Joe, 123–125
Urethane foam, 12

Van Andel, Tjeerd, 168
Vaughan, Roger, 154
Venus Products Inc., 10
*Very Willing Griffen*, 49
*Victorian and Edwardian Sailing Ships*, 143, 149
*Victorian Maritime Album*, 143
*Victory Ships and Tankers*, 147
Village Marine, 56
Villiers, Alan, 143

Virginia Sea Grant, 170
*The Visual Encyclopedia of Nautical Terms Under Sail*, 145
*VNR Illustrated Guide to Power Tools*, 18
Voyageur Motors, Inc., 71
*Voyaging With the Wind*, 143

Waine, Charles V., 140
Wallas, Eugenie, 136
Ward-Jackson, C.H., 142
Warren, Nigel, 69
Warren Tools, 22
Water, 5, 56, 138, 158; circulators, 138; heaters, 5; purification systems, 56
*Waterhouses: The Romantic Alternative*, 115
Waterline Shipmodeler's Planbook Series, 130
*The Waterman's Gazette*, 158
Waterproof grease, 39
Waters, D.W., 142–143
*Water Spectrum,* 158
*Waterways World*, 158
*Way of a Ship*, 143
Weather, 95, 149, 181
*Weather for the Mariner*, 149
Weathervanes, 171
West Beach Components Ltd., 70
*The Westcotts and Their Times*, 142
*Westcountry Coasting Ketches*, 143
*Westcountrymen in Prince Edward Island*, 143
Westfield Engineering Ltd., 106
West Marine Products, 51
Weygers, Alexander G., 23
Whalen, George J., 18
Wharfs, 134–135
*Where to Learn to Sail*, 166
Whetstones, 16
White, Mark, 37, 148
White, Walter, 142
*Whitney's Star Finder*, 91
*The Whole Air Weather Guide*, 95
*Who Values What? Audience Reaction to Coastal Scenery,* 160
Wicksteed, O.H., 142
Willard Brothers Woodcutters, 31
Williams & Hussey Machine Corp., 17
Willis, Lionel, 143
Wilson, Peter, 75
Wiskets, 46
W. Lawrence Allen Dory Builders, 106
Wood, 29–33, 142, 152, 156, 158; conservation, 142; finishing, 31; sources, 30–31; woodworking, 33, 152
Woodcraft, 131
Woodcraft Supply Corporation, 20
The Wooden Boat Foundation, 4
The Wooden Boat Shop, 101
Wooden boats, 101–107
*Wooden Fighting Ships in the Royal Navy*, 143
*Wood Finishing and Refinishing*, 31
*Wood Worker*, 158
Workmate, 12
Workshops, Boat Study, 4
World Multihull Symposium, 116
*World Ocean Floor Panorama*, 162
World Ship Society, 163
Wright, E.V., 142
W.S.T. Sales, 51

X-ACTO, 127

*Yacht Racing/Cruising*, 158
Yacht research societies, 114

*The Yachtsman's Wife*, 155
*Yacht Tenders and Boats*, 114
Yamaha headphones, 98
York Marine, 134
*"You Are First": The Story of Olin and Rod Stephens of Sparkman & Stephens*, 116

Yuloh, 111

Zephyr Products Inc., 77
Zephyr spinnakers, 78
Zinc coatings, 8
ZRC Chemical Products Co., 8

## BACK VOLUMES

*The Mariner's Catalogs* are a series, and almost all of the predecessors to this volume are still in print. All volumes are similar in scope to Volume 7, but contain completely different information. The original prices are still good: $4.95 for Volume 2, $5.95 for Volume 3, $6.95 for Volume 4, $7.95 each for Volumes 5 and 6. They are available at your bookstore or from:

**International Marine Publishing Company**
**21 Elm Street**
**Camden, Maine 04843**